THE GRAND STRATEGY OF THE UNITED STATES IN LATIN AMERICA

THE GRAND STRATEGY OF THE UNITED STATES IN LATIN AMERICA

Tom J. Farer

Transaction Books
New Brunswick (U.S.A.) and Oxford (U.K.)

Copyright © 1988 by Transaction, Inc.
New Brunswick, New Jersey 08903

All rights reserved under International and Pan-American Copyright Convention. No part of this book may be reproduced or transmitted in any form or by any means, electronic or mechanical, including photocopy, recording, or any information storage and retrieval system, without prior permission in writing from the publisher. All inquiries should be addressed to Transaction Books, Rutgers—The State University, New Brunswick, New Jersey 08903.

Library of Congress Catalog Number: 87-20596
ISBN: 0-88738-155-3
Printed in the United States of America

Library of Congress Cataloging in Publication Data

Farer, Tom J.
    The grand strategy of the United States in Latin America / Tom J. Farer.
    p.   cm.
    ISBN 0-88738-155-3
    1. Latin America--Foreign relations--United States. 2. United States--Foreign relations--Latin America. 3. United States--Foreign relations--1945- 4. Human rights--Latin America--History--20th century. 5. Intervention (International law) I. Title.
F1418.F26 1987
327.7308--dc19.   87-20596

Contents

Acknowledgments ix
Introduction: Ideology and American Foreign Policy—
   Confessions of an Agnostic xiii

PART I   Strategy, Morality, and the National Interest

1. The United States and the Third World:
A Matter of Perspective 3
2. Morality and Foreign Policy 18
3. The System 23
4. Reagan's Latin America 32
5. From Kennedy to Reagan: On the Management
of Liberal Contradictions 44

PART II   Human Rights

Introduction to Part II: Etiology of an Idea 63

6. The Inter-American Commission on Human Rights:
History, Structure, and Function 69
7. A Note on Terrorism and on the Relationship Among the Right to
Physical Security and the Right to Political Participation, and
Economic and Social Rights. 79
8. The Odd Couple: American Diplomacy and the
Inter-American Commission on Human Rights 86
9. The Torturer's Response 98
10. The Limits of Relativity 109
11. Human Rights and Human Welfare 124

PART III   Law and the Practice of Intervention

Introduction to Part III: On the Limits of Impartiality 155

12. On the Nature of Law in a Decentralized Political System 157
13. The Regime of the Charter 174
14. On Foreign Intervention in Civil Strife 190

15. The Dominican Invasion and the Cuban Missile Crisis	197
16. Nicaragua 1981-?	206
17. On the Decision of the International Court of Justice in *Nicaragua* v. *United States*	212

PART IV   The United States in Central America: Cosa Nostra

18. Central American Realities	219
19. Manage the Revolution?	232
20. Liberals and Duarte: Faith Over Reason?	249
21. At Sea in Central America: Can We Negotiate Our Way to Shore?	260
22. Contadora	280
Index	291

*For Carlos Fligler, Mary Crangle,
Sidney and Linda Rosdeitcher,
David Taylor and Sally Stote:
In friendship.*

Acknowledgments

Intellectual artifacts, however modest, cannot be anything other than an expression of the author's entire life. Acknowledgments must, therefore, be riddled with omissions. When, as in this case, a book reflects more than a decade of activity, the normal quota of omissions must rise sharply. One is reduced to naming only a few of those who have made the enterprise possible. Of course, if my reviewers are not generous, those who are unnamed despite their contribution may consider themselves fortunate, since the author's conventional claim of responsibility for whatever is awkward, foolish, or spurious may not entirely exculpate those whom he associates by name with his efforts.

The interior storms of middle age expose the rock of friendship and love that anchor one's life. Without the understanding and support of my wife, Mika, and my children, Paola and Dima, my attempt to be both participant in and observer of the social and political processes about which I write could have succeeded only at great personal cost, assuming it would have succeeded at all. They have borne much of the burden of that effort, borne it with such grace and generosity of spirit as almost to make it disappear.

My experience as a member of the Inter-American Commission on Human Rights of the OAS from 1976 to 1983 informs many of the essays collected here. The commission's executive secretary, Edmundo Vargas Carreño of Chile, enriched that experience with his wisdom, his kindness, and his unfailing good humor.

Three essays appeared originally in *Foreign Policy.* Bill Maynes, its editor, has few peers in detecting begged questions, loose connections, sloppy language, and insufficiencies of proof. Whatever the merits of their final form, they far exceed those of the original drafts. For that and that alone, I impute responsibility to him.

I set about selecting and organizing the enclosed pieces and writing the introductory chapter after I moved from the Presidency to the Law School of the University of New Mexico. Collegiality is a word frequently applied to but only occasionally experienced in professional schools. It exists to a peculiar degree at this law school. For their friendship, interest, and support, I want to thank Dean Ted Parnall and all of my other colleagues.

When I moved from the presidential office to the law school, Marj Griffin accompanied me across Lomas Avenue. Without her benevolence, her high spirits and marvelous good humor, and the speed and ease with which she has organized for me the infrastructure of intellectual production, this and other projects would have been long delayed. The constraints of tradition and the university's exchequer have now deprived me of her as an assistant. Happily, they have no effect on friendship, which will endure.

Finally, I must acknowledge my debt to the president of Transaction Books, Irving Louis Horowitz: for encouraging me to marshal the essays incorporated in this volume; for compelling me to reexamine and to refine my assumptions, and for demonstrating on his basketball court that when I chose to concentrate on tennis, I did so with an instinctive appreciation of my limitations.

Various chapters have previously been published. Where appropriate, I have made minor changes of an essentially formal character, while eliminating obsolete material that did not have even the minimal virtue of displaying shifts in my thinking over time.

Grateful acknowledgment is made to the following for permission to reprint:

American Academy of Arts and Sciences: Reprinted by permission of *Daedalus,* Journal of the American Academy of Arts and Sciences, "Human Rights and Human Welfare in Latin America." *Daedalus,* Fall 1983.

American Society of International Law: Excerpts from monograph *The Inter-American System: Are There Functions For Its Forms?* 1978. Reprinted by permission of the American Society of International Law.

The Carnegie Endowment for International Peace: Reprinted with permission from *Foreign Policy* 40 [52] [59] ([Fall 1980] [Fall 1983] [Summer 1985]). Copyright 1980 [1983] [1985] by the Carnegie Endowment for International Peace.

Center for the Study of Democratic Institutions: "The Inter-American Commission: A Personal Assessment," May/June 1984. Reprinted with the permission of *The Center Magazine,* a publication of the Center for the Study of Democratic Institutions.

The Hague Academy of International Law: Excerpted from "The Regulation of Foreign Intervention in Civil Armed Conflicts," *Recueil des Cours,* Vol. II, 1975.

Johns Hopkins University Press: Excerpted from "Human Rights and Human Wrongs: Is the Liberal Model Sufficient?" *Human Rights Quarterly,* May 1985. Reprinted with permission.

Pergamon Press: "At Sea in Central America: Can We Negotiate Our Way to Shore?" Robert Leiken, ed., *Central America: Anatomy of Conflict,* 1984, Pergamon Press. Reprinted with permission.

Princeton University Press: Excepts from "Law and War," Cyril Black and Richard Falk, eds., Vol. III, *The Future of the International Legal Order: Conflict,* 1971; "International Law and Political Behavior: Toward a Conceptual Liaison," *World Politics,* April 1973. Reprinted with permission of the Princeton University Press.

New York Review of Books: "Reagan's Latin America," *The New York Review of Books,* Copyright 1981 Nyrev., Inc. Reprinted with permission.

Introduction:
Ideology and American Foreign Policy—
Confessions of an Agnostic

The proposal to publish a collection of one's essays, unencumbered by the author's having to make a preliminary showing of imminent senility or death, first heats the ego, then chills it with a frisson of alarm over the possible consequences of spelunking about in his intellectual past. Those Dickensian turns of phrase; would they look now like limp cliches? That Flaubertian precision I had sought when pressing often swollen emotions into the austere forms of language; on returning to the scene of my efforts, would I find chiseled clarity or a great sprawling slop of a thing obscuring its original intent even from me?

And suppose, alternatively, I found just that clarity and grace of translation I had sweated to achieve. Would it now seem empty or alien, a tangible even if pretty failure of one's intellect and imagination? Since my themes had always been large, perhaps excessively so, I could escape H.G. Wells' indictment of Henry James whose intellect and style he much admired. James, Wells once wrote, is like a magnificent hippopotamus trying to pick up a pea lodged in the corner of a room. But to have written emptily or foolishly about large themes can hardly be less of an offense than to have explored arguably small ones in almost unexampled depth.

Eventually, both ebullience and alarm yielded to something rather more sober, yielded to curiosity: Curiosity about the impact of experience, some of it first hand, on the intellectual baggage I brought with me into the academic life and which, in my case, as in all others, doubtlessly influenced every facet of my work. And curiosity about the source of my conflicts with scholars sailing under nominally "conservative" flags.

In 1975, when I gave a set of lectures at the Hague Academy on the international law governing foreign involvement in civil armed conflicts, I began by sketching the political values and allied assumptions I brought to the subject. This was, apparently, a gambit unprecedented in the Academy's long and distinguished history. To me it seemed necessary on two counts. First, the law in this area is not well settled. Controversy among scholars and governments over its content had, in the course of the Vietnam War, become a screeching crescendo of irreconcilable assertions. But even in calmer times, the gap between state claims and state behavior has presented irreducible obstacles to consensus among scholars about the totality of relevant legal obligations.

The great volume of applicable legal materials—treaties, decisions of international and domestic tribunals, state claims and counterclaims, state action and counteraction, and the writings of scholars marshaling and professing to construe this motley assortment of acts and texts—left one with considerable scope to identify as controlling "law" whichever norms seemed most likely to promote his or her foreign policy preferences. Nevertheless, it seemed clear to me that certain forms of involvement, as well as certain efforts to deter or punish involvement, were by general understanding impermissible either under all or at least certain well-defined circumstances. But on a number of critical issues, the most you could say was that one rule would more effectively than another advance some stipulated set of values.

In trying to distinguish settled from contested norms, much less in assessing the capacity of norms to serve such broad objectives as minimizing the risk of general war or protecting human rights, no one could hope to quarantine private assumptions and values. Rather than allowing them a clandestine role, hidden to some degree even from me, I felt obliged to announce their presence, even at the risk of disarming my audience with such an aberrant display of candor. My compulsion to confess derived not only from the particular subject's *problematique,* but also from my previous criticism of colleagues whose judgment had, I believed, been twisted by the passions of the Cold War. Since I enjoyed no exemption from passion, at least in the realm of foreign affairs, candor alone might save me from inclusion in my own arraignment.

In viewing Third World civil wars, I was then and remain powerfully influenced by the conviction that changes of regime, however accomplished, in the poorer parts of the globe will rarely be very consequential for the East–West balance of power or for other pressing strategic interests of the United States. Those interests were threatened, however, by the perception that when, in the poorer regions of the world, a Soviet–aided clique replaced a United States client, something of consequence had occurred. As I saw it, the threat had three reciprocal dimensions corresponding to the perceptions of three different actors: The United States, its allies among the economically advanced states, and the Soviet Union.

If Washington imputed substantial importance to Dictator X's replacement by Comrade Y, it would misallocate national resources by diverting excessive amounts of them to the end of reversing this change in regime and/or preventing comparable change on the next relevant occasion. Moreover, to the extent it saw a Soviet hand behind the change, as a means of deterring Soviet aid to dissidents in other states, it might sacrifice mutually beneficial arrangements in such arenas as arms control and trade.

If the Politburo, on the other hand, convinced itself that the change constituted an important advance for Soviet interests, then the absence of any United States response, even if passivity reflected a Presidential judgment that the change lacked objective importance, might mislead the Soviets into adventures truly inimical to Western interests and thereby provoke a first-class diplomatic crisis. If our major allies either perceived the change as significant or believed that the United States deemed it significant, albeit erroneously, then United States political leaders would feel pressure to respond along the lines sketched above in order to maintain allied confidence in our guarantees of their security.

Since Chapter 1 sketches the assumptions supporting my continued conviction that changes of regime in the Third World will rarely have important, or where arguably important then predictable, material consequences for the United States or the Soviet Union, I will say a word about them here only because they seem so integral a part of my differences with notional Conservatives. These assumptions can usefully be organized under the following headnotes: science and technology, poverty and the idea of progress, nationalism, popular mobilization, and egotism. All I can do in the brief compass available to me here is suggest how these interacting features of the modern condition have altered radically the value of achieving or averting the displacement of governments in poor countries.

One of the classic motives for acquiring client states by installing or protecting complaisant rulers was use of the client's territory as a platform for projecting force. Through its impact on firepower, transportation, surveillance, and communications, to name four critical elements of the art of war, technological progress has dramatically reduced the strategic value of territory per se. Take the naval man's favorite frightener, the "choke point." Minus the metaphor, it is a narrow place through which commercial or military vessels must frequently pass. From the dawn of recorded marine history until very recently, occupation of the land bordering narrow passages no doubt constituted a substantial strategic advantage in part because the occupier had a natural platform for its weapons. Its adversaries had to expend assets both on weapons and on platforms to bear them. The blocking state, moreover, could employ qualitatively different weapons such as cheap fireboats and, later, mines.

For today's superpowers, those old asymmetries are essentially relics. By striking through the air with planes or missiles, they can annihilate forces attempting to block passage. And if they wish to impede naval movement, long-distance air power and powerful submarine fleets coupled with satellite surveillance enables them to attack anywhere on the high seas, as well as to mine straits and other narrows. Choke points exist and will continue to pose problems for naval strategists aiming to protect the resulting congregation of vessels. What has changed is the value of adjacent territory.

Other illustrations of the diminished value, for military purposes, of territory are: (1) For at least the first decade of the Cold War, before the massive deployment of intercontinental missiles, access to air bases abroad—for example, in Morocco—was an essential element of our nuclear deterrent strategy. Today it is irrelevant. (2) During the '60s, an Eritrean–based facility was both a key link in our worldwide military communications system and an important post for listening surreptitiously to the communications of other states. By the time of the 1974 Ethiopian revolution, communications and surveillance satellites had largely replaced its functions.

Scientific progress has altered the strategic value of territory in another respect. The invention of new materials and the multiplication of agricultural productivity has reduced the importance of natural resources, another classic inducement to great–power competition for influence in relatively weak states. In addition, the demands of mobilized populations for economic enhancement, elite and mass passion for progress, and nationalist aspirations, in that they require the import of technology for their satisfaction, drive governments toward exporting natural resources in response primarily to market rather than short–term political criteria.

My conviction about the strategic unimportance of regime change does not, however, rest primarily on my assessment of the contemporary value of bases or the difficulty of using political leverage to acquire natural resources at discounted prices. The conviction would survive the clearest demonstration of error in those assessments because its primary support is the judgment, powerfully backed by precedent, that the interacting elements of the modern condition enumerated above impede control of one state by another through local proxies and correspondingly raise the costs of control to the point where they normally exceed potential gains. At a minimum, they make all potential gains extremely problematical.

Regime change in China after World War II nicely illustrates my point. Greeted by many Americans and virtually all self–proclaimed conservatives as a disaster for the United States national interest, to this day its objective consequences for the balance of power or other global interests of the United States remain obdurately obscure. What is clear, however, is that neither the egotism nor the cultural consciousness of Chinese Communist leaders allowed them to become Soviet vassals, that divergent national interests quickly converted the supposed client regime into an antagonist, that the mobilization of the Chinese masses by war and revolution enabled the client to resist its former patron's pressure and that the elite's passion to alleviate poverty, foster modernization, and enhance national power have finally converted it to foreign and domestic policies utterly alien to the expectations of United States and Soviet decision makers two decades ago.

Since the Chinese precedent will be distinguished by some on grounds of the country's extraordinary size and age, the case of Somalia—a relatively new, thinly populated state—offers yet more telling support for the same set of points. In 1969, General Siad Barre seized power from a firmly pro-Western civilian government, announced his intention to establish a regime based on the principles of scientific socialism, imported Eastern Bloc security advisors, and successfully traded Soviet access to Somali territory for Soviet arms. By the mid-1970s Somalia seemed entrapped by dependence, particularly in the military sphere, on Soviet patronage. Inflated by Soviet aid to a size and technology far out of proportion to the country's locally generated wealth and expertise, at the same time representing a staggering local investment of resources and prestige, the Somali armed forces seemed to form an uncutable umbilical cord for the flow of influence from Moscow to Mogadishu. But when the centrifugal forces released by the Ethiopian revolution created a transient opportunity to regain territory lost to Amharite power in the previous century, the Somalis, rejecting Soviet pleas and threats, invaded their neighbor. And when the Soviets responded by suspending military aid, General Barre cut the cord and plunged onward alone to ultimate defeat, coincidentally providing another illustration of clientelism shattering on the rocks of nationalism.

While the Soviets were using Somali-based facilities for the support of their little Indian Ocean flotilla, an army of Western strategists, their voices magnified many times over by a compliant mass media, imputed dire significance to those facilities. But after the Soviets were expelled, rather than celebrating the loss of what had only a moment before been described as a strategically important, not to mention expensive, investment, most of the same strategists found new cause for alarm in the Soviet Union's incipient Ethiopian connection. Like the chorus of a Greek tragedy, they seem constitutionally incapable of recording good news.

Demonstrably erroneous predictions about the horrendous consequences of regime change litter the landscape of American political discourse. Fifteen years after the conclusion of the Chinese Civil War, the gloom brigade, by then a mirror image of propagandists in Peking seeking (successfully so far as we were concerned) to hide their country's appalling weaknesses, still envisioned all of Asia at risk to Chinese power. As much as any other force, that vision led us into Vietnam. When a part of the American elite began, however belatedly, to appreciate the extravagance of our Vietnamese adventure, the unregenerate residue envisioned the communization of the rest of southeast Asia in the event of a communist regime in Saigon. While there may be respectable reasons for reevaluating the assumptions of the antiwar movement, the fast-developing economies and stable polities of Thailand, Malaysia, Singapore, and Indonesia cannot be counted among them. The brigade's predictions of revolution sprouting like coca plants all over Latin America in the wake of Castro's accession similarly imply less a capacity for clairvoyance then a tendency toward hysteria.

And yet, as a force in American politics, it has gone from strength to strength, coming more and more to set the agenda of foreign policy discourse. Endowed like its most prominent adherent, Ronald Reagan, with the quality of Teflon, the brigade's reputation for sagacity endures as if it had been right about the consequences for United States strategic interests of regime change in China, Vietnam, and Cuba, not to mention such easily forgotten purlieus as Ethiopia and Angola.

From my dissenting views, which have in fact remained constant, it followed that, to the extent an American administration could handle the three-dimensional perceptual problem I mentioned earlier, it could be considerably more relaxed about Soviet transactions in developing countries than had been customary since the advent of the Cold War. Relaxation would, I believed, alter national security policy in several ways. In the first place, it would allow us to test Soviet motives and the limits of detente by tolerating within mutually applicable limits their search for influence and prestige.

If, as some Western students of Soviet policy claim, a compulsion for recognition as a coequal superpower helps drive Soviet policy, such a license might induce the Kremlin to moderate its view of diplomacy as a zero-sum game and to accept, even to embrace, certain offers for joint action to dampen or isolate threats to international order. At a minimum, we could generate a little cognitive dissonance among Kremlin leaders and learn more about their collective psyche without, on my assumption, placing valuable Western assets at risk.

From the onset of the Cold War to the present moment, successive administrations, Republican and Democratic alike, have treated as threatening and implicitly branded as illegitimate every Soviet effort to acquire influence beyond the borders of the Eastern Bloc. In effect, we have thought of Africa, Asia, and Latin America as a preserve in which only the West is licensed to hunt. I do not insist that such a view is either malign or necessarily imprudent. Monopolies can be pleasant to their holders as long as the cost of maintaining them is slight. I claim nothing more than the incompatibility of such a monopoly with recognition of the Soviet Union as a coequal superpower.

American determination to maintain this asymmetry did not flag in the era of detente. On the contrary, detente was, at least in part, an effort to reduce the costs and risks associated with the containment of Soviet influence in particular and revolutionary forces in general. Henry Kissinger's *White House Years* are quite clear on this point. Referring to a private meeting with Soviet Ambassador Dobrynin shortly after Kissinger and President-elect Nixon had announced that the new administration would take a businesslike approach to U.S.-Soviet relations, Kissinger writes of his difficulties in finding a satisfactory response to the ambassador's query about just what the United States was prepared to barter. On the score of geopolitical issues, the real though unspoken answer was "nothing." For instance, Kissinger ignored the Soviet Union's evident desire for recognition as a legitimate and important player in Middle East diplomacy because, as he writes, excluding Soviet influence in the area was an important goal of the new administration. In the end, he offered prospects for positive developments only in arms control and trade.

My judgment about the limited strategic importance of regime change leads also to the view that Presidents, in deciding whether to bolster, ignore, or undermine other governments, may employ humanitarian criteria not least among others without offending their presumed paramount obligation to enhance national security. To be sure, security and humanitarian criteria often will overlap. In fact, if you follow the party line laid down by Senator Patrick Moynihan and his erstwhile ideological allies, former Ambassador Jean Kirkpatrick and Norman Podhoretz, editor of *Commentary* magazine, they are indistinguishable, the theory being that whatever hurts Soviet interests and augments American power necessarily promotes human rights.

In defending this anodyne equation of national and humanitarian interests, its advocates have relied on two now notorious arguments. One, of course, is the contention that regimes of the left are almost invariably more cruel and more incapable of evolution in a democratic direction than their authoritarian counterparts on the right. The other is that, even in the event of an anomalous case where a Soviet-supported regime or Soviet-armed dissidents are less morally repugnant than adversaries claiming allegiance to the United States, since victory for the latter reinforces Soviet influence, the net global effect would be detrimental to the cause of human freedom.

The latter, in its airy generality, is less an argument than a declaration of faith and, like all such declarations, is essentially outside the bounds of reasoned discourse. Obviously, it is useless to invoke particular cases, since the nature of the argument renders them irrelevant. The former, to the contrary, depends on processes of cerebration susceptible to rational challenge. Chapter 4 contains the principal statement of my objections to Ambassador Kirkpatrick's extravagant claims. The harsh tone, emulating the ambassador's native style, is in part a reaction to the sneering brutality of her own polemics and in part a reflection of my judgment that the presumptions, prescriptions and rationalizations of the ideological faction she helps to lead have encouraged state-managed terrorism particularly in Latin America.

When attempting to institutionalize torture and murder, the practitioners of terror, whether they serve governments or rebels, look for psychological props as well as technical means. While it is often possible, particularly for governments (since they can sort through the wards of their prisons and asylums), to find a certain number of psychotics for whom the work of inflicting pain is its own reward, they are insufficiently numerous and dependable to staff a sizeable ongoing enterprise. In order to recruit and retain sufficient qualified personnel for even a small bureaucracy of terror, its administrators must first invent or borrow an appealing discourse of justification. An effective discourse will manage simultaneously to arouse an awful ferocity toward the targeted group and to numb any latent compassion which its torments might later evoke. Ideally, the discourse will fuse a positive appeal to idealism with a negative appeal to fear while simultaneously dehumanizing the victims by portraying them as a collectively vicious and irredeemable threat to the novice torturer's highest values. In short, the discourse must be Manichaean.

In our time, the United States rather than Europe is the preeminent external influence on the thought and sensibility of Latin elite and mass alike. Conservatives in particular look to us not only as a playground and sanctuary, but also as a source of funds, technology, and ideas for maintaining at least the fundamentals of the status quo. As in other parts of the world, there is normally a fairly broad spectrum of political instinct and opinion among conservatives, from those prepared to exchange dollops of reform for social peace to those who, by virtue of temperament and belief, view society as a state of war and equate concessions with treason.

Political and ideological forces radiating from the United States inevitably affect the balance of power and the choice of strategy within the conservative camp. Through word and deed, Mrs. Kirkpatrick has encouraged advocates of war *à outrance*. Her writings and speeches rationalize the Manichaean instincts of the hawks and her actions, such as defending Chile at the United Nations and publicly smiling on its brutish president, Augusto Pinochet, during a gratuitous visit to the country he rules with such conspicuous savagery, have been read as a sign of American support for harsh solutions to class conflicts.

The hallmark of her work and the work of like-minded writers is their refusal, which seems nothing short of a visceral incapacity, to impute the slightest benignity of motive to advocates of revolutionary change. Hers is an unqualified failure of empathy; she will not permit a view of the world which explains how people of ordinary decency might enter the nightmare life of armed opposition to established authority and, in the rare case of success, might seek to perpetuate power won by force of arms. Since she will not grant them the status of normal human beings containing the usual mix of selfishness and idealism, kindness and ferocity, since she consigns them to the status of monsters, she is equally incapable of imagining benign change in the regimes they will occasionally establish.

My differences with polemicists like Mrs. Kirkpatrick undoubtedly stem from temperament and experience. By instinct, I am a Tory in the sense summarized by the English Conservative who referred with pride to his party as "The Stupid Party." As he did, I distrust grand schemes for tidily organizing, first with the mind then with the knout, the huge, sprawling, complicated messiness of society. But my Toryism has always been flawed by an inability to get quite comfortable with the pain and humiliation which is the common condition of life in most of the world.

Beside temperament, there is experience. Like Mrs. Kirkpatrick, I have visited Latin America's presidential palaces and palatial clubs, the homes of its rich and the camps of its soldiers. Unlike her, I have granted equal time to its prisons and its prisoners, to the enemies and the victims of the prevailing order. Unlike her, I have found nobility and thuggery on both sides of the ideological line, just as I have found quite average sorts of people struggling as best they know how to secure some moral purchase for their lives.

Visiting Latin America unencumbered by dogma, it is not hard to see the conditions which drive an indeterminate but not trivial number of young men and women to scorn democracy, detest the United States, and embrace violence.

In Chapter 11 I have tried to describe the world as they see it (just as in Chapter 9 I have tried to reproduce the mind-set of their counterparts on the right). In some places it is a world in which elections would be meaningful, if they were not fixed. In others, it is a world where elections are not fixed because extraelectoral arrangements have always guaranteed that they will not be meaningful in terms of threatening any important feature of the status quo. It is a world marked by extreme concentration of land ownership and a tradition of intervention by the state on behalf of vested economic interests. It is a world where the protestant ethic never penetrated to leaven the arrogant ostentation of wealth and where military establishments, more often than constitutions, govern the limits of political change.

In these and many other respects, the countries of Latin America vary greatly among themselves and over time. But to the extent any summary can do justice, it seems fair to say that the dominant Latin pattern has been statist in the economic sphere, authoritarian in the political, inegalitarian in the social, and instrumentalist in its view of democratic politics and individual freedom. With rare exceptions, for almost a century the United States, despite its very different political traditions and cultural values, has appeared to left and right alike as the guarantor of the Latin status quo, particularly in the Caribbean basin. Naturally, therefore, opponents of traditional order have assumed the hostility of the United States.

As I suggest at the conclusion of Chapter 11, changes in the Catholic Church, economic and population growth and their associated dislocations, mass media, the gradual spread of education, and the values of advanced democratic–capitalist states all have worked to loosen frozen patterns of thought and society in Latin America. Coupled with often grim political experience, these changes offer unparalleled opportunities for the construction of working democracies. But much of the old right remains irreconcilably opposed to more than the mere form of democracy. By praising the right as the lesser evil, by encouraging the view that victory over the revolutionary left must precede reform, and by urging exclusion of the left from reformist coalitions, Ambassador Kirkpatrick and the entire administration she so accurately represented have, however unwittingly, given aid and comfort to the butchers at the gate of change.

I think even the casual reader will note, however, that I do not dissent from all parts of contemporary conservatism's canon. Authoritarian regimes that succeed either in coopting or disemboweling all the intermediate institutions of society (churches, the media, trade unions, universities, professional associations, etc.) tend, thereby, to increase their longevity and to eliminate nooks and crannies where heroic conservatives can maintain the tradition of critical thought. But unlike American rightists, I can see and have seen right– as well as left–wing governments employing this strategy of self–perpetuation. In order to accommodate its American patrons, the Right may have a somewhat greater inclination to mask its efforts to search out and destroy those nooks and crannies. During the late 1970s in Guatemala, no law or regulation prevented reformers from registering new political parties. Those foolhardy enough to do so were murdered. Theoretically, the law allowed workers to form unions. When, misled by theory, they did and elected leaders, the leaders died. Since the CIA–organized coup restored the army's right wing to power in 1954, after a brief hiatus of reform, its officer corps has ruled behind a facade sometimes of military, sometimes of civilian presidents, but always of pluralistic institutions resting silently in their respective graveyards.

Another difficulty with the authoritarian–totalitarian distinction as elaborated by Kirkpatrick and friends is the unpredictable relationship in practice between, on the one hand, the attempted absorption or neutralization of all potential loci of opposition and, on the other, either unusual brutality or the elimination of all open criticism of public policy. For roughly half a century, a single party has ruled Mexico. The Institutional Revolutionary Party (the PRI, as it is generally known) incorporates the leadership of all significant trade and peasant unions; keeps a tight leash on the armed forces; controls the electoral process at the local, state, and national levels; enjoys (as a consequence of various incentives, controls, and informal sanctions) a consistently positive relationship with the media; and selects the rector of the National University. Other parties are allowed to win a few seats in Congress and an occasional mayoral election, but not for decades has the PRI tolerated defeat in a single gubernatorial contest. Independent organizations of workers or peasants either are co-opted or neutralized. The Catholic Church, having first cast its lot with the old regime then suffered grave persecution in the early post–revolutionary period, keeps clear of politics.

The elite that runs the party is not exclusionary; on the contrary, it is eager to identify and assimilate able men and women. The same might, however, be said of communist parties in Marxist states. Since the country's other parties have hitherto formed an impotent minority, at least in part because of the PRI's monopoly of state power, characterizing Mexico as a "one–party state" would be literally accurate. It would also be misleading, conjuring as the term does a harsh, closed society, rather than one regarded as among the most open and pluralistic in all of Latin America.

At one level, the obvious and principal explanation for the coexistence of pluralism and one-party government is a powerful private sector within the economy able to provide alternative careers for the able and to constrain state power through its ability to devastate the economy and thus shake the foundations of public order by withholding investment capital and entrepreneurial skills. That this semi–independent principality could grow into the powerful force it has become is in turn attributable to the timing and consequent nature of the Mexican Revolution, unlike, for instance, the Cuban one. Although, like Cromwell's army, not without its Levellers, the men who gradually established dominance over the revolutionary coalition were middle–class people with, on the whole, matching ideas. They did not want to turn the world upside down. But living as they did in the early Twentieth Century, when socialist ideas had become a part of the educated Western man's intellectual universe, egalitarian claims did not have for them the same horribly threatening, alien aspect they had had for Cromwell and his lieutenants. So not only could they be incorporated into the revolutionary agenda and thus serve to rally peasants and an incipient working class to arms against the old dictatorial order, but after power had been won, they could be incorporated into the ideals of the new order where they have remained, legitimating, as they have continued to exert a certain pressure on, the party forged by the revolution's leaders to perpetuate the new order and their place within it.

Private enterprise is an important yet not, I think, the entire explanation for the Mexican phenomenon. The camaraderie, shared danger, and ecstatic idealism of revolutionary war suppress only for a moment, if at all, the irreducible contradictions of social life—contradictions of interest, of vision, and of personality. When the heights of power are won, the risk of counterrevolution may sustain solidarity a while longer. But once that risk recedes, division reassumes its natural place in the order of things.

If there is a rough balance of power among the various factions of the new elite, they may indefinitely accommodate their differences within a single political institution which will govern, as the PRI has governed Mexico, with continuing shifts in policy reflecting ever-varying power balances within the party and the seismic shift of economic and social forces in the outer world. Much the same thing has marked the politics of Yugoslavia, another one-party state with a relatively pluralistic society, relative, that is, to its Eastern Bloc neighbors, not to Mexico where political dissent enjoys far more tolerance.

My point, of course, is that neither one-party rule nor the absence of autonomous trade unions, an independent and vigorous clergy, and an adversary media signal the presence of a totalitarian or a notably brutal state. Yugoslavia suggests that, even where one-party rule is initially both harsh and rigid, the absence of autonomous intermediate institutions including a private sector does not preclude evolution toward a more open and relaxed system of governance. Evolution may proceed even toward tolerance of political competition, which is where Czechoslovakia seemed to be heading before the Russian winter overtook its brief spring.

Twenty years of professional devotion to the study of political systems has left me with confidence about little more than the irrationality of having much confidence in one's ability to predict the trajectory of intra- or interstate relations. Such confirmed agnosticism, however great its virtues in the academic life, generally disables one from consultancies for the powerful, since their temperament no less than their necessities, are better served by certainty. In the competition for vizierships, Ambassador Kirkpatrick is an archetype of the right stuff.

Another issue on which I feel some slight sympathetic vibration from the conservative canon is the relationship of the state to the economy in so far as it affects human rights and human welfare. Libertarian conservatives—the heirs of Nineteenth Century Liberalism—have contributed to the balance of contemporary thought by exposing the negative features of heavy state involvement in the economies of developing countries and the sometimes corresponding constriction of indigenous entrepreneurship. But, as was true of the authoritarian–totalitarian distinction, conservatives as a group, finding themselves in possession of a useful general idea applicable in varying degrees to different cases, were so determined to make it a perfect servant of their political ends that they hardened it into an iron rule impervious to context.

In Africa, south of the Sahara, the minimalist state, had it existed, would by virtue of its restricted scope have contributed mightily to economic development and individual autonomy. If, for example, farmers had been able to sell their produce at world market prices, millions of peasants would have remained in the countryside, growing gradually into a rural bourgeoisie rather than building bands of misery around the small urban cores inherited from the colonial era. Prosperous farmers would have induced growth in the class of entrepreneurs servicing them. If the village and rural town had not been identified with misery, if the private sector had offered expanding prospects of material comfort, if economic activity had not required government license, neither the attainment of political or bureaucratic power nor its retention would have been so desperate an affair.

Here, as elsewhere, many American conservatives are amnesic. They forget that such devices as state marketing boards, attempting to extract harvests from farmers at a fraction of the world price, were conceived not by Marxists or socialists, but by imperial bureaucrats determined to make the colonies pay for themselves. They forget that the colonial model of a modern society was intensely inegalitarian and statist.

Both for positive and negative reasons, minimalist government was and remains peculiarly relevant to Black Africa's needs and endowments. On the one hand, capital assets (for Africans almost exclusively land) were pretty broadly distributed among the indigenous population, while barriers to opportunity (e.g. vast disparities in education) were much less pronounced than in many other parts of the Third World. On the other, all the post–colonial states lacked a highly skilled bureaucratic class inspired by nationalist elan.

In much of Latin America, by contrast, where capital and education are extremely concentrated, private–sector–led development has tended to aggravate the misery of the poor. As in Europe during its industrial revolution, immiseration has elicited demands from ambitious and/or morally sensitive members of the middle class and lower–class leaders for government intervention to spread the burden and ease the pain of economic development. But the state to which they appeal is to a large degree colonized by the leading beneficiaries of skewed development. Indeed, the highly unequal distribution of new increments of wealth may be attributable in part to ongoing state action compounding inequality of opportunity and distorting market forces at the behest of the social and economic elite.

Other than in the wake of revolution (including externally induced revolutions from the top, exemplified by Japan, Taiwan, and South Korea), the activist state in developing countries is an unlikely contributor to enhanced welfare for the poorest sectors of the population unless a serious threat of revolution elicits a reformist strategy from the upper classes. The immediate human cost of a revolutionary effort is very high; the threat tends to elicit a passion for repression, not reform; most revolutions fail, and those that succeed are rarely led by people who see redistribution simply as a precondition for the more effective operation of free markets in the realm of power, goods, and ideas. No wonder reformers in Latin America often feel as if they were trying to answer a riddle wrapped in an enigma.

I think that it is precisely at the point of my accumulated pessimism about the prospects for rapid enhancement of human rights and welfare in Africa and Latin America (though not in southeast Asia) that I am closest to the conservative canon. Not age, I hope, but experience, accumulated in the years since I came down from Harvard to serve in the administration of John Kennedy, has worn away the sweet anticipation of grand achievements in far off places of which I then knew little. Conservative intellectuals have supplemented life in instructing us about the limits of politics. Where we differ, perhaps, is in the pleasure they seem to derive from confirming the bloody intransigence of the world.

Assuming I am right in believing, however provisionally, that crusades against the Left will not invariably promote human welfare, and in believing as well that regime changes in developing countries will rarely have much material consequence, we must then face the question, raised earlier, whether an American President can satisfactorily alter the appearance of materiality in the face of long–settled contrary convictions held by colleagues, competitors, and domestic guardians of the conventional wisdom.

Did Jimmy Carter demonstrate, as many observers believe, that it can't be done and that trying is likely to get you beat? Early in his term, the President and some prominent members of his administration, while attempting to expand the recognized agenda of critical international issues, certainly discounted rhetorically the importance of revolutionary change in developing countries. References to an "inordinate fear of communism" were a major innovation in public discourse. Nothing like it had been heard in the corridors of power since the onset of the Cold War.

Consistent with that rhetoric, the President and his CIA Director, Admiral Stansfield Turner, shrank the agency's covert operations section despite screams of rage from practitioners of the dark art, amplified by their friends in Congress and the media. A more conspicuous translation of rhetoric into action was the initially private, then increasingly public, pressure on an array of United States clients to improve their human rights record, although some, like the Iranian Shah, continued to enjoy immunity. When Carter refused either to supervise the transfer of power in Nicaragua by intervening directly or to back Somoza against a coalition in which the Left controlled the guns, to many political friends and enemies alike, his apostasy from key precepts of the Cold War faith seemed complete.

In fact, the President's deviance had always been partial and tentative. It soon yielded to the pressure of events in Afghanistan, the African Horn, Iran, and Central America, widely seen as reconfirming the truth of orthodox doctrine. Carter's acts and omissions appeared to challenge three articles of the faith: that revolutionary leaders are invariably hostile to the West; that their accession generally results in damage to important Western interests; that whenever the United States exhibits a flagging will to maintain the global status quo, the Soviet Union will move aggressively to alter the balance of power.

My own skepticism about the second proposition is recorded earlier in this essay and in Chapter 1. The best you can say for it is that the evidence of its truth is slight. That being so, the truth of the preceding article seems academic, even childish, in its implied anxiety about being unloved. As a statement of fact, it seems to me essentially correct, although uninformative about the etiology of the condition it describes. The hostility of revolutionary leaders reciprocates our own. It is the result not of *force majeure* but of human choice. In Africa and Asia, the first generation of revolutionary leaders, whether Marxist or bourgeois nationalist in ideology, did not regard the United States as a predictable enemy. Even Ho Chi Minh and Mao initially solicited American support. African leaders struggling for independence reasonably regarded us as an ally. Only in those parts of Latin America where we had long exercised the prerogatives of hegemony was Washington's hostility assumed.

Through our successive postwar choices—refusing to recognize the government of China; backing the French against Ho; orchestrating the overthrow of a reformist government in Guatemala; backing Portugal in Africa; conniving in the overthrow and murder of the Zairian political leader, Patrice Lumumba, and so on—we verified and globalized that assumption. Although our motives varied, the consistency of our acts led ineluctably to a view of the United States as the natural enemy of revolutionary change in all areas not under the control of Marxist regimes. Notwithstanding the Reagan administration's belated withdrawal of support from Marcos and Duvalier, the view corresponds closely with the fact. As it was made by human agency, so the fact can be changed. If it were, after a while the view would change.

The view central to my present inquiry is not that of revolutionaries lingering in mountains and mosques, but of the leaders of the Soviet Union. At issue is the third tenet of the Cold War faith for the transgression of which, however partial, Jimmy Carter has been arraigned. He is, of course, not the only figure the Right as well as a good part of today's Center as well have hauled before the grand inquest of the nation. Anyone who opposes aiding the contras or their Angolan counterparts or in any other way manifests "Vietnam Syndrome"—anyone, that is to say, who doubts the wisdom of devoting much national energy or wealth to determine the composition of Third World regimes or who exercises a strong, even if refutable, presumption against the use of force in that part of the globe—is included in the dragnet indictment. And although the persons originally responsible for detente, Richard Nixon and Henry Kissinger, have acquired immunity by clarifying their narrow purpose and by attributing its failure to Soviet perfidy and liberal funk, the doctrine itself with its unavoidable connotations of a more relaxed and regulated competition for influence and prestige is incorporated in the indictment.

What precisely must the prosecution demonstrate? That the Soviets would not have intervened at all in any of the named cases if Congress had given Kissinger a free hand in Angola and if Carter had reaffirmed the doctrine of global containment rather than implying and allowing people like Andrew Young to imply that the United States was relaxing its anti-revolutionary posture? That Soviet activity from Angola to Afghanistan represented a bid to alter the balance of power? That Soviet activity in the Third World already has or, if it were allowed to continue on its Carter-years trajectory, would alter the balance of power?

No one has yet made a persuasive case for the last proposition. For much the same reasons I find that indigenous revolutions affect the wealth and security of the United States trivially if at all, I regard Soviet efforts to acquire and sustain Third-World clients as a waste of their national resources except, conceivably, to the extent such efforts induce us to waste proportionally more of ours. Obviously this conviction is not fully shared by Soviet decision-makers. It is, however, quite unclear whether their various adventures are best explained in terms of: Bureaucratic compromise (i.e. giving every power center some opportunity to justify its existence); the perceived requisites for periodic relegitimation of party rule (by demonstrating both the claimed movement of historical forces in favor of proletarian revolutions and the Soviet Union's central role in accelerating those forces); belief that periodic demonstrations of will and capacity to project influence and cause trouble provide negotiating leverage with the United States on issues of greater intrinsic importance; and/or belief that the proliferation of Soviet clients could, in the very long run, really affect power relations between the Soviet Union and the Western Alliance.

Uncertainty about the sources of Soviet behavior in general aggravates inevitable uncertainty about the causes and meaning of the particular cases which form the gravamen of the complaint against Carter and company. Soviet intervention may have evidenced a gathering conviction of the erosion of American will and a coincident desire to probe its dimensions as well as to exploit it. On that view of the matter, Ronald Reagan deserves the Nobel Peace Prize for ratcheting up the defense budget, organizing the contras, savaging arms control and anathematizing the Soviet Empire, since by these means he quickly altered the Kremlin's perceptions and thus discouraged some intolerably provocative sally into the zone of Western interests from which the U.S.S.R. would have had difficulty withdrawing in the face of determined resistance.

But this is not the only possible construction of Soviet behavior. Even taking into account the activities of its ally Cuba, the U.S.S.R. had little to do with the revolutionary process in Central America and was as irrelevant as we turned out to be when Iran convulsed. The Soviets intervened prominently only in countries that either never had been or had ceased to be important to the West: Angola, Ethiopia, and Afghanistan. In Angola, they acted on behalf of an old client, in the face of Western resistance spearheaded by South Africa and, as a consequence of the South African presence, with the approval of a large bloc of black African states led by Nigeria. They appeared in Ethiopia after a marked contraction in United States interest in the country, at the express invitation of a revolutionary government that had seized power without benefit of Soviet aid and was resisting invasion by a Soviet client. Since the Somalis were attempting to alter a postcolonial boundary, most of black Africa strongly supported Ethiopia and did not therefore object to Soviet-Cuban involvement.

As for Afghanistan, it was an interest inherited, like so many other things, from the Czars. Among Western states only Britain had once palpitated to events up there on the world's roof. When India ceased to be the jewel in the British crown, Afghanistan ceased to trouble the sleep of Foreign Office mandarins. But as a territorial link with China and a Moslem country at a time when the adjacent, Islamized population of the Soviet Union was growing in size and importance, Afghanistan continued to attract Soviet interest. Without much complaint from Washington, the country's cautious rulers had practiced neutralism with a Soviet tilt until swept aside by a communist coup. Even the coup had elicited only *pro forma* complaints from the United States.

In sum, because of the geography and history of these countries, the Kremlin may not have regarded its varying forms of intervention as a revealing test of United States will in the wake of Vietnam. Nor is it by any means clear that if these cases had arisen after Reagan's militant restoration of that ol' Cold War religion with matching arms, the Kremlin would have eschewed the opportunity afforded by the peculiar conjunction of events in Ethiopia, the mixture of opportunity and challenge presented by Washington's bid to place postindependence Angola in the hands of its own client, and the risk in Afghanistan of a Marxist regime's replacement by a hostile fundamentalist Moslem government. Does historical experience suggest the likelihood of one great power, regardless of its ideology, accepting more constraining rules of the game than those by which the other plays?

In international relations, as in law, no cases are truly identical. But there is little doubt that Soviet leaders, in common with many noncommunists in Europe and Latin America, view United States occupation of the Dominican Republic as an assertion of hegemony similar in its fundamentals to their invasion of Afghanistan. Nor are they likely to see important differences between our coming to the aid of South Korea when it was invaded by the North and their responding to help Ethiopia ward off Somalia. As for Angola, Moscow would certainly insist that its Cubans were in principle no different than our Zairians (units of Zaire's army, such as it is, were in northern Angola aiding our man, Holden Roberto, before the arrival of large Cuban units) or South Africans.

When, years hence, historians review the seven years from the fall of Saigon to the election of Ronald Reagan, they may well conclude that its legacy of bitterness in U.S.–Soviet relations did in fact arise from Soviet misperception of the Carter Presidency. But the misperception was not the one commonly supposed, namely of a decisive slackening of American will to play the game of power on a global scale. It was, rather, a failure to grasp that Carter represented an accidental and, for that reason, fleeting opportunity to so restructure the terms of superpower competition that it could be conducted at a healthy distance from the precipice of crisis.

These days, to evince uncertainty about Soviet behavior is to be labeled a wimp by more courtly commentators, an apologist by many of the rest. Prominent Democrats vie with Republicans over who believes with greater conviction that the Soviet Union is an evil empire which would conquer the world if the United States were not rough, tough, and armed. I have, quite frankly, never met anyone, including Marxists, who thought that the U.S.S.R. had anything other than an ugly political order. But harsh governments inspired by an antidemocratic philosophy have not invariably pursued ferocious foreign policies. For there is no antithesis between harshness and prudence. Conversely, states with morally elevated domestic arrangements have been known to display considerable ruthlessness in dealing with the inhabitants of other states. It was Athens, not Sparta, which denied Melos the right to be neutral in the Peloponnesian War, secured its surrender through a relentless siege, and thereafter put to death all the city's grown men and sold the women and children into slavery.

Successful foreign adventures sometimes may help stabilize a shaky authoritarian government, just as they may restore electoral support for a democratic one. Unsuccessful power games, even stalemates, are likely to aggravate instability. The Soviet regime still seems solidly in place. No one claims that its Nomenklatura is fired by ideological passion. Under the circumstances, reason dictates a foreign policy designed to do no more than avoid humiliation, avoid further dispersion abroad of resources required for development at home, and, perhaps, to perpetuate recognizably communist systems in Eastern Europe.

The hubris endemic to the leaders of powerful states, bureaucratic competition for prestige and resources, competition for power among Politburo cliques, the felt need to occasionally exhibit belief in Marxist historiography and the Soviet Union's central role among communist states: These forces will no doubt encourage behavior not strictly necessary for maintenance of the extant political order, even somewhat dysfunctional from that point of view. But I expect the Kremlin to act on the whole cautiously and to be prepared for cooperation on terms of equality in areas where their interests coincide with ours. No one has yet made a persuasive case that the Soviet elite is either wildly irrational or self-destructive.

For better or worse, that perception of Soviet behavior is part of the background against which I have over the years assessed American policy. Why should a view so consonant with traditional conservative realpolitik, a view full of good old-fashioned cynicism about the motives of states, a view that imputes no value higher than self-interest to the Soviet elite, divide me so sharply from writers offering themselves as conservatives and their allies in liberal drag like those who run *The New Republic?* Can it be anything other than a compulsion to treat the Soviet Union like a state unlike any other state, a monster that must be pressed by threat of fire and sword onto ever more narrow ground until, caged at last, it becomes at last a normal state or splits into several of them? And then?

Would a capitalist Russian state sizzling with released creative energy discover a perfect symmetry of interest with the United States. Will we become the first great power in history unable to find a challenge to its security? I cannot help feeling that behind the contemporary Right's facade of sophisticated cerebration there squats that very American, pretty but primitive belief that somehow this City on the Hill can bring history to an end. Chiliasts and paranoids stand tall in the councils of the Republic. We do indeed have the means to bring an end to our history. But it is not an end at which the dead will rise and be made whole.

PART I
STRATEGY, MORALITY, AND THE NATIONAL INTEREST

1

The United States and the Third World: A Matter of Perspective

From the beginning of the Cold War until Jimmy Carter arrived in Washington, the United States had a lucid, coherent policy toward the Third World, one that gradually dissipated U.S. influence there and poisoned American politics.

It was characterized by a view of the Third World as an arena of unremitting competition between the United States and the Soviet Union and of Third World governments and people as pawns on the global chessboard. For Washington, the policy had two corollaries: first, a compelling preference for regimes that identified themselves strategically and ideologically with the United States; second, a willingness to use all the instruments of foreign policy, including force, to install and, in particular, to perpetuate such regimes.

The policy enjoyed a totalitarian grip on the hearts and minds of the American public and the foreign policy establishment. It governed the interpretation of domestic and interstate conflict, placing a Chinese, Russian, or Cuban hand behind every threat to friendly regimes and minimizing local sources of discord. It governed moral and intellectual perceptions as well. Complaisant, although no doubt sincere, academics elaborated the useful distinction between merely authoritarian and totalitarian regimes, and then assumed a morally anodyne equation between the former and governments that extolled capitalism and liquidated communists.

Virtually without dissent from within the grand salon of respectable opinion, the United States extended containment from its initial European venue to the entire world.

There was, of course, one critical and ultimately decisive difference between the two cases. In Europe, containment meant protecting well-integrated national states and consensual systems of government against alien occupation. In the Third World, however, containment could easily entail assisting one faction within a country—possibly a very ugly one—against another. Any moral qualms about a U.S. policy that called for perpetuating not a system of government but rather particular governments were eased by the comfortably paranoid assumption that Soviet, Chinese, or Cuban agents lay behind any violent threat to the status quo.

Until Vietnam, most Americans—leaders and followers alike—considered this a fine way to conduct relations with the Third World. Among other nice things, it reinforced traditional sensations of U.S. omnipotence. At little apparent cost, Washington restored Shah Mohammad Reza Pahlavi to power in 1953 by helping him depose a difficult nationalist government whose political and ideological descendants the United States would love to see in power today. Washington also extinguished a threateningly reformist government in Guatemala in 1954 and imposed a pliable tool of Western interests on the former Belgian Congo. U.S.-trained and -armed troops hunted down and killed Cuba's revolutionary hero, Che Guevara, in Bolivia in 1967, and crushed opposition to U.S.-supported governments everywhere else in Latin America, except Cuba. Cuban exceptionalism was particularly rankling, a cruel thorn piercing the American psyche.

America's involvement in Vietnam emerged ineluctably from the womb of this policy and underlined its legal gimcrack, its moral blemishes, and its material and strategic costs. The consensus unraveled, but the policy lingered on until the mid-1970s as Secretary of State Henry Kissinger and his two presidential accomplices ordered the bombing and invasion of Cambodia, encouraged and then rewarded—with a conspicuous program of economic aid—a coup against democracy in Chile, and tried to organize compliant anticommunist governments for Angola and Zimbabwe.

Alternative Approach

Trapped in a maze of unresolved, perhaps unrecognized, contradictions, Carter could neither express nor consistently implement a coherent alternative to the preexisting orthodoxy. But he did mark a watershed in policy—foreshadowed during the Kissinger years by such congressional action as the so-called Clark Amendment that ended U.S. intervention in Angola—by bringing advocates of a consistent, alternative approach to the Third World from the shadowy frontiers of respectability into the center of power.

Supported by former Secretary of State Cyrus Vance and eccentrically personified by Andrew Young, former U.S. Ambassador to the United Nations, the alternative sprang from a set of assumptions at odds with those that had guided the enthusiasts of global containment. Those assumptions were:

- that threats to the status quo in and among Third World states usually spring from volatile political, social, and economic conditions that exist independently of the Soviet–American competition;
- that transnational ideological commitments tend to be thin, inevitably subordinate to personal, group, and national interests;
- that the terrible problems of economic growth and distribution and the industrial democracies' overwhelming advantage in the deployment of markets, capital, and technology give the United States and its allies an enormous edge in East–West competition for influence in Third World states, including those run by ostensible Marxists;
- that national imperatives require Third World governments to distribute their resources through international markets;
- that the Soviet Union cannot permanently integrate Third World states into its strategic and economic system without conquering and occupying them;
- that most Third World states are of only trivial significance to the East–West strategic balance;
- that the costs of keeping Third World regimes in power are generally disproportionate to the potential gains;
- that the costs of armed intervention to promote or frustrate political change are high because the capacity of Third World states to resist coercion is increasing;
- that the costs of diplomacy that relies heavily on the threat and use of force will seriously aggravate the economic difficulties and social tensions already shaking America;
- that independently of East–West competition, the promotion of important U.S. national interests—such as expanding markets for American exports, assuring the stable flow of essential raw materials and the development of new sources, and halting the spread of nuclear weapons—requires forms and degrees of cooperation from Third World states inconsistent with a swaggering, violent diplomacy;
- that ideas and values have material consequences and that the complex of values incorporated in the major human rights texts therefore will play a crucial orienting role for the generation coming of age in the Third World, as well as for elites in the West; and
- that the regnant image of the United States as an opponent of major Third World blocs on issues of central importance to them limits the scope of present and potential cooperation along the whole range of international issues.

Of the cluster of policies spawned by these assumptions, four stand out. First, except in very special cases, the United States would no longer equate its interests with the survival of particular regimes or automatically intervene to preserve right-wing regimes against domestic opponents, even those flaunting Marxist rhetoric and Soviet guns. Second, it would be cooler to regimes that grossly violate human rights, and it would refuse to overlook those violations simply because a regime was anticommunist.

Third, it would establish businesslike, cooperative relations with regimes of the Left willing to practice nonalignment on strategic issues and to conduct their economic affairs in a manner that does not discriminate against the West. Fourth, it would treat Third World states as legitimate and significant negotiating partners in the management of the international political and economic systems and would trade balanced concessions rather than seek unilateral advantages by threatening to use force.

The New Diplomacy: Neorealism

While logically dictating a broad reorientation of policy, the assumptions—collectively constituting what I shall call "neorealism"—left open profoundly contentious questions. The administration was not writing on an empty slate. Having long identified with specific, sometimes brutal regimes, how could Washington distance itself and occupy the high ground of human rights without actively assisting in undermining former intimates? And how would Washington handle relations with unpalatable regimes whose countries possessed assets genuinely important to America if the very process of violent change might endanger U.S. interests?

In the case of the member states of the Organization of Petroleum Exporting Countries (OPEC), was there any basis for accommodation not entailing very damaging American concessions? Did it then follow that an effective diplomacy might still require background indications of the will to employ coercion where other means failed?

And what would Washington do if the Kremlin adopted a high-profile interventionary diplomacy at the very moment the United States was relinquishing it? To encourage Soviet acceptance of low-profile competition, should the United States practice linkage politics, using trade and technology as carrots and sticks? Or could the policy ever work unless the United States were prepared to treat the Soviet Union as a legitimate and equal participant in managing global issues?

In other words, even in the case of a president personally convinced of their truth, the assumptions behind the new diplomacy left a vast, poorly explored space for creative diplomacy or fatuous fumbling. However well he coped, such a president could anticipate venomous political resistance from the densely clustered forces committed by reason of interest, emotion, or intellectual conviction to the old way of doing business in the Third World.

This resistance would be reinforced and focused by influential actors and groups who found their particular oxen in danger of goring. Among those groups were beneficiaries of the former Shah's largess, business and social cronies of former Nicaraguan President Anastasio Somoza Debayle, investors dependent on the survival of repressive regimes, industrialists specializing in certain lines of weaponry, members of the operations section of the Central Intelligence Agency, and certain ethnic constituencies.

Yet Carter never fully accepted the assumptions of the new diplomacy. Much of the President's apparent ineptitude in managing and defending his foreign policies is attributable to this uncertainty. Oscillation among premises was an understandable response to the powerful currents of domestic opinion pulling against the new diplomacy; to the dreadful uncertainties surrounding any set of foreign policies; to the Nixon administration's heritage of reliance on regional hegemonies to safeguard Western interests; and to a Soviet Union able and apparently willing to follow or even enlarge the pattern of intervention woven by the United States during the preceding decades.

Distinguishing Losses from Defeats

A great chorus now proclaims the failure of Carter's foreign policy. Although persons of every ideological hue have enjoyed a good sneer over the President's tactical fumblings, the main burden of his prosecution is carried by characters ranging from the political center to the far right. Despite their differences on domestic issues, the members of this group now are working together to drive U.S. foreign policy back to global containment of the Soviet Union.

The message, at its crudest, is propagated by the man the Republicans hope will lead their posse to the White House. The Soviets, Ronald Reagan reiterates without blinking, are the true authors of every disagreeable challenge to the status quo. To ignore any challenge to the status quo is to encourage the Kremlin to additional provocations.

More cerebral critics concede that Western interests may be threatened by forces independent of the Soviet Union, most notably by Arab oil producers. But the whole chorus, from the crudest charlatan to the subtlest intellect, unites around two grand themes: the need to back diplomacy with conspicuous threats of force and the need to sustain friendly regimes against all comers. By sharply discounting the efficacy of force and failing to back friends, they argue, Carter has dragged the country to the brink of a full–fledged calamity.

Critics claim, in essence, that Carter embraced neorealism, that the doctrine is equivalent to appeasement, and that, by failing to practice a muscular diplomacy, the President has strung together a series of national defeats. The record shows, however, that Carter never resolved his ambivalence about neorealism and that its implementation is not necessarily passive or placatory. Moreover, practically all the defeats invoked by the accusers either were not defeats in any useful sense of the word or could not have been averted at any reasonable price by the use of force. Three of the most frequently cited examples—Iran, Nicaragua, and Ethiopia—illustrate nicely the void in the center of the prosecution's brief.

Iran

Could a president weaned on the wit and wisdom of the late General George S. Patton have, unlike Carter, preserved our Pahlavian asset? In order to think about Iran with some measure of rationality, it is necessary to begin by distinguishing losses from defeats. If some extraordinary natural convulsion, such as an earthquake, devastated the oil fields of the Persian Gulf, Americans would speak of a terrible loss, but not of defeat. Defeat implies human provenance. And in the case of a superpower, it also suggests results that prudent measures might have averted.

A social eruption of incredible force and remarkable spontaneity deposed the late shah. The Ayatollah Ruhollah Khomeini and his entourage cheered and exhorted the Iranian people and improvised tactics. But ultimately, historical forces, not any one man or group, drew hundreds of thousands, finally millions of unarmed citizens into the streets to face down the shah's massed troops.

The strength and depth of this movement seem to have stunned even the shah's most frenzied American supporters. They have drawn dubious if not perverse lines of causation between Carter's tremulous appeals for human rights and the shah's eclipse. They have muttered darkly about Carterian plots to restrain the Iranian military from a last-minute restoration coup. But virtually no one has suggested that the United States should have intervened to preserve the Peacock Throne. Even the hard-liners recognize the horrendous costs and probable futility of any intervention in the face of that volcanic eruption against Pahlavi rule.

The sheer material costs of occupying a country with 35 million highly politicized people are intimidating enough. Yet even those costs might seem minor compared with the impact on American military morale, on the cohesion of American society, and on the moral basis of the Western alliance. This explains why the shah's allies in the United States are reduced to cravenly vague arraignments of American policy.

But did the United States have to be so adversely affected by the shah's fall? It did not, if the President had moved early in his administration to put U.S.-Iranian relations on a footing of cool, pragmatic cooperation between states with overlapping geopolitical interests. Instead, persuaded by the geopoliticians among his advisors of the shah's indispensability to the stability of the Persian Gulf, Carter brushed aside his human rights policy and proceeded to court the shah with a passion unequaled by his predecessors.

Iran was an irreversible phenomenon transformed into defeat by a President clinging, albeit without much conviction, to the premises of global containment. The United States is still paying the price for his choice and will likely continue to do so for years.

Nicaragua

In Nicaragua, Carter—unlike the donkey in the Calvinist parable who, paralyzed by indecision, starved to death between equally succulent, equidistant bales of hay—oscillated, nibbling now at one set of premises, now at the other, and often, it seemed, just wandering about dreamily.

The country's strategic insignificance, the Somoza regime's notorious marriage of cruelty and venality, and American responsibility for its birth and longevity made Nicaragua a prime target for the application of Carter's new deal on human rights. But Carter, unwilling to face the prospect of a government installed and dominated by the Sandinista guerilla groups, futilely tried with dwarf carrots and brittle sticks to move the dictator toward reform. While Washington danced attendance on Somoza's canny maneuvers, the guerrillas catalyzed a massive popular rebellion that toppled the old order after roughly a year of bloody conflict.

Was this a defeat? In two of the senses suggested by political scientist Robert Tucker it was: The United States did not want and tried to prevent the eventual outcome; and others in the hemisphere and beyond perceived that outcome to be a U.S. defeat and an indication of a weakened U.S. position in Central America and the Caribbean.

How might defeat have been avoided? The administration might have thrown its support behind Somoza as soon as it became apparent that he was in serious trouble. An unequivocal commitment to his survival backed by a flow of weapons and military advisors might have saved the dictator, particularly if U.S. political pressure had led other states in the region, such as Panama and Costa Rica, to deny arms and sanctuary to the opposition. Still, the isolation of Somoza and the desperate fury of his opponents might finally have required direct U.S. intervention to avert his collapse.

Conversely, Carter might have raced to the front of the anti-Somoza parade with an unambiguous commitment to his removal. Carter could have suspended diplomatic relations pending the formation of a representative government and declared that the people of Nicaragua by their collective resistance had withdrawn the regime's mandate to rule. Then he might have cheered from the sidelines until Somoza fled and thus converted the appearance of defeat into one of victory. By so strong a commitment, he might also have precipitated an earlier loss of nerve in the Somoza camp and thereby saved Nicaragua from the final battles that cost 20,000 lives and completed the country's physical devastation.

Ethiopia

In the early and middle years of the last decade, hard-liners on foreign policy—some of whom are now Reagan advisors—trumpeted alarms about Soviet air and naval facilities in Somalia that were said to threaten Western oil routes. The Soviet Union lost those facilities in 1977 because it opposed Somali irredentist claims to the Ogaden region of Ethiopia, which is inhabited by ethnic Somalis. Yet the same experts then announced another American defeat. For when they broke with Somalia, the Soviets embraced revolutionary Ethiopia, a strong American ally until the fall of Emperor Haile Selassie in 1974. Washington now is free to negotiate its own way into the Somali facilities for a fraction of what they cost the Soviet Union, while Moscow must spend hundreds of millions of dollars to protect its investment in Ethiopia, a country in constant danger of flying apart.

Whatever Ethiopia may be worth to the Soviet Union—which is largely excluded from effective influence in almost all other significant African states—the price the United States would have had to pay to compete for influence there was grossly disproportionate to the potential gains. With the province of Eritrea on the brink of winning its war of secession and the Somali armies poised to smash into Ethiopia's eastern flank, Haile Mariam Mengistu, Ethiopia's strong man, needed more from Washington than a gargantuan transfer of arms rivaling the $2 billion worth ultimately dispatched by the Kremlin. He needed more than petrol, oil, lubricants, and a small army of technicians to keep transferred equipment functioning. For a brief but crucial moment, he needed what the Cubans provided: pilots and shock troops who would hold off the Somalis and the Eritrean freedom fighters until he could marshal and deploy Ethiopia's superior manpower. And had the United States committed itself to the Ethiopian revolution by providing such massive military aid, could it then have denied Ethiopia the immense additional resources required for reconstruction and economic transformation?

Great costs were compounded by serious risks. U.S. prestige would have been tied to a small clique of officers dominated by Mengistu, who rose to his position on a pile of corpses, favored methods of social transformation likely to infuriate both conservative and liberal opinion in the United States, opposed civilian rule, and lacked an established base in any large sector of the population. Meanwhile, the Soviet Union would have remained ensconced in its Somali facilities, more secure than ever in a country now ferociously antagonistic to the United States for snatching victory from its grasp.

Positive Developments

What then could people possibly mean when they speak of Ethiopia as an American defeat? In essence, they are saying that the Soviets are there in force while the United States would prefer that they were not. Thus, in their view, an American defeat occurs whenever and wherever the Soviet Union intrudes against U.S. wishes, no matter what the costs of the intervention are in proportion to the gains, or what the costs of blocking the Soviets are in proportion to the potential rewards.

But this definition of defeat works both ways. If deviation from an idealized world is the measure of defeat, the Kremlin tastes it every day. For the West exerts its power and influence all over the world, a condition the Kremlin would no doubt change if only wishes could be realized without cost. The refusal to bid for overvalued assets was a triumph of strategic restraint, just as the fall of Somoza was a triumph for human rights. But according to the theology of global containment, an enemy of Moscow must be a friend of Washington, and violence practiced by opponents of left–wing states is, by definition, defensive.

These cases, which are among those most commonly cited by critics of the new diplomacy, belie the claim that the United States has experienced calamitous losses that could have been averted by an armed defense of the status quo.

Because the doctrine of global containment was ascendant throughout the 1960s and had already begun to recede in the early 1970s, one way to assess its merits is to compare the relative position of the Western alliance and the Soviet Union at the end of the 1960s with their relative positions today.

In the Western Hemisphere, the situation is essentially unaltered. Almost all Latin American states and all of the major ones—including Columbia, Mexico, Venezuela, Brazil, and Argentina—remain conservative capitalist countries. Chile drifted to the left but was brutally dragged back to the right. Among the smaller states, Nicaragua has acquired a government of the left. However, up to now, it evinces no desire for, or expectation of, Cuban-style incorporation into the Communist bloc, and the Soviet Union appears neither to anticipate nor to encourage such a development. Grenada, before its occupation by U.S. forces, was both inconsequential and possibly cooptable.

Moreover, there have been at least two very positive developments for the Western Alliance. One is the discovery of huge, additional oil reserves here in the Western Hemisphere and hence far from the reach of Soviet power or Arab-Israeli fallout. Another is the growing capacity and will of states such as Mexico and Brazil to serve as influential actors elsewhere in the Third World. Whatever problems may exist between them and the United States, by interest and ideology they are U.S. allies on issues of first importance to East-West competition.

In sub-Saharan Africa, the West continues to enjoy economic and political preeminence and to absorb virtually all of the continent's mineral exports. The jury is still out on the net advantage of trading Somalia for Ethiopia. Soviet influence has decreased perceptibly in Guinea and has increased in the Congo and Angola. But the Marxist-sounding regimes of Angola and Mozambique (which has always been closer to China than to the Soviet Union) openly yearn for Western investment, and the former, possible the latter as well, would apparently prefer to follow a wholly nonaligned foreign policy if it could resolve its internal difficulties. The settlement in Zimbabwe opens up that country's resources for accelerated development by Western capital. And the emergence of Nigeria as a leading oil producer with a liberal economic model is a gain for Western interests.

Devastating Blows to the Soviets

The most important changes over the past decade (1970-1980) have occurred in the Middle East and Asia. Egypt, by far the most important Arab country in cultural and military terms, has moved in one decade from Soviet client to one of the Third World states that is most completely integrated into the strategic and economic systems of the Western Alliance. Ten years ago, it sheltered the Soviet Mediterranean fleet. Today, its ports and airfields and apparently even its armed forces are available to the United States for a whole range of missions, including regional intervention on behalf of friendly regimes. With Egypt's withdrawal from the Arab coalition, Israel is freer to deploy force on behalf of Western interests. These developments along, with Iraq's increasing coolness toward Moscow, have been sharp blows to the Soviet position.

The fall of the shah was a setback for the United States, but it was not necessarily a victory for the Soviets. Moscow enjoyed a substantial economic relationship with the shah's Iran. His successors interrupted natural gas deliveries and harshly denounced Moscow after the invasion of Afghanistan. For all the shah's grandiloquent claims, his troops were not a serious obstacle to a direct Soviet thrust against the Persian Gulf. And although successive U.S. administrations were blind to the danger, the shah's commitment to protect the gulf from revolutionary forces was as likely to precipitate a destructive conflict as to ensure stability.

Asia has been the scene of three strategically important developments over the past decade: American withdrawal from the Indochina war; the emergence of India as a guarantor of a relatively decent order in South Asia and, by virtue of its enhanced national power and its amiable diplomatic relations with the Soviet Union, as a solid barrier to Soviet penetration of the region; and the transformation of relations between China and the United States.

Critics of neorealism accurately record a sharp decline in the coercive power and prestige of the United States over the past decade. They err only in assessing the causes and larger strategic consequences of that decline.

American power has declined relative to other participants in the international capitalist economic system—not only advanced industrial nations, but also Third World countries such as Brazil and India. The enrichment of their human and material resources strengthens the system with favorable consequences for all participants, including the United States. Their strength and political maturity is the fruition of policies initiated years ago by the fathers of global containment. Restraints on American autonomy were always the foreseeable price. The United States is less powerful, but the system from which its wealth and security now spring is stronger.

The decline of U.S. military power relative to the Soviet Union is a less benign development. Globalists could argue that a President, passionately selling global containment to the American people, might have convinced them to support higher defense expenditures. However advocates of the new diplomacy could argue that global containment's monster child, the Vietnam war, destroyed public support for an escalating budget by sowing cynicism and mutilating the U.S. economy.

The more credible position lies with the advocates of the new diplomacy. But it is only a polemical sideshow to the central question of whether the unavoidable enhancement of Soviet military power has been translated into major strategic gains, as most hard-liners allege. The only possible answer is that it has not. The Soviet Union has lost a few facilities here, gained a few there. It may have helped marginally to enlarge the number of regimes calling themselves Marxist. But those regimes are impoverished, increasingly disillusioned by the limits of Soviet economic assistance, and as eager as ever to sell their resources to the highest bidder.

If Soviet military prestige is high, its prestige as a model for or partner in national development has never been lower. Furthermore, by flaunting its enhanced military means, Moscow has strengthened Western political forces favoring increased defense expenditures, reduced political barriers to Japanese rearmament, and precipitated Western military assistance to China.

No Ready Answers

Because Soviet gains are so problematical, why has American prestige dropped so stunningly, creating the pervasive sense of decline that fuels the current resurgence of American jingoism? Part of the responsibility lies with those who, feeling threatened by the premises and policies of the new diplomacy, have warred against it with hysterical allegations of failure. When many of the most influential American individuals, institutions, and publications relentlessly proclaim America's supposed defeats, the U.S. public and audiences elsewhere in the world, weaned on the assumptions of global containment, are inclined to believe them.

A large measure of responsibility also lies, therefore, with the first President to doubt the premises of global containment, Jimmy Carter. For only the President has the prestige and commands the attention required to refocus fixed ideas about the national interest. And only he has the power to act consistently on new premises and in so doing progressively to validate them.

A President with the intellectual independence and political courage to embrace the new diplomacy would have made Nicaragua a victory for American policy. He would not have cozied up to the shah. Once the Iranian revolution was under way, he would have advised the monarch to find refuge with some empathic tyrant. Then neither American diplomats nor U.S. prestige would have been hostage to the struggle for power inside Iran.

These and the many other expressions of the new diplomacy would have been preceded and accompanied by a clear and consistent statement of the premises that lend them coherence. Standing uneasily on the same bully pulpit Theodore Roosevelt used to impose his consistent if flawed image of American interests, Carter has spoken in confusing tongues, leaving his audience prey to its fears and to his enemies.

A consistent commitment to the new diplomacy and an open, principled rejection of the premises of global containment would have established the basis for the preservation of American prestige. But the effort could not stop there. For the premises of the new diplomacy only constitute a general orientation, a cluster of presumptions refutable in particular cases. They do not provide a ready answer for every contingency. In particular, they only set broad policy guidelines for dealing with Soviet behavior in the Third World and handling Third World states that threaten Western interests.

The new diplomacy counsels against reflexive opposition to beneficiaries of Soviet assistance, whether they be established governments or rebels, except in those few countries where domestic violence threatens imperative U.S. interests. Some leftist governments may arise. But the experience of the last 20 years demonstrates that they will pursue their own interests and eventually accommodate with the West, which normally has far more to offer. Only by assuming direct physical control of the country can the Soviets prevent this.

It does not follow, however, that the United States should never guarantee a particular regime's survival. But it should do so not because the regime's opponent disparages the free market or fires Kalashnikov rifles. Rather, the United States should help a government only if it is prepared to compensate U.S. assistance with a valuable concession that Washington could not obtain through the operation of international markets or if the recipients of Soviet assistance are so unrepresentative of local constituencies that, even after forming a government, they could survive only on the strength of Soviet bayonets. The United States should also support the Third World's few authentically democratic regimes, because any great alliance requires demonstrative reaffirmations of its ideological glue. It would also encourage opponents of brutal regimes, whether of the Left or the Right. From this perspective, Cuban aid to the Sandinistas in Nicaragua was unobjectionable, but the Soviet Union's physical conquest of Afghanistan intolerable.

A Recipe for Defeat

These generalizations imply several rather precise rules of the game. Each side would recognize that the other may choose to give sanctuary, advice, training, and arms to governments or their opponents. Where such aid is extended to unpopular regimes or subversives, the other superpower may make as much political capital as it can out of such involvement, but it will not treat the intervention as a basis for sanctions, except in a few specified cases, such as Saudi Arabia. Regular troops may, however, be dispatched only at the request of a recognized government to resist foreign aggression, not domestic turmoil, and they must depart when the invitation is withdrawn. Neither Washington nor Moscow would be condoning intervention. They would simply be agreeing to tolerate a degree of flexibility in recognition of the fact that each country may occasionally have special incentives to influence the outcome of domestic conflicts.

With far fewer nonmilitary assets to employ, the Soviets have a greater temptation to solicit influence by arming and training participants in parochial Third World conflicts. The United States can help them curb that instinct by more aggressively co-opting their erstwhile clients. The Organization for Economic Cooperation and Development, in collaboration with concerned oil-producing states, might even establish a fund that would offer concessional loans and investment guarantees for communist states that opt for strategic nonalignment and economic nondiscrimination and that are prepared to meet minimum humanitarian norms.

The new diplomacy also would probe the Kremlin's demand for recognition as a global actor equal to the United States. Without yielding on Afghanistan, Washington could propose formation of high-level U.S.–U.S.S.R. working groups, including representatives of the other industrial democracies, to examine possible bases for cooperative action to ensure the flow of Middle East oil, facilitate a settlement of the Arab–Israeli conflict, and accelerate the pace of change in South Africa.

As it implies distinct guidelines for U.S. competition with the Soviet Union in the Third World, neorealism also governs the instinct to coerce Third World states. Recognizing the collective sensitivity of such states to past instances of coercion and their growing power to retaliate through a variety of means, the new diplomacy requires the exhaustion of alternative remedies, the restriction of violent intervention to extreme cases, and the sanction if not of law then at least of widely recognized principles of equity. It opposes interventions that are not supported by allies, nor accepted by some prominent developing countries.

Today and in the years ahead, the international system will have to cope with regimes, such as the one in Zaire, that are politically, morally, and fiscally bankrupt. Within the premises of the new diplomacy, the United States can develop norms and structures to limit the resulting injury to the larger international system, as well as to the unwilling subjects of such regimes.

Several years ago, Americans might have thought that the Vietnam war, the subsequent U.S. rapprochement with China, and the exposure during the Watergate scandal of the domestic consequences of America's approach to foreign policy had finally interred global containment. Yet it has reappeared.

For a brief time, the United States enjoyed an indisputable global preeminence. The Vietnam war and OPEC brought a sudden realization of harsh limits on America's ability to dominate events. An adjustment of perspective does not come easily.

Defeat in other realms of policy—the persistence of poverty and racial conflict, the decline of traditional industries and the dollar, deep pockets of unemployment—has helped to fix in place a searing self-image of failure at the very time that individual Americans particularly need the satisfaction of vicarious participation in victory.

Americans are inclined to transcend a sense of personal inadequacy through identification with winners. Geographic identity with victorious sporting teams offers one source of personal fulfillment. National identity with a victorious diplomacy offers another. Foreign policy thus becomes the moral equivalent of sport, with other countries as irredeemable competitors. Cooperation spoils the game, and defeat aches. For the ultimate canon of American sporting life is that winning is not the most important thing: it is everything. But in international relations, the swaggering pursuit of triumphs torn by main force from the grasp of history, without reference to morality or cost, is a recipe for ultimate defeat or the collective destruction of the game.

2

Morality and Foreign Policy

The controversy over President Reagan's proposal to aid the Nicaraguan contras is merely another phase in the recurrent debate over the proper role of moral values in the conduct of U.S. foreign policy. While recently there has been a slight change in terminology, "human rights" having become more-or-less synonymous with moral ends, the underlying issues have not altered. Nor, with that modest exception just mentioned, are the contestants' labels any different. On one side are those who see themselves as heirs of the realist tradition with its stern emphasis on the statesman's duty to promote the national interest which in its essence is the same for all nations at all times. On the other are those who invoke the strain of idealism in American policy which mandates efforts to propagate American values beyond our shores.

Henry Kissinger may be the most notorious contemporary practitioner of realism, but its most distinguished and admired defender is George Kennan, the intellectual father of containment. Some thirty-five years after throwing down the realist gauntlet in an elegant little volume entitled *American Diplomacy, 1900–1950*,[1] Mr. Kennan has once again stoked the furnace of debate, this time by means of a brief, lead essay in a recent issue of *Foreign Affairs*,[2] quarterly journal of the Council on Foreign Relations. If it serves no other function, this essay nicely, albeit unintentionally, illustrates the realist position's difficulties.

Mr. Kennan opens his argument with the impeccable observation that "the functions, commitments, and moral obligations of governments are not the same as those of the individual. Government is an agent, not a principal. Its primary obligation is to the interests of the national society it represents, not to the moral impulses that individual elements of that society may experience." So far he is, of course, correct. The statesman has no more right to use his office to advance purely personal values than does a judge interpreting the Constitution or determining whether a contract violates public policy. But the judge obviously would fail in the performance of his duties if he were unwilling to enforce the values embedded in the Constitution, in legislation, or in the various sources to which he or she may legitimately repair in order to determine public policy. How, then, can the statesman fulfill his role as agent when he serves a people with a conspicuously evangelistic bent? Are his appropriate ends somehow insulated from common moral impulses? To put the matter more precisely: Can it fairly be argued that implicit in the statesman's pact with the American people is a directive to pursue ends and to employ means uninformed by conventional moral sentiments?

The classical realist has normally responded in two ways. The first is that, in serving the nation, a statesman acts on behalf of something larger than today's majority, even if that majority approaches consensus. The nation, he argues, is more than the sum of its present inhabitants whose identity is, after all, in a constant state of flux with some dying and others arriving. The nation is an historic entity that, unlike its inhabitants, can reasonably aspire to immortality. It is a culture limited in space but not necessarily in time. Of course, without people there is no culture. And of course, therefore, the statesman's pact is with people, not space. But among the people to whom he must answer are generations yet unborn. It follows that his supreme obligation is to assure the continuity of the state, its autonomy and political integrity, so that the great chain of living culture is not broken. He or she is, in other words, the trustee of an unwritten, intergenerational pact.

Contemporary American conservatives rarely use this sort of organic imagery, in part because, however fervently they embrace the label, their emotional and intellectual ties to traditional conservative ideology and feeling are loose at best. In any event, conservative metaphors clash with the dominant populism of American society, a society that associates political legitimacy almost exclusively with electoral majorities.

Even Ambassador Kennan, who probably comes as close as any public figure to the sensibility of a 19th century English conservative, does not openly rest his case on an organic view of the state. Rather, if I understand him correctly, he assumes that the great majority of people anywhere regard the production of morally pleasing outcomes for other peoples as a low priority in the conduct of foreign policy. That, at least, is how I construe the following passage:

> When the government of the sovereign state . . . accepts the responsibility of governing, implicit in that acceptance is the assumption that it is right that the state should be sovereign, that the integrity of its political life should be assured, that its people should enjoy the blessings of military security, material prosperity and a reasonable opportunity for . . . the pursuit of happiness.

Having said that, Kennan proceeds to the assumption which seems to me the key to his entire position. "Whoever looks thoughtfully at the present situation of the United States in particular," he writes, "will have to agree that to assure these blessings to the American people is a task of such dimensions that the government attempting to meet it successfully will have very little, if any, energy and attention left to devote to other undertakings, including those suggested by the moral impulses of these or those of its citizens."

Finally, as if in search of a clinching point however tenuously related to the logic of his main argument, he calls on us to "note that there are no internationally accepted standards of morality to which the U.S. government could appeal if it wished to act in the name of moral principles." Rather, there are various high-sounding words and phrases, incorporated in sundry solemn declarations and pacts and charters, all being of such "vagueness that the mere act of subscribing to them carries with it no danger of having one's freedom of action significantly impaired."

The division between realists and idealists is not nearly as neat as the terms imply, because many writers associated with the latter camp invoke national interest with no less fervor than their realist adversaries. The issue, they insist, is not whether governments should pursue the national interest. Of course they should and will! The real issue, however, is whether such pursuit should be informed by moral values, wheresoever derived.

As Kennan properly notes, the debate has two foci. One is the behavior of foreign governments in cases where that behavior, while not impinging on the material interests of the United States, does offend the moral sensibilities of some Americans. The other is the behavior of our own government as it seeks to augment national security and wealth. While this distinction has a certain analytical value, many though not all of the arguments arrayed against realpolitik apply to both cases.

The idealists, as I shall call them for want of a conspicuously better name, are able to assault the realpoliticans from several directions. One thrust is through the theory of democratic representation. In a society characterized by authentic political competition, the argument runs, diplomats are not entitled simply to assume the electorate's priorities. Rather, those priorities are expressed through the electoral process, a process tending to reveal the intensity as well as the breadth of support for particular policies. Just as individuals will sometimes risk both physical security and wealth on behalf of intangible goals, so in certain circumstances will large groups of people. In short, the claim in any given case that an electoral majority wants the government to employ means or pursue ends deemed moral by that majority, despite a coincident risk to national security or wealth, is not incredible and hence cannot be rejected out of hand on the ground that the claim is inherently unbelievable.

The principal difficulty with this argument lies not in its logical force but rather in its practical utility. In part because politicians in the industrial democracies normally struggle to allay rather than aggravate anxieties about the costs of alternative policies and, moreover, wrap their personal preferences in language which obscures the sharp edges of those alternatives, the substance of an electoral mandate is usually highly uncertain. Thus, even if one concedes that governments must heed the will of the voting majority, however perverse, in the vast majority of cases one has in fact conceded very little.

A second and more dangerous assault concentrates on the realists keystone concept, national interest. One thrust challenges Kennan's claim that the effort to assure the security and the economic interests of the United States in today's world is so extraordinarily problematic as to leave little time or energy for other undertakings, "including those suggested by the moral impulses of these or those of its citizens." On the contrary, some idealists argue, to the extent that security is achievable in a world of nuclear–armed states, the United States achieves it by means of an invulnerable retaliatory force. That force, together with the immense conventional superiority we enjoy all around the periphery of the country as a consequence of our relative national wealth and high technology, makes us more immune to physical threats than any great power of the last millennium. Nor, as *The Economist* pointed out editorially some years ago,[3] does the promotion of our national wealth require the feverish exercise of diplomacy. The age of mercantilism is past. Markets, not governments, allocate goods and services. If governments have a positive role to play it is largely by encouraging initiative and innovation at home.

Unbelievably rich and secure by historical standards, according to this view, the U.S. government is uniquely free to advance the moral visions of its polity. There is a broad realm of discretion within which it can act without serious risk to the material interests of this or future generations.

A second attacking force follows a totally different strategic vision. Rather than treating the promotion of moral ends as an affordable luxury for the United States, its proponents claim moral inspiration as an essential element of national security in an extraordinarily dangerous world. Leaders of this force normally subscribe to the seamless–web theory of national security. Every conflict of will (however minor the issue), like every country (however remote, small, or impoverished), matters. It matters in part because the ability to deter threats to interests of indisputable importance is a function not only of material assets but also of the perceived will to deploy them. Any sign of slackening in that will encourages the enemy to press forward until it encounters obdurate resistance. Coincidentally, it discourages allies. The market in national prestige is no less subject than the market in commodities to rapid and potentially disastrous fluctuations. Furthermore, since power derives from potential as well as presently deployable resources—that is, from industrial and technological capabilities as yet unallocated to martial purposes—questions of survival insinuate themselves into a vast range of issue areas, not simply those of immediate strategic concern.

The history of the Reagan administration illustrates with unusual clarity at least the rhetoric of humanitarian diplomacy in the service of a Hobbesian world view. For here we have a President who has restored the Cold War assumptions and the strategy of global containment to their traditional eminence in the conduct of American foreign policy and has done so in the name not of conservative realpolitik but rather in the declared pursuit of values usually associated with liberal Democrats.

Now that the administration has found itself able, despite the rhetoric and instincts of its leaders, to associate itself with a marvelous revolution against a right-wing villain, Mr. Marcos, and to claim some credit as well for the departure of the ineffable Duvaliers from Haiti, it has at least temporarily claimed the posture of a promiscuous crusader for democracy. Since few adults other than Saul of Tarsus and the protagonist of James Joyce's short story, "The Dead," have been known to experience genuine moral revelations, I am condemned to observe President Reagan's new departure in a spirit of high skepticism.

What I think prompted George Kennan to write the article I noted at the outset of this paper was an emotion more powerful than mere skepticism. It was, I believe, fear, fear that the fusion of moral enthusiasm with a foreign policy marked from the outset by a Manichean world view, a corresponding contempt for the cautionary advice of other democratic governments and paranoia about the balance of power could lead unintentionally to a superpower confrontation from which each would find it difficult to withdraw. If I am correct, then Kennan's article should be seen not as an attack on morality in the conduct of foreign affairs but rather as a reminder that the ultimate moral interest of the contemporary statesman is the avoidance of a Third World War.

Notes

1. Chicago 1951.
2. "Morality and Foreign Policy," Winter 1985–86 Volume 14, No. 2., p. 205.
3. "Which Foxholes to Fight In," August 28, 1976, p. 9.

3

The System

The Inter-American System is an idea corresponding never very precisely to a set of formal institutions and legal norms. It is also an association for mutual defense, political accommodation, economic development, and cultural exchange. But above all it is the still-evolving, tangled, and problematical relationship between the United States and its southern neighbors.

Over thirty independent states, they differ dramatically in size, density, history, race, culture, wealth, development, and just about any other facet of national existence the mind can conjure, with the partial exception of language. Yet it has long been assumed that history imposes on them a collective relationship to the United States that frames and colors their diverse bilateral ties with the northern behemoth, and often with each other as well. This is the so-called special relationship—variously defined, sometimes lamented, occasionally questioned, and perpetually present.

Although the great weight of U.S. economic and strategic concerns properly lies in other parts of the world; although American planners do not see the Western Hemisphere as the primary arena for confronting any of the great issues of contemporary international life—from pollution to nuclear proliferation to the allocation of wealth and the terms of resource transfers between developed and developing states—no President and no secretary of state has been prepared to renounce a special U.S. interest in and, as a corollary, preferred status for Latin America. President Jimmy Carter reiterated the traditional position in remarks before the Latin American foreign ministers and diplomats attending a session of the U.N. General Assembly: "As far as my stay in New York is concerned, I have saved the best for the last, because I feel closer to you than to any other region of the world."[1]

The Inter-American System is, as already suggested, far more than the cluster of formal agreements and official institutions that are its most concrete expression. They are only the official expression of a pluralistic system that comprises the much larger network of relationships between and among public and private entities—intelligence agencies, churches, trade unions, universities, armies, foundations, corporations. And then there is the idea itself, this way of thinking about the hemisphere that inevitably influences public policy. The formally bilateral question of the Panama Canal Treaty would not, for instance, have been so charged with political significance had it not been implicated in the larger relationship felt to exist between the United States and the totality of its southern neighbors.

Although their virtues have been absorbed into the conventional wisdom of the United States, becoming a point of intellectual departure for editorialists, politicians, and the portion of the public that imagines itself literate about foreign affairs, neither the idea nor the formal institutions that give it flesh are any longer sacrosanct. Heterodox opinion within the foreign policy community has on occasion gone beyond calling for reform to proposing institutional demolition. Before becoming Assistant Secretary of State for Inter-American Affairs, William Rogers wondered publicly if it were not time for the United States to withdraw from the Organization of American States (OAS).[2] Although withdrawal was too sharp a démarche for the State Department professionals, a policy of malign neglect has found supporters who imagine a time when the institutions are so clearly moribund that they could be interred, without commotion, virtually by unanimous consent.

Are the heterodox right? Have the norms, customs, and official institutions of the system lost their capacity to promote the interests of the United States or most of the other participants? Are they relics of another age, obstacles to the conduct of an enlightened diplomacy? Should they be reformed or should they rather be dismantled on the grounds that they help to perpetuate an outmoded conception of national rights and obligations in the Western Hemisphere?

The System's Progress: The Problematics of Success

The character of the system's formal institutions—principally the OAS and the Rio Treaty of Reciprocal Assistance—is premeditated. If, as critics maintain, the institutions need to be changed, it follows that the underlying reality of inter-American interests, relations, and beliefs that animated their architects already has changed. How has that reality altered in the course of the nearly four decades which have elapsed since the adoption of the Rio Treaty and the OAS Charter?

The Aims of the Founding Fathers

One begins, necessarily, with the original premises. Latin as well as American statesmen were concerned in the aftermath of World War II with external threats to the hemisphere. It was, after all, the Latins who, during the drafting of the U.N. Charter, tenaciously insisted on a quasi-autonomous security and peacekeeping role for regional institutions. In other words, it was not simply the United States that wished to "multilateralize the Monroe Doctrine."

However differently they may have appraised the prospect, U.S. and Latin American political leaders assumed the United States would play the central role on the Latin American stage. It was without rival as a source of investment capital and imports and as a market for southern exports. Its nationals had more investments in Latin America than in any other part of the world. And although the United States had not intervened militarily since the inception of Franklin Delano Roosevelt's Good Neighbor Policy, World War II had plainly strengthened its capacity to employ force throughout the hemisphere. Thus the United States represented at least a potential constraint on the autonomy of every Latin state.

Left-wing critics of U.S. policy in Latin America tend to see the institutions that grew from this premise as an elaborate sham designed to conceal the imperious thrust of American power. From time to time they have served that end, most notoriously in the cases of Guatemala, Cuba, and the Dominican invasion of 1965. But these instances of collaboration with imperial intervention hardly suffice to support the claim.

A striking feature of the seminal negotiations that finally produced the Rio Treaty and the OAS Charter was the evident enthusiasm of the Latin participants. Why would political leaders in countries so sensitive to the risk of American intervention have promoted institutions that, according to the critics, would serve merely to cloak or even thinly to legitimate American threats to their political independence? The simple answer, of course, is that they would not and did not. They devised the institutions of the Inter-American System not to legitimate but rather to contain American power. Containment was their dominating purpose. The Charter and the Treaty were its imperfect expression.

Unlike the U.N. Charter—which, by centralizing coercive authority in the Security Council and conceding vetoes to the Great Powers of 1945, frankly recognized the material inequality of states—the OAS Charter and the Rio Treaty collectively signify the triumph of formal equality: one state, one vote. There is, to be sure, a kind of veto power, since decisions compelling enforcement action by the member states require a two-thirds majority. But this was no concession. Rather, it was a counterweight to U.S. influence, a hedge against the anticipated capacity of the United States to marshal a friendly majority by one means or another.

The intent of the Latin founding fathers to circumscribe U.S. power—a power they could not in any event exorcise—also is apparent in the Charter's categorical and multiple prohibitions of intervention, except in the case of "measures adopted for the maintenance of peace and security in accordance with existing treaties," that is, measures adopted by a two-thirds vote. Article 18 states:

> No State or group of States has the right to intervene, directly or indirectly, for any reason whatever, in the internal or external affairs of any other State. The foregoing principle prohibits not only armed force but also any other form of interference or attempted threat against the personality of the State or against its political, economic and cultural elements.

The prohibition is echoed in Article 19's stricture that "No State may use or encourage the use of coercive measures of an economic or political character in order to force the sovereign will of another State and obtain advantages of any kind." And it is reechoed in Article 20, which precludes recognition of "special advantages obtained either by force or by other means of coercion."

The inhibition of U.S. power being its regnant aim, why was the charter acceptable to the United States? In part, no doubt, because the financial, moral, and political costs of a legally naked hegemony must have seemed even more onerous in 1947 than in 1933, when the United States renounced any unilateral right to impose its notions of propriety on the hemisphere. In part, as well, because U.S. statesmen saw no fundamental antagonism between the national interests of the United States and those of the dominant classes in Latin America. Fascism, which during the 1930s had flourished in some Latin states, had lost its allure—if not for its delinquencies, then certainly for its defeats. Communism was no more popular in Latin capitals than in Washington.

Economic interests also seemed essentially compatible. The Latins needed U.S. markets for their commodities and U.S. capital in lieu of the internal savings that most states still were unable to induce, even where there was much of a surplus to save. The Europeans, for many decades vigorous participants in the economic life of Latin America, had neither capital nor much capacity to import on the old scale.

But there were potential difficulties. Nationalism had lost none of its emotive force in Latin America. Although unalloyed with communist or explicitly fascist ideology, it could again threaten U.S. investments; Mexican oil nationalization remained a rankling memory for the U.S. business community. Moreover, as in the past, particularly some of the smaller states might prove feckless about repaying public debts to U.S. creditors. But with the Cold War already coming to dominate the view of the U.S. elite, these concerns must have seemed secondary at best. What really mattered was collective security against the emerging Soviet challenge. However it may have been perceived by U.S. statesmen, the challenge was defined in ideological terms: liberal capitalist democracy versus totalitarian, aggressive communism. A security system democratic in its form, resting on notions of equality, nonintervention, and mutuality of interest, nicely underlined the declared stakes of the competition.

Apart from the Cold War, the democratic forms of the OAS system appealed both to the self-consciously idealistic strain in U.S. foreign policy and to the natural inclination of a status quo power—necessarily delighted with the postwar dispensation—to consolidate and legitimate its position in terms of prevailing values. And the values that prevailed, in the aftermath of a war against their antithesis, were respect for the independence of small states and rejection of force as a tool of diplomacy.

Success and Its Discontents

The promise of converging political interests was essentially fulfilled. Whenever East-West issues surfaced at the United Nations or in other global forums, the bulk of the Latin states generally followed the U.S. lead. When Cuba broke ranks, a clear majority of the OAS supported U.S. efforts to isolate the apostate.[3] Within the OAS, few governments questioned the compatibility of the Bay of Pigs incident with the nonintervention norms of the charter. And as the issue of guerrilla-led revolution in the Third World became salient in U.S. strategic calculations, most Latin governments proved enthusiastic collaborators in Washington's effort to coordinate a global program of counterinsurgency. By formal resolution, the OAS anathematized Marxists and implicitly authorized relaxation of nonintervention norms as a means of cauterizing the revolutionary threat.[4]

Developments in the economic sphere coincided logically with the common struggle against the guerrillas. In most of Latin America, increasingly professional military establishments and a growing class of civilian technocrats opted decisively for the capitalist road to high-technology development. Among its other consequences, this choice entailed a relatively receptive attitude to foreign investors, heavy reliance on hard-currency financial markets, a drive for new or enlarged export outlets in the industrial West, tolerance of high levels of unemployment, and accelerating inequality between the upper one or two quintiles of the national population and those at the bottom.

By the late 1970s, however, that profound convergence of interests had succeeded in generating prickly differences between the United States and a large number of Latin governments. While in the late '50s and '60s, development aid and the struggle against the Left were the preeminent themes of hemispheric discourse, 15 years later they had been displaced: In the political realm, debate over issues of human rights agitated the hemisphere; in the economic realm, discourse was infused with the whole complex of North–South issues, though with particular emphasis on trade, the transfer of technology, and the regulation of multinational corporations.

The sometimes acerbic dialogue over human rights, muted since Reagan replaced Carter, related in at least two ways to the earlier successful effort to destroy the revolutionary Left. On the U.S. side, there was a sense of having strayed from the path of traditional American idealism and a kind of penitential desire to find the way back. Catalyzed in some quarters by remorse for the devastation inflicted on Indochina, the mood was rhythmically reinforced by reports of government-sponsored brutality in countries that the United States had encouraged and assisted throughout the 1960s under the banner of counterinsurgency.[5] The U.S. public was no longer comfortable with the worldly cynicism epitomized by a possibly apocryphal comment on the Dominican Dictator, Rafael Trujillo, frequently attributed to F.D.R.: "He may be an s.o.b., but he's our s.o.b."

Right-wing Latin governments, for their part, sensitive under the best of circumstances to "Yankee intervention" in what they might choose to regard as their internal affairs, greeted the freshet of American criticism with anger as well as deep concern, heightened by a sense of betrayal. As one young Uruguayan officer is said to have told a visiting American,

> We are doing precisely what you encouraged and equipped us to do—destroying Marxists and developing a free enterprise economy. The war against the Marxists requires exceptional means. You did not hesitate to use them in Vietnam. But you lacked the will to win. You gave up. This is our country. We will not give up. And we will win.

Comparative moderates in the more ruthless regimes justified the demolition of democratic institutions partially on grounds of the obstructions they pose to the anticommunist crusade and partially on grounds of their incompatibility with the pursuit of rapid development. Politicians, it was said, will cater demagogically to the masses, who lack the discipline and restraint required if the country is to be made safe for development. On the other hand, for hardline military and civilian groups in the most violently conservative states, the antidemocratic animus was neither tactical nor temporary. Rather, it was firmly rooted in a contempt for pluralist society comparable in intensity to the feelings of a hardened Stalinist. The fact that the officer corps in which corporatist or fascist views circulated were dotted with men who had studied in U.S. military establishments only contributed to the moral uneasiness of the United States. That uneasiness was further aggravated by the antiegalitarian consequences of *laissez-faire* development in Brazil, Chile, and many other places in the hemisphere.[6]

While the manifest thinness of the income trickling down to the lower quintiles of the Latin population had cost *laissez-faire* economic development much of its moral charm, development there had been. In Brazil, which contains roughly one-third of the 300 million citizens of Latin America, there was explosive economic growth. The average annual increase in the gross national product for the entire postwar period was more than 7%, with the annual rate of industrial growth at least 2% higher.[7] Mexico's growth, although less dramatic, still had hummed along at an annual rate of 6%.[8] The accelerating expansion of industry and large-scale, export-oriented agriculture in these two southern giants and in several other states—albeit on a more modest scale—had brought them into conflict with various U.S. interests experiencing the bite of an intensifying competition for markets.

Having preached the virtues of the international capitalist system, keyed to the theory of comparative advantage, the United States greeted the results of its evangelism with restrained enthusiasm. Brazilian soybeans threaten established U.S. markets in third countries. Shoes, textiles, and other labor-intensive products from Brazil, Mexico, and, prominent among the rest, Columbia, in conjunction with comparable products from the more advanced Asian countries threatening to monopolize the American market, were held tensely at bay by a variety of trade barriers. And the United States showed little inclination to dismantle the barriers despite the fact that Latin America coincidentally provided an expanding market for the sophisticated arms and other high-technology products in whose production the United States continues to enjoy a marked advantage.

Within the United States there was not only a clamor actually to toughen the barriers to manufacturers and competitive commodities from Latin America but also growing support for restraints on the export of capital, know-how, and technology. It was feared that if their exports continued to grow—encouraged among other things by a disciplined, docile, and poorly paid work force—the expanding industries of Latin America would strip the competitive edge from an ever-expanding list of traditional U.S. products. At the same time, the principal Latin states, faced with burgeoning populations, suddenly diminished growth rates, ineradicable unemployment, and a massive foreign debt, relentlessly pursued preferential access to markets in the advanced industrial countries, along with easier and less costly access to sophisticated technology.

These contradictions between Latin interests and those of certain influential sectors in the United States lent a new dimension to U.S.–Latin conflict in the economic realm. The traditional concern about limiting U.S. coercive power remained vital, as illustrated by the sharp collective reaction to the U.S. Congress's exclusion of Ecuador and Venezuela, because of their membership in the Organization of Petroleum Exporting Countries (OPEC), from the reduction in tariffs effected by the General System of Preferences (GSP). Beside this negative interest in constraining U.S. power, an affirmative desire to extract positive benefits from the United States had grown to at least equal stature. Not so many years before, the leading Latin states would have welcomed benign neglect. By the time of Jimmy Carter's Inauguration, it was by no means enough.

The effort led by Peru in the mid–1970s to place "collective economic security" on a par with military security as the primary shared objectives of the Inter–American System stemmed from both concerns. Behind the term lay an elaborate scheme that would have committed the United States to affirmative action in the economic sphere and have formally subjected both its domestic and foreign policies, insofar as they might seriously affect the economic health of other hemispheric states, to their appraisal. In 1975, by a 20–1 vote, its Latin allies trampled over U.S. opposition to an amendment of the Rio Treaty providing that "economic security" shall be "guaranteed" in a "special treaty." The amendment corresponded to a phrase in the Preamble to the Protocol of Amendment, which stated that the parties "recognize that, for the maintenance of peace and security in the Hemisphere, it is also necessary to guarantee collective economic security for the development of the American States."

Since the new article was clearly designed to bend the United States toward acceptance of a separate treaty on collective economic security, the United States reserved its position, declaring that by signing the Protocol of Amendment it accepted no obligation to negotiate such a treaty.[9] The issue also arose in the context of discussions concerning possible amendments to the OAS Charter, where it practically immobilized the draftsmen.

One other development bears significantly on any current appraisal of the Inter–American System. It is the sharply intensified transhemispheric perspective of the larger Latin states corresponding to the reduced economic role of U.S. capital goods and markets and the concomitant growth of economic links with other nations and regions.

European and Japanese multinationals hunt aggressively for an ever-expanding place in the Latin market. Volkswagen has the largest slice of

Brazil's auto market. France enabled Peru to break the sound barrier by selling Mirage aircraft. Japanese entrepreneurs are tying up big chunks of important commodities in long-term supply contracts. Reflective of their growing role in Latin America, Japan, Canada, Spain, and four members of the European Common Market—Belgium, France, West Germany, and the Netherlands—have joined the IDB and acquired observer status at the OAS.

The United States nevertheless retains great economic power in the hemisphere, but it does so as the first among equals, not as an unrivaled hegemon.

Notes

1. Oct. 6, 1977.
2. "Torpe y Confuso Hipopotamo," 41 *Visión* 24j-24k (Feb. 24, 1973).
3. Res. VI of the Eighth Meeting of Consultation of the Ministers of Foreign Affairs (Jan. 31, 1962), OEA/Ser. F/II. 8, Doc. 68, at 17-19, and 46 *Dept State Bull.* 281 (1962).
4. See the Declaration of Solidarity for the Preservation of the Political Integrity of the American States Against International Communist Intervention." at the 10th Inter-American Conference. 30 *Dept State Bull.* 420 (1954).
5. The degree of complicity is described by A.J. Langguth in his book, *Hidden Terrors* (1978).
6. See, e.g., A. Fishlow, "Brazilian Size Distribution of Income." 62 *Am. Econ. Rev.* 391-402 (May 1972); and see generally, I. Adelman and C. Taft Morris, *Economic Growth and Social Equity in Developing Countries* 192-94 (1973); H. Chenery *et. al., Redistribution with Growth* (1974).
7. G.F. Treverton, "Latin America in World Politics: The Next Decade," p. 29 (*Adelphi Papers* #137 1977).
8. International Bank for Reconstruction and Development, *World Tables* p. 169 (1976).
9. See "Report of the United States Delegation to the Conference of Plenipotentiaries," p. 10 (July 16-28, 1975 San José, Costa Rica).

4

Reagan's Latin America

Some of President Reagan's advisors believe that Jimmy Carter had a clear policy for dealing with Third World countries, and that it was wrong, above all in Latin America. Probably the most detailed and influential statement of their view is the article "Dictatorships and Double Standards," published last year by Jeane Kirkpatrick, the new ambassador to the U.N.[1] The central problem, according to Professor Kirkpatrick, is "that of formulating a morally and strategically acceptable, and politically realistic, program for dealing with non-democratic governments who are threatened by Soviet-sponsored subversion."

Drawing principally on Iran and Nicaragua, she describes what she takes to be a typical "non-democratic" government and the wrongheaded response to it she had come to expect from the Carter administration.

In such a government, a long-established autocrat is sponsored by a private army—which owes allegiance to him and his family rather than to some abstract idea of the state. The autocrat tolerates "limited opposition, including opposition newspapers and political parties." But because he is "confronted by radical, violent opponents bent on social and political revolution," he must sometimes invoke martial law to arrest, imprison, exile, "and occasionally, it was alleged [Kirkpatrick says, referring to the specific cases of Iran and Nicaragua] torture [his] opponents." The autocrat enriches himself in large part by confusing his own resources with those of the state and makes no attempt "to alter significantly the distribution of goods, status, or power."

In the past, this model autocrat was a good friend of the United States and successive American administrations gave him tangible and intangible support. But then came Jimmy Carter.

"The pattern [of response] is familiar enough," Kirkpatrick writes.

> An established autocracy ... is attacked by insurgents, some of whose leaders have long ties to the Communist movement, and most of whose arms are of

Soviet, Chinese or Czechoslovak origin. The "Marxist" presence is ignored and/or minimized by American officials and by the elite media on the ground that U.S. support for the dictator gives the rebels little choice but to seek aid "elsewhere."

Kirkpatrick goes on to elaborate this scenario, which turns out to be a tendentious but not crazily distorted version of the Nicaraguan case, cobbled together with incidents from the Shah's fall. As U.S. aid is steadily withdrawn, there are rising expressions of concern about the dictator's popular support and his failures in human rights, all echoed by "liberal columnists" and "returning missionaries."

As the conflict worsens, the United States calls for the autocrat's replacement by a broadly based coalition headed by a "moderate" critic of the regime. To hasten the friendly old retainer on his way, Washington cuts off aid entirely so the legitimate government becomes weaker while the rebels continue to accumulate weapons and intensify hostilities. Finally, either the dictator, effectively disarmed by the perfidious Carter, is overwhelmed by the rebels, or he dutifully abdicates to a moderate backed by the United States who is in turn replaced by radicals. In either case, Kirkpatrick argues, "the U.S. will have been led by its own misunderstanding of the situation to assist actively in deposing an erstwhile friend and ally and installing a government hostile to American interests and policies in the world" and even more repressive than its predecessor.

Kirkpatrick's remedies follow ineluctably from her diagnosis of Carter's errors. The United States must not undermine friendly authoritarian governments. It may encourage a "process of liberalization and democratization, provided that the effort is not made at a time when the incumbent government is fighting for its life against violent adversaries, and that proposed reforms are aimed at producing gradual change rather than perfect democracy overnight." When Marxists or other enemies of the United States seek violently to overthrow the traditional order, the United States should send aid, not excluding the Marines.

Of this proposal, it may be said that it rests on an almost demented parody of Latin American[2] political realities as well as on a grave misperception of Carter's policies and achievements. On the most elementary facts, Kirkpatrick is misinformed, for example, when she claims that Carter disarmed Somoza. Before the last round of the Nicaraguan conflict, Somoza's National Guard bristled with weapons supplied by Argentina and Israel. Passing to more important misconceptions, dictatorial regimes of the Somoza type are far less common today than they were twenty or thirty years ago, when Kirkpatrick's views seem to have been formed. A few relics survive: Duvalier Jr. in Haiti, Stroessner in Paraguay. But in number, population, resources, and strategic importance, such countries are inconsequential compared with the hemisphere's other nondemocratic, anticommunist governments, including those in Argentina, Bolivia, Brazil, El Salvador, and Uruguay. Nor, despite his success in eliminating all personal rivals, does her model apply to Pinochet's Chile.

In these authoritarian countries, the names at the top can and generally do change without any shifts in the pattern of wealth and political power. Formidable institutions are in control, usually the armed forces, a notable exception being Mexico's dominant political party, the PRI, and the huge state bureaucracy dependent on it. And these institutions work within a complicated setting of interest groups—including various sectors of the national business community, multinational corporations, the Catholic Church, professionals' guilds, the state bureaucracy, and, occasionally (and in most cases marginally), trade unions—all struggling to influence the regimes' economic and social policies. It is a political world very different from the one conjured up by Kirkpatrick.[3]

While the eccentricity of Kirkpatrick's account may raise doubts about her competence for public service, what matters more is the effect her account is likely to have on policy makers who confuse it with reality. Any political order sustained by little more than the force of a single autocrat's or family's prestige is bound to be precarious, especially where that prestige is linked to the ruler's bestial behavior or his special relationship with a feared or admired great power. Regarding such cases as the norm, Kirkpatrick not surprisingly demands we form a circle of fire around our proteges as soon as reformers of any kind appear armed in the streets. What would she do about those nuns and other "activists," as she calls them, who get in the way of hard-nosed policy? One possible hint appears in an interview Kirkpatrick gave just after the election of 1980. Commenting on the torture, mutilation, and summary execution of the civilian leaders of El Salvador's left-wing coalition, she said that "people who choose to live by the sword can expect to die by it."[4] So apparently any form of association with rebels makes one fair game.

If we turn from Kirkpatrick's model to the real world, we find, instead of the old-style caudillos, regimes of a very different character. Roughly half the members of the Organization of American States are recognizable democracies, including, for example, Venezuela, Columbia, Costa Rica, Peru, the Dominican Republic, and most of the Anglophonic states of the Caribbean. Kirkpatrick has little to say about democracy in such Third World countries other than to doubt its existence when it elects leaders who practice socialism, criticize the United States, and talk with Castro. While castigating Carter for tolerating the Manley regime in Jamaica, she refers to it as a "so-called democracy." One wonders whether the recent transfer of power there has shaken her implied assumption that Socialism is totalitarianism aching to be born. For her, the heart of our Third World problem is the regime that is anticommunist, but authoritarian, brutal, poor, corrupt, and hence unloved by liberals.

One redeeming feature of Kirkpatrick's essay is its demonstration of how a distinction that could be useful, between authoritarian and totalitarian regimes, is being subverted by dogmatists who assign practically all rulers professing capitalism and trying to liquidate leftists to the category of "merely authoritarian" while coincidentally expelling every revolutionary government and movement into the outer darkness of totalitarianism. In this way, the distinction has become simply a polemical weapon, useful for attacking Carter's human rights policy and for countering criticism of regimes that brutally crush proponents of reform, liberals, socialists, and Marxists alike.

In order to maintain their Manichaean vision, former liberals like Kirkpatrick must practice a heroic indifference to detail. The revolutionary who haunts their hysterical prose never acquires a face. Neoconservatives ask no questions about the particulars of time and place and program, about why a man or woman has assumed the awful peril of rebellion; they never ask because, for their crabbed purposes, they have all the necessary answers. Having taken up arms—some of them Cuban or Russian or otherwise tainted—against an anticommunist government, the revolutionary is either a totalitarian communist or a foolish tool, not to mention a "terrorist."

You find an equivalent coarseness of thought in the pages of *Pravda*, where the Soviet counterparts of our intellectual thugs ask not, "Who is Lech Walesa?" but rather, "Whom does Walesa consciously or unconsciously serve?" Since his opponent is a loyal communist government, for *Pravda* the only possible answer is "U.S. Imperialism."

Kirkpatrick herself admits that absolute monsters such as Hitler and Stalin or Pol Pot and Papa Doc Duvalier will occasionally appear at both ends of the imagined political spectrum. What concerns her, however, are the

> systematic differences between traditional and revolutionary autocracies that have a predictable effect on their degree of repressiveness. Generally speaking, traditional autocrats tolerate social inequities, brutality, and poverty while revolutionary autocracies create them.... Traditional autocrats ... do not disturb the habitual rhythms of work and leisure, habitual places of residence, habitual patterns of family and personal relations. Because the miseries of traditional life are familiar, they are bearable to ordinary people who, growing up in the society, learn to cope, as children born to untouchables in India acquire the skills and attitudes necessary for survival in the miserable roles they are destined to fill.

The other presumed moral advantage of anticommunist autocracies is their capacity for evolution toward more humane society.

> Although there is no instance of a revolutionary "Socialist" or Communist society being democratized, right-wing autocracies do sometimes evolve into democracies—given time, propitious ... circumstances, talented leaders, and a strong indigenous demand for representative government.

Nothing better illustrates the stupefying power of dogma than this attribution of permanence to revolutionary regimes and of an always latent fluidity to most conservative ones. In any fair test of durability, the latter make an impressive showing. The Somoza family, for example, lasted forty-five years. By monopolizing so much of the nation's economy, it had, by the time of its overthrow, actually reduced the possibility of democratic evolution.

Military rule in El Salvador, to take another current example, has endured since Franklin Delano Roosevelt's first election. If we use a measure more relevant to human rights and equate the "regime" with a very rigid structure of power and wealth and opportunity, then El Salvador had a stable autocracy from its independence in the early Nineteenth Century at least until the armed forces coup of 1979.[5] What was characteristic of this period was not "evolution" toward democracy but prevention of that evolution. In Peru, one hundred and fifty years of oligarchic control ended in 1968, not through democratic evolution but by means of reforms imposed by the armed forces.

Authoritarian governments of every ideological hue extend their jurisdiction as far as necessary to achieve their ends. They tolerate autonomous activity outside the formal state structure only when it is harmless or when it is informally but effectively integrated with the regime. In El Salvador before 1979, the military government and a small group of capitalists ("the fourteen families") consciously shared virtually the same interests and acted together. Though the press was nominally free, mass circulation newspapers in San Salvador conformed to the policies of the ruling groups.

"Preserving the existing distribution of wealth and power and poverty" is a deceptive summary of the goals of Kirkpatrick's "traditional autocrats." It is deceptive in that it implies that Latin American nations exist in a state of muscular placidity, as if society were ruled by a group of not necessarily good-natured but decidedly unambitious thugs who have no serious ambition beyond retaining control of their privileges and extorting protection money, and are willing to live and let live. When threatened by violent assault, of course they will actively hurt people—the violent malcontents and their sympathizers. But once the problem is liquidated, the "ordinary people" who want only to be left alone will come out of the cellar, where they have been hiding to avoid getting caught in the cross-fire, and docilely resume their "habitual rhythms."

This image is unreal because it misses the dynamic character of contemporary Latin American societies. When the masses are quiet, unambitious rulers can be placid. Today, their serenity is constantly disturbed. All the interconnected tendencies of recent years—urbanization, industrialization, rapid population increase, the vast spread of T.V. and transistor radios, revolutionary ideas about man and society—have unleashed a torrent of demands that may seem all the more terrifying because they cannot be suppressed by a government's administering exemplary punishment from time to time. Feeling a consequent need for sterner and more sweeping measures, rulers claim that national security requires them to impose comprehensive surveillance and more tightly controlled social institutions by increasing the power and reach of public authority.

This political project is "corporatism," fascism's cousin. As the political scientist Alfred Stepan notes in his penetrating study of Peru's corporatist experiment,[6] it has two poles. At the "inclusionary pole," the state offers working-class groups positive inducements to take part in its political and economic plans, as did the first Perón regime in Argentina, Lázaro Cárdenas in prewar Mexico, and Peru's military government before it turned to the Right in 1975. At the "exclusionary pole," the state elite relies heavily on coercion to break up existing working-class organizations and then to institutionalize docility. Chile under Pinochet is a particularly harsh example.

When the second of the two patterns predominates, as in Brazil and Chile following their respective military coups,[7] it follows that universities are purged, political parties dissolved, unions reorganized, dissidents murdered, the Church harassed, all as part of a huge effort first to demobilize the popular classes, and then to direct and strain their demands through new, purified institutions subject to manipulation by the state. In this effort, which has been analyzed with particular brilliance by the Argentine social scientist Guillermo O'Donnell,[8] the ruling groups can be said to be following, consciously or not, the example of empires like that of Rome, which for several centuries aggressively expanded its domain in a furious effort to liquidate threats to the status quo before they became unmanageable.

Seeking to preserve their own status quo, uncompromising right-wing governments ape the campaigns of classical revolutionary regimes to remove every source of dissent. They call themselves conservative. They are anticommunist. They will say nice things about the Free World. And, contrary to Kirkpatrick's optimistic speculations, they often take society on a road without any democratic exit.

The defense of right-wing authoritarian regimes finds a receptive, uncritical audience among many Americans because deeply ingrained ideological commitments affect their moral sensitivity. Anyone familiar with conditions in Haiti, for example, knows that its desperately hungry people would emigrate en masse if only a country able to provide life's basic needs would open its door. Although poverty and the nature of the Duvalier regime are linked, since that autocracy is noncommunist the U.S. government presumes that its refugees who reach our shores merely flee economic "conditions" and must therefore be turned back. On the other hand, practically all Cubans who arrive here are presumed to be fleeing political persecution rather than economic privation.

Another case of selective perception: If a revolutionary state commands people to move from one section of a country to another, we naturally condemn this ugly act as violating the right to travel freely and choose one's place of residence. But if the state enforces an absentee landowner's decision to expel sharecroppers who have tilled the land for generations, and if the landowner's choice was a rational response to market forces, even if those forces were themselves determined by political decisions about subsidies or the tariff on imported farm equipment, many economists will applaud it. Farming will be more efficient, free-marketeers will say, and sharecroppers eventually will find employment in more productive and hence better-paying activities. Or at least, it is claimed they would, if only markets could be fully liberated, for then they would function in accordance with theory.

The account of the Third World provided by Kirkpatrick and those who think like her obscures the realities of life under authoritarian governments—not only the torture and murder of political dissidents but also the more subtle yet often more comprehensively destructive acts carried out through the operation and manipulation of economic forces in societies with vast gaps between the power and education and wealth of a relatively few people and the rest of the population, a pattern of inequality often inherited from a precapitalist era. In countries like Brazil and Guatemala, these differences and the statist tradition that goes with them multiply the community-shattering impact of capitalism by placing the state at the service of relatively few people.

Acting through the state, the few can require proof of land tenure which illiterate peasants cannot produce. They can manipulate the exchange rate to encourage high technology imports at the expense of high employment. They can prohibit strikes and hold wage increases below the rate of inflation. They can subsidize large-scale agriculture and monopolize irrigation, while withholding subsidies for basic consumption goods. They can and do intervene in a thousand ways which have the predictable effect of uprooting whole communities, because neither they nor the state apparatus is a neutral arbiter guided by some abstract calculus of national interest. One certainly need not be a Marxist to see this. And one needs only a minimum of candor to admit it.

Quietly and anonymously, economic and social forces unleashed or at least aided by the state can eliminate entire cultures. Sylvia Hewlett notes in her study of Brazil that there remained during the 1950s "a major concentration of indigenous tribes (numbering approximately 200,000 people) in the Amazon and central regions. . . ."[9] As a consequence of the decision to open up these regions through highway building, colonization schemes, and other means, the indigenous population is disappearing. Some Indians will survive disoriented, adrift on the edge of an alien world. As for their "habitual patterns of family and personal relations," soon the world will forget that they ever existed.

Honest scholarship would have to ask what is the difference between a revolutionary state that decides to eliminate a group with bayonets and one that proceeds to do so by indirection. Both claim that they are promoting modernization and advancing national interests as defined by those who rule. Yet one case rightly horrifies us and will command the attention of Walter Cronkite, while the other passes almost unnoticed.[10]

Conservatives are properly impressed by Brazil's rapid expansion and the deepening of its industrial base during the era of intense political repression—1968 to 1973. They used to be silent about its record in producing equity or welfare. A recent World Bank study using 1977 figures estimates that 65% of the Brazilian population age fifteen and above is functionally illiterate; the figure runs close to 90% in rural areas.[11] Roughly 20% of the children in Brazil are in a state of second- or third-degree malnutrition (body weight 25% or more below normal).

According to figures cited by Hewlett, between 1960 and 1973 the rate of infant mortality in Sao Paulo (the richest part of Brazil) increased 45% to a high of ninety-seven deaths per thousand live births.[12] Life expectancy for the middle and upper classes of Sao Paulo is estimated to be around sixty-seven. The poor in parts of the rural northeast will have a life expectancy of only about forty years. Such misery is no doubt "familiar," as Kirkpatrick claims, but unlike our new ambassador to the U.N., even a minister in the Brazilian government wonders if it is bearable. In an interview with *Veja,* Brazil's equivalent of *Newsweek,* the present Minister of Industry and Commerce, Joao Camilo Penna, said:

> The country possesses today a social stratum with high managerial capacity that has, however, a great debt with 40 million humble Brazilians. A debt that, if it is not paid, will result in these humble people being turned into humiliated people. And after humiliated people, I don't know.

Preoccupied with such games as distinguishing between the "authoritarian" and the "totalitarian," many people concerned with U.S. diplomacy have failed to notice changes in Latin American institutions that have been unfolding in the shadows cast by state and private terrorism. Perhaps the most important of these is the emergence of national human rights movements. Under a variety of names, often supported by the Catholic Church, these movements have united hereditary political enemies in alliances reminiscent of wartime France. In countries where the armed forces agree to return to their barracks, these Latin analogies to the Resistance could emerge as stable, center–left political coalitions able to carry out orderly programs of economic and social reform. In most of the Western Hemisphere today, moreover—unlike postwar Western Europe—the orthodox Moscow–oriented party is only a fragment of the Left, in many countries a trivial one.[13]

The experience of modern authoritarian government has enhanced the prospects for such coalitions. Frustrated in the 1960s by the obduracy of vested interests, their imagination fired by illusions about the Cuban revolution, susceptible to a rigidly Marxist view of norms and political institutions, reformers in such countries as Brazil, Columbia, and Chile tended to see democratic politics only as the means of preserving privilege. They became correspondingly insensitive to the violence lying beneath the accumulated restraints and tolerance of relatively decent social orders.

They have since learned how ferociously competent modern security forces can be and how private leftist terrorism can evoke deep antipathy throughout societies with liberal if not always strictly democratic traditions; the result in such countries as Argentina, Uruguay, and Brazil has been increased support of unrestrained counterterrorism. However, moderates and conservatives who have seen their children ground up in the state's security machine also have had a lesson in the difficulty of stopping violence once it rushes into the streets.

The failure of Cuba's economic model is another factor in the education of the Left. Fidel Castro himself has helped to disseminate the bad news and has drawn one of the appropriate conclusions. In conversations with Alfonso Robelo, leader of the political opposition to the present Nicaraguan government, and with Sandinista leaders, Castro emphasized the importance of preserving a significant private business sector. Some Central and South American leftists still may be reluctant to admit it, but they cannot indefinitely evade the fact that a commitment to a private sector is also a commitment to some species of political pluralism.

Advocates of democratic reform face enormous difficulties. In many Latin American countries a demographic explosion is taking place while the economy relies on a capital–intensive technology that was developed in the labor-scarce states of Europe and North America—a combination that usually creates very high levels of unemployment. Also imported from the developed states are consumer appetites that stimulate the greed of the well-to-do. Because international capital is hard to obtain, politicians and businessmen feel they must compete for it by suppressing every sign of social disorder; and modern technology provides an apparatus for official terror beyond the dreams of Nineteenth Century rulers. Western stagflation meanwhile threatens export markets and consequently the ability to finance growth of any kind.

The rush to authoritarian governments in the 1960s and early 1970s heightened academic appreciation of these and related obstacles and encouraged a pessimistic determinism about projects for social and political reform.[14] But the failure of countries like Chile and Uruguay to reproduce the Brazilian economic "miracle" by combining assaults on the working class with an open door to international capital has helped to undermine confidence in the stability of that formula for social order. It received another blow recently when Uruguayan voters rejected a constitution designed by the armed forces to perpetuate their rule. The democratic impulse has not yielded to competing claims to legitimacy.

The great question is whether reform coalitions can increase equity and welfare without sacrificing the long-term growth necessary for peaceful relations between classes. If they can, they should satisfy the demands of the Latin American military officers who have seized power in order to halt class warfare and the consequent disintegration of all traditional institutions, including the armed forces themselves. Plausible blueprints are available.[15] In the case of Brazil, for instance, a recent confidential study shows how moderate changes in government policy designed substantially to reduce inequality also could do much to relieve the shortages of energy and foreign exchange that threaten the country's future. A more equitable distribution of income coincidentally would benefit domestically controlled private businesses, because they enjoy a comparative advantage over multinational corporations in producing basic consumer goods.

Most of Latin America is now open to renewed projects for democratic social reform, or could soon become so. Carter helped to shape this more promising situation by insisting that the way a regime treats its own people has to affect the quality of its relations with the United States. Having initially disarmed himself by foreswearing intervention in trade or private capital as a means of defending human rights, he could offer few incentives, and he used few convincing threats. By 1977, only a derisory amount of bilateral economic aid was available to reward good behavior.

In a few cases, Carter did block or delay aid to authoritarian states, such as Argentina, from international financial institutions, but various, partially self-imposed, constraints made this a rarely used and only marginally threatening weapon. In cautioning authoritarian governments against repression, Carter drew mainly on the accumulated prestige of the United States among Latin American military establishments and the upper classes. His considerable achievements, including fair elections in the Dominican Republic, are partly owing to the weight of American influence, but primarily to the gathering force of human rights as an ideal that cuts across deep divisions of class and ideology in Latin America. That force powerfully multiplied the effect of Carter's efforts.

Simply by acting to demonstrate some continuity in Washington's support for human rights, Ronald Reagan could easily match Carter's achievement. He needs to act quickly. His victory has particularly encouraged the predators in those few remaining social jungles where an alliance of corrupted soldiers, industrialists, and landowners would rather fight to the last worker, peasant, politician, and priest than accept reform.

While campaigning for the presidency, Mr. Reagan allowed certain ideologues who were vindictive toward all critics of traditional capitalist order to speak in his name. Responsible Republicans should urge the President to reject associating American power with conservatism that relies on vicious repression. They should act because it is the right thing to do; and because it is in the national interest that Latin Americans succeed in establishing capitalism with a human face.

Notes

1. *Commentary,* November 1979, p. 34.
2. For the sake of brevity, I will use "Latin America" to refer as well to English-speaking states of the Caribbean.
3. Even outside Latin America, Kirkpatrick's model fits reality poorly. While it covers the little states of the Persian Gulf and Saudi Arabia and a few African states like Zaire and the Ivory Coast, it does not apply to such "Free World" allies as Indonesia, Thailand, and South Korea.
4. *The New York Times,* December 7, 1980, p. E3.
5. For my views on post-coup El Salvador, see chapters 18 and 20 below.
6. *The State and Society: Peru in Comparative Perspective* (Princeton University Press, 1979).
7. Brazil in 1964 and Chile in 1973.
8. *Modernization and Bureaucratic Authoritarianism: Studies in South American Politics* (Institute of International Studies, University of California, 1979 ed.).
9. *The Cruel Dilemmas of Development: Twentieth Century Brazil* (Basic Books, 1979, p. 171.
10. Perhaps the results would be approved if either state held a national referendum. Minorities standing in the way of progress are generally despised whether the regime is democratic, as in Nineteenth Century America, conservative authoritarian, or authoritarian socialist. We should at least recognize moral parallels where they exist.

11. "Brazil: Human Resources Special Report," World Bank Staff Working Paper (Washington, D.C., 1979) pp. 28-31.
12. This might have something to do with the fact that, in the ten years following the coup of 1964, the percentage of national income obtained by the wealthiest 10% of the population increased from 39 to 50. Sri Lanka's per capita income is roughly one-eighth of Brazil's, or about the same as that of a town in the rural northeast of Brazil; its infant mortality figure is about half that of Sao Paulo. Life expectancy in Sri Lanka is sixty-eight. See tables in James P. Grant's *Disparity Reduction Rates as Social Indicators,* Overseas Development Council, Monograph No. 11, 1978.
13. Moreover, unlike some leftist groups, the Communist Party during the past two decades with few exceptions—e.g., recently in El Salvador—has generally sought popular front alliances and opposed armed revolution. For that reason, particularly during the 1960s, romantic followers of Che Guevara despised the orthodox communists. In the El Salvador case, most of the likely participants in a conventional popular front, including the Social Democrats, had already decided to back an armed struggle for social change.
14. O'Donnell's study, first published in 1973, led the way. For an intellectually impressive critical reassessment of O'Donnell's hypotheses, see David Collier, ed., *The New Authoritarianism in Latin America* (Princeton University Press, 1979). Certain essays in the Collier book offer a basis for less gloomy expectations. The four-volume set, edited by Juan Linz and Alfred Stepan, analyzing *The Breakdown of Democratic Regimes* (Johns Hopkins University Press, 1978), is implicitly optimistic in the emphasis of its authors on the margin for political choice and one human error, as opposed to the iron hand of economic circumstances. See particularly Stepan's essay on Brazil in the volume entitled *Latin America.*
15. For a fairly persuasive blueprint, developed under the auspices of Robert McNamara, for growth with equity within an essentially capitalist framework, see Hollis Chenery, et al., *Redistribution with Growth (Oxford University Press, 1974).* Another useful how-to-do-it book is *Income Distribution and Growth in the Less Developed Countries,* edited by Charles R. Frank, Jr., and Richard C. Webb (The Brookings Institute, 1977).

5

From Kennedy to Reagan: On the Management of Liberal Contradictions

A notable feature of contemporary political life is the failure of Democratic presidential aspirants to present a well-defined alternative to the policy of the Reagan administration for handling essentially domestic conflicts within Third World States. Their failure reflects the practical difficulty of managing contradictions stemming from the liberal tradition, aggravated, perhaps, by Ronald Reagan's presentation of himself as a more pure and effective expression of that tradition.

One of the defining characteristics of liberalism has been its concern for the autonomy of the individual within a single political community and for the autonomy of peoples organized as political communities in a world of states; in brief, individual and national self-determination.

In its innocent youth, liberalism assumed their complementarity. The state, seen as a voluntary association of free individuals linked by some sense of common identity, protected the association and its members from subordination to the will of other nationally organized groups. Hence, the United States by respecting the autonomy of other nations was coincidentally respecting the freedom of their citizens.

When history proved to be a two-way street on which states could and frequently did move back and forth between democratic and authoritarian rule, liberals had to choose between respect for state autonomy, formalized in the doctrine of nonintervention, and the promotion of individual freedom. Since liberalism's bedrock is the individual, wherever governments have not been able to invoke the legitimacy of selection through a competitive political process, nonintervention has lost its allure as a self-evident value. Rather, it has had to be justified in terms of its *service* to liberal ends.

How might nonintervention serve liberal ends in a world pocked by nondemocratic governments? Or, more specifically, why shouldn't the United States intervene to promote "freedom"? To begin with, a liberal might argue, because in the process of trying to liberate the citizens of another state, it might prove necessary to destroy many of them. After all, throughout this century authoritarian governments have demonstrated an impressive capacity to mobilize and motivate their populations for self-defense and for aggression too. Some authoritarian regimes—the early days of Nasser, Hitler, and Peron, for examples—appear authentically popular. That is one reason not only the elite guardians of the regime but even conscripts may fight well against an invading force. They may also fight because of the instinctive assumption that invaders, whatever their stated aims, have come to pillage. This is why even unpopular governments may sometimes rally support in the face of an external threat. A third reason is sheer self-preservation: If the regime's cadres are numerous enough, they can force a conscript to choose between certain death at their hands and the mere risk of death if he obeys orders and fights.

Moreover, even if the regime deploys only its committed supporters, the most benevolent invader will do what is necessary to minimize casualties to its own forces, including artillery and air strikes against such legitimate targets as roads, railroad lines, ports, and munitions factories, despite the consequent injury to the civilian population. Who knows if the people of occupied France would have voted in favor of the Normandy landing had they known the price they would pay for liberation? The discovery of how much we would have to destroy in order to save Vietnam from communist rule fueled opposition to that war.

A second arguable utility of adherence to nonintervention stems from the limited zeal for self-sacrifice. Representative governments do not have a broad mandate to impose large sacrifices on their constituents to render the blessings of liberty to another community. To justify the cost of intervention, evangelism must be alloyed with crasser interests, such as promoting the security, wealth, and influence of the United States.

A further disincentive for liberals contemplating crusades for freedom is the fact that welfare liberalism does not exercise an ideological monopoly in America. It has always had to compete with its bastard sibling, social Darwinism, which treats freedom as a merely useful condition for the emergence of the fit at the top of society. Social Darwinism, aspiring to nothing more than being number one among states, appeals to the competitive ethos of a capitalist society, an ethos liberal institutions attempt to domesticate. So in creating the means for intervention—including covert operatives and regular armed forces—and when intervening for impeccably liberal purposes, liberals provide means and precedents available to conservative successors zealous only in the pursuit of commerce and power.

Postwar competition with the Soviet Union initially eased the creedal tension between concern for the spread of liberal institutions and respect for the moral utility of nonintervention. Easing occurred by means of a definition of nonintervention tailored to the perception of a two-dimensional Soviet threat. One dimension was external aggression. The other was subversion: Soviet (later Chinese) arms, advice, training, and sanctuary to violent minorities which, as parts of the community of believers (in Marxism), served Moscow's aims and were therefore to be deemed agents of the Soviet Union rather than nationalists who happened to believe in state capitalism and one-party politics. On the assumption that they were simply foreign agents and that, if victorious, they would impose nonliberal institutions backed by Soviet power, U.S. opposition to their triumph served both tenets of the liberal creed, as long as the target state already possessed liberal institutions.

The assumptions perfected the fit between U.S. means and ends. Openly extending economic assistance to the recognized government of Italy was a normal, unobjectionable essay in diplomacy. Secretly funneling money to Italy's Christian Democratic Party was less easy to reconcile with the putative virtues of nonintervention. But we justified it, not implausibly, as simply balancing the rubles presumably flowing from Moscow into the treasury of Italy's Communist Party. We sought, in other words, to reinforce liberal institutions, not to subvert them. From the outset of the Cold War, nonintervention was lawyer's idiom for "containment." Functionally, it meant: (1) a U.S. shield against direct Soviet threats; and (2) assistance to recognized governments fighting off rebels bearing Marxist flags—Law, liberalism, and old-fashioned national security locked up in one neat package.

Communist parties, though large in France and Italy, were nonetheless minorities. And after the experiences of Poland and Czechoslovakia, the American elite assumed that communists in government would quickly become a government only of communists backed by Soviet force. Being able, therefore, to marry liberal values with the imperatives of geopolitics, containment inevitably commanded consensus, the Cold War consensus that would carry America into the killing ground of Vietnam.

The debate within the Truman administration and the liberal community at large over American policy toward the Chinese Civil War prefigured the rending tensions of the Vietnam era. Reports from our resident diplomats—the old China hands—could not be reconciled with the assumptions committing liberals to containment. They demonstrated that neither side was attached to liberal institutions and that, as far as one could tell, the communist enjoyed more widely based support. In addition, the communists were winning without benefit of much aid or advice from Moscow and, in any event, with less aid than the Kuomintang continued to receive from Washington. In the face of an authentic civil war between equally illiberal contenders, respect for national autonomy required nonintervention; while concern for individual freedom seemed to dictate indifference. A liberal democratic administration nevertheless chose unilateral assistance to Chiang over principled neutrality, in part, no doubt, on grounds of electoral prudence: The congressional elections of 1946 seemed to auger a conservative renaissance and Chiang was only the first of many anticommunist dictators to manage deep penetration of the American political process.

At roughly the same time the Truman administration was ignoring messages from Mao proposing friendly relations, it took the first little step down the long road to defeat in Vietnam by spurning Ho Chi Minh's pleas for diplomatic support against the French. Rather than using its overwhelming economic and political leverage to block France's reassertion of colonial control, Washington flashed signals of tolerance to the French, who promptly responded by blasting their way back into Hanoi. It would cost the Vietnamese eight years and a delta of blood to drive them out.

In the Chinese case, arguably we had only bent liberal principles: However much they might differ in every other respect, both Mao and Chiang were nationalists, and neither championed pluralist democracy. So in terms of liberal principles there seemed little basis to choose between them. We had nevertheless chosen and adhered to that choice even after it became clear that the balance of indigenous power rested with Mao. But by that time it was also clear that our assistance would not suffice to distort China's rough and ready process of self–determination.

In the case of Vietnam, however, liberal principles simply broke against the administration's interest in the resurrection of Western Europe. Paris offered Vietnam neither pluralism nor self–determination; but in pursuit of a cooperative anticommunist French government, the United States catered to France's still–undiminished appetite for empire. Perhaps if the left wing of the New Deal had not been preoccupied with the task of rationalizing Stalin's tightening grip on Eastern Europe and clinging to toeholds in the Democratic Party, some noise might have been made about this small, yet portentous, betrayal of liberal principles. In fact it passed almost unnoticed.

Had they been harried into explicit defense of their policy, Truman and Acheson might have justified their indifference to France's imperial taste by invoking the larger liberal interests at stake in Europe. In context—a perceived threat to the prospect for liberal government in Western Europe—this sort of explanation carried weight. It also, unfortunately, carried the potential for that wider claim with which conservatives would assault liberal policy in the wake of Vietnam—the claim that every act that enhances

American power relative to Soviet power coincidentally serves liberal values, a proposition to which I will return later.

The Truman administration's deviations from the letter of liberal principle seem trivial beside the delinquencies of its Republican successors. An American President who connives in the subversion of freely elected governments does not simply bend liberal principles, he fouls them.

The Eisenhower administration was a two-time offender—Iran in 1953, Guatemala in 1954. Of course, both governments had many flaws and powerful domestic enemies; otherwise, the President's agents, John and Alan Dulles, could not have so easily arranged the fall of Prime Minister Mossadeq and President Arbenz. So, alas, do many governments established by reasonably fair elections (as, for instance, conservatives were quick to remind anyone who voiced doubt about the Rhodesian election which brought Bishop Muzorewa to a fleeting encounter with office under Ian Smith's auspices). In the context of their time and place, the Mossadeq and Arbenz regimes had indisputably democratic credentials. Certainly, their claim to be representative governments was, at a minimum, no less persuasive than that of the present government of El Salvador.

If history had stopped in 1954, one might have dismissed the argument that all the Democrats lacked was temptation and preceded to conclude that the subversion of representative government during the Eisenhower years epitomized the distinction between liberals and conservatives in the conduct of American foreign policy. Liberalism, after all, is a creed which treats representative government as a universal right, in part at least on the assumption that there is no rational basis for favoring one person's right to liberty over another's. Conservatism takes the world as it is, riven by conflict, greed, and the will to dominate. What we're against, an aid to Jesse Helms said some years ago, is rationalism, that cold elitist view of the world which disparages the ordinary man's gut instincts, like patriotism. To the modern American conservative, what is natural is good and preference for one's own people at the expense of others is natural. Moreover, unlike liberals, conservatives have never been inclined to see a natural harmony and potential synergism among states. For conservatives, it is a Hobbesian world where the strong take what they will and the weak endure what they must. So if the destruction of democratic institutions, whether perfect or flawed, promotes the interest of the United States, a genuine conservative should not hesitate.

Despite these creedal discrepancies, after 1954, when temptation tested liberals' faith, they too succumbed albeit in more ambiguous cases: the Belgian Congo and the Dominican Republic. Patrice Lumumba may have been all the things then and subsequently said of him—demagogic, irrational, irresponsible—but he achieved the Prime Ministership through an authentic electoral process and led the only party able to transcend lines of tribal cleavage. That did not prevent the U.S. from conniving in his removal, if not his death, thus triggering the complicated course of events which would produce today's Zaire, the world's largest Kleptocracy. That Lumumba might have fallen without any aid from us and the Congo fallen into that Conradian horror for which the Belgians had so admirably prepared it are speculations of moment only to those concerned with questions of moral judgment. They are irrelevant to the question whether the liberal creed gives distinctive shape to the foreign policy of liberal Presidents.

It didn't in the Congo, and it didn't in the Dominican Republic in 1965 when Lyndon Johnson used Marines to swing the momentum of civil conflict against the ascendant faction committed to restoring Juan Bosch to the presidency he had won by fair means and lost through a *coup d'etat*.

From their occasional betrayals, however, it does not follow that liberals are simply conservatives with a sunny rhetoric. Both oppose the spread of Soviet power and of left-wing authoritarian regimes. Both seek a world of nations open to American business and cultural penetration. But in practice, as well as in theory, they differ sharply over means. Liberals believe that, in the great generality of cases and always in the long run, economic reform and expanded political participation are goods in their own right, antidotes to revolution, and avenues to more harmonious and cooperative relations with the United States. Liberals embodied this belief in the Alliance For Progress with its insistence on reform as a condition to aid, its bias toward democratic governments, and its initial policy of withholding recognition from usurping military regimes.

The alliance was Conrad's Kurtz, noble work gone rotten in the doing of it, ending not in a whimper but a shriek from the chambers of torture established by the officers supposedly learning democracy as well as counterinsurgency in our military schools.

The impact of Vietnam on liberal thought is relentlessly exaggerated. By the time its lessons became clear, the wreck of the alliance had already laid bare several sharp edges of the liberal's dilemmas. Architects of the alliance assumed: (a) that bilateral economic assistance would be used both as a positive inducement and a negative sanction, encouraging Latin liberals and intimidating conservatives; and (b) that material and training for Latin soldiers would inculcate democratic values and enhance professional competence, thereby giving Latin armies a role other than meddling in local politics while coincidentally strengthening their capacity to shield reform from leftist subversion.

Reality refused to conform. Latin governments took aid but were unwilling or simply unable to initiate the sweeping reforms required to eliminate the sources of violent opposition. An immediate reduction in mass poverty could not be achieved by moderate means. The countries were too poor, poverty too entrenched, for a few hundreds of millions in aid to catalyze quick results. Only a major redistribution of productive assets, particularly land, could conceivably have had the desired impact. But the principal beneficiaries of redistribution were either wholly outside the political system or controlled by local bosses, "caciques," serving elite-dominated political parties. Even in the Latin democracies, radical reform had no electoral base. It was, moreover, both susceptible to indictment as "communistic" and certain to stir ferocious resistance among adversely affected groups in the middle and upper classes. Therefore, it would have to provoke the armed forces, institution of social mobility for middle-class men, trained to search out every seed of communist subversion and to equate national security with domestic tranquility.

Nothing less than the prospect of a guerrilla victory could have moved these massed obstacles to change. Latin politicians and officers quickly discovered that, on that score, they had nothing to fear except fear itself. In most of the hemisphere, the preconditions of revolution did not exist. And in the few cases where perhaps they did, governments also discovered that in the end they could rely on the United States for survival. The Alliance, after all, was not a hemispheric welfare program, it was a means to the end of preserving noncommunist governments, preferably liberal ones, but, in any event, noncommunist.

Latin elites appreciated the dilemmas of Washington's liberals. The political movements in their countries committed to that radical reform which, as Castro had demonstrated, could quickly raise living standards for and mobilize the very poor (at least if they were landless) were precisely the movements liberals were determined to defeat, in part because such movements were presumed hostile on East-West issues and in part because they proposed to achieve reform through the medium of a powerful, unelected state bureaucracy. So Washington was doomed to seek its liberal ends through governments unable to achieve and often fiercely determined to thwart them. Or perhaps it would be more accurate to say that Washington's end—draining pools of discontent—could not in the circumstances of Latin American society be achieved by means acceptable to democratic governments, to their politically organized constituents, *or* to American liberals themselves. Our choice of partners and means was simply incongruent with our ends. And once it discovered that Latin America was not dry brush awaiting the revolutionary's torch, and that repression worked, Washington achieved a better fit by removing reform from the agenda of its purposes.

The election of Jimmy Carter restored international reform (and its attendant contradictions) to the national agenda, this time under the rubric of human rights. For those who worked closely with him, the President's personal commitment to the defense of human rights is indisputable. Many of his critics agree, indicting him precisely for pursuing a personal moral obsession by means which on balance, they argue, failed to enhance either human rights or the national interest.

Notwithstanding the President's objective commitment, the human rights campaign also was intended to serve perfectly traditional national interests, above all the rehabilitation of that collective sense of high moral purpose which had helped drive American foreign policy after World War II. As *The Economist,* bellwether of sophisticated Establishment thought on both sides of the Atlantic, suggested at the time, an exclusive emphasis on physical security and economic prosperity could not rally support for the expensive instruments required to service security commitments all over the noncommunist world. American foreign policy, declared this champion of private economic interest, also required a dose of idealism. It might have added that throughout modern American history, liberals and liberal ideas have mobilized the population for the sacrifices incident to great exertions beyond our frontiers. Perhaps it is natural that in a state protected by wealth, organization, and above all geography from the realistic threat of invasion, the Left should be the party if not of war then certainly of adventure.

No cynicism need attend this attribution of instrumental value to the human rights enthusiasm which coursed through Establishment circles in the mid–1970s. In theory, the national and human interests are not necessarily incongruent. The trick is to make them congruent in practice. It was precisely when it came to practice, however, that the contradictions which had plagued the Alliance for Progress resurfaced. Once again, the countries on which we could exert the greatest influence were in most cases countries closely aligned with us on East–West issues. Their elites were committed to such alignment as a means of preserving a structure of privilege often incompatible with the human rights dimension of U.S. policy. President Carter sought progress on economic and social rights coincident with a halt to violations of political and civil rights. The former challenged privilege itself. The latter challenged means increasingly used to suppress domestic challenge to privilege. While, by guaranteeing a regime's security, the United States might reduce its propensity to kill, the guarantee removed an important, in some cases the only powerful incentive to political and economic reform.

Old contradictions also haunted the renewed search for domestic agents of reform with whom to cooperate. In some countries elite closure or control of all formally democratic channels of change reduced liberal reformers to impotence or drove them into alliance with the authoritarian Left. In such cases the coalition of once moderate figures and violent revolutionaries seemed the only plausible challenger to the status quo. It was, however, an implausible partner for the United States.

To begin with, there was a deep reservoir of mutual suspicion. The United States cannot easily shake a heritage of intervention on behalf of foreign economic interests, hostility to revolutions of all kind, collaboration with monsters (such as the unspeakable Trujillo), intimacy with Latin military establishments, tolerance of deposed dictators, and collusion in the overthrow of democracies. The militant Left, for its part, has a heritage of contempt for liberal institutions, apologetics for Soviet foreign policy, and, in some cases, indiscriminate violence. Mutual ignorance heightens these entrenched obstacles to dialogue, much less cooperation. United States law and practice discourage, when they do not prevent, entry into the United States of left-wing students, intellectuals, and politicians. Patterns of recruitment to the U.S. diplomatic, military, and intelligence services, bureaucratic ethos, the ease of contact with local business and military elites, and deference to the sensitivity of local governments all discourage efforts by U.S. official personnel to cultivate dialogue with leftists in their own countries. Each side assumes the other's irreducible hostility.

The assumption is over-determined, not baseless. For liberals do inevitably oppose the substitution of one form of authoritarian rule for another, even if the new form is more likely, in some cases, to manage a successful assault on mass poverty.

The creedal principle and the prudential policy of nonintervention add a final deterrent to alliance with militant entrepreneurs of change. Intervention like terrorism is now a term of casual invective, but no Gresham's Law of rhetoric has driven out its hard-core denotation of coercive action by one government intended either to subvert another or to deny it choice over matters of essentially domestic policy. Military assistance to rebels is the extreme case. In giving it we would violate a core norm of the international system. But without arms from some source, can dissidents hope to overcome a tough authoritarian regime? The latter, by virtue of its control over the major centers of economic activity in the society and its recognition as at least the *de facto* government, enjoys both financial means and the legitimacy to equip itself luxuriously from the international arms bazaar.

If, for all the reasons just enumerated, we, unlike the Cubans or Russians, cannot find partners on the far Left, how can the United States hope to promote human rights in a society where their violation is an integral feature of the existing social, economic and political structure? As academ-

On the Management of Liberal Contradictions 53

ics like to say: It is a good question. The case of Nicaragua revealed that Jimmy Carter was one among many liberals without an answer.

Logically, he had two alternatives other than doing what was necessary to sustain Somoza or aiding the Sandinista guerrillas. One was strict neutrality. The other was trying to assemble from the available human materials in Nicaragua an acceptable agent of reform, one committed to nonalignment in foreign policy and to pluralism at home.

The proposition, retailed by Jeane Kirkpatrick and others, that Carter disarmed Somoza and/or did nothing to oppose the Sandinist victory is simple mendacity. Administration policy from January 1968, when the riots and businessmen's strike sparked by the assassination of Pedro Chammoro suggested Somoza's vulnerability, until the dictator's resignation and flight in July 1979, had only two themes: Opposition to a Sandinista-dominated Nicaragua and opposition to perpetuation of the Somoza dynasty. These ends were in fact reconcilable almost to the end of the dictator's reign because, for most of the civil war, even perhaps as late as the summer of 1979, the Sandinistas were unsure of their ability to win an outright military victory. Rather, they hoped that, with the aid of their moderate civilian allies and by naming as Shadow Minister of Defense a former Colonel of the National Guard, they could split off from the guard career officials who were not personally implicated in its crimes. Sandinista uncertainty about victory coupled with their desire to minimize the human and material costs of prolonged civil war gave the United States powerful leverage, assuming it could force the departure of Somoza and his principal civilian and military cronies or itself split the guard.

Means far short of Marines were available to the President. By some combination of the following threats and inducements he could have broken the regime's will to fight:

1. Threats to freeze U.S.-based assets of the Somocistas and deny them visas;
2. A promise of American asylum for any officers of the guard wishing to leave Nicaragua immediately;
3. Declared willingness to organize and fund a multinational force which would guarantee due process and civic order after Somoza's departure pending a national election;
4. A flat declaration of U.S. refusal to aid the survival of the Somoza regime under any circumstances;
5. Threatened recognition of the Sandinista-supported government in exile unless Somoza and its top lieutenants left the country and the National Guard accepted a cease fire and immediate negotiations with the rebel coalition over the conditions for ending the conflict and preparing the country for elections.

In the end, Somoza resigned under conditions less favorable to his clique and before a military defeat was certain, but after it was clear that the United States would not save him and actually wanted him to depart.

Once Carter conveyed to the opposition his determination to behead the Somocistas, the moderate civilians allied with the Sandinistas would have immediately endorsed negotiations for a transitional regime. As long as they were allowed to establish their own military cantonments within Nicaragua and retain their arms pending demobilization of most forces on both sides, the guerrillas—pressured by hitherto friendly governments in Panama and Costa Rica and fearing U.S. annointment of their former allies as the transitional government—would have had to accept negotiations under auspices of the Latin democracies leading to elections and a pluralist government.

This is no essay in hindsight. Within the Carter administration one faction urged steps to produce Somoza's early resignation, repeatedly warning that a prolonged civil war would dim the prospects for post-Somoza democracy. But the President sided with advisors who opposed a U.S. diktat to the Somocistas while hoping to persuade Somoza to resign and turn power over to a coalition of his less monstrous supporters and his more conservative opponents, leading ultimately, they perhaps prayed, to elections and a new, democratic start.

In part, the President was constrained by domestic politics—Somoza's supporters in Congress threatened to block legislation required to implement the Panama Canal Treaties if Carter actively sought to displace him. But in larger part he constrained himself, fiddling to the tune of nonintervention while Nicaragua burned.

Then, already weakened by a thousand political cuts, obsessed with careening debacle in Iran, Carter seemed unable to muster the attention or mobilize the resources needed for a possible salvage operation in Nicaragua. To be sure, he tried, dispatching a canny professional diplomat and such dollops of aid as he could wring from Congress; but relations already showed signs of curdling by October of 1979 when young officers of El Salvador's armed forces, chastened by the defeat of their Nicaraguan counterparts and sensing the seismic slide of social forces in their own country, seized the government from their superiors, announced a new era of reform, and invited the political leaders of reformist parties to join them.

Along with Nicaragua and Guatemala, El Salvador had been near the top of the Carter administration's list of Western Hemisphere human rights violators. Rushing at speed through the door the coup had seemingly opened, the administration quickly collided with familiar dilemmas. Shrewd calculation rather than moral revulsion had directed the coup. Over the years, young men with a taste for social mobility, not reform, gravitated to the military academy. Hitherto El Salvador had belonged to a few families and successive generations of senior officers. The coup leaders felt competent enough to dispense with the oligarchs and their own superiors. Now El Salvador was their thing. And it could stay that way, they apparently assumed, as long as they stuck together and liquidated every potential source of armed opposition while tolerating that degree of reform which would reduce the pool of guerrilla recruits while enticing Washington back into the old alliance.

Some officers may have had a more generous vision. Some may have actually imagined the armed forces purged of corruption and brutality, transformed into a truly national army rather than a sophisticated Cosa Nostra. To act on the basis of that vision, however, meant to split the armed forces, a risky and psychologically wrenching prospect and one which no consequential group of officers would contemplate, except as an alternative to the prospect of military defeat. So once they concluded that Carter would not risk their defeat, the tradition of respect for each field commander's discretion to feather his nest and eliminate undesirables was not likely to be disturbed.

As one of the Carter administration's final acts, it authorized the renewal of military assistance to this curious partner in the defense of human rights. All in all, a fitting epitaph to Jimmy Carter's management of liberal contradictions.

Orthodox conservatives assume office unencumbered by the liberal's creedal dilemmas. If a Third World government generally aligns with the United States on East-West issues, declares itself anticommunist, and maintains an agreeable environment for American business, it is a friend. Preserving such friends by all necessary means is in turn a policy imperative. Their domestic delinquencies are irrelevant in principle and important in practice only to the extent they complicate the task of saving them.

With all of the difficulties imposed by liberal sentimentality planed away, an honest conservative's policy has about it a harshly elegant simplicity. It can appeal to minds tired of contradictions. But it does not touch the heart. And so it seemingly cannot inspire the American electorate to "pay any price, bear any burden" to sustain agreeable and demolish unfriendly governments. In order to mobilize support for the cost of intervention on a global scale, either an administration must scare the electorate to death or inspire its episodic zeal for good works.

The appeal to fear seems to have lost much of its force. Small wonder, after Americans have been exposed so frequently to wolf's syndrome. There was the 1960 missile gap, fabricated by political adventurers out of imaginative Air Force intelligence projections, analog of today's "window of vulnerability." There were two whole decades of waiting for the Chinese hordes to engulf Southeast Asia. There were the post-Vietnam years, in which the American people awaited the fall of those Southeast Asian dominoes supposedly doomed by our failure in Indochina. Today, even the flat-earth minds among us have noticed that Thailand, Malaysia, Singapore, and Indonesia have never been more securely upright.

When fear fails, conservatives must turn to ideals more inspiring than power and commercial prominence. The Reagan administration is not, moreover, entirely orthodox. Though allied with conventional business conservatives, the President himself and his avid supporters have emotional ties to the imagery and recipes of Nineteenth Century liberalism and to our enduring evangelical tradition. The pulse of redemptive enthusiasm could be felt from the inception of Reagan's campaign. Together with bursts of liberal rhetoric, it lent authenticity to his invocation of Rooseveltian optimism about the American future.

In light of those affective ties, as well as the instrumental value of liberal rhetoric, there is nothing astonishing about Jeane Kirkpatrick's claim in a recently published collection of speeches that "liberal beliefs and practices lie at the core of the Reagan Administration's orientation toward politics" and that "the President and many of his principal advisors see themselves as purveyors and defenders of the classical liberal tradition. . . ."[1]

The Reagan Phenomenon, to which the title of the book alludes, is nothing less than the end of Vietnam-induced national self-denigration and a renewed consensus, embodied in the President, about "the relevance of our nation's basic principles to the contemporary world" and the centrality of American power "for the survival of liberal democracy."

This appropriation of liberal ideals, evidenced by the President himself on many occasions, notably in his democracy-on-the-march speech to the British Parliament, was bound to impose on this administration labors of contradiction management hardly less onerous than those which have tormented liberals. How, without loss of credibility, could the Reagan administration reconcile on the one hand its claim to embody liberal values—which it properly equates with human rights—and on the other both its visceral hostility to socioeconomic reform and its desire to collaborate with brutal but enthusiastically anticommunist regimes? Ambassador Kirkpatrick's essays and speeches, including those collected in *The Reagan Phenomenon*, illustrate several facets of the administration's strategy of reconciliation. One tactic in the overall strategy is to imply that, since illiberal beliefs lie at the core of the Politburo's policies, whatever measures enhance American power ultimately promote liberal ends. This proposition is, of course, the mirror image of Kremlin apologetics[2] and deserves about equal shrift. Neither Kirkpatrick nor other like-minded patriots ever

On the Management of Liberal Contradictions 57

put the matter quite so boldly. Robert Nisbet comes uncomfortably close in his gaseous introduction:

> No one has spoken more eloquently than Ambassador Kirkpatrick in support of democratic ideals, of human rights in the world, but no one has seen more shrewdly than she the crippling hypocrisy of so much of the liberal intellectual's advocacy of human rights: A stern, uncompromising insistence upon full human rights in nations we are obliged for strategic reasons to ally ourselves with, but, with this an indifference that approaches sheer blindness to frightful assaults upon human rights in the Soviet Union and in the growing number of countries which, spurred on by the Soviets, make the rhetoric of socialist humanitarianism camouflage for, not simply abuse, but obliteration of human rights.[3]

No one has managed quite so well as Nisbet to capture in one sentence, albeit long, the links among the several features of the reconciliation strategy. To demonstrate the moral dimension of "strategic reasons," the right employs a two-step argument. In step one it declares that Marxist regimes are qualitatively worse violators of human rights than non-Marxist ones. In step two it claims that the incidence of the former is a function of the U.S.-Soviet power relationship: more power for the United States equals fewer Marxist regimes.

In order to make the first step credible, the Right has relied in part on the theoretical distinction between "totalitarian" regimes (treating totalitarian as synonymous with Marxist) and "merely authoritarian" ones, in part on the general claim that liberals reflexively exaggerate the defects of right-wing regimes while ignoring or mitigating Marxist delinquencies, and in part on imprecise accounts of right-wing behavior.

The claim that liberals employ a double standard in appraising left-and-right wing regimes, an established feature of right-wing polemics, was probably true in the 1930s, when I was born. Repeating it today evidences either ignorance or malice. Liberal-dominated committees of Congress for example, have produced scrupulously detailed reports on human rights violations in Marxist states. Damning accounts of human rights violations in the Soviet Union, Vietnam, Poland and Afghanistan, among other places, have appeared in the *New York Review of Books,* the central organ of the liberal intelligentsia. Mainstream human rights organizations, such as Amnesty International—inevitably staffed largely by liberal volunteers precisely because conservative activists, being committed to the abstract distinction between left-and-right-wing regimes, are unwilling to indict the latter—have displayed an unimpeachable commitment to even-handed appraisal. Nor is it entirely irrelevant that the President who first invited a Soviet dissident to the White House was Jimmy Carter, not his conservative predecessors.

The careful arrangement of reality to suit political ends equally characterizes the Kirkpatrickites' handling of particular cases. Were it not for the fact that a non–Marxist regime satisfying the criteria for a totalitarian one would inconvenience Ambassador Kirkpatrick, her description of South Africa as "a democracy on top and an authoritarian system on the bottom" might have surprised me. Here is a regime which from one day to another uproots whole communities, bulldozes their homes and transports them to "homelands" they have never seen; a regime which governs minutely the movements of every black person in the country; a regime which can and does imprison people indefinitely—white, colored, and Indian, as well as black—without charge or trial, a regime which by executive fiat transfers people to any part of the country or confines them to their homes bound, under threat of harsher measures, to silence and isolation; a regime in whose interrogation chambers people die for unexplained reasons because its interrogators torture with impunity. As the leading publicist for the authoritarian–totalitarian distinction, Mrs. Kirkpatrick has remarkable difficulty recognizing a paradigmatic instance of the latter.

In order to facilitate sanitizing the behavior of favorite governments, Mrs. Kirkpatrick repeatedly insists on the importance of judging events in context, but her own insensitivity to real contexts is stupifying. For instance, in a statement before the Third Committee of the United Nations she referred to Guatemala as a country whose economic and social progress has for the past several years been threatened by ruthless terrorists.[4] Who would know from her description that the regime which ruled that country until March 1986 was Murder Incorporated with a flag?[5] All-in-all, Mrs. Kirkpatrick's work is brute testimony to the force of Orwell's dictum, she herself paradoxically invokes, that the whole tendency of modern thought is away from concreteness.

The claim to be quietly championing human rights in Central America and everywhere else is itself an enormous retreat from the swaggering contempt for Carter's policies that marked Reagan's postelection behavior. Hardly were the results in before gorillas from the campaign train fanned out through Central America with assurances to their local counterparts that the new administration would have no interest in how they went about maintaining order.

The stridence of their claim that human rights was dead alarmed even *The Economist*'s anonymous editorialists who arraigned this mandate for massacre being delivered by persons they delicately labeled "self-proclaimed emissaries" for the President–elect. Perhaps that issue of the magazine escaped Mr. Reagan's notice. It did not, in any event, inhibit a purge of the State Department's Latin American Bureau. Out went any professional diplomat judged guilty of fervor in defending human rights during the Carter years. And, as if to assuage any lingering doubt about his personal views, the President, normally quick to correct his ebullient Secretary of State, remained mute after Mr. Haig, at his first press conference declared: "International terrorism will take the place of human rights in our concern."

When, however, it became apparent that neither national security tocsins nor omnibus moral claims (American power equals more human rights) could rally support for unconditional guarantees to right-wing regimes, the administration nominally rehabilitated Carter's policy of conditioning, or at least threatening to condition, aid levels on good behavior.

This observer remains skeptical that Ronald Reagan has had a conversion experience in the manner of Saul of Tarsus. One reason for doubt is that the societal reforms required in most developing countries, if "human rights" is to be more than a slogan, cut right against the grain of his administration's whole social philosophy, which is nicely epitomized by its attitude toward VISTA. Constance Horner, who as director of the organization seemed more interested in dismantling than managing it, explained her activities by noting that conservatives aim to discourage an activist "form of community organizing which is designed to elicit a confrontation between poor people as a group and government or nongovernment institutions in their communities." The reason: "Such confrontations are usually designed to encourage expansion of programs, entitlements, rights which only serve to enhance dependency, not self-reliance."[6]

Revolutionar-preempting reforms in the Third World must do exactly what Social Darwinism says must not be done: They must alter preexisting inequality in access to health, to wealth, and to government itself whose favors have, of course, so largely determined the existing structure of inequality. Frightened oligarchs and frustrated officers begin to contemplate reform when poor people begin with the help of priests or middle-class activists to establish organizations (peasant leagues, labor unions, and so on) which can confront the power of wealth with the power of numbers and which can forcefully claim the kinds of entitlements that have hitherto been the exclusive province of the rich.

El Salvador is only one of a number of countries, not all of them in Latin America, whose long-term potential for liberal government cannot be realized solely through the interplay, peaceful or violent, of domestic forces. Having begun to realize that the character of government and society in most Third World countries is of little consequence to American security, the electorate is not inclined to large sacrifices on their behalf. But as the Reagan administration reluctantly discovered, there remains in the body politic an impulse to encourage liberal government where it can be done without great risk and cost. The Caribbean Basin offers several countries which satisfy this test in part because Latin partisans of reform, despite (or possibly because of) their historic sensitivity to all forms of unilateral American intervention, are ready to join us in sponsoring social and political change.

Probably the Reagan administration is ideologically disabled from seizing this opportunity. Probably we must wait for a new, liberal President who has learned two lessons: First, that we will not reform brutal social orders by guaranteeing their survival and, second, that a successful transition to real participatory institutions in countries where such institutions have a constituency but not a tradition requires sustained attention and material aid from the United States.

Presumptions are guides to action in the average case. For reasons I outlined earlier, nonintervention—whether by more-or-less direct applications of force or by the use of economic instruments—is an appropriate presumption for liberals. And, like all presumptions, it is refutable in exceptional cases.

Notes

1. *The Reagan Phenomenon and Other Speeches on Foreign Policy* (Washington: American Enterprise Institute for Public Policy Research 1983).
2. I.e., the theory that every increase in Soviet power promotes the liberation of the laboring classes.
3. *Supra* note 1, at xiii.
4. Press Release USUN 167–(82), December 7, 1982.
5. If the "government" consists of those people who systematically exercise decisive power over the central issues of national life, the seat of government in Guatemala continues to be found not in the office of President Marco Vinicio Cerezo Arévalo, but in the cantonments of the armed forces. Cerezo himself claims to exercise "twenty-five percent" of governmental power.
6. See Ann Hulbert, "VISTA's Lost Horizons," *The New Republic,* August 30, 1982, p. 18.

PART II
HUMAN RIGHTS

INTRODUCTION TO PART II: ETIOLOGY OF AN IDEA

At his first news conference, Alexander M. Haig—United States Secretary of State under President Ronald Reagan—achieved the unenviable distinction of communicating at a uniquely early point in his tenure contempt for the values which knit up the Western Alliance. The medium for this unintended message was the following statement:

> International terrorism will take the place of human rights in our concern because it is the ultimate abuse of human rights. And it's time that it be addressed with better clarity and greater effectiveness by Western nations and the United States as well.

In the coderoom of international diplomacy, a declared priority for terrorism over human rights is effortlessly deciphered as an invitation to put on the brass knuckles and never mind the Marquis of Queensberry. Whatever Secretary Haig's actual intentions (and I am not reluctant to attribute to him the best of motives), his language was an incitement to governments to massacre present or potential rebels.

The historical setting of Secretary Haig's remarks make this conclusion inescapable. Until the Second World War, most legal scholars and governments affirmed the general proposition, albeit not in so many words, that international law did not impede the natural right of each equal sovereign to be monstrous to his or her subjects.[1] Summary execution, torture, arbitrary arrest and detention: these were legally significant events beyond national frontiers only if the victims of such official eccentricities were citizens of another state. In that case, international law treated them as the bearers not of personal rights but of rights belonging to their government and ultimately to the state for which it spoke. In effect, for the purposes of interstate relations, the individual was nothing more than a symbol and a capital asset. Assaults on his person carried out or acquiesced in by representatives of another state were deemed assaults on the dignity and material interests of his state, requiring compensation.[2]

Guardians of the spiritual realm were episodically less permissive. Virtually from the start of that bloody enterprise known as the Spanish Empire in The New World, some priests struggled to moderate the awful cupidity and grotesque caprice of the Conquistadores, their secular associates in Spain's civilizing mission.[3] In addition, Christian missionaries worked to alert decent opinion in Europe, such as it was, to the genocidal features of the trade in African slaves[4] and, thereafter, to such abominations as the Belgian King Leopold's personal empire in the Congo.[5]

Even Europe's colonial powers thought, or at least found it convenient to appear to think, that the Congo's indigenous population required some guarantee of minimally decent treatment. And so, while negotiating the orderly division of Africa at the Congress of Berlin in 1984–85, they announced and Leopold nominally accepted, arguably as a condition of his suzerainty over the Congo, an obligation to look after the well being of its inhabitants.[6] Since the conferences provided no enforcement mechanism, relying rather on the good faith of the ineffable Leopold, the people of the Congo did not quickly hear of or experience the good news.[7] Nevertheless, the very recognition of limits on a fellow sovereign's discretion in the disposition of his human assets was a phenomenon.

The effort to inhibit Leopold was one among a number of events in the latter part of the Nineteenth Century and the first part of the Twentieth expressing an epochal shift in moral sentiment that would ultimately find expression in law. Heralds of this shift had appeared a good deal earlier to trumpet its arrival. While historians will always dispute when the first faint notes could be distinguished, the American and French revolutionists, by invoking on their own behalf universal and inalienable rights, unmistakably declared the new age. The often vacillating but finally decisive Anglo-French intervention in the Greek War of Independence from Ottoman rule,[8] justified in part by the allegedly peculiar cruelty of the Ottoman administration, reenforced the evangelical message of the French Revolution, as it poured across national frontiers, that, in the spirit of human solidarity, one state might choose to liberate from perceived oppression the people of another.

During the remainder of the century, the Ottoman Empire continued to serve as a magnet for essays in "Humanitarian Intervention" by Great Powers: the Russians, on behalf of Orthodox Christians, and the French, on behalf of Catholics.[9] In addition to evidencing the power of transnational solidarities, these interventions demonstrated the possible contradiction between such claims and harmony in the relations of states. World War I tragically underscored the potentially destructive impact on interstate relations of claims for liberation and justice asserted by people against the political structures containing them. At the same time, however, because the Allies sought to marshal support by characterizing their exertions as a struggle to defend and promote freedom,[10] one consequence of the War was to enhance the perceived legitimacy of individual and group claims against the state.

The process of unpacking the individual from the state went on with the inclusion in the post-war settlement of provisions purporting to guarantee fair treatment for minorities principally in the infant countries carved out of the Austro-Hungarian Empire's corpse. Subsequent experience suggested both the importance of such guarantees and the diffidence of guarantors on those common occasions when compassion did not manage to coincide with more traditional state interests.

The minority provisions in the post-War treaties[11] created a special regime for the protection of a limited cluster of interests of carefully circumscribed peoples. In this respect they were not unique, having been preceded by the capitulations[12] coerced from the Ottoman Sultan, the Chinese Emperor, and other non-European dignitaries by Western governments determined to insulate their citizens, primarily traders, from local jurisdiction. But the capitulations were simply a discriminatory expansion of each state's acknowledged right to fair treatment for its own subjects when they were abroad, a right equally operative in relations among the great powers.

Even in making the treatment of the subjects of one sovereign a matter of legitimate concern to other sovereigns, the minority-protection clauses did not open entirely new ground: Under duress, the Sublime Porte had conceded rights of protection over the Empire's orthodox and Catholic populations respectively to the Russians and the French.[13] But when, in the final stages of the Second World War, the victorious allies decided to prosecute Nazi leaders not only for waging aggressive war and massacring people in occupied territories, but also for the slaughter of German citizens ("crimes against humanity"),[14] they were opening new territory.

German nationals did not enjoy the protection of any special treaty regime. So if they had unconditional rights subject to violation by the Third Reich, it had to be under customary rules of international law or general principles to be found in every civilized society. Thus, the judgment of Nuremberg, and the General Assembly declaration affirming the legitimacy of the principles supporting that judgment,[15] implied a core of obligations concerning the treatment of their citizens applicable to all sovereigns. In this way, the realm of human rights became available for general occupation.

In the ensuing decades, both through formal agreements and declarations evidencing the consensus necessary for customary law,[16] states have bound themselves not to torture or summarily execute or enslave their citizens, or to convict them without due process of law, or to dissolve their trade unions, or to discriminate among them on the basis of race or religion, or to do other things that today, as in the past, are the authors of despair. Many nations, going beyond declarations of self-restraint, have rallied with varying degrees of rhetorical commitment behind the claim that the state has an affirmative obligation to protect its citizens from economic, social, and cultural impoverishment.

Today the normative regime of human rights, envisioned by idealists at the close of World War II, is largely completed. With respect, however, to achieving near universal congruence between norms and official behavior, we have only begun.

Notes

1. Richard Bilder, "An Overview of Human Rights Law," in Hurst Hannum, ed., *Guide to Human Rights Practice* (Philadelphia 1984) pp. 4-5. See also Elihu Lauterpacht, ed., *International Law: Collected Papers of Hersch Lauterpacht*, Vol. I (Cambridge 1970): "The Predominant theory is clear and emphatic. International law is a law of states only and exclusively. Individuals are only the objects of international law." p. 279. But he goes on to demonstrate that, over the course of the Twentieth Century, the predominant theory has become riddled with exceptions to such a degree as to require a far more qualified and nuanced statement of it. pp. 141-149 and 279-285. "It may now be submitted, by way of summary, that these examples show that there is nothing in the existing international system [i.e. post-World War II] which makes it impossible for individuals to be directly subjects of international duties [and correspondingly rights] imposed upon them as such. . . . Secondly, reasons have been given why even in those cases in which States are formally made subjects of international duties, the actual centre of legal and moral responsibility is in the individual and not in the metaphysical personality of the State. Decisive reasons of progress in international law and morality seem to favour that construction." p. 285.
2. See L. Oppenheim, 1 *International Law: A Treatise* (Hersch Lauterpacht 7th ed. London 1948) pp. 304-06, 310; on reparations see pp. 318-19.
3. See, *e.g.,* Roger Merriman, *The Rise of the Spanish Empire,* Vol. II (New York 1962) pp. 656-63.
4. See, *e.g.,* D.B. Davis, *Slavery and Human Progress* (New Haven 1984) pp. 304-05. See also Paul Lovejoy, *Transformations in Slavery* (Cambridge 1983) pp. 253-61. "[The missionaries] were firmly opposed to the slave trade and enslavement; indeed, the missions were intimately associated with the abolition of the trans-Atlantic slave trade." But, he adds, "on the other hand, they generally concluded that [in Africa] conversion to Christianity should precede the abolition of slavery. Slave holders, for example, were allowed to become Christians. Slavery was to be tolerated temporarily, so that the Christian church could be established. Only when Christians were a majority of the population would it be safe to abolish slavery." pp. 253-54. The struggle for abolition, particularly when it assumed the form of pressure by Great Britain on other states and the stopping and boarding of vessels on the high seas, was, of course, an augury of movement in the architectonic plates of moral and legal sentiment.
5. See generally Neal Ascherson, *The King Incorporated* (London 1963).

6. Lauterpacht, Vol. II, *supra* note 1 (1975), p. 103. To be precise, pursuant to Article 6 of the Berlin Act, all the powers exercising rights in the Congo Basin undertook to care for the moral and material conditions of the natives. Similar provision in the Act concluding the Brussels Conference of 1890 was thought, Lauterpacht says, to require "positive measures for the improvement of the natives' lot."
7. Massacre, mutilation and forced labor continued at least through the first decade of the Twentieth Century. Ascherson, *Id.* at 241–260.
8. See generally Dakin, *The Greek War of Independence 1821–33* (1973).
9. See generally Stanford and Ezel Shaw, *History of the Ottoman Empire and Modern Turkey,* Vol. II (Cambridge 1977).
10. "[W]e shall fight for the things which we have always carried nearest to our hearts,—for democracy, for the right of those who submit to authority to have a voice in their own governments . . ." Woodrow Wilson, Speech to Congress, 2 April 1917, quoted in Frederick Calhoun, *Power and Principle* (Kent State 1986).
11. See Lauterpacht, *supra* note 1, Vol. II, at 49, 147, 506.
12. Lord Kinross, *The Ottoman Centuries* (London 1977) pp. 427 and 479; see also Shaw and Shaw, *supra* note 7, at 131, 300, 367.
13. See Kinross and Shaw and Shaw.
14. Lauterpacht, *supra* note 1, at 470–71.
15. G.A. res. 95(I) (11 December 1946).
16. See generally Anthony D'Amato, *The Concept of Custom in International Law* (Ithaca 1971).

6

The Inter-American Commission on Human Rights: History, Structure, and Function

Background and Introduction

The Inter-American Commission on Human Rights (IACHR), founded in 1959, is one of the principal organs of the Organization of American States. The commission is empowered to receive complaints from individuals, organizations, and groups alleging violations of human rights in any of the member states of the OAS and to make findings of fact and recommendations designed to effect the vindication of those rights.

Its purposes, though not its form, were foreshadowed in the charter of the OAS, adopted in 1948, which announced, albeit in the most general and unconstraining terms, the Western Hemisphere's shared humanitarian values. Specific rights were set forth in the American Declaration of the Rights and Duties of Man, approved in Bogotá at the time of the adoption of the charter some seven months before the adoption of the Universal Declaration of Human Rights by the General Assembly of the United Nations.

A resolution was also passed at Bogotá charging the Inter-American Juridical Committee with the preparation of a convention for the establishment of a Court of Human Rights for the hemisphere. In 1949, however, the committee reported that there did not exist at the time a sufficient basis in positive international law for the creation of such a court.

There the matter rested for some time, to be sure under continued, or one might more accurately say intermittent, study. It was not until renewed democratic winds began to fan the continent in 1958 and 1959 that the movement for the establishment of a Court of Human Rights gathered any momentum.

In late 1958, the dictatorial regime of Perez Jimenez was overthrown and democracy was restored in Venezuela. It also was in 1958 that Juscelino Kubitschek of Brazil proposed the establishment of an "Operation Panamericana," adding a strong stimulus to the rather incipient enthusiasm for social transformation. The conceptual linkage between democracy and social change was reflected in the creation of a Social Progress fund and the Inter-American Development Bank in 1959. These programs, initiated in the last days of the Eisenhower administration, were the immediate precursors of the Alliance for Progress.

At their fifth meeting, held in Santiago in August 1959, the hemisphere's foreign ministers resolved in the "Declaration of Santiago" to establish the Inter-American Commission and called for the drafting of an American Convention on Human Rights. The "Statute" of the commission was approved by the Council of the OAS on May 25, 1960, and its first meeting was held in that year.

The commission broadly construed its then somewhat ambiguous charter to allow consideration of individual complaints. It began to issue general reports, including the contents of individual communications and commission comments thereon. The commission also devoted a good deal of its attention to the tense situation in the Caribbean.

Following the American intervention in the Dominican Republic in 1965, the commission, with the consent of both factions, played a particularly useful role in mediating differences between them and in actively protecting the human rights of large numbers of individuals on both sides. In the wake of this unanticipated and somewhat improvised success, the commission's mandate was strengthened by Resolution XXII of the Second Special Inter-American Conference, held in Rio de Janeiro in November 1965. The broadening of the commission's powers mandated by Resolution XXII was formalized in 1966 by the Council of the OAS through amendments to the statute of the commission. Among other things, they confirmed the power to consider individual complaints.

The Protocol of Buenos Aires amending the charter of the OAS, adopted in 1967 and in effect since 1970, further enhanced the commission's authority by establishing it as one of the "principal organs" of the OAS. In a transitory provision, it declared that the commission was to continue its efforts to ensure the observance of human rights until such time as the American Convention on Human Rights was to enter into force. The effect of these amendments to the charter was to incorporate by reference the commission's existing statute, Article 2 of which defines "human rights" as those established in the 1948 American Declaration on the Rights and Duties of Man. The result was to complete the process of incorporation of the Statute of the commission and the American Declaration on the Rights and Duties of Man into positive law of the charter. In short, the Protocol of

Buenos Aires established the human rights commitments of the member states as a part of the body of binding positive hemispheric law.

One final historical note: In 1969, the American Convention on Human Rights ("Pact of San José") was signed by eleven states at the Specialized Inter-American Conference on Human Rights held in San José, Costa Rica. It entered into force almost nine years later, on July 18, 1978, with deposit of the eleventh instrument of ratification by the member state of Grenada. As of January 1, 1987, sixteen states are parties to the convention: Bolivia, Columbia, Costa Rica, the Dominican Republic, Ecuador, El Salvador, Grenada, Guatemala, Haiti, Honduras, Jamaica, Mexico, Nicaragua, Panama, Peru, and Venezuela.

As stated in the first paragraph of its preamble, the purpose of the convention is "to consolidate in this hemisphere within the framework of democratic institutions, a system of personal liberty and social justice based on respect for the essential rights of man."

The first part of the convention establishes the obligation of the states to respect the rights recognized in the convention and to ensure to all persons subject to their jurisdiction the freedom to exercise those rights. It then goes on to define the rights and freedoms protected, which are mainly civil and political rights, since with respect to economic, social, and cultural rights, the states only undertake to "adopt measures, both internally and through international cooperation, especially those of an economic and technical nature, with a view of achieving progressively . . . the full realization of the rights implicit in the economic, social, educational, scientific, and cultural standards set forth in the Charter of the Organization of American States by legislation or other appropriate means" (Art. 26).

Special mention should be made here of the important innovation that Article 43 of the convention introduces into the system: It requires member states "to provide the Commission with such information as it may request of them as to the manner in which their domestic law ensures the effective application of any provision of this Convention." This differs from the provisions of the commission's previous mandate, which merely authorized it to urge the OAS member states to provide information on any measures that they had adopted with respect to human rights.

Another important innovation that the convention introduces into the Inter-American system is its opening up of the complaint process to states. Until the convention came into force, the commission was empowered to consider complaints only from individuals and nongovernmental entities. However, this innovation is limited by Article 45's requirement that both the state exercising that right and the state against which the petition is filed have recognized the competence of the commission to receive and examine this type of communication.

The Composition, Authority and Activities of the Commission

Seven members, each a presumed authority in the field of human rights, compose the commission. Members serve in their personal capacity, not as representatives of their respective governments. Nominated by member states, they are elected to four-year terms by the General Assembly of the OAS. No more than one national may be elected from any one country. Members may be reelected once. The chairman is elected by the vote of an absolute majority of the members.

Under its regulations, the commission is authorized to hold up to eight weeks of regular meetings per year and such extraordinary sessions as may be required. Members receive only their expenses and a modest honorarium.

The seven members of the commission are backed up by a full-time staff or secretariat, headed by an executive secretary who is appointed by the Secretary General of the Organization of American States, in consultation with the commission.

In addition to working closely with the members when the commission is in session, the permanent staff carries out the commission's day-to-day work, processing complaints, soliciting information from governments, preparing special studies, and so forth. Under the terms of the statute, the staff forms a part of the General Secretariat of the OAS and is subject to the rules and regulations of the General Secretariat as a whole.

The work of the commission consists basically of three activities:

1. Consideration of individual complaints regarding specific violations of human rights by a given member state;
2. Preparation and publication of country reports on the general situation regarding human rights in a given country; and
3. Other activities aimed at the promotion of human rights, including preparation of studies and reports on general themes related to human rights; preparation of the Annual Report; management of an extremely modest fellowship program; the organization of seminars; and the publication of an Inter-American Yearbook on Human Rights.

The examination of individual complaints and the preparation of country reports constitute the most important work of the IACHR. The two activities are intimately related, for the value and persuasive force of the country reports depend to a large degree on information obtained through the processing of individual complaints received by the commission.

Any person, group of persons, or legally recognized nongovernmental entity may submit petitions to the commission. The petition may be in any of the OAS official languages, on the petitioner's behalf or on behalf of third persons, with regard to alleged violations of human rights recognized in the American Convention on Human Rights or in the American Declaration of the Rights and Duties of Man.

The Requirements of Prior Exhaustion of Domestic Legal Remedies

The commission normally cannot accept a complaint unless it provides some basis for concluding that internal remedies have been exhausted. However, the exhaustion of remedies requirement is not applicable when:

a. The domestic legislation of the state concerned does not afford due process of law for the protection of the right or rights that allegedly have been violated;
b. The party alleging violation of his rights has been denied access to the remedies theoretically available under domestic law or has been prevented from exhausting them; or
c. There has been unwarranted delay in rendering a final judgment under the aforementioned remedies.

In other words, this requirement is not applicable when there are no effective and expeditious remedies to exhaust.

The prior exhaustion of domestic legal remedies is required by international law. The International Court of Justice, for example, applied this rule in the Interhandel Case between Switzerland and the United States, declaring: "The rule that local remedies must be exhausted before international proceedings may be instituted is a well-established rule of customary international law."

The exceptions built into Article 46 of the convention reduce much of the possible inconvenience presented by this requirement, if they are construed humanely. In this respect, allocation of the burden of proof can be crucial. Who will have to produce the evidence showing that internal legal remedies have been exhausted? Initially, the European Commission was too severe in applying the exhaustion rule, in that it demanded from the complainants proof that domestic legal remedies had been exhausted. After some years, the European Commission amended its statute. Under that amendment, complainants simply must enunciate in their petition the domestic legal remedies they have pursued. From this information and that furnished by the government, the commission then decides on the admissibility of the denunciation. In many instances, the European Commission has even acted as if the rule of prior exhaustion of domestic legal remedies were an exception that must be invoked by the state being accused.

The experience of the European Commission, which tends to underline the necessity for equality among the parties, could be used in the future by the Inter-American Commission on Human Rights to liberate the complainants, when the circumstances so indicate, from the burden of proof. In actual practice to date, the requirement has rarely presented serious difficulties, perhaps because within the worst delinquents the inadequacy of local remedies is apparent.

The Requirement that the Subject of the Petition or Communication not be Pending in Another International Settlement Proceeding

Article 46 of the convention further requires that the subject of the petition or communication not be awaiting settlement in another international proceeding. The same limitation exists in both the European Convention and the Optional Protocol to the United Nations Covenant on Civil and Political Rights. Nevertheless, this limiting requirement in some degree threatens the efficacy of the convention.

What happens when someone is arbitrarily detained, tortured, or kidnapped by the security forces of the state? Often their relatives or friends plead these facts before all of the international organs for the protection of human rights. By coordinating their efforts, rather than operating on the case serially, the concerned organs can significantly enhance the prospect for a successful intervention on behalf of the victim.

The Procedure

If the petition satisfies the few preliminary requirements for admissibility, the commission will communicate to the government in question the pertinent parts of the petition, withholding the identity of the petitioner or petitioners unless they expressly authorize disclosure, and request information. In serious or urgent cases, the commission may request the government in question to allow the commission to conduct an on-site investigation.

If the government fails to provide the requested information within a period of 180 days, and provided the evidence does not lead to a different conclusion, the commission will adopt a decision declaring the facts related in the denunciation to be true and formulating the suggestions and recommendations it deems appropriate. If the government provides information tending to disprove the complainant's charges, the latter is then informed about the response and given an opportunity to make observations and present evidence in rebuttal.

The pertinent parts of those observations and the evidence presented by the petitioner will be forwarded to the government in question so that it may make its final observations within a period of thirty days.

In order to reach a friendly settlement of the matter, the commission will place itself at the disposal of the parties concerned at any stage of the examination of a petition, either at the request of any of the parties or on its own initiative.

Once these measures have been taken or once the indicated time period has elapsed, and if no friendly settlement has been reached, the commission will examine the case, taking into account the observations and evidence presented by the petitioner and the government in question and any evidence the commission obtains from witnesses, documents, records, official publications, or those resulting from the on–site observation, if it has conducted one. On the basis of these, it will formulate conclusions and make any suggestions or recommendations it considers appropriate. Conclusions and recommendations then are transmitted to the petitioner and to the state in question.

If the state fails to adopt the measures recommended by the commission within the stipulated time period, the commission may publish its conclusions, recommendations, and suggestions, either by including them in its annual report to the General Assembly or through such other means as the Commission considers appropriate.

The number of individual cases considered by the commission has grown at an exponential rate in recent years. In 1968, the Commission opened fourteen new cases and had approximately eighteen pending. Five years later, those figures had changed only modestly: in 1973, approximately twenty-six cases were opened while twenty-four were pending. By 1976, however, the corresponding figures were 139 and 145. In 1980, the number of new cases reached 2,900, while there were approximately 4,730 cases in process.

The Country Reports

The Commission bases its country reports on information obtained through the processing of individual complaints, as well as other available information. Typically, a country report begins with a chapter on the legal provisions affecting human rights in the country concerned and follows up with chapters dealing with the observance of the rights to personal security enumerated in Article 9(a) of the commission's statute. Reports usually deal as well with civil, political, economic, and social rights.

While the practice of issuing reports on the general situation of human gifts in particular countries dates back to the early 1960s, such reports were rare before 1974. Since then, they have multiplied dramatically. The commission has published one or more reports on Chile, Cuba, Nicaragua (before and after the revolution), Argentina, Bolivia, Colombia, El Salvador, Guatemala, Haiti, Paraguay, Surinam and Uruguay. Special reports are normally updated in chapters of the Commission's Annual Report to the General Assembly of the OAS.

Ideally, the country report should include information gathered during a visit, technically referred to as an *observation in loco,* during which the commission can, among other things, meet with a wide range of individuals and groups, inspect places of detention, and observe the operation of the judicial system. In the past, a few governments have been adamant in their refusal to grant the consent necessary to conduct an on-site inquiry. Those that have welcomed the commission, including countries that initiated the idea of a visit, may in a few instances have been influenced by the perceived opportunity to dispel false allegations and to draw upon the expertise of the commission which, through recommendations and direct discussions, can point out where deficiencies exist and improvements can be made. In this way, the commission can assist the government in its own efforts to improve the protection and observance of human rights within its borders.

The Observations in Loco

The visits of the commission may have their origin in a spontaneous invitation on the part of the government, or they may be the result of a request by the commission for that government's consent to carry out a visit. The latter situation generally arises when, in the judgment of the commission, there is reason to believe that the situation of human rights in that country warrants investigation.

No other intergovernmental organization for the protection of human rights had the experience of the Inter-American Commission with regard to on-the-spot investigations. A major purpose of such visits is to speak with persons who are in a position to provide the commission with information concerning the protection of human rights. Such persons normally would include detainees and their families and friends, former detainees, representatives of religious, social, labor, and professional organizations, members of the judiciary and the bar, and government officials. Another important activity of the commission during an *observation in loco* is the reception of complaints from persons who allege that their human rights have been violated.

Conclusions: The Impact of the Commission's Work

Little has been said here about living bodies wrested from the hands of torturers or of determinate human beings resurrected from the status of the "disappeared." Nothing has been said of a liberated trade–union movement, a free press, or pluralistic politics. Nothing has been said about these end products, in part because I cannot offer you conclusive evidence that these are the results of the Commission's work.

Governments still do not admit delinquencies. If individuals are freed, their liberation, if it is advertised at all, is presented as an act of official grace. It also is difficult to measure achievement outside the paper world of reports and communications because the commission has no absolute right of access to the prisons, detention camps, and interrogation centers where hope is crushed and identity extinguished. Without the permission of governments, the commission remains at a vast distance from the ultimate subject of its concern: individual human beings. Being unable to communicate directly with them or, frequently, with their wives, children, friends, and others intimately familiar with the facts, it can reach a firm and final conclusion in particular cases (the kind of conclusion to which governments would feel a considerable compulsion to respond directly) only in a limited number of instances, usually where governments tacitly concede the charges.

Having said that much, one may retain the belief that the commission does have an impact in the real world, that lives have been saved and democratic freedoms nurtured. Even if one were doubtful on that score, however, he or she still would be justified in believing in the utility of the commission's work. Decent, pluralistic societies cannot be built in a day. Indeed, it is not inevitable that they will be built at all. The commission is the embodiment of an ideal. Ideals that remain for long divorced from an institutional base generally prove evanescent. For many years, there seemed to be a gentlemen's agreement among member states of the OAS to overlook each other's atrocities. As long as the members of the commission are true to their obligations and as long as the commission's existing degree of autonomy is preserved, it will obstruct any slide, blatant or subtle, back to the days when a conspiracy of silence prevailed.

In concluding, note should be taken of a fact which, though it seems obvious enough, is frequently ignored. By itself, the Commission can only be one modest element in the process of realizing the ideals of the various human rights texts. At best, it can be an effective finder of the facts and propagator of the good news that such ideals exist. But it cannot by itself translate those ideals into the real world where vile crimes against elemental human right are an everyday reality. What is to be done with those facts after they are found? That is the question which the member states of the OAS and other interested parties—particularly Canada, Japan, and Western Europe—must individually and collectively address. The commission cannot bear more than a small part of the freight of the human rights movement. The real sanctions and incentives remain at the disposal of states.

7

A Note on Terrorism and on the Relationship Among the Right to Physical Security, the Right to Political Participation, and Economic and Social Rights

Mr. President:

On behalf of my colleagues and myself, I should like to thank you for the opportunity to communicate the views of the Inter-American Commission on Human Rights concerning several issues which I believe are also of great interest to this commission.

In briefly elaborating the views of the Inter-American Commission, I hope to contribute to that ongoing exchange of ideas among the various intergovernmental organizations concerned with human rights, which, if carried on in a frank and constructive manner, can only aid in the defense and promotion of the values to which we all aspire.

In the commission's most recent annual reports, because of blatant violations of the rights to life, personal security, liberty, and due process of law, and the phenomenon of "missing persons," the commission thought it necessary to focus its concern on the tremendous wave of murder, torture, and arbitrary detention in the hemisphere.

But while examining the state of the human right to personal security in the various countries, the commission recognized a relationship—by no means a perfectly symmetrical one, but nevertheless a distinct relationship—between the violation of the right to personal security on the one hand and, on the other, neglect of economic and social rights and suppression of political participation.

That relationship is in significant measure one of cause and effect. In other words, neglect of economic and social rights, particularly when political participation has been suppressed, produces the kind of social polarization that then leads to acts of terrorism by and against the government.

Right to Political Participation

Article 20 of the American Declaration of the Rights and Duties of Man:

> Every person having legal capacity is entitled to participate in the government of his country, directly or through his representatives, and to take part in popular elections, which shall be by secret ballot, and shall be honest, periodic and free.

Article 23 of the American Convention on Human Rights: Right to Participate in Government:

> 1. Every citizen shall enjoy the following rights and opportunities:
>   a. to take part in the conduct of public affairs, directly or through freely chosen representatives;
>   b. to vote and to be elected in genuine periodic elections, which shall be by universal and equal suffrage and by secret ballot that guarantees the free expression of the will of the voters; and
>   c. to have access, under general conditions of equality, to the public service of his country.
> 2. The law may regulate the exercise of the rights and opportunities referred to in the preceding paragraph only on the basis of age, nationality, residence, language, education, civil and mental capacity, or sentencing by a competent court in criminal proceedings.

This right, naturally, leaves every state a very broad range of discretion concerning the distribution of power within the state and the means through which power can legitimately be acquired.

Whether power is highly centralized or, as in some federations, diffused among constituent elements, whether there shall be a strong executive and a weak parliament or the reverse—these and a host of other choices which face the people of every sovereign state are purely matters of national discretion beyond the reach of external judgment. But Articles 20 and 23 do impose some limits. They are not meaningless. What are those limits? The answer is clear:

Every national state houses within itself a variety of interests that are in some degree competitive: ethnic interests, regional interests, class interests, to name only three. Articles 20 and 23 must be construed in light of other human rights, including those of association, assembly, and petition. In that light, if not by themselves, the governing articles guarantee to every faction or interest the right to organize itself for political competition and the right to compete fairly for political power. This right is a corollary of the truism that no class, no party, no man, no race, and no professional group—lawyers, soldiers or even diplomats—has a monopoly on truth, wisdom, or virtue. Having no such monopoly, none has a moral or prudential right to monopolize power.

The right to political participation makes possible the right to organize parties and political associations which, through open discussion and political struggle, can improve the social level and economic circumstances of the popular classes and prevent a monopoly of power by any group or individual. A democratic framework is an essential element for establishment of a political society where human values can be fully realized.

The 1980 General Assembly of the Organization of American States, in its resolution on the Annual Report of the Commission, recommended to those member states which still have not done it to reestablish or to perfect the democratic system of government, in which the exercise of power derives from the legitimate and free expression of the popular will, in accordance with the characteristics and circumstances particular to each country.

Economic and Social Rights

Article 26 of the American Convention on Human Rights: Progressive Development:

> The States Parties undertake to adopt measures, both internally and through international cooperation, especially with those of an economic and technical nature, with a view of achieving progressively, by legislation or other appropriate means, the full realization of the rights implicit in the economic, social, education, scientific and cultural standards set forth in the Charter of the Organization of American States as amended by the Protocol of Buenos Aires.

Neglect of economic and social rights is another cause, though one that is more diffuse and problematic, of violence and social conflict.

Some scholars and diplomats have argued that economic and social "rights" are not true rights in the sense of categorical present claims on governments. They are, rather, mere aspirational values.

Adherents of this position fail to grasp the essential nature of the legal obligation assumed by all governments; the obligation to work in good faith for the realization of these aspirations *in a sequence which gives priority to basic health and nutrition.* The priority of "survival rights" or "basic needs" is a virtual corollary of the right to personal security. For there is neither a moral nor practical difference between a government which executes innocent people and one which tolerates their death by sickness or starvation when it has the means to obtain the food or health care that could save them.

One suggested difference between political and civil rights, such as claims against the government for personal security, and mere aspirational welfare values is that violations of the former stem directly from governmental action, while welfare claims arise as a consequence of acts of God (for example, drought) or the impersonal international market. The distinction is neither accurate nor relevant. It is inaccurate because governments can violate rights of physical security by negligently or maliciously failing to act against private persons bent on murdering their fellow citizens. The government in such cases is not directly responsible for the infliction of unjustified pain. It is, nevertheless, legally and morally delinquent.

Aside from failing to express logical differences, what is morally or legally interesting about the supposed distinction? Governments are endowed with the right, the resources, and the obligation to protect their subjects. Their legitimacy is rooted in that very function. Governments that simply refrain from crippling their populations are mere parasites without any secular basis for their claimed authority.

The commission has been extremely cautious in this sensitive area because it recognized the difficulty of establishing criteria that would enable it to measure the states' fulfillment of their obligations. It has also seen the very difficult choices that governments face when allocating resources between consumption and investment and, hence, between current and future generations. Economic policy is near the very center of national sovereignty. However, in light of the competence it has been given, the commission wishes to make the following observations with respect to economic, social, and cultural rights:

1. The essence of the legal obligation incurred by any government in this area is to strive to attain the economic and social aspirations of its people, by following an order that assigns priority to the basic needs of health, nutrition, and education.
2. According to development experts, life expectancy, infant mortality, and illiteracy are the best indicators for evaluating the progress being made toward higher levels of economic and social well-being for the general populace.
3. In view of the extremely unequal distribution of wealth in many countries, an increase in national revenues does not necessarily mean an improvement in those indices. The premise that a better national income helps to reduce poverty at the lowest levels of the social scale in a

country is only true in those cases in which priority attention has been devoted to the disadvantaged sectors.
4. Efforts to eliminate extreme poverty have been made under radically different political, economic, and cultural systems. In turn, those efforts have produced spectacular results in those developing countries that have expanded public health care services at the lowest level of society, that have tackled systematically the problem of mass illiteracy, that have undertaken comprehensive agrarian reform programs, or that have extended the benefits of social security to all sectors of the population.

At the 1980 General Assembly of the Organization of American States, the member states resolved to share the concern of the commission in emphasizing the importance of economic, social, and cultural rights in the context of human rights for the integral development of each human being. They also resolved to reaffirm that the effective protection of human rights should include economic, social, and cultural rights.

Terrorism and Human Rights

In contemporary international relations, few "issues," i.e., few associations of words, are so capable of producing profound and dangerous misconceptions.

One danger arises from the increasingly indiscriminate use of the word "terrorism." Many people and many governments are now using the term to characterize any movement of rebellion which they happen to dislike. In this fashion, the word is being emptied of its proper moral and juridical content and becoming a mere instrument of ideological and national polemics.

The commission has not explicitly defined the word terrorism. But implicitly we have been faithful to the historical conception by emphasizing terrorism as a cluster of barbaric methods, methods which are intolerably cruel and viciously indiscriminate, methods which even in the midst of civil or international armed conflict are forbidden by international law. These methods may be used by enemies of the government seeking its overthrow or by governments trying to repress opposition.

You will recall, for instance, the term's intimate historical association with the French Revolutionary Government which executed persons merely on suspicion of disloyalty or simply because they had offended influential figures.

The commission has often been asked: Does the existence of terrorists and threats to subvert the public order influence the commission's evaluations concerning respect for the observance of human rights in a given country? Within the limits to be described below the obvious answer is yes.

The commission repeatedly has emphasized the obligation of governments to maintain public order in order to preserve the human rights of all citizens.

In the life of any nation, threats to the public order or to the personal safety of its inhabitants, by persons or groups that use violence, can reach such proportions that it becomes necessary, temporarily, to suspend the exercise of certain rights.

The majority of the constitutions of the American States provide for the temporary institution of states of emergency or states of siege in such circumstances. Of course, the institution of such special legal regimes must be in response to the necessity of preserving those rights and freedoms which have been threatened by the disturbance of the public order and personal safety.

When the situation is grave, certain restrictions may be imposed—for example, on freedom of information or on the right of association—within the framework established in the constitution. In even more extreme cases, persons may be detained for short periods without it being necessary to bring specific charges against them.

It is true that such measures threaten the rule of law, but the threat can be contained provided that governments act responsibly: if they register arrests and inform the families of the detainees of the detentions; if they issue strict orders prohibiting torture; if they carefully recruit and train security forces, weeding out sadists and psychopaths; and lastly, if there is an independent judiciary able to correct swiftly any abuse of authority.

However, it is equally clear that certain fundamental rights can never be suspended, as is the case, among others, of the right to life, the right to personal security and integrity, and the right to due process. In other words, under no circumstances may governments employ summary execution, torture, inhumane conditions of detention, or conviction by a process that does not adequately distinguish guilt from innocence.

In this regard, it is important to recall the words spoken by His Holiness Pope John Paul II at the OAS on October 6, 1979. After acknowledging that at times special measures may be adopted, he added the following:

> ... they never, never justify an attack on the inviolable dignity of the human person and on the authentic rights that protect this dignity. If certain ideologies and certain ways of interpreting the legitimate concern for national security were to result in subjugating man and his rights and dignities to the state, they would to that extent cease to be humane and would be unable, without gross deception, to claim any Christian reference. In the thinking of the Church it is a fundamental principle that social organization is at the service of man, not vice-versa. That holds true also at the highest levels of society, where the power of coercion is wielded and where abuses, when they

occur, are particularly serious. A kind of security with which people do not identify, because it does not protect them in their very humanity, is only a farce; as it grows more and more rigid, it will show symptoms of growing weakness and rapidly approaching ruin.

Each government that confronts a subversive threat must choose the path of respect for the rule of law or the descent into state terrorism.

In light of the basic nature of terrorism, I was surprised and disappointed when a very senior official of one state which is a member of both the OAS and the United Nations Human Rights Commission recently declared: "International terrorism will take the place of human rights in our concern. . . ."

The suggestion that concern about terrorism and the defense of human rights are somehow competitive, so that one must be subordinated to the other, reflects at best a remarkable confusion. The violation of basic human rights, i.e., of those rights which can never be suspended, is the essence of terrorism whether practiced by private individuals or by governments themselves.

Politically motivated terrorism is carried out in a democratic society with the precise intention of provoking a terrorist response from the security organs of the state. Such a response tends to polarize the society and fuel sympathy for subversives.

A just and self–confident society has the toughness and resilience to fight back within the limits of law and morality. In waging war against a society which honors those limits, the terrorist campaign manages only to consolidate the community and to reinforce its value and its morale. The campaign therefore must fail. A society already divided by injustice and riddled with merited guilt usually will respond with counterterrorism and thereby fertilize subversion while sapping the strength and authority it struggles to preserve.

The work of the Inter–American Commission is not merely an institutional expression of our hemisphere's highest aspirations. It is also a contribution to the defense of democratic societies from the impulse to terrorism among the enemies of freedom and within our own hearts.

Note

This chapter originated as a statement on behalf of the Inter-American Commission on Human Rights to the United Nations Commission on Human Rights, February 22, 1981.

8

The Odd Couple: American Diplomacy and the Inter-American Commission on Human Rights

I was asked to explore the ways in which the work of the Inter-American Commission on Human Rights has interacted with the movements of U.S. diplomacy. That interaction is obviously intricate and ultimately problematic. What follows here is a preliminary effort to suggest, by means of a few salient examples, its contours and complexity.

Before turning to the specific roles the commission has played in several of the past decade's most arresting Latin American dramas, I think I need to say something about the commission itself.

The bulk of its work falls into two categories: investigation of individual cases (which may involve more than one victim) and inquiries into the general state of human rights in particular countries.

The inquiries are the more controversial and, seemingly, consequential aspect of its work. Occasionally precipitated by an unsolicited invitation from a government, in the great majority of cases the inquiry stems from the commission's finding prima facie evidence of generalized and severe violations. The terms "finding" and "prima facie" may exaggerate the formality of the commission's procedures in this respect. Being not a judicial institution endowed with coercive authority backed by state power and subject to precise jurisdictional constraints, but rather an investigating body with a broad, loosely drawn mandate, the commission properly reserves to itself ample discretion to decide when such an inquiry is appropriate. In some instances, a dramatic rise in the number of complaints about a country may trigger the commission's decision. There is, however, no consistent relationship between the incidence of complaints and the extent and severity of violations. Income and literacy levels in a country sharply affect the incidence of complaints. So do expectations. Where violations are endemic, the commission may not receive many complaints until government-sponsored terrorism ascends sharply from an already high plateau.

Complaints are, therefore, only one index of trouble. The commission staff and commission members have many sources of information about the conditions in member states. Trouble in the realm of human rights has a distinctive smell. When the odor reaches the commission, it usually has resolved to prepare a report.

That decision is immediately communicated to the concerned government. The communication also urges its recipient to invite the commission to undertake an observation *in loco*. If an invitation is not forthcoming, the commission then formally requests permission to enter (the *anuencia*). And if that is denied or if, though granted, the government evades agreement on a date for the prospective visit, the commission goes public with the rejection and declares its intention to proceed with the preparation of a report drawing upon its many sources of information.

Chile was the venue of the commission's first observation *in loco*. The observation produced evidence for a report presented to the General Assembly of the OAS which was, appropriately enough, held in Santiago, Chile.

Before that assembly, the commission's practice had been to present a fairly innocuous annual report to the gathering of foreign ministers who would dutifully "take note" of the commission's work and coincidentally appropriate for it an exiguous budget. The hemispheric shocks set off by the Pinochet government's orgy of centrally organized murder broke that procedural mold. It moved the commission to seek entry, to carry out an aggressive investigation, and to prepare a document frankly detailing the ugly conditions in Chile. It also moved the OAS to invite the commission's president to defend its report before the assembled ministers. The result was an open and bitter debate among governments, with Chile in the role of a snarling wolf hemmed in by hunters.

Public and elite opinion in states with democratic or at least ostensibly populist governments had in varying degrees opposed holding an OAS meeting in Santiago in the midst of Augusto Pinochet's long night. At first, cries of opposition had not penetrated the clubby atmosphere of the OAS. According to tradition, invitations to host the annual meeting were to be accepted simply in order of receipt. Cuba apart, any proposed distinction on the basis of human rights delinquencies would normally have been deemed both dangerous and bizarre. Aware of their own glass houses, accustomed to regard nonintervention as their highest value, the professional diplomats—usually left at peace to run the organization—had thus followed tradition in accepting the Chilean government's calculated invitation.

In Washington, support for General Pinochet's effort to enhance his legitimacy by hosting the region's ministers drew on sources beyond the professional's reflexive taste for chummy relations. General Pinochet had a friend, probably at Chase Manhattan and certainly in the largest office on the seventh floor of the State Department, since, by destroying the government of Salvador Allende, he had satisfied one of Henry Kissinger's obsessions. Dr. Kissinger already had rewarded General Pinochet's good works by opening the American exchequer. Direct U.S. bilateral economic aid rose from $10.1 million in 1973 to $177.3 million in 1975, despite indisputable evidence of mass murder and savage torture authorized at the highest levels of the Chilean government. In fiscal year 1975, after General Pinochet had already begun to export his version of state terrorism, Chile received $57.8 million in assistance under P.L. 480's Food for Peace Program. The rest of Latin America, with thirty times Chile's population and huge deposits of malnourished people living on the rim of starvation, received only nine million dollars. When an increasingly restive Congress sought to restrain U.S. largesse by prohibiting assistance other than that which would "definitely benefit the needy people," the State Department found that condition satisfied by a large housing guarantee program, the bulk of which could not possibly benefit directly the lowest 30% of the Chilean population.

Advised by his more liberal, more expert, and less emotional Assistant Secretary for Inter-American Affairs, William D. Rogers, Dr. Kissinger had, by 1975, become sensitive to the wounding consequences of unveiled support for General Pinochet. Hence, although he would not endorse rejection of Chile's invitation, he did see the need to make gestures in Santiago which would allay congressional criticism. Endowed, therefore, with some room to maneuver, the U.S. delegates supported open debate. (However, when Robert White—later ambassador to Paraguay and El Salvador—appeared to associate the United States with a frank indictment of the Pinochet regime's behavior, Dr. Kissinger, who had left Santiago after delivering a generalized encomium to human rights, cabled a stinging rebuke and arraigned Mr. White for exceeding his mandate. Rogers' intervention, by saving White's career, enabled the ambassador to continue serving his country until Ronald Reagan's first Secretary of State, Alexander Haig, drove him out of the government.) The General Assembly debate culminated with a resolution urging Chile to cooperate with the commission and to carry out the commission's recommendations.

This meeting lifted the commission from obscurity and established a precedent for serious debate and frank resolutions. Whether it coincidentally did much to alleviate General Pinochet's terrorism is doubtful. Although Washington might not have been able to avert the coup of 1973, Chile's desperate economic straits had given the United States potentially enormous influence over the military junta's postcoup behavior, a point overlooked by those who search relentlessly for a Kissinger tie to the coup itself. Of course, rather than using that influence, Dr. Kissinger had rewarded the coup masters, meanwhile saving his reprimands for the U.S. ambassador who urged Chile's tyrant to practice moderation.

Neither the commission's findings—implicitly confirming a system of torture and summary execution authorized by Pinochet—nor other pressures fundamentally altered administration policy in the United States. Congress itself finally began cutting off aid. In the face of congressional restraints on aid to Chile—restraints presaging increasingly close review of executive branch behavior—Dr. Kissinger grudgingly followed Mr. Rogers' lead in urging the Chileans to reduce their savagery.

By this time, of course, practically everyone marked for elimination was dead or in exile, and opposition was intimidated. All congressional sanctions and State Department advice could accomplish was the release of some political prisoners. Now in unchallenged control of Chile, General Pinochet was willing to throw his critics a few bones. Pressure on him and his American sponsor came from so many "respectable" (i.e., unequivocally non–Communist) sources, the commission's role was marginal, at least until the late 1970s when the flowering of state terrorism in Argentina somewhat obscured Chile's achievements. Since then, the commission's periodic updates may have helped to keep the Chilean situation fairly high on the agenda of international concern. But far greater credit must certainly go to the "Chicago–school" economists who designed Chile's economic disaster, which encouraged open opposition. Nor can one overlook the contributions of General Pinochet himself. His taste for murdering opponents complicated the efforts of Reagan administration stalwarts like Jeane Kirkpatrick, Ambassador to the United Nations, to slip his regime back into the realm of moral legitimacy.

Since 1975, the commission has conducted on–site observations in roughly one–third of the member states of the OAS. Applying the dual criteria of commission impact on human rights and the actual or potential consequence of Commission action for U.S. diplomacy, perhaps the most salient cases are El Salvador, Nicaragua, and Panama.

Panama

In 1977, during one of its periodic meetings, the commission received a long cable from General Omar Torrijos, "Chief of Government" (*Jefe de Gobierno*), urging it to visit Panama and decide for itself what was the actual condition of human rights in that country. Not so coincidentally, the Panama Canal Treaty was then awaiting the Senate's advice and consent.

Opponents of the treaty on the Senate floor and in the public at large, most of them hitherto insensible to signs of savagery in Free World states, had, apparently through some sort of divine inspiration, developed an irrepressible concern for alleged human rights violations in this particular non–Communist regime. Well, that may be stretching a point; true–blue conservatives had some difficulty distinguishing the populist Torrijos, who enjoyed amiable relations with Fidel Castro, from the real red stuff. Be that as it may, one of several objections to the canal treaty was its supposed contribution to the perpetuation of the Torrijos era and hence, treaty opponents claimed, of singularly grave delinquencies. I believe that the idea for a visit originated with a member of Zbigniew Brezinski's staff.

At the time of the invitation, Panama was not high on the commission's list of states in need of investigation. There were very few cases and little extrinsic evidence of massive human rights violations. From the commission's perspective, then, this was a genuinely unsolicited invitation.

Before the event I thought it likely that the Commission's report, whatever its contents, would have a substantial impact on U.S. public and senatorial opinion. I was mistaken.

Several factors appear to have limited the report's effect. First, the human rights issue never weighed very heavily with the anti–treaty constituency in America. It was looking for arguments, not facts. Second, as a consequence of our then very limited staff and the lack of any felt urgency among my colleagues, the report was slow to emerge. By the time it did, opinion in the United States was pretty well fixed; only the most dramatic indictment of Mr. Torrijos might have shifted it.

Third, the report was not dramatic. On the one hand it confirmed the obvious: Panama was not a democracy; hence it violated the rights of its citizens to participate in government. And, as in the case of virtually all nondemocratic regimes, rights of opinion and association were not consistently upheld. On the other hand, after carefully investigating cases of alleged political murder and systematic torture—cases brought to the commission in richly bound volumes prepared by anti–Torrijos organizations in the United States—the commission found the charges to be baseless.

In light of the accusations passing for fact on the floor of the Senate, that finding might seem dramatic enough. But it was flattened by the format of the commission's report. By tradition, we never compared countries. A statement saying that, compared to Chile, Paraguay, Uruguay, Haiti, and Guatemala, to name only some, Panama was the peaceable kingdom, might have been picked up by the media. What the media in fact saw was a bureaucratic–looking document divided neatly into chapters corresponding to articles of the declaration. What was good about Panama was apparent largely through what was not there, namely, evidence of murder, torture, and disappearance. It was a case of the dog that didn't bark. Neither the media nor the public nor the Senate has the acuity of Mr. Sherlock Holmes.

A final factor explaining the report's light touch is that in 1977 the commission still had a low profile. Nevertheless, if the Carter administration had chosen to serve as its sounding board, the report might have had considerably greater resonance. In fact, the administration largely ignored it, I think for the reasons enumerated above: by itself, the document did not speak clearly. And there was no precedent for the president of the commission offering press backgrounders to explain reports and underline their significance.

Though it largely ignored the report, the Carter administration in other ways focused unprecedented attention on the commission. Beginning with the 1977 General Assembly, the administration became conspicuous among those states that warded off assaults on the commission's powers, defended its reports, echoed the indictments implicit in those reports, and supported resolutions congratulating the commission for its works, incorporating commission doctrine and urging delinquents to follow the commission's recommendations.

El Salvador

President Carlos Humberto Romero's invitation, which arrived at the commission in the fall of 1977, was unsolicited, but a slightly unpleasant odor had preceded it, and that was enough to make the invitation as welcome as it was surprising. Here again, I think, the invitation had its roots in the White House.

Among the many myths spun by the media about the Carter administration was its supposed taste for confrontation with human rights delinquents. As far as one could tell from the outside, President Carter's style was distinctly nonconfrontational, particularly in face–to–face encounters. This was in part a matter of personality. In part it was a natural concomitant of a centrist's effort to advance deeply felt moral positions without challenging conventional wisdom about the national interest. And in part it reflected President Carter's self–imposed weakness: he had announced at the outset of his tenure that he would not impede trade or interfere with the flow of private capital. Above all, perhaps, the Carter administration operated without benefit of any systematic theory about social and political change.

In this setting of impulses and constraints, the Inter–American Commission had inherent charms. Since the commission was an official multilateral institution, the United States could support its activities without seeming to violate President Carter's almost theological norm of nonintervention. Moreover, since the commission could neither deploy sanctions of its own nor trigger compulsory sanctions by members of the Organization of American States, its efforts did not risk creating conditions in which the United States would be forced to choose between an ugly bilateral diplomatic confrontation with some delinquent nation on the one hand and apparent collusion on the other.

Nevertheless, although a commission indictment might have no concrete consequence, President Carter and his aides no doubt believed that the very operation of an official human rights mechanism and the coincident exposure of delinquencies must be a "good thing" which had to have long-term benefits. Though castration and homicide might continue in certain countries, U.S. officials could find solace in the view that they had contributed to "institution-building." Not surprisingly, therefore, a common administration response to human rights violations in Latin America was a suggestion to the delinquent dictator or junta that he or it authorize an observation *in loco*.

As late as 1978, Latin American governments could persuade themselves that a commission visit posed manageable risks. They were, after all, members in good standing of that gentlemen's anti–Communist club, the OAS. As such they had participated in the creation of the commission and the election of its members. The members themselves were people whose "moderation," "respectability," and sensitivity to the OAS tradition of "live and let live" seemed confirmed by the very fact of their nomination. Most had held high governmental positions; more than one still did. Many had diplomatic experience, and diplomats understood the conventions. Like guests, they did not make awkward demands or bite the host. These, I suspect, were the more-or-less conscious calculations of President Romero and his colleagues in the government of El Salvador.

At first, they seemed well-based. The chairman of the three-man team authorized by the full commission to conduct the observation, in addition to being one of its most conservative members, was the member most easily awed by authority. Arriving in advance of his colleagues, he played the role of compliant guest while Mr. Romero and company pursued a two-front strategy. On one front they used the media—controlled by the oligarchical families and their retainers—to convey the impression that the commission came as a friend of the government to vindicate its reputation. On the other front, they organized the families of soldiers and policemen to present complaints alleging human rights violations by antigovernment groups. In other words, the government sought not so much to neutralize the commission as to secure its cachet of good behavior in the face of a terrorist assault.

Press and television pictures of the subcommission's chairman exchanging toothy grins with the normally dour General Romero buttressed government claims, broadcast by the compliant media, that the commission had come to praise it. Together they would probably have succeeded in discouraging government opponents from talking to the commission were it not for the coincidental presence in El Salvador of Father Robert Drinan, former dean of the Boston College Law School and then a member of Congress, together with John McAward, the Unitarian–Universalist Church's Latin American expert. Encountering them in the hotel where we had set up offices, I expressed concern about the distorted picture of the visit the government was retailing. They immediately contacted Archbishop Oscar Romero (no relation to President Romero) and vouched for our bona fides. As a result, the archbishop granted us a long interview and, through his clerical network, gave us entrée to persons and groups who would otherwise have dismissed us as government pawns or worse.

One other means for breaking out of our initial isolation was Christian Democracy. Because of its transnational character, the Christian Democratic movement periodically brings together leading figures from the national parties. Consequently, the commission's executive secretary, a Chilean who had been active in Christian Democratic politics since his university days and had held diplomatic posts under Eduardo Frei, knew several Salvadoran party members.

Despite the government's best efforts, word that the commission could be trusted passed quickly to many opposition groups who proceeded to lay their case before it. Persuasive evidence of murder and torture and of a vast system of intimidation organized at the peak of government and relentlessly implemented by the various security forces rapidly accumulated, culminating in our discovery of secret cells where a group of recently "disappeared" persons had been held and tortured.

At the next meeting of the full commission, we offered our impressions of the situation in El Salvador. It sounded as if Dr. Carlos Dunshee de Abranches had visited one country, perhaps Italy when the Red Brigades were at their zenith, while Fernando Volio and I had visited another. Dr. Abranches grudgingly yielded to the weight of the evidence, but not without exacting as inducements more emollient adjectives. The final report was, nevertheless, a harsh indictment of the government and of the whole system of domination from which it emanated. Sent to San Salvador for comment, it came back with a violent, lengthy, tendentious, and largely irrelevant rebuttal. We agreed among ourselves to present the report without significant change to the next meeting of the OAS General Assembly.

In September, 1979, just weeks before the assembly convened in La Paz, young officers rose and swept away the Romero regime. According to some informants, the coup originally had been timed to coincide with the report's presentation at the assembly. It does appear, in any event, that the report's strongly negative conclusions were known to the plotters who doubtlessly assumed that it would accelerate erosion of the regime's legitimacy and bar U.S. support even as armed opposition intensified. Frightened by the recent demise of their Nicaraguan sibling—the National Guard—they decided to violate the norms of hierarchical control in order to preserve the military institution.

And so, after Andrés Aguilar, the president of the commission, presented the cónclusions of its report on El Salvador, the figure who sought the floor to respond, El Salvador's foreign minister, was none other than Hector Dada, a Christian Democrat politician whom I had met secretly during the subcommission's visit. Instead of the violent denial and coincident assault on the commission's integrity we would otherwise have expected, Dada confirmed the facts. On both sides it was a triumphal moment, a moment that kindled a transient optimism about the country's future.

Nicaragua

Nicaragua's popular eruption against Anastasio Somoza's rule pushed the commission onto a route which closely paralleled and occasionally intersected the movements of U.S. diplomacy.

The popular demonstrations set off by the assassination of Pedro Chamorro, editor of the opposition newspaper, *La Prensa,* President Somoza's most effective and tenacious opponent, and the regime's increasingly harsh response, catapulted Nicaragua to the top of the commission's list of states in need of investigation. As the violence crescendoed through the first half of 1978, the commission informed the Nicaraguan government of its decision to prepare a report on the situation and requested an invitation to visit.

Apparently in response to direct pressure from Washington, President Somoza finally agreed. Whereupon President Carter sent him a personal note—exuberantly leaked by President Somoza—commending him for the decision to invite us. Though consistent with President Carter's policy of rewarding repellent regimes for any positive response, however marginal, to U.S. expressions of concern about their behavior, its dispatch was a singular diplomatic gaffe. On the one hand, it strengthened President Somoza's conviction that no American administration, not even one so anomalously sensitive to his means of keeping order, would tolerate his replacement by leftist opponents. On the other hand, it confirmed the ingrained assumption of his leftist opponents that any American administration preferred thuggery to revolution.

Initially, the commission negotiated an October date for the visit. Then came the popular rising of early September. After local units of the National Guard retreated to their fortified barracks, Somoza sent his elite units to reoccupy the liberated towns. To save himself, he methodically destroyed large parts of them. National Guard planes skimmed over residential neighborhoods hurling rockets through flimsy roofs. Tanks lobbed shells into suspect neighborhoods. After the bombardment the Guard came and killed. Any male between the age of ten and senility who was not known as a Somoza supporter was presumed hostile.

Neither President Somoza's unsavory reputation among Latin governments nor his crimes might have spurred an OAS majority to break with its traditional indifference to merely domestic events. But these particular domestic events were having international repercussions. Costa Rica's political elite—enemies of Somoza by instinct and history, sympathetic and familiar with the middle-class Nicaraguans who, in the wake of Chamorro's assassination, had moved toward alliance with the Sandinista guerrillas—began to bend the norms of neutrality. Costa Rica became, first, a guerrilla arms entrepot and then progressively a training and mobilization center and sanctuary. Incensed, Somoza threatened retaliation. Costa Rica's appeal to the OAS for protection activated the latter's peacekeeping machinery. Foreign ministers or their delegates hurried to Washington to constitute the Organ of Consultation. It was already functioning when Somoza crushed the first rising. With U.S. encouragement, the ministers treated events within Nicaragua as an integral part of the threat to hemispheric peace. The Organ of Consultation called on the commission to accelerate its trip. With Somoza's approval, the commission complied, arriving in Managua on October 3, 1978.

After a week of exhaustive investigation—including lengthy conversations with Somoza, his Guard officers, and his judges, congressmen, and ministers; after interviews with persons representing every organized sector of the population, with political prisoners, Red Cross officials, priests, nuns, medical personnel, journalists, members of the local human rights organization, residents encountered in long walks through devastated neighborhoods while we were shadowed by government agents; and after visual inspection of practically every area in the country where fighting had occurred—five of the six commission members agreed that the scale, indiscriminateness, awfulness, and overtness of the violations, together with the prospect for continuing carnage, called for unqualified condemnation of the Somoza regime and acceleration of the commission's characteristically stately pace. We instructed the staff lawyers who had accompanied us to have a draft report ready by the end of the month when we would convene a plenary session in Washington.

Debate on the draft demonstrated a hitherto unexperienced degree of consensus about both the substance and the form of our report. Lashed by a sense of collective outrage and the felt possibility of affecting directly the situation in Nicaragua, we produced an indictment of the regime unparalleled in the force and clarity of its conclusions. The report was without precedent in another, still more dramatic respect. In earlier reports, after a finding of gross violations, the commission had recommended that unnamed officials be tried and punished. In other words, the commission had avoided treating the regime itself as the criminal. The logical implication was that lesser officials had acted outside the scope of their authority or with the mere acquiescence of the regime. Of course, in a sense, this was a mere convention and it was understood as such by OAS diplomats. At the same time, it reaffirmed the unwritten norm that decoupled legitimacy from conformity with the rules of civilized behavior.

The commission's report on the Somoza regime broke with that tradition. It traced the violation of human rights to the very character of the regime and its Guard. Consistent with that conclusion, we dispensed with recommendations. This meant that, in the Commission's view, the violations would continue as long as the regime survived.

By virtually calling for President Somoza's removal and the reform of the National Guard, the commission was getting far ahead of U.S. policy. The counteraccusation, hurled by Jeane Kirkpatrick, among others, that President Carter had disarmed Somoza and had done nothing to oppose the Sandinistas is simple mendacity. From the assassination of Mr. Chamorro in January, 1978, until Somoza's flight in July, 1979, administration policy had a major and a minor goal. The major goal was preventing the emergence of a Sandinista regime; the minor goal was mitigation of Somoza's rule or, ideally, his replacement by a coalition of his civilian retainers and the middle-class opposition.

Given President Carter's determination to avoid U.S. military involvement in any form, he could achieve his principal goal only by guaranteeing the survival of the Guard (somehow purged of its worst elements), for the middle-class opposition had no armed forces. If the Guard disintegrated or was overwhelmed, the Sandinista guerrillas would fill the resulting military vacuum. Thus, throughout 1978 and far into 1979, the tactical purpose of U.S. diplomacy was to separate the middle-class opposition from its alliance with the Sandinistas by persuading President Somoza to devolve the forms, and some of the substance, of political power onto the envisioned coalition.

This tactic failed primarily because the administration's evident priorities confirmed Somoza's belief that, if faced with a stark choice between him and the Left, President Carter would choose him. He therefore saw no reason for making concessions that carried the slightest risk to his power. But since those were exactly the concessions required to produce a split in the opposition, Washington's diplomacy foundered.

While President Somoza's obduracy was, I think, the primary cause of his regime's failure, the commission's graphic, detailed exposure of the Guard's savagery hardly helped U.S. efforts to build a regime dependent on a somehow cleansed Guard for its survival. Widely disseminated in Latin America, the commission's conclusions helped consolidate Latin American opinion against the last-minute effort of the Carter administration to marshal support for collective intervention under the OAS Charter. The Organ of Consultation called instead for the dictator's resignation, citing in justification the conditions documented by the commission. In his later autobiographical musings, Somoza cited the commission's report as an important component of the pressures to which he finally succumbed.

The commission's work need not have clashed with U.S. goals. Perpetuating Somocismo without Somoza—the inevitable consequence of fabricating a coalition including President Somoza's creatures and dependent for security on his praetorians—was not the only way to avoid an exclusively Sandinista government. During most of the civil war—even perhaps as late as the summer of 1979—the Sandinistas were unsure of their ability to win an outright military victory. Rather, they hoped that, with the aid of their moderate civilian allies and by naming as shadow minister of defense a former colonel of the National Guard, they could split off from the Guard career officers who were not personally implicated in its crimes. The Sandinistas' uncertainty about victory coupled with their desire to minimize the human and material costs of prolonged civil war gave the United States powerful leverage, assuming it could force the departure of Somoza and his principal civilian and military cronies, or itself split the Guard. Means far short of sending in U.S. Marines were available to President Carter.

During the 1970s, the independent actions of the commission and the U.S. government sometimes reinforced each other. But as these cases accurately suggest, the commission marched under its own flag to the beat of a different drummer. If, in the next few years, they begin to march in lockstep, I fear that such coordination will be attributable to changes not so much in the purposes of American diplomacy as in the character of the commission.

9

The Torturer's Response

The topic, "Why Torture?" has, it seems to me, a flaw nicely captured by the performance of a professor who some years ago acquired a considerable reputation stemming from his lengthy study of sex in American culture. After the publication of his book, he was invited to disseminate his observations before a large audience and for a handsome fee. According to a friend who happened to be there, the professor received a long, adulatory introduction which prepared all except the most hardened agnostics among those present for a host of penetrating observations. Finally Professor X shambled to the microphone amidst anticipatory acclaim, smiled down at his audience, and began: "Ladies and gentlemen, it is a pleasure." And having thus exhausted the subject, he shambled off backstage and was not again seen in those parts.

In the spirit of that laconic colleague, I said to the scholar who invited me here: "It hurts, and it works. And that's about all there is to say other than declaring your position for or against it." But he was nothing if not tenacious. The sort of people likely to attend a conference at Princeton sponsored by Amnesty International, he said, "unlike those who take courses at our training camps in Panama and Honduras, probably never thought about torture from the point of view of a torturer in the service of a conservative Latin American regime. The natural flow of their empathy is to the tortured. What we need is someone who can understand and explain the other side of the equation. And you," he concluded, "are that someone."

An allegedly preeminent capacity to comprehend the mind of the torturer struck me as, at best, an ambiguous compliment. And I couldn't help wondering what I had done to earn it, although I suppose I am unusual among people in the human rights community in having once trained a Third–World police force in the mysteries of unarmed self–defense and criminal procedure.

The fact is that the force I trained did not torture and did not make people disappear and was the only efficient, meritocratic, and admirable public institution in the entire country. Its qualities were attributable not to me but to the general who commanded it, a man who spent a year at this University and for the sake of his humane and democratic beliefs would later spend ten years in solitary confinement. But that's another story for another day.

It is true that in the course of my eight years as a member, two of them as president, of the OAS Human Rights Commission, I often found myself shaking the hand or warmly patting the shoulder or discoursing civilly with organizers and practitioners of torture and other forms of bestiality, men as different as the bull-necked colonel in battle fatigues with whom I dined in the highlands of Guatemala and the tall, imperially slim, sad-eyed ex-general in the elegant, double-breasted flannel who was President of Argentina while middle-aged men in hidden rooms had their mouths pried open and cattle prods jammed against their tongues. The ugly paradox is that in my work outside this country, in all those meetings with men operating systems of state terror, I never met one who would admit to torture or even defend its use. They spoke of dirty wars with "terrorists" and "subversive delinquents" as they invariably refer to the opposition; they spoke of the abuses that inevitably occur in such conflicts, the excess of zeal or anger in isolated cases. But they did not admit to the systematic employment of terror. They spoke, in other words, with the reticence and evasion of people who, though they feel justified, know they are operating outside the formal and moral law of that Western Christian civilization in the name of which they conduct their wars of extermination. They did not doubt their delinquency; but in their hearts and among their own kind, they successfully pleaded extenuating circumstances.

In order to hear the frank, unashamed defense of torture and mass murder I have to come back to my own country, to this country where, during President Reagan's first term, our United Nations ambassador appealed to Congress for an El Salvador aid package without human rights conditions. Not for her the unctuous mendacity of the then Assistant Secretary of State for Human Rights, Mr. Elliot Abrams, or the President's other spokesmen who claimed that congressionally imposed conditions somehow restrict our ability to apply quiet but effective pressure. El Salvador, Mrs. Kirkpatrick is reported to have said, has too much strategic importance to allow considerations of human rights to impede the pursuit of victory. If this small boil on the neck of the hemisphere requires our collusion in murder, can Upper Volta be far behind?

You asked me to put myself in the place of the men and women in the trenches of Western Civilization, the Major Bobs and Generals Montt and Lucas and other great men of our time. All right, here is what one of them might say if he had had the benefit of that capacity for lucid orderly exposition imparted by an Ivy League education.

Here is the statement of General Roberto Menendez:

"The world is at war, though the war is undeclared. Ferocious battles erupt, often unexpectedly, now in one country, now in an other, often in several at once. Battles are won; others are lost. The war goes on. There are grounds neither for compromise nor pity. The stakes are too high for pity. Pity makes you weak. And there cannot be compromise because the antagonists hold utterly incompatible views about the ends of life and the organization of society.

"We are defending a social order that has evolved over two millennia. We are defending the fundamental institutions of our civilization: the family, religion, private property, and the whole system of ordered liberty which they support and in turn supports them. The enemy, Marxists of one liturgy or another, are bent on destroying those institutions and abolishing liberty.

"Because your societies are richer and more developed, because you have filled out all the empty spaces and imbued most citizens with respect for the civil order into which they are born, you can deal with the problem largely as an external threat. You do not need extraordinary measures. We are not so fortunate.

"All the crises a body politic must pass through before it achieves an effortless order—crises of legitimization, participation, distribution—are hitting us at once, while you were able to handle them slowly and more-or-less sequentially.

"And then there are the demographics of the problem. Your bleeding hearts talk as if we've butchered half of our population and the rest are starving to death. Then how, I ask you, is it that our towns and cities are awash with people, young people for whom we have no houses, no schools, and no jobs? Meanwhile the priests and other agitators, Marxists and their fellow-travelers, go around telling everyone he has a right to these things. The best of them are just irresponsible and dangerous fools throwing sparks onto tinder.

"To build up the economy, we need capital. To get the capital, we need social peace. To get that peace, we need to insulate the masses from the agitators. When the cancer of subversion has already penetrated into the healthy flesh of society, we have to cut out the cancerous tissue, quickly, before metastasis.

"In societies like ours, ordinary measures don't work against clandestine groups. Torture does. You talk about us as if we were animals, subhuman, or you say we use these methods because we're not professionals, not well-trained. As if we invented torture. Were the Gestapo badly trained or the S.D. or other German units? Not on your life. But they knew that when you are dealing with organized political movements capable of energizing much larger groups if they go undetected, if you are dealing with such movements rather than isolated criminals, you need shortcuts, and you need to discourage those who have not yet committed themselves to the life of subversion.

"You call us thugs and incompetents. Well, there's nothing unprofessional about the French security services; but they failed to root the terrorist cells out of the Casbah during the Algerian war. Then the paratroop units were sent, the elite of the whole French army, as fine a group of professional troops as exists. And they failed too, at first. Then they turned to torture, and when they finished, the Casbah was secure.

"Someday, maybe, we'll be able to do it gently. Someday, we'll just have to strap someone in a chair, attach some electrodes to the forehead, and every image in that mind will flash on a screen. No pain. No screams. Let us know if you develop something along those lines. Until then, we'll do what works. And until then, we would prefer a little less hypocrisy. You sometimes overlook the fact that we are doing what consistent majorities in *your* Congress and consecutive Presidents of *your* country have been training and arming and urging us to do, namely win.

"You think the situation in El Salvador is precarious now? How do you think it would be if the death squads hadn't been operating in 1980 and 1981? They annihilated the guerrilla networks in San Salvador. They secured the capital. And they scared the hell out of a lot of potential collaborators.

"All right, maybe they also drove some people into the subversion. That is a risk. Terror doesn't always work, particularly if it is applied half-heartedly, as the Salvadorans have been forced by pressure from Washington to apply it. The Guatemalans, on the other hand, told you to go to hell. They butchered everyone they thought needed butchering, terrified the Indians, and they've got the problem under control again.

"I know I've been talking about killing, not just torture. Of course, in many cases we do both, particularly when the torture confirms what we suspected, namely the guilt of the detainee. If we fill our jails with them, the next thing you know their friends have seized the American ambassador and want to trade him for imprisoned colleagues.

"As far as the killing is concerned, I take it your only possible objection is the lack of due process, not the killing itself. After all, these people are rebels, usually with links of one kind or another to foreign governments. Rebellion is treason. Capital punishment is not unusual in the case of treason. (Need I remind you that you executed the Rosenbergs, husband and wife?) So I take it that you think torture is worse than execution, that torture is something special.

"I admit that, as a matter of law, you have a point. Article 3 of the

Geneva Conventions of 1949 does ban torture, while not preventing a government from executing its opponents during or after a civil war. All right; that's the law; but is this a morally compelling distinction? You could argue, you know, that torture has a far clearer military justification. The only justification for executing rebels at the end of a civil war or spies in time of peace is some very problematic idea about the long-term deterrent effect. But taking up the gun against the state is such a dangerous gamble to begin with, I doubt people do it unless they expect to win. With torture, on the other hand, you are seeking information directly related to reducing your casualties. The connection between this supposedly illegitimate means and the clearly legitimate end is much closer.

Moreover, society does not normally value freedom-from-prolonged-pain more than it values life. In many of your states, capital punishment has been outlawed. But what is life imprisonment in conditions of maximum security other than torture? Even if a person prefers death, you won't let him have it. Just as your courts wouldn't allow a person in a state of acute pain and humiliating dependence to choose death. Indeed, you are prepared to force-feed a person to keep her alive.

"Torture, summary execution, all the apparatus of terror is ugly, no doubt. And as a child of the enlightenment, I share with you a presumption against their use. But like all presumptions, it has exceptions. And we are not the only ones who have carved them out. You North Americans have done your part.

"I remember a few years ago, on some anniversary of the atomic bombing of Hiroshima and Nagasaki, the survivors among those who had been involved in the decision to drop the bomb were asked whether they had repented. I can't remember one who admitted he had. Moreover, various eminent intellectuals who had not been involved were prepared with the wisdom of hindsight to defend the incineration of those two Japanese cities. Why? Because it saved lives. Classical utilitarianism: Maximize the sum total of happiness and minimize the pain.

"The bomb was indiscriminate, a terror weapon, like torture and disappearance and mutilation and the other instruments we have found it useful to employ in times of grave national emergency. And who among you would not do the same in the right circumstances. Suppose you arrested a man a few days before Christmas who told you mockingly that he had planted a bomb in a department store which would go off in three hours. And suppose you were able to confirm that he had set off bombs in the past. So there was every reason to believe his claim. Maybe some among you would not have the stomach to torture the location of the bomb out of him. But how many would not feel the thrilling hope that there was someone willing to take on the job? As I said earlier, in North America and Europe, these extenuating circumstances don't yet arise very often. *We* are less fortunate in this respect.

"We who preserve order in Latin America and our friends and colleagues faced with similar challenges in other parts of the world—in South Africa, South Korea, Zaire, Indonesia—we recognize that either we are being subjected to some kind of double standard or the alleged concern with our means conceals hostility to our ends, above all, the preservation of a stable anticommunist order with potential for economic growth and ultimate legitimization among the great, volatile masses.

"First this matter of a double standard. No doubt you think I am going to insult your intelligence by claiming that human rights organizations and the media dramatize problems in countries like my own far more than in Communist countries. I leave that sort of adolescent mendacity to American supporters of our cause. We see that the mere denial of a visa and discharge from government employment of a single Jewish dissident in the Soviet Union is more likely to galvanize American, particularly congressional, opinion than the execution of a thousand peasants in one of the countries for whom I speak. Of course, I endorse this discrimination. The Soviet Union is an enemy state and one hits it with whatever weapons are available. But I appreciate that that double-standard argument works well only with some American audiences.

"But when I speak of a double standard, I have a different comparison in mind. Chile, Guatemala, El Salvador, Argentina before Alfonsin: We are not the only allies of your country facing subversion and terrorism and using means we find not only efficient but necessary. I admit now, perhaps implicitly I have done so already, that in a sense these means are somewhat indiscriminate. Sometimes the people we torture know nothing useful and have no *direct* connection to the guerrillas. But even in those cases can it be said that there is "innocence?" We do not pick up people who are with us, who support us, who sympathize with our efforts. No, my friends, obviously we pick up people who have identified themselves as at least latent enemies of order: People who fertilize the ground for guerrilla recruitment by telling peasants they have all kinds of economic and social rights (by the way, the Reagan Administration has been quick to recognize this problem and has assisted us by rejecting, as dangerous and statist, the notion that there are such things as economic and social rights); people who give ammunition to international campaigns against our countries by accusing us of human rights violations. We pick them up because objectively they are helping the enemy. Or peasants who choose to live in guerrilla-dominated areas where inevitably they provide cover and food and infrastructure for the subversive delinquents.

"I appreciate you will not share my point of view about the dimensions of culpability. And, you doubtless think, since our methods foreseeably subject to torture or death people *you* deem innocent, they should be condemned. Indeed you go further, urging suspension of the aid we need in some cases to survive the assault against our capitalist and Christian civilization. And this, I respectfully suggest to you, is where the double standard appears. For how many of you or your clones in Congress were demanding a punitive suspension of aid to another friend of the United States faced with terrorist assaults on its society when it has found itself driven to measures you label indiscriminate when we employ them?

"Obviously I refer to Israel. You understand that I do so not for the purpose of criticizing Israel or urging you to support sanctions against that country. On the contrary, the Israelis are good friends of ours. When I recently visited my fellow officers in Guatemala, I found practically all the elite troops equipped with Israeli Galil assault rifles, excellent weapons by the way. My old comrade-in-arms Anastasio Somoza probably could not have held out as long as he did, after the Carter administration cut off his arms supply, if Israel had not helped fill the gap. Along with the weapons—for which, to be sure, we pay market rates—we get excellent technical advice. We do not criticize our friends. We ask only for equal understanding.

"When the Israelis bombed PLO headquarters in Beirut, before the Lebanese invasion, many so-called civilians were killed. That was foreseeable. The Israelis are excellent pilots; but there are limits to the degree of surgical accuracy anyone can achieve. But most or all of those civilians were Palestinians who probably sympathized with the cause of the PLO and no one forced them to live where the PLO operated.

"I know there was criticism of the bombing even in the pages of *The New Republic*. Well, if it makes you feel better, criticize us. But just as Mr. Peretz, who owns that magazine, did not suggest that Israel should be punished with sanctions that could threaten its existence, he should not call for sanctions against us when we do what is necessary. For us, nothing is excused. For Israel, everything. Some people said it was wrong of the PLO to locate its headquarters and its weapons in refugee camps and civilian buildings. Well, by the same process of reasoning, our guerrillas should not seek to swim in the peasant sea. But that's like asking fish to walk.

"When the Phalangists slaughtered the Palestinians in their camps and an Israeli tribunal found Sharon and Eytan "indirectly responsible," *The New York Times,* which never misses an opportunity to calumniate us, which has never expressed a single word of sympathy or understanding for our difficulties, proclaimed this a vindication of the Israeli political system.

"Some of my colleagues were a little bitter. 'Indirect responsibility,' they snapped at me. As if anyone who had spent one week in that part of the world, as a number of them had, did not know what the Phalangists would do once they were allowed into the camps. Sharon was condemned for failing to take into consideration the danger of a massacre, when the truth is that of course he took it into consideration.

"And where is Sharon now? In prison, like some of my Argentine colleagues, or is he still a Minister? Nor is it necessary to look outside the core group of capitalist democracies to find an impulse toward extraordinary measures whenever the social order is threatened. Look at your reaction to Pearl Harbor. You rounded up citizens of Japanese ancestry and dumped them in concentration camps.

"I understand these things. I laughed at my colleagues for their naivete. But I appeal to you to be less unfair in the future, to appreciate that in our minds, we are fighting a war for survival: The survival of the military institution; the survival of the capitalist mode of production; the survival of the small-town values of family and church and order and accepted hierarchy that we were born into, that are the warp and the woof of our identity.

"Are you hostile to these ends? Is that what makes us different? Is that what justifies your anger? I know that Amnesty never calls explicitly for sanctions. In a formal sense, it merely exposes torture and pleads with the accused government to take corrective measures. But who is deceived by this shadow play? A call for sanctions is implicit in the process of exposure, because, as Amnesty knows, we do not torture and kill gratuitously. We are not savages. We act out of a sense of extreme necessity. We feel justified. And unless we are faced with sanctions more dangerous to our success than the loss of terror as a means of defeating the subversives, we will continue, albeit moderating our operations from time to time to coincide with executive branch certification to your Congress that we are making progress in the human rights realm. In any event, even if Amnesty does not appeal for sanctions, many other human rights zealots do. So, I repeat, my colleagues and I are left to draw one of two conclusions: either you think you know more about antisubversive operations than we do, or you are hostile to our ends.

"Let me assure you that the efficiency of our means—above all, torture, disappearance, the public exposure of mutilated cadavers, in short, terror—cannot be doubted. Terror, you see, is a strategy of disorientation. It is designed to deprive potential subversives of the ability to calculate and foresee the consequences of their actions. Terror disrupts and dissolves the ability of people to act in concert. The occasional error and the variable definition of the enemy is in this respect immensely useful. For it helps to chill even the most latent opposition; it multiplies the force of each individual blow against the subversive enemy.

"To illustrate my point, let me quote the instructions of Carl Theodore Dreyer, the Danish director of horror films, to his crew:

> Imagine that we are sitting in an ordinary room. Suddenly we are told that there is a corpse behind the door. In an instant, the room we are sitting in is completely altered; everything in it has taken on another look; the light, the atmosphere have changed, though they are physically the same. This is because *we* have changed and the objects are as we conceive them. That is the effect I want to get in my film.[1]

"The success of my Salvadoran colleagues in achieving this effect is nicely captured by your writer, Joan Didion, in her book on that country, where the subversive forces are so powerful. From the moment she arrives in the airport of San Salvador, she is enveloped by an atmosphere of anxiety. That apprehension remains with her, like an excruciating pain, throughout her two-week stay. She recalls an evening when she and her husband were sitting on a porch by candlelight, against a backdrop of shadowy night-raiders. 'Nothing came of this,' she writes, 'but I did not forget the sensation of having been in a single instant demoralized, undone, humiliated by fear, which is what I meant when I said that I came to understand in El Salvador the mechanism of terror.' And here was someone protected by the almost impermeable armor of an American passport reinforced by celebrity.

"Not only torture but the signs of it on randomly distributed cadavers that mark the face of a new day heighten the chill which, if it is successful, will spare us still more extreme measures. As one of our enemies, the scholar Juan Corradi, has so aptly put it, they 'remind the provisionally living that they too might fall at any moment . . .,' that everyone who is not with us is, ineluctably, a hostage. If, despite that, resistance endures, can you imagine how perilous our cases would be if we fought by rules you announce from the sedated comfort of societies where capitalism has achieved ideological hegemony over the entire population?

"We who live in the jungle and we alone know the paths that lead to safety. Do not presume to instruct us. For if I may paraphrase another enemy of our cause, you are like the professor who knows a country only from the bare figures in his books about the gross national product or the per capita output of wheat, trying to describe that place to a man who has thirsted in its deserts and shivered on its mountains. You cannot reasonably believe that you have a superior grasp of our tactical requirements.

So at bottom, you must feel hostility to our ends. Assuming you are not Marxists, we believe this hostility stems from a misapprehension of our ends. Do you think we want the poor to be hungry and the upper classes to be obscenely rich? Do you think we are opposed to free institutions? Do you think we want the armed forces to occupy the same omnipotent, all-pervasive position in our societies that the Communist Party occupies in Marxist states? If you believe those propositions, you do misapprehend our ends. And that is because you do not understand our problems.

"I will admit to the existence of countries, very poor and underdeveloped countries—places like Paraguay, Haiti, Zaire—where the armed forces and the family or clique they serve are purely parasitic and the population is mere prey. However, let me point out, as your former ambassador to the United Nations has done, that, even in those countries, people are free to go about their day-to-day business and family life without interference. The government may tax them a little, but basically it leaves them alone—as long as they are quiet and do not aid subversion. Still, those are governments that are often gratuitously cruel and always corrupt. I give you that. But like us, they are not totalitarians. They do not want to organize the population into youth groups and homemakers groups and construction brigades. They do not seek to replace sacred elements in people's lives. Christian, voodoo, animist, and nativist cults and creeds are untouched. We are not mobilization societies. On the contrary, our purpose is to keep the population demobilized. Why? Because, within a capitalist framework, we cannot now satisfy the demands a mobilized population makes.

"Here again I see a double standard. For your own society, you accept a marginalized sector of the population because you recognize the costs in material and institutional terms of trying to absorb that sector. But for our societies you postulate millenarian goals and treat them as if they were presently realizable, and as if we did not have constraints far greater than those you coexist with comfortably.

"Let me put it very simply. Our population is growing quickly. It is urbanizing even more quickly. Its appetite for material goods may grow quickest of all. The fundamental task of any political order is to regulate the demands of the masses so that they are compatible with the capacity of governing elites to respond without violating the society's values and traditions and long-term security. Overload leads to instability and civil war.

"Traditional methods of demand control do not work well under current circumstances. Urbanization debases the symbolic currency in patron-client relations which at one time substituted in part for material benefits. Alien ideas—Marxism, Liberation Theology, so-called economic and social rights—aggravate this tendency to demand material rewards for political support.

"Nor is it possible in most cases to mobilize the masses around nationalist issues. In the first place, mobilization is a two-edged sword. While for a time it may distract the population from distributional issues, it also may create a heightened sense of competence, may facilitate communication and the discovery of common concerns and, if actual sacrifices are required, may heighten expectations of improved conditions after the national crisis is resolved. In the second place, wars are dangerous to the social order because only we, the armed forces, stand between civilization and chaos followed by Marxism. The military institutions cannot risk defeat. Thirdly, within the Western Hemisphere, the U.S. has imposed a kind of Pax Americana. Our economies are too vulnerable for us to resist serious economic sanctions. Finally, in our epoch, ideological fraternity is more important than common citizenship. Would it not be grotesque for me to feel hostility toward fellow officers in other countries with whom I have shared the firing range at your training camps, with whom I have exchanged intelligence information, who fight the common enemy, merely because they live on the other side of a geographic frontier? It would be unnatural and it would be dysfunctional.

"While on the one hand, then, our traditional control mechanisms are weak, on the other, we need control to create the conditions of economic growth, the ultimate key to a stable social order. Today, capital knows no national loyalties. If we do not create an attractive environment in our countries, indigenous capital flows out and foreign capital stays out. This generation must serve as the cannon fodder of the war against underdevelopment.

"A final word to you so that you will better understand us and yourselves. You call us savages, thugs, barbarians. But to us you are weak, pathetic, and decadent. You have lost the capacity even to imagine causes for which it is worthy to torture and to kill, even at the risk of one's immortal soul. Perhaps you never had it. Martyrdom is not native to your history, as it is to ours. In this respect, even the subversive delinquents—the anarchists and the Marxists—are more akin to us than are you, the unworthy beneficiaries of our holy struggle.

"So, now you know what is the appeal of torture. Whether you will benefit from this knowledge, whether you can benefit from this knowledge, remains to be seen."

Having said all that and being able, therefore, to assume my normal role, I am free to discuss with you, if you wish at some later point, why I remain unmoved by the torturer's appeal for understanding.

Notes

This chapter originally appeared as a lecture delivered at a Conference on "Why Governments Torture," held at Princeton University's Woodrow Wilson School, April 11, 1984.
1. Quoted in an unpublished paper of Professor Juan Corradi.

10

The Limits of Relativity

Through the people it honors, a nation declares its ideal conception of itself.

We come together today to honor Eleanor Roosevelt. Death, with all its amnesiac force, has lifted her into the pantheon of great Americans. So no discord attends this event, at least not openly. But if she were still among us, even the deaf would hear the clamor of furious battle.

Within our country, we wage unrelenting ideological war, a war reminiscent of the early days of the New Deal. After its confused beginnings, the New Deal came to stand for the proposition that a nation is more than a collection of isolated, ruthlessly acquisitive individuals. It is, rather, a community, a dense network of reciprocal responsibilities—at its best a place where compassion moderates pride and where no human being, whatever his or her achievements or capacities, is trivial.

Unprotected by the majesty of the presidential office, more conspicuously committed than her husband to the compassionate elements in the New Deal synthesis, a woman with an unashamed commitment to public life, Eleanor Roosevelt was an easier target than Franklin Delano Roosevelt for the apostles of social Darwinism. They abused her with the twisted malice inherent in their world view.

Adolph Hitler incarnated the application of social Darwinism to the entire globe. The ruthless, acquisitive individual was writ large by him as the ruthless, acquisitive nation. That vision led inexorably to war and dialectically to a countervision, the vision of a community of nations knit together not only by a sort of enlightened prudence but more profoundly by respect for the common humanity of the individuals whose collective will the various nations theoretically embodied.

Revulsion triggered by the exposure of the Holocaust, compounded by the glory always attached to martial achievement, and reinforced by a belated sense of guilt lent the idea of universal human rights an enormous momentum. Within fifteen years after the close of the war, the idea had assumed elaborate, mutually reinforcing normative and institutional forms which survive to this day essentially unchanged, though not entirely unchallenged.

Eleanor Roosevelt, more than her husband, more than any American associated with the effort to realize the declared war aims of the allies, came to personify the struggle for human rights both at home and in the world at large. The ideological forebears of today's rightists loathed her concern for the human consequences of high policy, despised her equation of the human and the national interest, and reviled her belief in the obligations of governments to act in the interest of human fraternity. For her enemies, as well as for her ideals and a life in their constant service, I have come to honor her.

The Inter-American Commission on Human Rights: The Relevance of Context in Assessing the Behavior of States

In this hemisphere, the Inter-American Commission on Human Rights of the Organization of American States has, since 1960, been a principal instrument for the defense and promotion of human rights. Its seven members, nominated by governments and elected by the member states of the OAS for four-year renewable terms, have over the years achieved a remarkable degree of consensus. Assisted, no doubt, by their at least formal independence, they have bridged chasms of ideology, personality, and culture to produce a series of reports on the situation of human rights in various countries which in their candor, detail, and balance find few if any parallels in the product of other official bodies.

The commission has been charged with rectifying and, where necessary, exposing violations of the substantive norms contained in the hemisphere's two principal human rights texts: the 1948 Declaration of the Rights and Duties of Man and the American Convention on Human Rights.[1] Since 1978, when the eleventh ratification brought the convention into force, the commission has applied the Declaration's norms to the remaining non-ratifying states.

Except with respect to the issues of capital punishment and abortion, there is no important difference between the two texts. Nor do they enjoin significantly different procedures. Under both, the commission has drawn on every credible source of information—including, in many cases, on-site observations—to develop an accurate, comprehensive and balanced picture of the condition of human rights in those countries it has chosen or been requested to study.

The commission's efforts have always been shadowed by the question: Under what circumstances and to what extent can and should it take into account the social, political, and historical context of alleged violations? In more strictly legal idiom, the issue is the relevance of context to the proper interpretation of substantive human rights norms.

Absolute Standards

Paradoxically, it is precisely in those cases where context is irrelevant that its relevance has been most stridently asserted. The issue was joined with particular virulence in connection with the commissioner's report on the situation of human rights in Argentina during the period 1976–1979[2] After extensive negotiations and, apparently, bitter internal debate, the country's military government had agreed to an on-site investigation by the commission. Arriving in September of 1979, we conducted exhaustive discussions with representatives of every organized sector of society, with detainees and petitioners by the hundreds, with judges and, of course, with high officials of the government. Both the officials and spokesmen for associations of agriculturalists, industrialists, and other groups sympathetic to the government presented us with an essentially homogeneous description of events in the country during the six years preceding our visit. Its main elements were as follows:

By 1973, when a democratically elected government led by Juan Peron assumed office, two very powerful and well organized subversive movements were engaged in a coordinated assault on the basic institutions of Argentine society. The ferocity of their means and the extremity of their ends induced the formation of groups at the other end of the political spectrum prepared to meet violence with violence. The counterterror of the Right added to a pervasive sense of insecurity among the general population, a sensation of the entire society spinning out of control into the abyss of anarchy.

In the face of this supreme threat to Argentine civilization, a broad spectrum of the population called on the armed forces to intervene and restore order. The military institution responded to this appeal and initiated a full-scale campaign against the terrorist organizations. The latter—well armed and financed, secretly present in almost every institutional nook and cranny—furiously resisted the assault and thereby produced a conflict of such dimension that it could fairly be described as a civil war.

But, given the clandestine character of the subversive organizations, it was a peculiar war, a war of secret engagements and secretive tactics, by its nature a dirty war: *Una guerra sucia.* In the course of any armed conflict, "abuses" will be committed in the heat of battle by terrified or enraged men. Overzealous officers may on occasion exceed appropriate limits. If abuses will occur in a conventional conflict, obviously they cannot be avoided in a war against urban guerrillas. No doubt some abuses did occur in the course of this dirty war. The armed forces have disciplined the guilty parties. A commission report which did not place those abuses in context would not be worth the paper on which it was written.

The commission, of course, noted that the very reference to abuses conceded that there were limits to the means which could be legitimately employed. The basic issue, then, was whether violation of those limits had been sporadic and random or, conversely, a conscious ingredient of strategies adopted or authorized at the highest levels of the armed forces. It soon became apparent to every member of the commission that the version of events maintained by the government and its supporters (and acquiesced in by great numbers of honorable men and women who quite naturally flinched from the moral dilemma that would arise if they rejected that version) was insupportable.

The immense body of direct testimony and circumstantial evidence we were able to accumulate admitted of only one conclusion: President Videla and his colleagues had authorized the detention, torture, and, in the great majority of cases, summary execution of persons suspected of involvement in the left-wing subversive opposition. The thousands of "disappeared persons" were simply people who had been seized by the security forces acting on the basis of whatever information local commanders deemed appropriate and processed through a nationwide clandestine torture system. Although the armed forces had smashed the spine of opposition in the very first year of their campaign, the system continued to function even after the arrival of the commission.

Consistent with its traditions, the commission resisted every effort by an avid press, by government officials, and by other interested parties to extract at least a preliminary declaration concerning the main issues of fact. On the other hand, we were sensitive to the importance of clarifying our criteria for evaluating the facts, of facing up, in other words, to the demand that we place events in their proper context.

The occasion for doing so was a meeting between several commission members and the directors of the Argentine Federation of Bar Associations. We began in an atmosphere marked by formal propriety and muted hostility. Like many other prominent Argentinians, our hosts felt that the very presence of the commission in their country was an implicit indictment of actions and events that could be appreciated only by those who had lived through the terrible experience of civil society transformed into a Hobbesian jungle.

The leaders of the Bar spoke first, offering the now familiar narrative of events during the period 1973 to 1979. Then it was our turn. The commission has repeatedly affirmed, I began, that governments have not only the discretion, they have the duty to maintain that degree of order requisite for the practical realization of human rights. To that end and under exceptional circumstances, governments may find it necessary temporarily to limit the full exercise of certain rights including freedom of speech and association. In extreme cases, governments even may exercise the power of preventive detention, that is, arresting and holding persons temporarily either without recourse to the courts or on the basis of evidence that would under normal circumstances be insufficient to justify a detention order. However well motivated, the use of those extraordinary measures always threatens to undermine the very freedoms they are at least nominally designed to preserve. Nevertheless, both domestic legal systems and international law allow their use under appropriate circumstances.

Article 27 of the American Convention, for example, states that "[i]n time of war, public danger, or other emergency that threatens the independence or security of a State Party, it may take measures derogating from its obligations under the present Convention to the extent and for the period of time strictly required by the exigencies of the situation. . . ."[3] But, with equal explicitness, the convention provides that certain rights can never be suspended, and those nonderogable rights include, as one would surmise, the right to life, the right to humane treatment, and the right to a fair trial. In short, governments enjoy a very broad discretion in the selection of means for the maintenance of order. During periods of emergency, they can prohibit political meetings, ban strikes, censor the mass media, and even detain large numbers of persons merely on reasonable suspicion of their involvement in subversion. What governments cannot authorize or tolerate for any purpose and under any circumstances is summary execution (murder), torture, cruel conditions of detention, and conviction by means of a procedure which deprives the accused of the opportunity to conduct an effective defense.[4]

These limitations apply in time of war as well as in time of mere domestic turbulence. Indeed, their application to wartime conditions, including civil war, antedates the American Convention. Common Article 3 of the Geneva Conventions of 1949 expressly and categorically prohibits summary execution, torture, and other inhumane treatment.[5]

It is from this perspective, I concluded, that the commission must appraise the human rights situation in this or any other country. Appreciation of the historical setting is essential to a fair appraisal of those many extraordinary measures governments are authorized to employ. It is also essential to a fair appraisal of responsibility for the actions of subordinate officials who transgress categorical prohibitions. But context is utterly irrelevant in cases where it can be shown that persons in control of the institutions of the state have themselves ordered, authorized, or acquiesced in the violation of nonderogable rights.

I had finished. Broad smiles washed over the faces of our hosts. "We are in complete agreement," said their principal spokesman, who thereupon invited us to cocktails and dinner. Impressed by the hostility-reducing power of this formulation, I trotted it out for appreciation at most of my subsequent meetings with government officials, only to find that it induced a subtle and revealing variation on the Bar Association's response. Yes, officials would say, that is a proper statement of the law, but you must realize that this was *una guerra sucia*.

I realized that, of course, just as I realized that those three words were the accepted formula for justifying the unspeakable. The leaders of the armed forces and many civilians who had urged them on or at least managed acts of heroic unconcern writhed with ambivalence. On the one hand, they seemed to feel the guilt or fear characteristically experienced by sane people who have knowingly violated sacred norms. On the other, they clung to the belief that their case was in some sense unique and their actions therefore justified. The violence of their feelings is suggested by their denunciation of a paragraph in the commission's report declaring that governments enjoying popular support could defeat even powerful, clandestine subversive movements without resort to state terrorism. The government appeared to object to the inclusion of that proposition while carefully avoiding an explicit statement of its own position.[6]

The unspeakable remained unspeakable.

Beyond the Minimum: Criteria for Comparing Degrees of Compliance

Argentina was by no means the only case where, for the reasons outlined above, context was irrelevant to the question of whether the government should in effect be indicted for grave crimes against human rights. Chile, Haiti, Guatemala, and El Salvador were among the others. Context is not irrelevant, however, in all instances where violations are prolific and barbarous and where the highest officials of the state know the identity of the delinquents. Suppose formal authority and real power do not coincide? This is, after all, a condition endemic in states where a civilian government does not exercise effective control over the armed forces who, in fact, arrogate to themselves the ultimate power of political decision.

Since the commission neither deploys nor proposes sanctions, it can pretty well satisfy its mandate simply by reporting the facts accurately. In doing so, it must identify the institutions and, where possible, the officials responsible for the delinquencies it narrates. The position of governments with the capacity for influencing events in the target state is, of course, quite different. To the extent they directly or indirectly reinforce the capacity of the delinquents to continue or increase their violations, they become complicit. Where power and authority are not united in a single institution, it may be possible to promote human rights by strengthening those elements in the apparatus of government that are trying to reduce violations or by transferring aid through nongovernmental organizations directly to civilian beneficiaries. However, where the division between power and authority is extreme, the donor will find it extremely difficult to transfer assets to the concerned state without enhancing the strength of delinquent powerholders. Clearly this is one facet of the U.S. dilemma today in El Salvador and Guatemala. In my judgment, the Reagan administration has yet to offer a plausible theory for escaping it.

Although the bulk of the commission's work since the mid-1970s required the members to be indifferent to context, in a number of important cases appreciation of the setting of alleged violations seemed to me essential for any fair judgment. Though essential, it was difficult and potentially divisive. For it is precisely in the effort to take account of context that differences in experience and political values are most likely to intrude. I think that our generally successful efforts to contain these differences is instructive particularly with reference to the question of whether human rights provides a means for bridging the ideological chasms of our time.

Perhaps the most dramatic, certainly the most celebrated, of the cases I have in mind is that of the Miskito Indians in Nicaragua. Various members of this ethnic group and their foreign supporters have charged the government of Nicaragua with practically every delinquency in the human rights book. Some charges simply involve questions of fact, but the one most relevant to my present purpose is essentially a question of law. I refer to the forced resettlement of Miskitos living along the Rio Coco on the Honduran border and the concomitant destruction of their villages, crops, and livestock. In some circles, this action has been treated as it if were morally indistinguishable from such punitive forced migrations as Stalin's expulsion of the Tatar people from their ancestral lands.

Neither the suddenness nor the coercive character of the Nicaraguan transplantation are in dispute. As one who visited the resettlement camps and interviewed persons resident there, I can attest to the resulting trauma. Not every painful and coercive action of the state, however, violates human rights. Article 22 of the American Convention guarantees to "every person lawfully in a State Party . . . the right to move about in it, and to reside in it." But his right may be limited, "to the extent necessary in a democratic society to prevent crime or to protect national security, public safety, public order, public morals, public health, or the rights or freedoms of others." In addition the freedom of movement and residence "may also be restricted by law in designated zones for reasons of public interest."[7]

At the time of the forced migration, the so-called "contras" had already begun launching attacks across the Rio Coco from bases in Honduras.

Disaffected Miskitos composed a significant element of their forces. United States involvement in organizing and arming the contras was conspicuous and growing exponentially in conjunction with declarations from the highest officials of our government which seemed to rule out the possibility of a *modus vivendi* with the Sandinistas on any terms short of their capitulation. The government in Managua claims to have believed that a Bay-of-Pigs-type assault designed to seize land on which a government of contras would be declared and immediately recognized by the United States was imminent.

Even putting that claim aside, it is indisputable that the Sandinistas faced a not trivial and rapidly growing security problem along much of the Honduran border, particularly that part occupied by ethnic Miskitos, many of whom undoubtedly sympathized with the dissidents. Removal of the population from a guerrilla-infested area, scorching of the earth and establishment of no-go zones are classic antiguerrilla tactics and thus fall clearly within the national security exception to the right of residence, an exception that would be assumed by any competent lawyer even in the absence of Article 22's explicit qualifying language.

Could one nevertheless argue that a regime should not be able to invoke the national security justification if violent opposition arose as a consequence of its prior violations of human rights, such as the right of association and the right to participate in government? Whether such a causal connection can be established in the Nicaraguan case is a not altogether easy question. With respect to the more general issue, there is an immediate moral charm to the proposition that delinquent governments should have no legitimate right of self-defense against domestic opponents. But I do not think that charm can survive moderately close inspection.

What we have here is a formula for treating the great majority of governments as outlaws. Since its appeal is therefore limited, it can never become part of the corpus of international law or even of regional law outside the North Atlantic area where, arguably, it already exists in some inchoate form. Nor, on reflection, is it likely to be a very helpful moral guide for the capitalistic democracies in their dealings with nations of the Second and Third Worlds. For, by lumping together all regimes which in varying degrees violate any human rights and declaring them outside the moral pale, we seemingly eliminate that discriminating moral censure which under present circumstances tends to restrain violations of human rights. If a threatened government can anticipate equivalent hostility regardless of whether it detains or liquidates its opponents, it may be inclined to choose the more definitive alternative.

In addition and more fundamentally, the formula is an invitation to foreign intervention in domestic armed conflicts and therefore threatens to accelerate the disintegration of the system of world order established in the wake of World War II. Intervention in extreme cases, such as Cambodia under the Khmer Rouge or South Africa—intervention, for instance which assumes the form of aid to insurgents—may be desirable in part because our extant nuanced discriminations help sharpen perception of the special character of such cases. For right-wing manichaeans, the formula has a different blemish: It fails to distinguish between odious clients of the United States and those attached to the Soviet Union.

Advocates of the left-right dichotomy often seem interested only in the forms of a society's macroinstitutions, not in their day-to-day human consequences. If, for example, they see a country holding elections with candidates from more than one party, they conclude that the right to participate in government is fully realized. They do not seem interested in such questions as why one party always wins; or, where the winners alternate, why parties favoring redistribution of capital assets, particularly land, never win or even attract substantial support in countries filled with desperately poor people. Under those circumstances wouldn't it be reasonable to speculate that subtle but powerful forms of coercion may be operating to deprive poor people of the power to organize, inform themselves, and make authentic choices? Isn't this a question on which a person concerned about human rights might want to be agnostic pending some probes into the living body of society?

A single-minded commitment to form seems equally to govern right-wing appraisal of press freedom. If the media are in private hands, they are deemed free on the assumption, I suppose, that competition will promote diversity absent an explicit system of state censorship. But just as corporations in many fields find it possible and profitable to scramble for market shares without competing over prices, media entrepreneurs may choose for reasons of class solidarity not to compete in the dissemination of certain data and ideas. Informal censorship may reinforce or substitute for class interests. Argentina has a large and in many respects diverse press. Yet, for over two years preceding the visit of the commission, not a single mass circulation newspaper found newsworthy the fact that thousands of Argentinians were being seized—in the street, the home, the workplace, often before hordes of witnesses—and then disappearing.

To be fair and to be honest, satisfaction with the mere forms of liberal society is not uniquely a condition of right-wing fanatics. In their case, satisfaction scales the dizzy heights of infatuation. But I often felt that we on the commission were not guiltless. In our report on Columbia,[8] for example, we did not attempt to peer behind the form of party competition to determine whether, as alleged by far-left opponents of the political system, the right to participate in government was inhibited by such factors as:

1. Limited access to the mass media by left-wing parties and spokesmen;

2. Conditioning neighborhood and village access to various government services on the basis of "appropriate" voting behavior;
3. A gentlemen's agreement among leaders of the two major parties to keep certain potentially popular programs off the political agenda;
4. The sharing of governmental power, regardless of the outcome of elections, only among national and local leaders of the two major parties.

The text of the American Convention neither compels nor precludes deep analysis of the political process as a condition for assessing compliance with the right to participate. Its history is equally mute. Nothing of particular relevance can be found in the negotiating history or the debates over signature and ratification because, I am sure, none of the participants ever envisioned being subjected to such scrutiny in depth. That failure of imagination is arguably not decisive for the commission. But it is hardly surprising that men and women nominated and elected by the member states of the OAS should for the most part reflect the assumptions of their constituency. Obviously, there are few assumptions more central to the liberal ethos that has nurtured the human rights movement in this hemisphere than the assumption that in a state where associational rights are reasonably well protected, the right of political participation is realized in all cases where formal political power coincides with electoral achievement. As long as the franchise is not arbitrarily restricted and the ballots are accurately counted, traditional liberal criteria are satisfied.

From a classical liberal perspective, the political arena parallels the economic one. In both, entrepreneurs compete to identify and satisfy the demands of consumers. In both, consumers are assumed to be rational, uncoerced actors with sufficient knowledge of all alternatives to allow them an informed choice. In both, the possibility of new entrants where existing entrepreneurs do not adequately service consumer preferences also is assumed.

Evident deviations from the model in the economic sphere led to demands for corrective action by governments. Fair-trade, pure food and drug acts, and antitrust legislation were some of the most important responses. Irreconcilable assessments of the actual and potential efficacy of piecemeal efforts to eliminate impurities from the market model have been a central feature of twentieth century political conflict. Since World War II, unprecedented prosperity and the system of social welfare made possible by sustained economic growth softened that conflict in advanced capitalist states. It also may have encouraged the broad, though largely implicit, consensus that, whatever its flaws as a mirror of reality in the economic sphere, it is sufficiently faithful to political reality to legitimate the distribution of formal political power.

Of course, deviations in the political sphere have been recognized and corrective action attempted. Limits on campaign spending and the "fairness" doctrine are two American examples. It nevertheless seems to me that skepticism about the political model has been qualitatively less intense than skepticism about its economic counterpart. Merited or not, that confidence in the efficacy of political laissez faire is, together with affluence and the welfare state, the foundation of civic peace in the Western world.

The liberal ethos of Western hemisphere human rights is probably a sufficient explanation of the commission's failure to push behind the forms of political competition. To begin with, the ethos determines the intellectual formation of most commission members. In addition, the power and importance of liberal assumptions about the political process would make any such effort on the commission's part seem not so much quixotic as subversive. Even if they could transcend their own and their principal audience's predispositions, the commissioners still would be restrained by an impoverishment of means. Whether because of liberal hegemony (in the Gramscian sense) or the intrinsically problematic nature of the subject, there exists no cluster of widely accepted criteria for identifying, much less assessing, the subtler foms of restraint on the exercise of a free and reasonably informed political choice.

The liberal model validated by the commission is not entirely without official challengers. President Pinochet of Chile, echoing right–wing sentiment in other Latin American states, has repeatedly declared his commitment to restructuring his country's political process in order to eliminate, prior to the restoration of electoral competition, a leftist electoral option. Aside from the crude decimation of leftist cadres, he apparently hopes to achieve this end by redefining the limits of government so as to make the acquisition of political power largely irrelevant to advancing the economic interests of the popular classes. If gross restraints on the government's power to redistribute wealth—whether through expropriation with partial compensation, progressive income taxation and associated welfare transfers, or any other means—are incorporated into the constitution and sealed there by a scheme of weighted voting, and if electoral competition is then restored for "non–Marxist" parties, he will at least manage to underscore the limits of the liberal model.

The exceptionalism of Pinochet's candor testifies to that model's enduring strength, as does the impending election in Nicaragua. Sandinista leaders do not profess liberalism. But they nevertheless feel compelled to conduct an electoral test which with all its deficiencies is not entirely unthreatening, if the tally is going to be checked by independent observers. For in that event it might reveal substantial public disaffection.

In this instance, the felt need to dissemble should not, I believe, be equated with moral unease. If I read them correctly, a majority if not all the Sandinista leaders are guided by the Marxist conception of electoral success as a sign of, rather than a primary means for, achieving victory in the conflict of classes. Upper- and middle-class coalitions may win nominally free elections, I believe they would argue, because they have succeeded in confusing the popular classes about the nature of and most efficient means for advancing their true interests. The power to confuse derives in turn from millennia of control over not only the political and economic but also the idea-generating and -disseminating institutions of society. Even after the revolution, a considerable measure of control persists. This perspective explains in part the regime's feverish efforts to penetrate and transform or to replace intermediate social institutions, efforts which led quickly and ineluctably into a collision with the hierarchy of the Catholic Church. The effort also aggravated Miskito suspicions about the new government's intentions and thus helped foster the dialectic of hostility that culminated, with encouragement from Washington, in ferocious armed conflict. It lent support, moreover, to the conservative claim that this revolutionary movement—and, indeed, all such movements—pursued totalitarian control.

Conservatives may be right about the elective preference of the regime. Moreover, whatever the subjective values of regime leaders, objectively the elimination of autonomous, nongovernmental institutions could produce a condition approximating totalitarian control, at least if the United States collaborated by maintaining an external environment of isolation and threat rather than relying on its vast capacity for cultural and ideological penetration to offset regime closure of indigenous ideological competition.

To this date, the course, capabilities, and intentions of the regime are ambiguous. It has not tried to eliminate the most inherently powerful autonomous institution, the private sector of the economy, although it has tried to fence entrepreneurs off from political influence. Despite their affection for Castro and respect for what they see as salutary achievements in Cuba, the island's economic stagnation has not been lost on the Sandinistas. And, according to a well-informed opponent of the Nicaraguan regime, Castro himself drew the connection between stagnation and his assault on the private sector. There is, therefore, reason to believe that preservation of a private sector is not a consciously short-term expedient. Soon the regime will discover that political enfeeblement is incompatible with entrepreneurial dynamism. At that point, it will have to choose between some sharing of political power and enhancing the material welfare of the popular classes.

Another ambiguity in the regime's present posture arises from the absence of a consistent correlation historically between the castration or absorption of autonomous institutions in the wake of revolution and the subsequent imposition of totalitarian controls. The heirs of the Mexican revolution emasculated the Catholic Church, expropriated powerful foreign investors, and placed the armed forces firmly under the control of the party (the "PRI") they constructed to institutionalize their rule. The party served also as a means of absorbing peasant and labor organizations. While the PRI has tolerated, sometimes even encouraged, the formation of other parties, it has never allowed them to mount a significant threat to its rule, just as it has not tolerated the emergence of powerful, autonomous competitors for the PRI-related unions and peasant associations. Yet even its sternest critics do not label Mexico totalitarian. On the contrary, it is generally seen as one of the more pluralistic countries in Latin America, in part because the PRI itself is an arena for contending social groups rather than a tightly controlled, sharply defined hierarchy.

Of course, the men who made the PRI were in most cases middle-class pragmatists. Uninhibited by Marxist-Leninist ideology, they could improvise a political structure consistent both with the mixed economy they intended to encourage and the political control they intended to maintain. In varying degrees, the Sandinistas appear constrained by self-imposed Leninist blueprints. But, particularly since their recovery from the intoxication of victory, they also have evidenced some capacity to appreciate the constraints imposed by history, culture, and geography. Moreover, the country's relatively favorable ratio of people to resources and two endowments from the Somoza era—limited foreign investment and the dictator's economic empire—make redistribution of capital assets and satisfaction of demands of the popular classes potentially easier to accomplish in Nicaragua than in post-revolutionary Mexico. In Nicaragua, moreover, the preexisting officer corps has utterly ceased to exist. Hence, at least in the absence of a threat from the United States, the ideological proclivities of regime leaders in comparison to their Mexican predecessors may be partially offset by reduced incentives to impose Procrustean political controls. A regime paralleling the PRI will not be totalitarian, nor will it be a paragon of representative democracy. One ingredient of tragedy in post–World War II Latin America has been the absence of a non-Leninist model, propagated by a powerful state, for radical or revolutionary reform.

Conclusion: Between Darwinism and Leninism

Given the current social and economic conditions in most Latin American states, the 19th Century liberal model could not serve as the exclusive blueprint for humane reform. Moreover, its employment as an ideological weapon by local conservatives and agents of United States imperial power made it unattractive to many latent reformers even as an intellectual point of departure. Liberation Theology was an effort by the most admirable forces in the Latin Catholic Church to fill the void between social Darwinism and Leninism. While its clerical origins probably limited its appeal, its principal defect as a model has been its failure to provide a fairly well defined and coherent economic program. Moreover, its actually very traditional skepticism about market capitalism has tended to reinforce the tendency toward *etatism* that has often dominated the Latin Right, as well as the Left.

This is not intended as a criticism of Liberation Theology. Neither the Catholic nor any other church is an appropriate source of economic or political models. It is, rather, the source of moral criteria for judging secular models of political and economic organizations. The courageous and creative men who fashioned and propagated Liberation Theology intended to flagellate the conscience of the rich, such as it is, and to liberate the poor from that reflexive apathy and servility to the perpetuation of which the Church had for centuries contributed. Their effort has not been in vain.

It has helped prepare the soil for a model that disaggregates the tasks of storming the political heights and establishing a more just social order. To achieve the former, power must be concentrated; to achieve the latter, it must be diffused. Diffusion must occur in the economic as well as the political sphere, which is only another way of saying that relatively free markets can be instruments of liberation—liberation from want and liberation from the will of others. But they are likely to serve that purpose only where opportunities for participating effectively in all markets are widely available, in other words, only where political power has been exercised to moderate extreme concentration of capital assets, to disseminate health and education and technical skills, to disintegrate private monopolies, and to facilitate cooperation among individually weak market units, particularly peasants and workers.

Like Liberation Theology, the human rights norms recorded in the various conventions and declarations are not a model or program for reform but rather a measure of achievement. As such, however, they imply the model sketched above. The implication springs from the declaration that there are economic and social as well as political and civil rights. Even the most minimal definition of the former requires in most countries a significant degree of redistribution both of private assets and government services. And it springs as well from the fact that the exercise of civil and political rights is radically unequal in a society marked by extreme poverty.

Eleanor Roosevelt knew this instinctively and fought with all her formidable powers to shape liberal doctrine in light of her knowledge. That is why we honor her best by rededicating ourselves to the continuing struggle.

Notes

This chapter originated as a paper delivered at Vassar College on the occasion of its Eleanor Roosevelt Centennial Conference in October 1984. Published as "Human Rights and Human Wrongs: Is the Liberal Model Sufficient?" *Human Rights Quarterly* Vol. 7, No. 1, May 1984.

1. Declaration of the Rights and Duties of Man, O.A.S. Res. XXX, adopted by the Ninth International Conference of American States (March 30–May 2, 1948, Bogota). O.A.S. Off. Rec. OEA/Ser. L/V/1.4 Rev. (1965); American Convention on Human Rights, O.A.S. Treaty Series No. 36 at 1, O.A.S. Off. Rec. OEA/Ser. L/V/11.23 doc. 21 Rev. 6 (1970). The United States has signed, but not ratified, this convention.
2. Report on the Situation of Human Rights in Argentina, OEA/Serv. L/V/11.49, doc. 19, 11 April 1980 (original: Spanish).
3. American Convention on Human Rights, Art. 27(1).
4. Ibid. Art. 27(2).
5. Convention Relative to the Protection of Civilian Persons in Time of War, Art. 3, 12 August 1949, 6 U.S.T. 3515, 3518; T.I.A.S. 3365; 75 U.N.T.S. 287; Convention Relative to the Treatment of Prisoners of War, Art. 3, 12 August 1949, 6 U.S.T. 3316, 3319; T.I.A.S. 3364; 75 U.N.T.S. 135; Convention for the Amelioration of the Condition of the Wounded and Sick in Armed Forces in the Field, Art. 3, 12 August 1949, 6 U.S.T. 3114, 3116; T.I.A.S. 3362; 75 U.N.T.S. 31.
6. Report on Human Rights in Argentina, note 2 above.
7. American Convention on Human Rights, Art. 22(1), (3) and (4). For a study on the meaning of similar limitation clauses in the International Covenant on Civil and Political Rights, see Bert B. Lockwood, Jr., Janet Finn, and Grace Jubinsky, "Working Paper for the Committee on Experts on Limitation Clauses." 7 *Human Rights Quarterly* (February 1985): 35.
8. Report on the Situation of Human Rights in the Republic of Columbia, O.E.A./Ser. L/V/11.53, doc. 22, 30 June 1981 (original: Spanish).

11

Human Rights and Human Welfare

My mandate was to pose the central dilemmas of human rights in Latin America. As a novelist begins by finding the voice, the point of consciousness, appropriate to his tale, I began by considering whose dilemmas to dissect: The dilemmas of traditional oligarchs feeling the seismic shift of social forces and wondering how best to contain them? The dilemmas of military cadres caught between the temptations of power, which grow inexorably from the barrels of their guns, and the risk of disunity that lies in wait on the political heights? The dilemmas of social democrats committed by instinct and interest to plural societies, but committed as well to a measure of social justice that the more pluralistic political orders of Latin America often seem unable to yield? The dilemmas of the rural poor, torn between the pain of exit and the dangers of voice? Latin America is a sea of dilemmas in which moral visions drown.

Being a member of the Inter-American Commission on Human Rights makes one a vicarious participant in other people's dilemmas. It also imposes a personal one, namely, how to relate the work of the commission—enforcing the hemisphere's formal humanitarian norms[1]—to the lives of ordinary people, the popular classes, with their vast numbers yet slight weight on the scales of what victors in the social wars call "justice." The following fable suggests the dimensions of that dilemma.

I

Imagine first a country, let us call it Tierra Linda, that for one hundred years, ending two decades ago, had been governed by a succession of military dictators, supported by or allied first with local landowners and ultimately with an alliance of landowners and large industrialists.

Twenty years ago, the combination of a succession crisis brought on by the assassination of the reigning dictator and intensified by pressure from a liberal American President, who had suspended military aid some months before the assassination, and an economic crisis, resulting from the discovery of a competitively priced substitute for guano, the country's chief export, gave the democratically inclined leaders of the country's two traditional political parties—the MRP (Movement for Progressive Reform) and the MDP (Movement for God and Country)—a long-awaited opportunity. They contacted several of the country's most prominent industrialists and landowners and proposed a joint effort to institutionalize civilian rule.[2]

The spokesmen for the oligarchy agreed to the proposals, subject to inclusion of the following conditions in a new national constitution: (1) members of the Supreme Court would be appointed for life; (2) as a precondition to the expropriation of land or businesses, the government would have to pay the full value of the expropriated property as determined by a Court of Property Assessment, the judges of which would receive life appointments; and (3) the maximum tax rate on income would be 20%. The party leaders acquiesced and, in addition, said they would accept a slate of Supreme Court justices and Property Assessment justices chosen by the national associations representing industrialists and landowners. Furthermore, the traditionally more populist MRP consented to purge its left-wing youth movement and to refuse, under any circumstances, to enter into coalition with any left-wing parties that might participate in the envisioned elections.

As for the parties themselves, they agreed to have the presidency alternate between them during the next sixteen years and to divide, more or less equally, all ministerial and senior bureaucratic posts. Patronage at the regional and municipal levels also would be shared. After this time, real competition would commence; the winner, however, would continue to allocate a fair share of ministerial and other positions to the loser.[3]

The newly united civilians then approached military leaders and demanded their withdrawal from politics. After intensive bargaining, the generals agreed to adopt an apolitical role so long as the political parties abided by the following conditions: (1) military expenditures would never fall below 7% of the GNP, except with the consent of the Minister of Defense; (2) the Minister of Defense would always be selected by majority vote of the general officers of the armed forces; (3) the new constitution would extend military jurisdiction to all crimes against the security of the state, even if committed by civilians, and the new penal code would define such crimes to include assaults against public officials or any member of the armed forces, kidnapping, arson, and rebellion.

Twenty years have passed, during which five presidential and congressional elections have been held, and all parties to the original understanding have met their commitments. The country has, until recently, experienced steady, modest economic growth and a gradual expansion of the middle classes. But poverty in the rural areas, where land ownership remains highly concentrated, is intense, despite the heavy migration to the cities, now ringed by squatter communities and penetrated by vast slums. Underemployment and unemployment are estimated at no less than 40% of the population. Persons in this category live on the the margin of subsistence. Infant mortality among families in the top 10% of the population is under twenty per thousand, not much higher than the rates in developed countries. In poor areas, and especially in the countryside, it is close to one hundred. The top 10% of the population receives half the national income; the bottom 40% of the population receives 12%.

In recent years, import–substitution-led growth has slowed as the market tends toward saturation. Locally made goods, protected by high tariffs, are relatively costly. The worldwide recession and growing protectionism have hurt export industries. A combination of steady inflation, slow growth, and continued high birthrates has increased the number of unemployed and underemployed persons and visibly reduced opportunities for secondary school and even university graduates.

Political leaders detect a growing sense of popular frustration. It coincides with the emergence of still small, but apparently well-organized, subversive groups. By agreement, the leading newspapers print very little about the exploits of these groups, other than an occasional army bulletin describing some "outrage," or a report on the capture, trial, and conviction of individuals for crimes against national security.[4] Allegations of torture during the interrogation of suspects, made by the handful of left-wing deputies, have been ignored by the press but published abroad. There is no censorship. The leading newspapers and magazines are controlled by four families.[5]

Perhaps partially in response to charges, made recently by the Conference of Bishops, concerning the mistreatment of detainees and condemning any deviation, however slight, from the rule of law, the president of Tierra Linda invites the Inter-American Commission to conduct an observation *in loco*[6] and prepare a report on the general situation of human rights in his country. With the full support of the government, the commission carries out an on-site inspection and finds the situation as described above. Can it do anything other than conclude that Tierra Linda is a model of compliance with human rights norms? The press is in private hands and is free of official restraints. The judiciary is independent of the executive power; it recently found unconstitutional a new land reform law providing for payment in five-year government bonds at fixed interest rate. Elections are free. Even Marxist parties are allowed to participate. Freedom of religion is strictly observed, although because the national conscription law has no provision for conscientious objection, Jehovah's Witnesses are imprisoned for refusing to serve. The commission does find some evidence of abuse during interrogation, but it does not appear to be institutionalized, and in one extreme case, where two persons accused of attempted kidnapping died during interrogation, the officer in charge was court-martialed and given a brief prison term.

In the course of confirming that elections are free, the commission asks a well-respected Tierra Linda intellectual why the left-wing parties failed to rally powerful support among the poor. He replies, in essence, as follows.

First, the rural poor are deeply dependent on the local land-owning oligarchy. Of course the ballot is secret, but returns are broken down by village. The leaders of these small, cohesive social units believe that any community which fails to turn out a large vote for the party of the landowner on whom it is principally dependent will suffer. Moreover, most of the potentially rebellious younger men have left for the cites by the time they reach voting age. In addition, the traditional parties have roots in the countryside. Local party bosses maintain support by doling out patronage. The Left has nothing material to offer. Therefore, as long as the conditions of life for those who remain behind do not deteriorate dramatically, the rational, "mini-maxing" peasant, if he votes at all, votes for the parties of the status quo.

In the rich sugar-growing areas along the coast, where plantation labor was originally organized by MRP activists, workers are comparatively well paid and covered by the social security system, which provides a small pension on retirement and affordable vacation centers.[7] As for the cities, the analyst continues, here too the traditional parties are well organized, even in many of the squatter settlements. They identify and co-opt natural leaders, often giving them jobs in the municipal government. Leaders who refuse to join one of the parties are conspicuously unable to secure any services—water, electricity, occasional garbage collection, medical dispensaries—for their followers.

Finally, he concludes, the poor are both tired and cynical. They spend enormous amounts of time and energy searching for or commuting to work, and scrounging for food and building materials. They often suffer from malnutrition and gastrointestinal illnesses. People in this condition have little time or energy for attending political rallies. Many, moreover, are illiterate. And even the established parties make attractive promises. But nothing changes.

The commission publishes a final report stating, in effect, that the situation of human rights in Tierra Linda is excellent.

Shortly after its publication, the government of Golfo Profundo, a neighboring state, invites the commission to evaluate its achievements in the human rights realm. Until 1975, Golfo Profundo had an economic, social, and political profile very similar to that of Tierra Linda. But in 1975, responding to worsening economic conditions and incipient rural and urban insurgency, a military junta seized power in the name of tranquilization and reform. After some maneuvering, General Omar Hernandez emerged as the dominant figure and assumed the presidency. Close associates took over key commands in the armed forces. Having consolidated power, General Hernandez introduced a set of wholly unanticipated reforms.

For rural areas, he promulgated a comprehensive land reform involving the expropriation of all holdings in excess of one hundred acres and all underutilized land. Compensation was to be paid principally in the form of twenty–year government bonds with fixed interest rates. Experts estimate that, given the rate of inflation, owners will receive about 25% of the actual value of their land.

Second, he converted all manufacturing enterprises to "social property."[8] Owners were left with 25% interests in management and profits. The other 75 was transferred to workers in the enterprises. The value of the transferred rights would be compensated out of enterprise profits at a rate to be determined by the new worker–dominated boards of directors, according to values established by special assessment tribunals; but the period of compensation could not exceed twenty–five years.

Finally, on the political front, General Hernandez prepared a new constitution for submission to the electorate, one replacing the old parliament with a People's Congress. Proposed congressional districts were many and small, and candidates had to have lived in them for a minimum of five years prior to seeking office. The congress would have the power to block legislation, which could only be initiated by the president, who would be popularly elected for a term of five years, no more than twice. As a transitional measure, however, the constitution provided that, upon its adoption, General Hernandez would remain as chief of government for four years.

Prior to the beginning of the referendum campaign on the new constitution, General Hernandez took a number of significant steps. First, he purged the Supreme Court, replacing its members with primarily younger men and women who had rallied around his reform proposals. In addition, he converted all newspapers into employee cooperatives,[9] and founded a government–owned paper. Finally, he nationalized the hitherto private radio and television networks and placed them under the control of a board ultimately responsible to the minister of the interior.

The reform decrees and the proposed constitution were announced simultaneously. On the same day, all banks were nationalized and foreign currency transactions limited to those strictly necessary for the conduct of commercial, industrial, and agricultural enterprise. Severe civil and criminal penalties were decreed for the violation of currency controls. Currency-control crimes and all crimes against "national security," as well as disputes stemming from the agrarian and industrial reform laws, were placed under the jurisdiction of special three-person tribunals set up by General Hernandez. Members of the tribunals were selected by meetings in rural and urban barrios. They included lawyers, students, ordinary workers, and peasants. At least one member of each tribunal had to be either a lawyer or a law student.[10]

The commission finally arrives in the country, interviews representatives of all sectors of opinion, holds full and frank discussions with government officials, visits sessions of the special tribunals, visits industrial and agricultural enterprises, and then, having returned to its base in Washington, prepares a report with the following conclusions: (1) the government has violated the right to a fair trial and the right to judicial protection, since the popular tribunals have a fluctuating membership, include nonlawyers, and in general lack the elements required to satisfy Articles 8 and 25 of the American Convention on Human Rights, to which Golfo Profundo has adhered;[11] (2) the government has violated the right to property by failing to pay just compensation as required by Article 21 of the Convention;[12] (3) the government has violated Article 23 of the convention, which deals with the right to participate in government. In particular, the postponement of presidential elections violates the requirements of Article 23 that "every citizen shall enjoy the right to vote and to be elected in genuine periodic elections, which shall be by universal and equal suffrage and by secret ballot that guarantees the free expression of the will of the voters."[13]

As is its custom, before publishing the report, the commission sends it to President Hernandez for his comments. He reads it and then dispatches his principal advisor, the distinguished author Gabriel Garcia-Machado, to reply on behalf of the government. Garcia-Machado flies to Washington, appears before the commission, and delivers the following statement.

"With respect to the courts," he begins, "we had to bypass the old judicial system. Of course, it was formally independent; but it was so wedded by class and family ties and ideology to the oligarchical society we are trying to alter that the judges could not be entrusted with enforcing laws designed to block a foreign-exchange hemorrhage and to repress armed conspiracies by the oligarchy. The fluctuating and partially nonprofessional membership of the new tribunals reflects our belief that the judiciary should be responsive to the needs and enduring values of ordinary people, who should feel that the courts exist to serve them.

"As to the alleged failure to pay just compensation, we reject categorically the equation of 'justness' with market value. Was it just that so few should have had so much? And how do you think these families, who remain obscenely rich even after our expropriations, acquired their holdings? Do you think they found unoccupied land, or that they bought it at fair market value? Let me tell you, my friends, they were the original expropriators, and they paid no compensation. Whatever they may subsequently have contributed is certainly reflected in the compensation we are paying.

"Finally, with respect to our supposed violation of political rights, I ask you: Who has more control over his life? Our peasants, who now own their own plots or are shareholders in cooperatives, and our workers who now govern their own plants, or the popular classes of a land you call a democratic model, our good neighbor, Tierra Linda. There, once every four years, as required, the population marches to the polls to chose between two men whom they know not and who know not them. What does that ballot have to do with the day-to-day reality of their lives? What does it have to do with their sense of personal value? You don't know. You don't know because you don't *want* to know. It would be information irrelevant to your mandate as you define that mandate. Political rights must be related to the reality of participation in the decisions that govern the day-to-day quiddity of your life. Without that connection, these rights are lifeless forms.

"The reactionaries are right [he smiled at the pun]. Freedom is property. Without property, a man is a helpless thing. And he knows it and feels the self-contempt that goes with that knowledge. We have acted to equalize the power people have over their lives. If your convention cannot recognize that, then you may need a new convention.

"Let me add that you criticize us also for delaying elections and then limiting congressional power. Let me ask you: Who would win if fair elections were held today? Probably the General. But he has not had time to organize a political party and to identify a new class of leaders stemming directly from the people. So the parties of the middle and upper classes, funded now by the oligarchy, which still has plenty of money, would dominate Congress. Even by the most generous definition, the middle classes— of course, I include our labor aristocracy—make up less than 30% of the population. They would support redistribution of wealth from the oligarchy to them. Full stop![14] If the choice, for instance, is between increasing their social security benefits and extending the reach of social security at existing benefit levels, of course they will oppose extension. They will not even support the land reform, because initially it is causing some disruption of production. Moreover, the peasants are growing more food than export crops. This has hurt our balance of payments and therefore our import capacity. So we have placed heavy taxes on nonessentials like television sets and cars. And we limit the foreign exchange that can be taken on holidays. So no more shopping sprees in Miami, despite the cheap fares. In short, gentlemen, free elections today, when the majority are still disorganized and distrustful of all governments, even this new one, will be a test of organizational skills and political sophistication, not a test of informed popular will."

The commission is moved by Garcia-Machado's eloquence, but I am by no means certain that it will alter the report.

How serious are the dilemmas posed by Garcia-Machado? Is he persuasive in the context of my hypothetical countries? Is he persuasive in the context of the real world of Latin America? Even if he is, what should we conclude about the relationship between the human rights of the legal texts and the ideals of social democracy?

Despite their profound importance, the issues raised by Garcia-Machado must remain on the periphery of concern to institutions directly engaged in the defense of human rights. Representative democracy may conceal scarifying injustice. People may fairly dispute the most appropriate means for promoting participation in government and distributive justice. But no one at all these days will defend torture, murder, and arbitrary detention as acceptable means to any ends, however nominally noble.[15] Conservatives, liberals, and social democrats agree on the categorical prohibition of these devices. Thugs use them—in self-indicting clandestinity, to be sure, but they use them. And it is these violations of incontestable rights, transcending ideological differences, that are naturally at the very heart of the human rights defense effort. Legitimate dispute about the relative humanity of various political projects begins only after we move outside the zone of barbarism.

II

The points sharpened, it is hoped, by my little allegory can be restated in terms of the following questions: What are the prospects for the amelioration of mass poverty under Latin political systems characterized by party competition and periodic, relatively free elections? Do authoritarian regimes of the Left enjoy an acute comparative advantage as instruments for constructing a floor under extreme poverty? What sorts of humanitarian costs are incurred by recourse to authoritarian methods? Are conventional interpretations of human rights texts insufficiently responsive to political reality in Latin American states? My responses to these questions will be both schematic and tentative, intended more to provoke debate and research than to convince; for how can I reasonably hope to produce a higher level of conviction than I myself have achieved?

Turning to the first question, my discomforting conclusion is that no regime in Latin America which has achieved power and ruled according to the norms of the political game practiced in North America and Western Europe has succeeded in altering significantly either the distribution of income or power; nor has it succeeded in placing a floor under extreme poverty and integrating a large proportion of hitherto marginal persons. The Chilean experience haunts every democratic reformer in Latin America. It showed just how quickly a major effort to redistribute power and property can polarize a society, to the point where even a strong tradition of civilian and constitutional rule cannot contain unleashed social passions. Chile suggests, but only suggests, that democratic processes may not be tough enough to withstand the pressure of a redistribution that seriously affects the status or income of the middle and upper classes.[16]

Yet it remains far from clear just how much Chile has to tell us about the prospects for democratic reform. The absence of a congressional majority for the reform coalition, the coalition's at least rhetorical ambiguity about its long-run commitment to democratic institutions, its failure to discipline its extremist wing, its decision to expropriate alien property without payment of *any* compensation, the fallen copper prices, the coalition's assumption of office at a time when the American presidency was in the hands of harsh and amoral conservatives—all of these factors simply constitute too many idiosyncratic elements to allow much confident drawing of conclusions.

Chile certainly demonstrated that a government with the will to effect a fundamental transformation of class relations could come to power in a Latin American state. Whether any such government could survive the effort remains unclear. Other Latin societies have not been tested because they have not produced governments with the will to try.

The leaders of Venezuela's *Acción Democrática,* for example, as part of their arrangement with the Christian Democrats (COPEI) and upper-class leaders, an arrangement that preceded—and probably was a precondition for—the reestablishment of democratic rule after the dictatorship of Perez Jimenez, openly eschewed the effort.[17]

With the exception of Chile's *Unidad Popular,* successful democratic politicians have solicited support without challenging the essentials of the status quo. In the absence of such a challenge, particularly in the countryside, is it possible to improve substantially the conditions of the poorer classes, that proportion of the population—varying from roughly 30 to 60% and even higher in the poorest countries like Bolivia—who live on the edge of subsistence?

A small number of so-called populist regimes—the first Peronist government being the most notable—after achieving power through electoral coalitions of import-substituting industrialists and workers in the modern sector, have enriched the income shares of the latter. Such regimes have coincidentally enhanced the capacity of workers to function as an autonomous political force. Because Argentina is highly urbanized, Peronism's typical populist bias against the rural sector did not have the usual consequences of deepening peasant misery, that is, of plundering the many to pay a relatively affluent few. In less urbanized countries, the short-term balance of populism's welfare consequences has been problematical.

The tendency of populist leaders to ignore, if not to ravage, the countryside is a symptom of their fundamental flaw—an unwillingness or inability to deal comprehensively with the linked problems of late-industrializing states marked by an inheritance of narrowly concentrated power and profoundly divided societies.[18]

III

A decade ago, *Redistribution with Growth*,[19] that classic exposition of strategies for ameliorating poverty in developing countries, pointed out that the Latin American context is distinguished by relatively high per capita income and, compared with the other great centers of pauperism, a uniquely high concentration of productive assets, most conspicuously land. Economic growth and the concomitant penetration of capitalist relations of production into every corner of society tends, at least initially, to aggravate inequality:[20] where capital, skills, and influence are already sharply concentrated, the growth of inequality is correspondingly more acute.

The only sizable nonsocialist states that have resisted this powerful by-product of rapid growth are Taiwan and South Korea. Both carried out sweeping land reforms before their economies began to swell, and thereby produced a class of highly productive, labor-intensive capitalist farmers who fed the cities, generated foreign exchange, and formed a substantial market for the countries' infant industries. In addition, their numbers, financial independence, and economic importance gave them leverage to combat the sorts of urban-biased price restraints and foreign exchange manipulations that have savaged the local food-producing portion of the agricultural sector in much of Latin America.

The concentration of land ownership in Latin America is no doubt related to the character of Iberian imperial appropriation, though not in any single, indisputable way. While in some countries latifundia is a lineal descend of the colonial order, in others it followed independence. During the latter part of the Nineteenth Century, under the generous patronage of the Mexican dictator, Porfirio Diaz, both domestic and foreign interests constructed great estates by the simple expedient of confiscating the communal lands of the Indian peasantry. Though the Mexican Revolution in its turn displaced many of these owners, the estates survived in the hands of a successor oligarchy for another two decades.

The great redistribution managed by President Cárdenas in the second half of the 1930s seemed to complete the revolutionary process. Thanks to Cárdenas and his supporters, the old hacienda with its quasi–feudal relations was in fact dead. But those who believed that a strong, independent peasantry would rise in its place were mistaken. Within one decade, the large farm began to reemerge as the dominant actor on the rural stage,[21] though this time in the form of a high–technology capitalist enterprise.

Like the old haciendados, the owners could summon to their aid the resources of the state. No pistoleros were needed to tranquilize an army of dependent peasants, because modern agrobusiness does not need many workers and can choose from a reserve army of the rural unemployed. Instead, the state provided the overhead of a successful agriculture: research, irrigation, subsidized credit, cheap energy and fertilizer, and roads. Where more land was needed, it could be bought or leased at firesale prices from impoverished peasants, who had been left to rot on their very own withered ground. Under such felicitous conditions, only fools would bother to steal it.

Mexico is not the only country where land reform has not stabilized a powerful middle–class peasantry. Contemporary land concentration seems to me more a symptom than cause of inequality and absolute need. The decisive assets in Latin America's power game are liquid wealth (often accumulated over many generations), inherited social prestige, entrepreneurial and organizational skills, and connections with foreign (primarily American) centers of power and wealth. It is the intense concentration of these assets in most Latin countries, coupled with the extreme deprivation of the popular classes, that limits so sharply the deployable power of theoretical majorities and tends to rip the substance out of electoral politics.

The difficulty of achieving the more balanced class relationships that have developed in the welfare democracies of North America and Western Europe is compounded by the fact that, in the culturally heterogeneous countries where most Latins live, possession of these assets correlates significantly with being white. As in the United States, race tends to reinforce the inherited structure of inequality.

Putting race to one side, is the context of Latin American industrialization really very different from Western Europe's on the eve of its industrial revolution? Certainly not insofar as the distribution of land is concerned. The enclosure movement radically concentrated land-holding in the century preceding England's pathbreaking takeoff. And if concentration did not actually intensify, it certainly underwent no marked diminution in other European countries as they hastened after the British vanguard.

Today's theories about the income-concentrating effects of industrialization derive initially from the European experience. It is now agreed that British income-inequality intensified at least until the middle of the Nineteenth Century, more than sixty years after the revolution's first spasms.[22] Thereafter, distribution appears to have remained fairly stable for several decades. Not until the far end of the century did a reverse trend take hold. And only in the middle of the Twentieth Century did the combined effects of economic growth, the redistributive efforts of government, and possibly, the natural working of the mature capitalist economy manage to place a floor under extreme poverty.

Drawing on this experience, optimists—in most cases, paradoxically, political conservatives—have urged serenity in the face of contemporary misery.[23] The late-industrializing countries, they argue, are simply passing through a necessary stage. Moreover, by virtue of the dramatic increase in human knowledge about the workings of economies, the technological revolution, and the mobility of productive factors, the several phases of the modernization process can be drastically telescoped.

Pessimists,[24] on the other hand, respond that certain features of contemporary economy and society, including the technological revolution, the mobility of capital, and the general porosity of frontiers, preclude reproduction of the European pattern, much less allow any reduction in the length of its phases. To summarize (without mutilating, I hope) an elaborate and subtly defended set of arguments, the central obstacles to reproduction of the Euro-North America experience are the following:

First, the population explosion, reinforced by the disappearance of empty land, has created a huge surplus labor force, one that has apparently outstripped the capacity of Latin American economies to generate productive employment. In Europe, for example, the wage share of national income began to rise only when, as a consequence of overseas migration, sustained economic growth, and mortality rates that remained high, labor became relatively scarce. In peripheral, late-industrializing states, the importation of a capital-intensive technology, developed in the tight labor markets of the developed world, compounds the difficulties of labor absorption, just as it exemplifies the peculiar problems of managing equitable growth.

Second, when neither technology nor capital could move so easily across national boundaries, and when the extant technology was rather simple, local entrepreneurs had far greater incentives to develop their own variations—which, as rational profit maximizers, they inevitably did, taking into account relative factor costs. The operation of today's integrated world economy discourages indigenous technology creation despite the huge gap that has opened between the cost of labor in developed and developing states. Why? Because foreign technology is often available at marginal production costs; because the exogenous stimulation of a premature consumerism produces an insatiable hunger for high technology goods developed in and for the relatively rich inhabitants of developed states (and not readily duplicable, if duplicable at all, by more intensive labor techniques); because many local manufacturers are subsidiaries of multinational corporations that can generally maximize global profits by transferring, often at inflated costs, their own technologies developed in the more labor–scarce centers of corporate activity; because artificially high exchange rates and low tariffs on capital equipment, championed by increasingly dominant industrial elites, understate the real cost of imported technology; because the multinational manufacture of components—an important source of industrial activity in some countries—requires a uniform technology; and because, particularly for parastatal corporations able to draw on public revenues, installation of the newest technology appears to induce a satisfying sense of economic progress.

A third factor cited by the pessimists, and implicated in choice–of–technology decisions, is the development, in advance of a modern economy, of a swollen state structure. Being colonized by the dominant classes, it is inclined to distort market forces and to repress the popular classes on their behalf. Modern technology facilitates repression. Tear gas grenades and a machine gun would have saved the Bastille.

The fourth source of pessimism, one that is in some respects paradoxical, is the muting of nationalist ambitions brought about in part by the post–World War II normative assault on armed diplomacy, in part by a sense of class solidarity in an ideologically polarized world, in part by the hemispheric *Pax Americana.* In Nineteenth Century Europe, interstate rivalries encouraged the upper classes to instill a sense of nationhood in the lower classes; without that effort, the elite would have found it difficult to conscript them as cannon fodder for the wars of national aggrandizement that the ruling classes saw as a natural feature of international relations.

A fifth verse in the litany of pessimism emphasizes the immense fluidity of capital. The ability to move capital quickly from one place to another, combined with ready access to information about global investment opportunities, has opened a wide vista of alternatives to the owners of capital, and has consequently forced governments to compete in the provision of investment incentives. Among favored incentives is a docile, low-wage work force.

To be sure, there are countervailing forces, among them, *ideas*: The obligation of governments to satisfy basic needs as a condition of their legitimacy, as opposed to the watchman, noninterventionist state of Nineteenth Century and contemporary Chicago School mythology; equality, at least of opportunity and merit rather than inherited status, as justification for unequal rewards; and *institutions*: The enhanced competence of state structures in the late-industrializing states, making them potentially more efficient tools for equity-enhancing intervention; the defection of the Catholic Church from the oligarchic coalition.

Even some of the factors invoked by pessimists have a Janus-like form. The invention of means for dramatically enhancing output per worker creates opportunities for governments, anxious to do so, to confront the equity issue. The diffusion of information about lifestyles in developed countries, though it seeds a morbid consumerism, also strengthens demands for human rights among once quiescent sectors of the populations. And by stimulating the migration of the poor in droves toward the source of opulence, it thereby creates incentives for the United States to encourage social reform in Latin countries. Although the policy of the current administration in Washington is instead to bolster reactionary regimes, such perverse ideological fixations may not endure as national policy.

IV

The belief that, without profound institutional change, steady growth in the GNP by itself can do little to ameliorate the conditions of the poor clearly lies behind the uneasy sympathy of the democratic Left in the United States and Western Europe toward revolutionary reformers. Cuba is both their model and the source of their ambivalence. What has it in fact accomplished? As Nelson Valdez notes, there is a consensus among scholars of a wide variety of ideological positions that, on the level of life expectancy, education, and health, Cuban achievement is considerably greater than one would expect from its level of per capita income.[25]

A recent study comparing 113 Third World countries in terms of these basic indicators of popular welfare ranked Cuba first, ahead even of Taiwan—which is probably the outstanding example of growth with equity within a capitalist economic framework. Data in the 1981 World Development Report of the International Bank for Reconstruction and Development also support the consensus. Cuba excelled, according to all main indicators of human needs satisfaction. For instance, out of the 124 countries studied in the survey, with 124 as the top ranking in each category, Cuba ranked 103rd in life expectancy, 98th in infant mortality, 122nd in primary school enrollment, and 102nd in adult literacy—yet its GNP ranking was only 76th.

Even before the revolution, Cuba surpassed most Latin American countries in its levels of health and education. What has changed remarkably is not so much the gross indicators as those that reflect the changed conditions of the poor, particularly the rural poor. In 1958, for example, the one rural hospital in the entire country represented about 2% of the hospital facilities in Cuba; by 1982 there were 117 rural hospitals, or about 35% of all hospitals in Cuba.

Also revealing is the shift in the major causes of death in Cuba. Before 1959, the majority of illnesses that led to death were those traditionally associated with underdevelopment: diseases of the digestive system and of early infancy, and respiratory problems such as tuberculosis. "At present," Valdez concludes, in his exhaustive survey of the data, "Cubans die for basically the same reasons as people in the developed world: congenital abnormalities, lesions affecting the central nervous system, diabetes, etc. . . . Cuba has eradicated polio, diphtheria, and malaria."

The achievements are undeniable. Could they, however, have been accomplished in a more open political system with a market economy? Skeptics about the asserted relationship between authoritarian socialism and the eradication of pauperism speculate that a capitalist Cuba would have enjoyed high growth during the international boom years of the 1960s and 1970s, particularly in light of its proximity to the United States, its large middle class, and relatively good infrastructure. And, skeptics conclude, the benefits of such growth would have trickled down sufficiently far to raise the poor up to or above the level they have achieved under Fidel Castro.

Since the revolution, Cuba's economy has grown markedly more slowly than those of most other Latin countries that are at roughly comparable levels of development.[26] It could therefore be argued that the distributional efforts in the fields of health, nutrition, and education have been necessary to compensate for the Cuban government's initial failures in the realm of economic management. Or, as a Polish wit put it recently, communism is a system of political economy that mobilizes the citizenry for heroic sacrifice to overcome the inefficiencies of the system. Since the stagnant 1960s, however, there has been steady, though unspectacular, growth. The CIA estimates that in 1982, a year of absolute shrinkage in most of Latin America's fast–growth economies, Cuba's GNP grew approximately 4%.

Skeptics nevertheless insist that, with respect to the satisfaction of basic needs, Cuba is a special case because a significant part of the social surplus used to place a floor under extreme poverty is earned through political and military service to the Soviet Union. Without a Soviet subsidy, estimated to have run as high as $3 billion in some years,[27] Cuba would have come nowhere near compensating for its inefficiencies and the departure of human capital, the result, at least in part, of its adoption of an authoritarian political system and from its policies of redistribution. As Salvador Allende and, more recently, the Sandinistas discovered, the Soviet Union is not prepared to provide comparable subsidies for new Latin recruits.

Despite claims to the contrary by such distinguished authorities on the global economy as Ronald Reagan, authoritarian–socialist regimes do *not* as a group display a strong tendency to produce economic stagnation. The CIA recently estimated Soviet growth over the past thirty years at roughly 5% per annum. Since the end of World War II, several East European countries also have grown steadily under varying economic arrangements. Therefore, one must argue either that growth, in the generality of cases, will be slower under state capitalism, despite its diversity of economic strategies, or that authoritarian socialism is peculiarly stifling to growth in the Latin American context.

Certainly, other factors enter into Cuba's failure to match Brazilian and Mexican growth rates. Among them are the country's deep prerevolutionary dependence on the United States and the romantic egalitarian policies the Cuban leadership pursued in the early postrevolutionary years. Castro himself has said that his greatest error was to eliminate the private sector. In fact, he had gone even further by trying to eliminate virtually all material incentives. If Castro can learn something from his experience, so, *a fortiori,* can revolutionary leaders who have no vested interest in confirming their omniscience. Furthermore, we should not lose sight of the fact that Cuba alone among Latin states consciously subordinated overall growth to equity and the refinement of human capital.

We can, with good reason, be skeptical about the claim that under a liberal–capitalist regime, the Cuban economy could have grown very rapidly, and thereby have met basic human needs without a significant redistribution of income shares or social power; there has been little reduction, if any, in the number of people living in conditions of absolute poverty in the fast-growing economies of Latin America, most notably Brazil and Mexico. Since the 1950s, both countries have had, by historical standards, extraordinarily high income growth rates. Growth rates in excess of 6% per annum enlarged the middle class and, at least in the Brazilian case, increased the income shares of the upper middle class. Yet shares of the lower 30 or 40% actually shrank, since growth by itself could not compensate for the cumulative consequences of an initial concentration of capital, income, and education, a capital-intensive technology, and a demographic explosion.

In light of this, is it likely that a capitalist Cuba would have introduced the reforms necessary to spread the growth dividend to all sectors of society? Indeed, given Cuban dependence on the United States—political, economic, and psychological—and the extent to which U.S. interests would have been affected by rural reform, wasn't the prospect of such reform even lower in Cuba than in many other Latin states whose governments failed to overcome the entrenched power of rural interests?

V

Under any definition, regimes of the Cuban variety, and certainly the Cuban regime itself, plainly diminish the political and civil rights of intellectuals, businessmen, the professional classes, and workers in the modern sector of the economy, at least those who have made a relatively secure place for themselves, either because of their skills or because of their membership in independent and relatively powerful trade unions. When one turns to the previously marginalized classes, the balance may be less clear, and the arguments about autonomy made by Garcia-Machado, my hypothetical leftist intellectual, are rather more plausible. The sheer experience of physical health might easily enhance a person's sense of efficacy and hence autonomy. Guaranteed access to employment, medical services, and at least minimally adequate nutrition also would be expected to increase one's sense of security, an important element, one would suppose, in the subjective experience of autonomy.

Perhaps paradoxically, the institutionalization or bureaucratization of the revolutionary regime also may enhance autonomy for those marginal sectors previously dependent on wage labor and sharecropping. In their former existence, they were probably subject to the largely uncontrollable whims of employers and owners. In the early postrevolutionary stage, they may be no less subject to whim, in this case, that of party enthusiasts. But after chaotic fervor and voluntarism yield to organization, a dense network of rules will tend to replace discretion. Left-wing authoritarians will introduce socialist "legality," their version of *estado de derecho* (a government of laws, not men), if not for reasons of morality and legitimacy, then certainly to enhance efficiency.

Rules are two-faced: as they restrain, they necessarily demarcate areas of freedom. But even the restraining aspect of rules may enhance freedom. Knowing what is demanded, one can chose either to obey or to evade—and risk the consequences. Where, however, continuing employment turns on unpredictable factors, ranging from the master's whim to shifting patterns of world demand for a crop he produces, then one lives outside the realm of choice, and hence of autonomy in any sense—assuming there are neither alternative forms of employment nor other means of support.

The evenhanded, predictable application of well-defined rules is one autonomy-enhancing result of the revolutionary interest in efficiency. I should add, however, that the interest in predictability may not apply when the state is dealing not with formally marginal and depoliticized persons, but with those who are politically aware. To keep them in a state of perpetual intimidation, the state may prefer to maintain a broad area of uncertainty about the correctness of one's conduct, defining crimes in such vague and comprehensive terms—for example, "subversion of the revolution" or "violations of the interest of the proletariat"—that even those who wish to maintain a low profile cannot avoid punishment.

The state's interest in efficiency also may lead to some enhancement of autonomy of the previously marginalized classes, in that instrumental concerns may produce the organization of political participation—the capacity to influence the allocation of public goods and services—at the bottom of the political pyramid.

One of the intrinsic weaknesses of an authoritarian regime is the lack of adequate feedback mechanisms. Having eliminated all political competition, how can the leadership monitor the performance of officials at the end of the chain of command? Of course, they can and do set up a duplicate structure of party and state to verify performance. But this is expensive and filled with the promise of debilitating bureaucratic conflict. Moreover, it does not rule out collusion between officials and party monitors. Thus it may be very useful, even necessary, to empower ordinary citizens to discipline errant officials. Empowering the objects of governments to evaluate their immediate governors serves to enhance bureaucratic performance and helps build active loyalty to the regime. In addition, the revolutionary elite may see it as another way to transform social consciousness from individualistic toward more communal conceptions.

Perhaps all these considerations were at work in the Cuban decision to create the Organs of Popular Power that made their national debut in 1976.[28] They were designed to invest the general citizenry with power to oversee governmental activity at the local, provincial, and national level, but so far have shown signs of efficacy at the local level only.

Municipal delegates are nominated at open meetings held in the barrios. Apparently, party activists closely monitor the nomination process, but they do not exclude all nonparty members. Candidates chosen by majority vote in these gatherings then compete for selection as delegates from a large urban unit to Municipal Popular Power. In the end, about 75% of delegates are members of the Communist Party or affiliated organizations.

Without going into detail, let me say that this institution does provide some participation, in two respects. One of its functions is to take care of the needs of citizens. For example, citizens can go to delegates or members of Municipal Popular Power in much the same way that citizens of, say, Chicago can go to ward leaders to obtain assistance from the state to carry out some personal task or to fulfill some personal need, such as obtaining building materials. The other is to monitor the operations of municipal government. Delegates are required to report to their constituents periodically with respect to promises made at earlier meetings. Even the obligation to admit to and explain failure must have some disciplining effect. Beyond that, the election process goes on, and it is possible to remove delegates at the local level. There is no indication at this time of Popular Power gradually extending its influence up through the provisional and into the national level, where the most important allocations of public goods continue to be made by a very small elite.

Let us suppose that by distributing land and strengthening the infrastructure of small-scale agriculture, by creating jobs, by generalizing social security, and by opening Cuba's recreational centers to urban marginals and rural proletarians, that by doing all these things Castro's revolution actually enhanced some people's sense of autonomy, dignity, and well-being. That supposition rests on assumptions about the relationship between changes in material conditions and changes in subjective states, assumptions that, through a process of introspection and projection, external observers like myself find plausible. The remarkable anthropologist Oscar Lewis was struggling to test this assumption when premature death cut short his research. Without the benefit of his completed study—which at best would have been only suggestive—we fall back on projections from personal experience and from the negative self-images, documented by Lewis and others, among marginalized people in several Latin communities.[29]

But accepting my initial assumption about the subjectively liberating effects of Castro's reforms, and assuming further that these effects required a radical transformation of state–society relationships imposed without broad consultation and consent, is it then possible to construct a satisfactory moral calculus for the Cuban Revolution? Certainly the calculus must take account of the reduced freedom and, in many cases, exile for the upper classes. It must, in addition, incorporate, as best it can, speculations about the future course of the revolution, about what happens to intellectuals no longer absorbed in the struggle for elementary social justice, and former marginals, now literate and economically secure, ready to exercise their new freedom. The former will inevitably return to their natural role of social critic; the latter, having been endowed with the security and dignity of a bourgeoisie, will be drawn into the universal culture of consumerism, seeking satisfaction in material acquisition and the space to express idiosyncrasy and ambition. If the regime cannot respond by creating space for its former supporters and by establishing competitive channels to resolve the allocative and other contradictions inherent in every social organism—if, in brief, the regime attempts to maintain the social and political solidarity and consensual hierarchic structure of the revolutionary moment—its claim to having once served as a liberating force will be drowned by the cries of its new prisoners. Beyond losing any present claim to moral esteem, it would thereby compel us to recalculate the value of its original achievement.

Jeane Kirkpatrick and her acolytes, in hawking the distinction between authoritarian regimes of the Left and Right,[30] refuse, in their rabidly dogmatic way, to impute to the former any possible initial contributions to human dignity and autonomy. Instead, they indict the leftist variant, not only for its presumed stability, but precisely because of its supposedly *unalterable* vocation for the comprehensive elimination of autonomous institutions and individual space. The empirical base for this claim has always seemed to me reminiscent of George Bernard Shaw's description of metaphysical inquiries: it is, he said, like searching in an unlit cellar for a black cat who is not there.

Regimes that acquire power through force of arms and with the intention of transforming both society and economy for egalitarian ends continue to assume a remarkable diversity of forms and tolerances. They include Albania's Gothic tyranny; Yugoslavia, with its decentralized economic system, ongoing experiment in worker control, and considerable tolerance of ethnic and religious diversity; Poland, with its large private–farming sector; consumerist Hungary; Nicaragua, where 60% of the economy remains in private hands; China, once derided as the land of blue ants, whose leaders, dismissed at one time as crazed ideologues, are reexamining some (but, unfortunately, not all) fundamental tenets of the society; and of course that arthritic giant, the Soviet Union, which fanatics persist in regarding as the natural or archetypical revolutionary Marxist state. None are democratic. All constrain the autonomy of their citizens in ways that violate liberal conceptions of civil and political rights. But the comparison proposed is not with democracies; it is with authoritarian regimes consecrated to the maintenance (if necessary—as it often is—by unspeakable means) of levels of inequality that in operation exert broad and powerful restraints on human autonomy. Anyone who thinks that human dignity enjoys wider scope and better protection in Guatemala than Yugoslavia must have spent her life screwed to a chair in an otherwise empty room at The Heritage Foundation.

The claim that authoritarian regimes of the Left, precisely because they seek to transform frozen societies, are peculiarly resistant to liberty-enhancing revolution is equally without foundation. Though still very tight, Party control over the lives of the Chinese population has palpably eased. Moreover, by moving, as they apparently are, to a partially privatized small business sector and to the substitution of market forces for political commands to drive large areas of the economy, Deng Xiaoping and his associates are beginning to open wider spaces for the expression of individual preference, however little they may like the prospect.

Yugoslavia, emerging from the horrors of German occupation as a rough, highly centralized autocracy, with Tito as its Stalin, has evolved into what most observers regard as one of the less coercive authoritarian states. Nor does Yugoslavia set the limits of possible evolution. At the time of its displacement by the Red Army in the spring of 1968, the Czechoslovakian Communist Party seemed headed toward the restoration of political competition and the relinquishment of monopoly power. Neither a generation of indoctrination nor the perquisites of power nor the fear of Soviet intervention prevented the emergence, at the apex of the Communist party, of leaders with a passion to open the system. If any counterfactual proposition can be deemed certain, it is that, were it not for invasion, today's Czech government would be a social democracy, the form natural to the country's tradition and its phase of socioeconomic development.[31]

The evolution of Latin America's two extant revolutionary regimes, Cuba and Nicaragua, remains problematic. Revolutionary regimes founded by a charismatic leader tend to remain frozen in their initial posture until the leader dies or, as in the case of Tito, he himself chooses a new course. The likelihood of that occurring in the Cuban case, or in any other where the revolution confronts a credible external threat, is slight. If Cuba and the United States achieved rapprochement, then a major liberalization of the regime would not be astonishing, at least in the wake of Castro's death.

Cuba has in place many preconditions of an authentically liberal regime. Its population is healthy and literate and socially integrated. The majority are workers, teachers, and civil servants, the normal constituency of social democratic regimes in developed countries. The army has evolved within a tradition of civilian control, and as a consequence of its experience, ideology, and indoctrination, is closely linked to civil society. So it offers a considerable contrast to the airless, alienated, generally parasitic military institutions endemic to most of Latin America. Finally, the aspiration to republican government is an enduring feature of Latin America's political culture. Cuba would, in this respect, be an improbable exception. As a country located ninety miles off the coast of Florida, it cannot forever resist the magnetic attraction of a neighboring society devoted to competition and consumption.

Senior party leaders probably would continue to play important roles in a more pluralistic Cuba. They have grounds for confidence in sustained electoral success should they open the political process to competition. Though the population now wants more comfort, more individual opportunity, more space for self-expression, the great bulk of those who remain on the Island seem committed to the achievements of the revolution. The men and women who made that revolution therefore would begin electoral life with enormous advantages. Under conditions of immaculate electoral freedom, the Swedish Socialist Party, unaided by any heroic mystique, won steady electoral majorities for over four uninterrupted decades. With the head start they have achieved, the Cuban revolutionary elite, reconstituted as a democratic socialist party, could well match that record. By contrast, as literacy and urbanization spread, right-wing authoritarian governments, being coalitions of self-aggrandizing military establishments and wealthy minorities, cannot face free elections with equanimity unless they have previously succeeded in liquidating the leadership and destroying the institutions of the popular classes.

The fact remains, however, that, whatever the immediate achievements of revolutionary elites in enhancing the dignity and autonomy and the physical conditions of the marginal classes, and whatever their capacity for evolution, their initial triumph and subsequent consolidation will be paid for in the coin of human pain. The scope of the desired transformation precludes interclass compromise. The revolution cannot be negotiated.

The awful hostilities generated by civil war tend, in its aftermath, to spill over the constraints of the reconstituted system of justice into merciless vendettas. Moreover, to consolidate the revolution, the new regime must mobilize the popular classes to guard against counterrevolution and thus entrust power to leaders with neither the means, the training, nor the incentive to achieve an at least rough-and-ready due process. In sum, though there are certainly cases where advocates of revolution can make a strong moral claim for support against an intransigent and ruthless regime, the cost of revolution cannot be casually discounted.[32]

I suppose that for most American audiences, whose selective vision is inimical to revolutionary claims, the caveat is gratuitous. President Reagan warns that, in the event of successful revolutions in Central America, "feet people" will inundate the country's southern border, all the while blithely ignoring the fact that if the United States opened its doors to the Haitian victims of Duvalier's political economy, no one would remain in Haiti other than the butcher, his court, and his thugs. Conservatives conjure images of future bloodbaths as if the forty thousand dead noncombatants in El Salvador were a mere drip.

In subtler cases, even liberals can be myopic. During Peru's first Belaunde administration, a competitively elected civilian government of the center, the armed forces, in the course of their successful efforts to suppress rural guerrilla movements sparked by or at least associated with peasant land hunger, killed hundreds of Indian peasants. Subsistence farmers with a life expectancy a little over half that of the haute bourgeoisie of Lima, these peasants died because of their passion for land that had doubtlessly belonged to their ancestors and whose redistribution was already favored in theory by a majority of Peru's political elite. The reform bill was stalled in a congress riven by personal feuds and manipulated by a tiny landed elite that exploited to the full its wealth and prestige. It remained stalled until the armed forces suspended party politics, promulgated even more sweeping reforms, and implemented them before landowners could complete the decapitalization of their estates that had been initiated in anticipation of the congressional reforms.

Admittedly, the areas where the massacres occurred were remote. Admittedly, they occurred before the international human rights movement had developed to the point where it had become a force capable of driving issues onto the diplomatic agenda and into the mass media. Yet the mild reaction of Western liberals and moderates to news of the killings hints at an almost visceral inability to perceive the degree of official violence that can coexist with a competitive politics.

VI

Land redistribution was the most celebrated and apparently the most enduring of the reforms managed in Peru by the government of General Juan Velasco Alvarado.[33] The regime's declared purposes were to break the hegemony of the old landed oligarchy, promote national integration, reduce dependency on foreign centers of economic power, improve the distribution of wealth, and accelerate the process of economic modernization. In the course of its seven-year tenure, it decreed sweeping changes in the structure of industry and the press similar in character to those carried out by General Hernandez in my hypothetical Golfo Profundo, changes that did not proceed very far while Velasco held power and that did not long survive his fall.

Whether, as some commentators argue, the net effect of General Velasco's effort to impose reform has, despite its many failures, enhanced the authentically democratic potential of Peruvian politics is an issue beyond the scope of this essay. As I suggested earlier, what interests me primarily here is whether attempts like the Peruvian one to alter quickly and decisively a highly unequal distribution of social power and personal welfare must inevitably come into conflict with human rights norms. Or, conversely, can and should those norms be construed in ways that provide space for egalitarian reform?

My conclusion is that they can and should—if the reformist or revolutionary project passes two threshold tests. First, it must fully respect those rights that, according to the constitutive legal documents and our regnant moral consensus, cannot be qualified or suspended under any circumstances. I refer, of course, to the rights to life, to freedom from brutal treatment during arrest, interrogation, detention, or at any other time, to due process of law, to the free exercise of religious belief, to freedom from discrimination on the basis of race, sex, creed, or culture, to free opinion, and finally, the right to maintain the autonomy and integrity of the family unit. Second, it cannot regard the sudden, sharp concentration of power generally required to carry out radical reforms as anything more than a brief transitional expedient. Prolonged suspension of political competition would be clear evidence of bad faith on this account.

A revolutionary government satisfying these threshold conditions should be able to carry out its vocation without conflict with human rights norms. For example, the American Convention on Human Rights simply requires "just compensation" where property is expropriated and adds, moreover, that "the law may subordinate . . . use and enjoyment [of property] to the interest of society." Partial compensation, progressive income taxes, a bias toward the poor in the allocation of public works, and subsidized credit seem to me equally legitimate methods for promoting social justice and national development. They are, as well, means for realizing the rights consecrated in the American Declaration on the Rights and Duties of Man that was unanimously adopted by the member states of the Organization of American States in 1948. Article XIV of the declaration recognizes that "every person has the right to work [and] to social security which will protect him from the consequences of unemployment, old age and disabilities arising from causes beyond his control."

General Hernandez's effort to break the oligarchy's control of Golfo Profundo's mass media also should survive normative assault. Nothing in the American Convention equates untrammeled private ownership with "Freedom of Thought and Expression." On the contrary, Article XIII condemns restraints on the exercise of this freedom even if they emanate from the private sector: "The right to expression may not be restricted by indirect methods or means, such as the abuse of government or private controls over newsprint, radio broadcasting frequencies . . . or by any other means tending to impede the communication and circulation of ideas and opinions."

The human rights norms of this hemisphere codify not the practice of governments, but the ideals governments feel compelled to concede. As such, these norms are no obstacle to revolutions that seek, by means respectful of fundamental rights, the more equal distribution of power, wealth, and freedom.

Notes

1. American Declaration of the Rights and Duties of Man, adopted by the Ninth International Conference on American States, Bogota, 1948; American Convention on Human Rights, signed at the Inter-American Specialized Conference on Human Rights, San Jose, Costa Rica, November 22, 1969, entered into force on July 18, 1978 (having in that year obtained the requisite eleventh ratification), and, as of September, 1983, ratified or adhered to by seventeen member states of the Organization of American States. States not parties to the convention are subject to in most respects equivalent provisions of the declaration (See Article 20 of the Statute of the Inter-American Commission on Human Rights of the OAS, hereinafter cited as IACHR). The declaration, the convention, the statute, and the regulations of the commission, plus the statute of the Inter-American Court of Human Rights, are contained in the *Handbook of Existing Rules Pertaining to Human Rights,* published by the OAS.
2. The inspiration for this scenario stems in part from Terry Karl's description of the 1957–58 transition to democracy in Venezuela in her working paper for the Latin American Program of The Woodrow Wilson International Center for Scholars, "Petroleum and Political Pacts: The Transition to Democracy in Venezuela" (no. 107, 1981).
3. The sixteen-year power-sharing agreement is obviously based on the Columbian arrangement, the National Front, which restored civilian rule after the terrible *violencia* of the 1940s and 1950s and the resulting military government of General Rojas Pinilla. For a useful description and evaluation of The National Front, see *The Politics of Compromise,* edited by R. Albert Berry, Ronald G. Hellman, and Mauricio Solaun (New Brunswick, New Jersey; Transaction Books, 1980).
4. When the IACHR arrived in Buenos Aires in September 1979, we were informed that during the prior two years, when people were being picked up all over the city, never to reappear, not one of the city's Spanish-language newspapers published any reports about this phenomenon. No formal governmental directive commanded their silence.
5. When the IACHR visited El Salvador in January 1978, I was struck by the uniform approach to that country's impressive human rights problems taken by the leading newspapers, both in their "news" and their "editorial" pages. In essence, they seemed resolutely insensitive to the existence of any human rights problems.
6. The rules governing observations *in loco* are contained in Chapter IV of the Commission's Regulations.
7. Rather, as in the United States, Latin American social security systems have evolved incrementally, reflecting ad hoc elite concessions to politically mobilized groups rather than a general functional or ethical conception of public responsibility to ease deprivation.

8. For Peruvian efforts to promote worker managements, see Peter T. Knight, "New Forms of Economic Organization in Peru: Toward Workers' Self-Management," in *The Peruvian Experiment*, edited by Abraham F. Lowenthal (Princeton: Princeton University Press, 1975), pp. 350–401.
9. Peru's reformist military government (1968–74) seized the country's leading daily newspapers for the declared end of creating "an authentically independent press." A useful analysis of the problematic consequences is Dennis Gilbert's "Society, Politics, and the Press." *Journal of Inter-American Studies and World Affairs,* August 1979, pp. 369–92.
10. The tribunals established by the government of Nicaragua, following the overthrow of the Somoza regime, to try persons accused of crimes allegedly carried out on behalf of the deposed regime had a somewhat similar structure.
11. Article 8, *Right to a Fair Trial.* Paragraph 1. Every person has the right to a hearing, with due guarantees and within a reasonable time, by a competent, independent, and impartial tribunal, previously established by law, in the substantiation of any accusation of a criminal nature made against him or for the determination of his rights and obligations of a civil, labor, fiscal, or any other nature.
12. Article 21. *Right to Property.* 1. Everyone has the right to the use and enjoyment of his property. The law may subordinate such use and enjoyment to the interest of society. 2. No one shall be deprived of his property except upon payment of just compensation, for reasons of public utility or social interest, and in the case and according to the forms established by law. 3. Usury and any other form of exploitation of man by man shall be prohibited by law.
13. Article 23. *Right to Participate in Government.* 1. Every citizen shall enjoy the following rights and opportunities: (a) to take part in the conduct of public affairs, directly or through freely chosen representatives; (b) to vote and to be elected in genuine periodic elections, which shall be by universal and equal suffrage and by secret ballot that guarantees the free expression of the will of the voters; and (c) to have access, under general conditions of equality, to the public service of his country. 2. The law may regulate the exercise of the rights and opportunities referred to in the preceding paragraph only on the basis of age, nationality, residence, language, education, civil and mental capacity, or sentencing by a competent court in criminal proceedings.
14. Cf. *No Easy Choice,* by Samual P. Huntington and Joan Nelson (Cambridge: Harvard University Press, 1976), p. 22: "If the bourgeois model is followed [in the early stages of industrialization], political participation is expanded to encompass the urban middle class and economic growth proceeds reasonably rapidly. Economic inequality also increases, both as a concomitant of economic growth *and as a result of the utilization by the middle class of its political power to further its own ends."* (italics added)
15. See, for example, OAS General Assembly Resolution 371, adopted July 1, 1978, in which the Assembly resolved: "5. To reaffirm that, in the search for economic and social justice, human dignity and the freedom of the individual as expressed in the American Declaration of the Rights and Duties of Man must be preserved and the rule of law respected. 6. To reaffirm the conviction that there are no circumstances that justify torture, summary execution, or prolonged detention without due process of law, and to deplore these transgressions, which would violate the fundamental rights of man."
16. On the fall of Chilean democracy, see Arturo Valenzuela's "Chile," in *The*

Breakdown of Democratic Regimes, edited by Juan J. Linz and Alfred Stepan (Baltimore: Johns Hopkins University Press, 1981); and Paul Sigmund, *The Fall of Allende* (Pittsburgh: University of Pittsburgh Press, 1977).

17. Karl, "Petroleum and Political Pacts."
18. Within the large and still growing literature on the interplay of politics and economics in contemporary Latin America, two high points are *The New Authoritarianism in Latin America,* edited by David Collier (Princeton: Princeton University Press, 1979) and Alain de Janvry, *The Agrarian Question and Reformism in Latin America* (Baltimore: Johns Hopkins University Press, 1981).
19. Hollis Chenery, et al., *Redistribution with Growth: Policies to Improve Distribution in Developing Countries in the Context of Economic Growth* (Oxford University Press, 1974).
20. See, for example, Simon Kuznetts, "Economic Growth and Income Inequality." *American Economic Review,* March 1955, p. 45: "Widening in the early phases of economic growth when the transition from pre-industrial to the industrial civilization was most rapid: becoming stabilized for a while, and then narrowing in the later phases." Quoted in Sylvia Ann Hewlett, "Human Rights and Economic Realities," in *The Future of The Inter-American System,* edited by Tom J. Farer (New York: Praeger, 1979), p. 86.
21. Susan Eckstein, "Revolution and Redistribution in Latin America," in *The Peruvian Experiment Reconsidered,* edited by Cynthia McClintock and Abraham E. Lowenthal (Princeton: Princeton University Press, 1983), p. 359.
22. Kuznetts, "Economic Growth and Income Inequality."
23. Harry Johnson, *Money, Trade and Economic Growth,* p. 153: "There is likely to be a conflict between rapid growth and an equitable distribution of incomes and a poor country anxious to develop would probably be well advised not to worry too much about the distribution of income." Cited by Hewlett, "Human Rights and Economic Realities," p. 27.
24. Hewlett is typical. See generally *ibid.* and her book *The Cruel Dilemmas of Development: Twentieth Century Brazil* (New York: Basic Books, 1979).
25. An unpublished paper prepared for the Inter-American Commission on Human Rights.
26. On the development of the Cuban economy, see Carmelo Mesa-Lago, *The Economy of Socialist Cuba* (Albuquerque, N.M.: University of New Mexico Press, 1981) and Jorge I. Dominguez, *Cuba* (Cambridge: Harvard University Press, 1978), pp. 173-90, 383-91.
27. The amount of the subsidy has varied over time, and the subsidy has assumed a variety of forms—which is one of the reasons estimates of the extent of the subsidy are both rough and problematical. See generally, Mesa-Lago, *The Economy of Socialist Cuba,* pp. 186-87 and Dominguez, *Cuba,* pp. 149-59. To put the Soviet subsidy in some perspective, U.S. grant aid to the State of Israel for fiscal year 1983 is $1.485 billion. Israel's population is approximately one third the size of Cuba's.
28. For a concise description of the Organs of Popular Power in operation, see Elden Kenworthy, "Dilemmas of Participation in Latin America," *Democracy,* Winter 1983, pp. 72-83.
29. See, for example, Oscar Lewis, *The Children of Sanchez* (New York: Random House, 1961).
30. See "Dictatorships and Double Standards," *Commentary,* November 1979, p. 34; my critique of Kirkpatrick's manipulation of the authoritarian-totalitarian distinction appears in *The New York Review of Books,* March 19, 1981.

31. See James R. Kurth's remarkably perceptive essay "The United States and Central America: Hegemony in Historical and Comparative Perspective," in *Central America: International Dimensions of the Crisis,* edited by Richard E. Feinberg (New York: Holmes & Meier, 1982), pp. 39–57. He compares the hegemonic crises experienced by the Soviet Union and the United States growing out of the changing political telos in their respective spheres of influence.
32. For a sophisticated systematic effort to test the human rights balance of the Cuban revolution, see Jorge I. Dominguez's essay "Assessing Human Rights Conditions," in *Enhancing Global Human Rights* (New York: McGraw Hill, 1980s Project/Council on Foreign Relations, 1979), pp. 21–116. A less systematic but equally interesting effort to sketch a moral calculus for the whole process of political and economic development is Peter Berger's *Pyramids of Sacrifice* (New York: Basic, 1974).
33. For diverse assessments of the Velasco regime's achievements, see McClintock and Lowenthal, *The Peruvian Experiment Reconsidered.*

PART III
LAW AND THE PRACTICE OF INTERVENTION:

INTRODUCTION TO PART III:
ON THE LIMITS OF IMPARTIALITY

The subject of foreign intervention in civil armed conflict invites partisan essays not only because it implicates many of the great moral issues which infuse contemporary life, but also because its normative contours are so uncertain. A stunning diversity of international agreements, multinational declarations and resolutions, state claims and acts—a veritable potlatch of "evidence"—endows both scholars and governments with an insidiously broad discretion in the identification and application of governing norms.

Despite the relative indeterminacy of the norms and intensity of the passions which surround the phenomenon of foreign involvement in civil violence, some scholars still insist on the obligation—and hence, presumably, on the possibility—of impartial judgment. At the conclusion of a deliciously astringent review of a book on the legal aspects of the Indo-Chinese war, an eminent colleague, Professor George Ginsbergs, having congratulated the author on his capacities as an advocate, announces his own continuing commitment to the tradition of objective scholarship.[1]

Professor Ginsbergs, if taken literally, urges us to an inhuman perfection. Given the uniqueness of the actions which are the raw material of legal analysis, as well as their emphatic moral resonance, we cannot reasonably expect to discover incontestable truths. Epistemological assumptions, hunches, political and moral preference all must accompany and influence the investigation of the existing normative order and, of course, proposals for its progressive development.

But there are standards! And they go beyond Kenneth Boulding's impish observation during a discussion of international fact finding: "Of course, there are no facts . . . but there are lies." An honest effort to adduce all of the evidence that legal scholars, regardless of political and jurisprudential affiliation, deem essential to the identification and application of authoritative norms, is the obvious first condition of scholarly integrity.

Unfortunately, its satisfaction will never be indisputable. Life itself is short and books, you will be gratified to recall, are shorter still. Selection is unavoidable. Inevitably, someone somewhere will denounce the neglect of bits of data he or she deems relevant. So be it.

Respect for antagonistic analysis of the evidence—respect that is for competing summaries of trends in decision, usually expressed as conclusions about the state of the law—and respect for the policy appraisal offered either to support or to urge modification of the perceived trends is the second canon of academic integrity. Respect is evidenced by fair presentation of and detailed response to antagonistic positions. Which is only to reiterate the almost banal perception that where the subject is man, the appropriate form of discourse is dialectical.

I harbor no illusion that a dialectical process will carry us ineluctably to the true or truly just norms. But it can clarify the nature and consequences of choices bequeathed by historical processes to contemporary participants in the society of nations.

My announced appreciation of the subjectivities of legal scholarship should not disarm you, although for all one knows that might be its subconscious intent. I should be treated as if I were the scientist hypothesized by Allen Wheelis, the scientist who tells us:

> I am so skeptical of every assertion . . . so likely to find uncertainty in even the best established theory, so inclined to hold back truth, to keep it tentative, that you may leave your doubts with me. When I say *fact* you can be sure.

"So he lulls us," Wheelis concludes, "so we are beguiled."[2]

Notes

1. George Ginsbergs, *American Journal of Comparative Law,* Vol. 21 (1973), pp. 337-38.
2. *The End of the Modern Age,* 1973, p. 42.

12

On the Nature of Law in a Decentralized Political System

Most international lawyers are committed to the belief that law, rather than being a mere fig leaf for the raw thrust of national power, is an independent variable exerting, in Tony D'Amato's apt phrase, a certain pressure on national decision makers. This fraternal consensus fractures, however, as soon as discussion turns to the questions: What is the exact nature of the phenomenon generally called law which influences decision, and how or why does it achieve the asserted effect?

The Traditionalists

With respect to the former question, traditionalists accept, at least implicitly, H.L.A. Hart's description of any complete legal system as a union of primary and hierarchically ordered secondary rules that are treated by the system's administrators as compelling guides to decision and are generally obeyed by ordinary citizens.[1]

By primary rules, Hart means a society's agglomeration of authoritative normative statements governing social behavior such as the prescriptions of criminal and tort law. By secondary rules, he refers to the corpus of normative statements that communicate the means by which primary rules can be identified, applied, enforced, and changed. They are, in other words, rules about rules. Of these secondary rules the "Rule of Recognition" is necessarily preeminent in that only by recourse to it can we determine the legitimacy or authoritativeness of competing claims with respect to the existence, application, enforcement, or modification of both primary and other secondary rules.

If a given social system is sufficiently complex so that there is more than one criterion for distinguishing authoritative norms from other kinds (e.g., rules of etiquette or moral standards), then the imperatives of order require that there be, within the Rule of Recognition, a further hierarchy culminating in a single ultimate criterion of legitimacy. Its existence assures, at least in principle, that every dispute about the law can be resolved definitively, since competing claims logically cannot enjoy equal validity.

For the traditionalists, "consent" is the ultimate criterion of the international legal system. Its claims to ascendancy have rested on both deductive and inductive grounds. Deductively, it is seen as a corollary of the doctrine of the legal equality of sovereigns that emerged after the Treaty of Westphalia to order the European political system. The imposition of rules—even by commanding majorities—is perceived to be inconsistent with equality, except where there is prior consent to accept the results of a "legislative" process. Inductively, the consent theory is based on recurring governmental manifestations of a ferocious insistence on a state's discretion to select ends, and means for their fulfillment, except where limitations have been assumed voluntarily.

Under the criterion of consent, most treaties were clearly "binding" or "valid" as express manifestations of the concordance of sovereign wills. Customary law was rationalized as a case of implicit consent.

Traditionalist scholars and governmental leaders both realized, no doubt, that an extreme consensual rationale for international law nullified the phenomenon's cardinal virtue: a capacity to lend greater stability to intergovernmental relations. It was therefore essential to interpret consent in such a way that it would not be perpetually susceptible to withdrawal at whim. This was accomplished by the dictum that states could consent to the relinquishment of their freedom to withdraw their consent. With respect to customary law, consent to relinquishment was presumed to coincide with initial consent to the rule in question.

By this means, customary rules were rendered obligatory. But before they could operate, they had to be identified. Consent being implicit, intermediate evidentiary criteria had to be developed in order to distinguish legal rules both from mere coincidence in state behavior and from relational norms which have not yet hardened into rights and duties.

Two such criteria have achieved wide scholarly recognition. In order to negate the danger of a rule being inferred from identical means of dealing with domestic problems, one criterion requires that the subject matter of any alleged rule must fall within the domain of international relations.[2] Thus, even if, for example, every nation–state were to eschew the death penalty, so long as the individualized deprivations employed to maintain domestic order are not perceived to raise issues of substantial international concern, a state might revert to capital punishment without fear of challenge.

The second criterion is, in theory, subjective: Concurrent practice is legally relevant only where it can be shown that the practice is motivated by the belief that it is legally obligatory or, in the more moderate articulation, that the practice is at least consistent with prevailing law (the so-called *opinio juris*).[3]

As a group, the traditionalists have not evinced a deep interest in the behavioral mechanism by means of which their perceived regime of rules has affected or governed the ultimate act of political decision. They seem to have regarded this problem as one raising essentially extralegal questions best left to the political scientists. On the whole, therefore, they have been content to assert that states, as a consequence of their participation in the international legal order, are "obligated" to obey its rules.

Although the reference to obligation might be construed simply as a reference to a deductively necessary consequence of the hypothesized legal order or as a vivid way of invoking alleged long-run self-interest in the face of each day's temptations to seize a unilateral advantage, it has in addition always carried the suggestion of moral adjuration. And, given the central role played by consent in the moral systems of most societies, the human tendency to transfer compelling moral perspectives to new contexts and the fact that in the epoch of its inception international law was conceived to govern the relations between identifiable human sovereigns or small homogeneous elites connected by personal relationships, the attribution of moral significance to legally conforming behavior seems to have been ineluctable. It also was desirable in that it lent international law a certain compulsion beyond that engendered by the sanction of retaliation and the putative long-run advantage of preserving the integrity of a means for reducing provocation and facilitating cooperation.

Every gain has its cost. By identifying consent as the fountainhead of international law, the traditionalists buttressed the latter's defenses. But in so doing they sacrificed, among other things, a fully developed—some would even say coherent—theory of legal change.

The main obstacle to coherence was the insistence on *opinio juris*. Professor D'Amato has sketched the concept's difficulties:

> How indeed can [it] help to explain 'the emergence of a principle or rule of customary international law.' ... Any new rule of customary law would be based on practice that by definition could not be "required by" or "consistent with" prior law. More importantly, [the] formula cannot explain how existing laws could change, for a change in the law would again by definition be based on practice that was not "consistent with" prevailing law. [p.8].

When a theory of law cannot provide a completely intelligible account of change in the content of legal norms, one may entertain doubt about either the efficacy of the theory or the reality of the order it purports to describe.

There are observers who have inclined toward the latter alternative, seeing the international legal system as a system *manqué*, lacking developed rules of change and, by implication, wholly realized criteria of recognition. But most academicians have conceded the inadequacy of theory. Some have coped with that concession by exploring alternative strategies of explanation, including in at least two instances the bizarre proposal that the initial momentum of a developing customary rule must originate in a government's erroneous belief that a certain practice is already obligatory. Others—noting that, despite conceptual inadequacies, courts and governments use, in varying combinations and emphases, the postulated elements of customary law in making claims and deciding cases—have discounted the importance of an entirely coherent theory. It is sufficient, they imply, simply to note that, for a variety of "extralegal" reasons, both verbal support for and behavioral consistency with a given norm will sometimes flag until it is demonstrably replaced by a new norm commanding respect at the levels of rhetoric and deed.

The Yale School

In the early decades of this century, while the mandarins of international law were fretting over the inelegance of their postulates, a small, pugnacious group of American legal philosophers concerned primarily with domestic legal phenomena were laying the foundations for a massive assault on the verities of international law. Launching themselves from Holmes's dictum that law is merely a prediction of what the courts will do, these "realists" derided the capacity of norms either to predict or explain decisions and insisted that the main subject of scholarly attention must be the entire value–allocative process. Through their persistence, law found itself being dragged from the serene realm of language into the grubby republic of human behavior.

As a center of legal realism and of its sibling, the behavioral school of political science, Yale was a natural incubator for the two great bulls, Harold Lasswell and Myres McDougal, who some three decades ago plunged into the china shop of international legal thought and began smashing up the carefully husbanded piles of conventional wisdom.[4]

Where the traditionalists have always conceived their function to be that of identifying norms and measuring state conduct against them, Lasswell and McDougal claim a more ambitious vocation for international lawyers, namely that of maximizing the rationality of authoritative decision. Law properly understood is for them a policy science, the practitioners of which play vizier to a nation's sultans. In essence, their declared function is to clarify the decision makers' value preferences and, by analyzing in light of decisional trends the relevant facets of particular decisional contexts, to predict the value–allocative consequences of the behavioral choices open to national leaders at any given time.

Rules are reduced to receptacles of useful information, mere summaries of past decisional trends. As such, they suggest, with varying degrees of accuracy, the expectations of relevant audiences concerning behavior and their attitudes towards authority. In this capacity, rules, like other kinds of data, might influence decision;[5] but being nakedly instrumental, they can hardly command it.

If rules are only data, where then can one find the "law"? It consists, Lasswell and McDougal conclude, in the convergence of perspectives of authority and expectations of control.[6] *Authority,* according to Michael Reisman, a leading disciple of the Yale masters, "is a set of conditioned subjectivities shared by relevant members of a group; when operative, when tripped so to speak by outside events, these subjectivities provide the individuals concerned with an indication of appropriate behavior. Authority can be considered a significant determinant of individual or group behavior, not necessarily when it compels a certain course, but when it indicates that course with a degree of clarity sufficient to excite internal tension or psychic dysphoria if an incompatible course is followed."[7]

Control, he writes, "refers to resources that can be employed to secure a desired pattern of behavior in others."[8] By itself, control is, in other words, raw power.

This and comparable definitions employed by the Yale School—e.g., "Lawful decision must be both authoritative and controlling" and "Law is a delicate balance of authority and control"[9]—are not designed to suggest that prescriptions become "binding" or "legal" when they cross some magical threshold on the respective continua of a society's perceptions of authority and expectations of control. The point to remember is that, for the McDougalites, there is no brooding reality beyond those perceptions and expectations. "Law" is simply a summary reference to cases where the perceptions are fairly intense and uniform and expectations rather high. Lawfulness thus becomes a question of degree.

Some may wonder why, having shaped a technical language to their special purposes, the Yale School's devotees have not abandoned the term "law" altogether, encrusted as it is with a plethora of traditionalist connotations. I suppose the answer is that, however they may deplore the term's ambiguity, they concede its continued force as a symbolic value in social relations. By invoking its name, they domesticate and thus encourage adoption of their methodology for decision making.

It may also be asked why, in light of McDougal's acknowledgment that the layman tends to equate law with authority alone,[10] followers of the Yale

School insist on adding the factor of control. The answer lies in their conception of law as a guidance device for decision makers and also, of course, for those affected by decision. By defining law or, more to the point "lawful decision," in terms of authority and control, they guide the decision maker to a consideration of both factors. If he ignores the relevant audience's conception of the requisites of authoritative decision, he can anticipate resistance to the value allocation which the decision purports to effect and he may reduce the efficacy of subsequent efforts to clothe decision with authority. Similarly, decisions which comport fully with authority expectations but which will not be enforced—i.e., which are unsupported by the value allocations required to overcome anticipated resistance—also may reduce the efficacy of authority. Although, if asked, people generally will equate authority with law, this is so at least in part because of their subconscious expectation that authoritative decisions will be controlling. If this expectation is consistently disappointed, the perceived focus of authority will necessarily shift, probably after an extended period of uncertainty.

Once one accepts this account of what law is all about, customary law is stripped of that elusive quality that has frustrated the traditionalists. Since rules are not "binding" in any event, there is no reason to relate them to a particular source, such as consent, which could endow them with autonomous power. And one need no longer subscribe to an epistemology shaped by the need to prove the reality of an immaterial phenomenon. Every index of prevailing authority subjectivities and control perspectives may be recognized and employed. Authority and control may converge for a great variety of political, economic, social, and ideological reasons. Those reasons are the "sources" of the law.

The Practical Consequences of Theory?

Despite dramatic verbal dissimilarities between traditionalist and Yale–School conceptions, is it clear that the latter's account of the nature of law frequently will yield distinctive operational results? Consider, for instance, the question of whether there are customary rules of law governing the conduct of military operations in a civil war. During a recent discussion of war crimes in Vietnam, one distinguished traditionalist flatly denied the existence of a customary law of land and aerial warfare applicable to civil war. I imagine he would concede that most authoritative decision makers and private individuals concerned with international affairs would be outraged and shocked if, for example, nuclear weapons were employed by either side in a civil conflict. I suspect he would also concede that outrage might well be backed up by various forms of deprivatory behavior such as the suspension of credit to purchase arms and delivery vehicles. Nevertheless, his subsequent comments indicated that, even if he were to accept the accuracy of these predictions about perceptions and expectations, he still would not be convinced of the existence of customary rules, apparently because one cannot point to any explicit concession by national governments that the restraints that have in fact been exhibited in various contemporary civil (and mixed civil–international) conflicts are occasioned by a feeling of legal obligation. Hence, however strongly one might, on grounds of prudence and morality, advise participants in a civil war, against recourse to nuclear weapons, one could not maintain that they were under any legal restraint.

It is impossible to prove that this traditionalist's refusal to characterize proposed behavior as "illegal" would degrade his chances of dissuading the potential users of nuclear weapons or persuading other decision makers to respond with effective sanctions. But there are reasons why it might, even if one discounts the word's symbolic force.

First, decision making time always is limited. An advisor may not have the opportunity to elaborate his assessment of the international consequences of a proposed act. Reference to its illegality is a summary way of justifying the prediction of an intensely hostile response. Moreover, by fixing the decision maker's attention on the question of international response, the legal advisor may gain a more extended hearing than he would with advice couched in moral terms. Finally, particularly in the matrix of crises, leaders may be responsive only to dramatic, categorical statements such as "that proposal calls for blatantly illegal conduct."

A second reason relates to the problem of specialization in the advising function. Once the lawyer has opined that behavior is "legal," or at least not "illegal," decision makers may feel that his utility is exhausted and may therefore deny him any opportunity to explore the range of reciprocal behavior that proposed action may generate. Yet, by training and disposition, the international lawyer may well be preeminently sensitive to the provocative and destabilizing nature of the planned behavior, for his work consists in large measure of anticipating the response of other governments to initiatives of his own.

On the other hand, some foreign policy decision makers appear indifferent or even antagonistic to "legal" criticism of policy proposals. Perhaps this reaction is largely explicable in terms of the law's traditional association with morality, the popular foreign policy decision making style in many leading states being, after all, one of genteel amorality. If the Yale School's account of international law achieves widespread penetration of elite consciousness, this association of law with morality should be weakened and the informational features of law more fully appreciated.

Even assuming that the difference in perspective between my traditionalist professor and a behaviorist would lead to different conclusions about legality in the postulated case, I am not convinced that this difference flows inevitably from their respective jurisprudential commitments. As Professor D'Amato demonstrates, not all traditionalists impose tremendously onerous standards of proof on those who invoke the law. Traditionalists can be and often are more impressed with what states do than what they say. The truth is that, whether one seeks a quasi-mythical manifestation of consent or an ensemble of perceptions of authority and expectations of control, the primary problem remains epistemological.

In Search of an Intermediate Posture

A number of younger scholars have attempted to stake out independent positions somewhere between the perceived polarities of the traditionalists and the Yale School. They are united, I believe, not by any comprehensive alternative account of international law but rather by shared misgivings about certain features of the Yale School's approach.

The main focus of their concern is McDougal's transformation and, in their mind, evisceration of the idea of a prescription.[11] Professor D'Amato, one of the abler among those who pay only qualified tribute to Yale, expresses that concern when he writes:

> As H. L. A. Hart has demonstrated, it is central to the concept of law that the rules themselves are a *sufficient reason* for punishing one who disobeys them. On the other hand, Myres McDougal and his associates have maintained that international law is merely and solely a *process* of authoritative decision making and that . . . rules are only helpful guides to possible policy alternatives, [guides which] "exhaust their effective power when they guide a decision-maker to relevant factors and indicate presumptive weightings." [p. 11; emphasis in original.]

Unfortunately, the basis of Professor D'Amato's Hartian sympathies remains coyly veiled. Just prior to his invocation of Hart he asserts that "legal prescriptions indicate to man that which he ought to refrain from doing. In this latter usage as a prohibition and not a power, *legal rules communicate to the receiver the expectations of others (society, other nations) who might retaliate if he disobeys the prescriptions.*" [p. 11; emphasis added.] That seems to mirror McDougal's contention that rules function as prohibitions only in the sense that they warn the receiver about the content of other people's demands, that is to say, their expectations and their probable willingness to defend them. Hence, the difference between McDougal and D'Amato seems reduced to the assertion that "rules themselves are a *sufficient reason* for punishing one who disobeys them."

Unless we can divine what he means by that proposition, it is impossible to test the accuracy of Professor D'Amato's contention that his adherence to it distinguishes him from the Yale School. Perhaps he is simply asserting that in the real world of international relations, legal rules evoke a subjective response which, prior to any calculation of the danger of retaliation or of the long-run national interest in a relatively stable order or any other conscious appraisal of the consequences of rule violation, inclines officials to comply with their commands. This reflexive reaction may be reinforced by, or may in part be an internalized expression of, two conscious calculations: That, in general, widespread recognition by state officials that a body of authoritative norms exists promotes the national interest; and that there is consequently a presumption in favor of adherence, since deviation by one actor encourages deviation by others, thereby reducing the prospect for continued recognition. Both the reflex and the calculations will exert a certain pressure on the decision-making process. And even if they are not decisive, they may still affect the shape and dimension of the policy that is ultimately chosen.[12]

I am speculating, then, that Professor D'Amato is drawing a phenomenological distinction, a distinction between the scholar's perception and the operative perceptions of the men who govern the fate of nations—the former seeing rules as data banks, the latter seeing them first and perhaps primarily as prescriptions which in general ought to be obeyed.

Professor McDougal is, of course, aware of the tendency among international lawyers and political elites to think of legal rules as "binding" prescriptions. Although he hopes to eradicate that tendency, in part by educating lawyers and decision makers to see the world as he does, he couches his briefs in the traditionalist terminology in deference to its continued existence. Hence, the shape of his polemical statements does not, as Professor D'Amato contends, "attest to a different view of 'law'" or rules than the one he openly espouses (p. 12), but rather evidences a firm grasp of the distinction Professor D'Amato appears to arrogate to himself.

To be sure, the McDougalites do tend to equivocate. Sometimes they disparage a rule-oriented jurisprudence not primarily because it degrades the potential for value-maximizing decisions, but rather on the asserted grounds that, in practice, decisions are guided by value-oriented contextual assessments and not by verbal prescriptions. Since Professor D'Amato would concede that many decisions are not rule-governed, their respective positions cannot be distinguished in terms of a radically different perception of actual decision making. Where they do differ is in their appraisals of the desirability of rule-directed decisions.

D'Amato believes (as I do) that McDougal's insistence on minimizing the guidance potential of verbal prescription[13] facilitates myopically chauvinistic decisions unresponsive to collective interests, and thus leads to obliteration of the line between legality and political expediency. Indeed, he seems to feel that, in large measure, McDougal himself has already abandoned the distinction between acts which are politically expedient and those which are legal. McDougal is alleged to have preserved little more than the extremely plastic criterion of "reasonableness," i.e., what is reasonable is therefore lawful (pp. 215–29), except perhaps in the case of highly detailed and recently ratified treaty obligations. My own reading of McDougal leads to the conclusion that there is, at least in his mind, a clear distinction between authoritative decision and decisions which are merely effective. A man who writes—"Effective control . . . when it asserts decision, in the sense of imposition or threat of severe deprivation, without regard for community expectations about how and what decision should be taken, is not law but naked power or unilateral coercion"[14]—is evidently sensitive to the distinction between community–sanctioned and proscribed behavior. But, however clearly he may himself grasp the distinction, it remains perfectly possible that his jurisprudence obscures it for others.

The most interesting and important difference Professor D'Amato is trying to express concerns the possibility and desirability of promoting greater uniformity and hence predictability of decision by limiting the variety of contextual factors that a decision–maker, functioning in a claim–conflict situation, should be encouraged to take into account. This is, I think, what is really at stake in D'Amato's insistence that his conception of rules is distinguishable from that of the Yale School.

One way of perceiving a primary rule is as a two–dimensional artifact consisting of a directive to behave in a specified way and a context with certain specified features. The ambiguity of rules is partially a function of their contextual dimension, for in the nature of things there will never be a context which contains only the specified features. Any human interaction is, after all, an extraordinarily complicated mosaic of tangible and intangible phenomena. The details of time and place and participants, and related past, present, and future relationships are effectively infinite. Considered in its fullest detail, every interaction is unique;[15] indeed, even if only a small number of its potentially describable features is considered, no interaction is like any other.

A world of unique events is stupefying. We are driven to act by a belief in the relationship of things; but there is no way to relate unique events. The problem has been summarized with customary brilliance by Edward Said, the Columbia University critic and philosopher. In an unpublished paper on the nature of norms, he refers to Edmund Burke's speech *On Conciliation with the Colonies,* which

> is shot through with a powerful desire, at once moral and intellectual, to make the Parliament see everything . . . to present America as what he calls a whole object. . . . The anomalous and tragically conservative nature of Burke's effort is at once apparent when it is remarked that for Burke to have seen the whole meant always a consequent recommendation by him to withhold action. . . . He concedes everything to the solidity and particularity of an object, whose quiddity practically stultifies any action on it that one might take. . . . Burke . . . illustrates, in a particularly eloquent way . . . how thought that attempts to suit action to the full realities of a situation cannot stop until the realities overwhelm the possibility of action.

Rules are a means for reducing the overwhelming bulk of reality to socially useful proportions by attaching special significance to a few phenomena. If the phenomena are not present, the behavioral directive does not apply. But where they are, there also may be present phenomena identified as crucial by some other rule or by norms of greater generality, such as principles. Or there may be contextual features the importance of which is established by other types of rules, such as moral ones.

The contextual features included in a rule of law are selected on the assumption that where they are present, the demanded conduct will promote optimally a public policy or value. Therefore, a rule's capacity to influence decision deteriorates in cases where the presence of other, presumably unanticipated, contextual features defeats that assumption: that is to say, where the end the rule was presumably designed to achieve can be promoted more effectively by not behaving in the prescribed manner. Pressure to ignore the behavioral directive also is experienced when there is a change in the weighting of competing policies or values. If, for example, states began to be more concerned with preventing major human rights deprivations than with avoiding armed conflict, the rule inhibiting armed intervention for humanitarian purposes without U.N. authorization gradually would be reinterpreted, formally replaced, or ignored because of the pressure exerted by the shift in values.

As noted above, Professor McDougal's position is that decision-makers should treat rules only as items of evidence that can be more or less helpful in identifying the act or acquiescence which, in a given encounter between states, will maximize realization of the preferred values of the international community. A rule can almost never settle this problem in advance. The contextual features attached to the rule's directive were selected on the basis of experience with prior decisional contexts. Subsequent contexts will be different, and, their potential variety being infinite, they inevitably will present many unanticipated configurations. To promote optimal value realization in every decisional context, decision–makers are urged to engage in elaborate contextual analysis using categories developed by Lasswell and McDougal to identify and organize features which enjoy recurring importance. Thus the participants, their objectives, strategies and resources, and the immediate and long–range consequences of decisional alternatives must be examined in light of the value outcome demanded by the consensus of the international community. Where the analysis does not yield one clearly preferred outcome, in order (apparently) to balance anticipated egotistic decisions by antagonistic elites, the decision maker may legitimately choose from among the behavioral candidates the one that best promotes his own value preferences.

Professor McDougal appears to concede that analysis can be foreshortened by explicit agreement. Thus, when arguing for a broad contextual reading of the United Nations Charter's proscription of force except in cases of individual or collective self–defense "if an armed attack occurs against a member of the United Nations," he notes that the provision does not read "if, *and only if,*"[16]—thus implying that the latter articulation would have precluded the interpretative posture he proposes. In effect, then, the Yale School seems to presume a mandate for an elaborate contextual analysis except in cases where it is explicitly rejected.

Perhaps Professor D'Amato is implying that we should reverse the presumptions, except perhaps in cases where contextual features are identified at a very high level of generality. It does not follow that contextual features other than those identified can never be taken into account. An intermediate position would emphasize a rebuttable presumption of applicability whenever the specified contextual features are identified, which could be overcome only by a clear showing that the value allocation which would be effected by following the directive would conflict grossly with community preferences manifested in other normative articulations such as widely recognized principles, widely ratified multilateral treaties, and so on.

Underlying this approach to the application of rules is the fear that the prophylactic value of primary rules will be lost if their content is not stabilized by secondary rules that rigorously systematize the mechanics of rule identification and interpretation. It is assumed that the pressures of a claim–conflict situation degrade each party's capacity to identify community demands and provide incentives to ignore those demands even when they can be identified with substantial accuracy. It is also assumed that the presumed consequences of flagrant disregard of community preferences exercise some measure of restraint. That restraint is diminished to the degree that accepted modes of interpretation facilitate diverse identifications of community demands. There is, therefore, a clear community interest in shaping rules that will encourage uniform identification of those demands. To achieve this end, the community must sacrifice the theoretical possibility of value optimalization in each decisional context.[17]

The two-dimensional conception of legal rules and the related presumption of contextual exclusivity described above is only one possible means to that end. Alternatively, one might conceive of rules as communications which can be decoded only by treating the prescription and the specified contextual features as an integrated index of community demands and expectations. In this view, the contextual features are not necessarily intended to be exclusive. Rather, in conjunction with the behavioral directive, they convey a legislative purpose from which the acts or omissions required in a given context can be inferred. It is assumed that at any given point in time a manifest core of intention is effectively communicated by particular associations of behavioral directives and contextual stipulations.

While this conception may encourage a freer inventory of contextual features than the two-dimensional alternative, it remains outside the Yale dispensation in that it still emphasizes the centrality of normative language as a guide to decision and insists that for each rule there are cases which fall clearly within its directives—that is to say, its manifest purpose—and hence can be characterized without the aid of an elaborate contextual analysis.

Even if the presumption theory were generally accepted as a means for stabilizing primary rules, its potential contribution to the reduction of normative indeterminacy obviously is limited to those cases in which a *recognized* rule is opposed by a claim for a concededly novel exception. If a rule emanates from a single source—for example, a legislative act in domestic society or a widely ratified multilateral treaty in its international counterpart—the distinction between an established rule and its novel qualification assumes an apprehendable form. One can then point realistically to a moment in time when the relevant community's consensus crystallized in a specific behavioral directive which, supported by the demand for stability, may enjoy a subsequent life of its own. But how often does this occur in the domain of international customary law? Today, radically altered means of communication and transportation, coupled with the uniquely menacing consequences of unbridled competition among nation-states, encourage and facilitate codification whenever a substantial international consensus emerges. An issue's consignment to the domain of customary law is not infrequently a sign of the failure to achieve consensus.[18] As a consequence, in a specific claim-conflict situation, the parties may adduce rules with identical contextual features but conflicting behavioral directives.

This case is the main concern of Professor D'Amato's book—*The Concept of Custom in International Law*.[19] He proposes a methodology for identifying the authoritative rule (see particularly pp. 73–102), a methodology which, he asserts, will promote uniformity. Under this theory, a credible identification of applicable law must rest on proof of both a "qualitative" and "quantitative" element. The qualitative element consists of the *articulation* of a rule alleged to be a rule of international law authorizing or compelling a certain act or acquiescence (pp. 74–87). The articulation gives a state notice that its actions or decisions will have legal implications.

The quantitative element consists of one or more acts that find their justification in the articulated rule, or abstentions in the face of acts so justified, by states with the requisite interest and capacity to resist them (pp. 87–98). No specific number of acts or abstentions is

> necessary to satisfy the material element of custom formation. . . . There is no international "constitution" specifying when acts become law. Rather, states resort to international law in claim–conflict situations. In such instances, counsel for either side will attempt to cite as many acts as possible. Thus we may say that persuasiveness in part depends upon the number of precedents . . . (p. 91).
>
> Two acts are significantly more persuasive than one, since in the third situation there would be no effective way of cancelling the rule by acting differently (p. 94).

It is clear from D'Amato's subsequent discussion that conflicting claims are to be resolved primarily by a grossly quantitative comparison. Two other factors are referenced, but in so casual a manner as to suggest their secondary or tertiary importance. One is temporal; more recent precedents may be more persuasive (p. 93). The other is the identity of the parties to the earlier precedents, where they are in conflict (pp. 96–98). Professor D'Amato suggests that the comparative legal sophistication of the parties, more than their relative power, may affect the precedential weight attributed to their behavior. Despite these refinements, it certainly appears to be his position that after a few precedents (perhaps only two) have accumulated, the first subsequent deviation should be regarded as a violation of customary law. However, he says it is simultaneously a "disconfirmatory instance" which will facilitate future deviation. "The number of disconfirmatory acts required to replace the original rule is a function partly of the number of acts that established the original rule in the first place, the remoteness in time of the establishing act, the legal authoritativeness of the participating states, and other possible factors, including the argumentative skill of the proponent or opponent of a claim of custom. At any rate, the theory that has been suggested here allows for the smooth working of change in customary international law" (pp. 97–98).

Professor D'Amato's claims are not entirely persuasive. One may doubt whether a rule that requires the first few deviations from earlier "precedents" to be deemed illegal "allows for the smooth working of change." In this respect, as in others, Professor D'Amato's approach does not differ significantly from (although it certainly helps to clarify) the traditionalist formulation he purports to displace. The quantitative and qualitative factors he enumerates are well-established features of the traditionalist method for identifying legal rules.

D'Amato's assumption that conceptually his is a distinctly different approach apparently rests on the belief that under traditionalist theory there was no means of legitimately replacing the established rule because deviations, no matter how numerous, could never be "consistent with prevailing law" (p. 93). He concedes that no one has ever asserted this, but suggests a tension between explicit theory and the implicit conception which has organized the vast body of traditionalist work—the conception that, although initial deviations probably will be deemed illegal, as disconfirming instances multiply and as attendant claims of legitimacy are accepted, consent to a new normative dispensation becomes demonstrable.

Actually, there is nothing in traditionalist theory which requires all customary rules to begin life as criminals. Suppose over a period of years the vast majority of states verbally repudiated an established rule and announced their adherence to a new one, and on the first subsequent opportunity to fit deed to word, a state acted in accordance with the newly acclaimed norm. Must its first behavioral deviation be deemed a delinquency?

D'Amato's somewhat mechanistic reformulation of traditionalist theory may seem to require an affirmative response. Consequently, while aspiring to facilitate change and bring normative and behavioral reality into a more intimate relationship, he has introduced a rigid threshold of legitimacy which in certain circumstances could utterly divorce formal legitimacy from community perceptions of desirable behavior.

This ironic twist stems, I believe, from D'Amato's necessary ambivalence about the virtues of normative flexibility. There are obvious dangers for a system whose rules of recognition and legal change require behavioral norms to lag well behind the vectors of societal change. Political, economic, social, and moral forces will push against the law's restraints. Accommodation between conservatives and progressives will be impeded by the former's perception of every challenge to their position as a threat to the fundamental legal structure. Some measure of efficacy will be squeezed out of authority.

On the other hand, particularly in international society where the sense of community, at best exiguous, is constantly threatened by national egotism, there may be more than balancing advantages in skewing the legal order toward the perpetuation of an old consensus by placing a comparatively heavy burden of proof on those who proclaim a new one. This policy bias does not mandate the straitened epistemology employed by some traditionalists. Signs of a new consensus may be sought in every cranny of international life and by the application of the full technical resources of the behavioral sciences—resources so relentlessly extolled by Professor McDougal and his cohorts.

What finally distinguishes those who resist the gravitational pull of the Yale School is a commitment not to legal alchemy, but rather to a belief in the possibility of clarifying and contributing to the sustenance of consensus by the utilization of verbal prescription. This is one conservative faith that has yet to be extinguished.

Notes

This chapter is taken from review articles: "International Law and Political Behavior: Toward a Conceptual Liaison," published in Anthony A. D'Amato, *The Concept of Custom in International Law,* Ithaca, Cornell University Press, 1971, xiv, 286 pp.

1. See generally H. L. A. Hart, *The Concept of Law* (Oxford 1961).
2. See, e.g. Judge Manley O. Hudson's formula for the derivation of a customary rule of law prepared at the request of the International Law Commission, in International Law Commission, *Yearbook, II,* 1950 (New York, 1957), 26.
3. *Ibid.*
4. The principal published works of the Yale School of International Law are as follows: Myres S. McDougal and Associates, *Studies in World Public Order* (New Haven 1960); McDougal and Florentino P. Feliciano, *Law and Minimum World Public Order* (New Haven 1961); McDougal and William T. Burke, *The Public Order of the Oceans* (New Haven 1962); McDougal, Harold D. Lasswell and Ivan A. Vlasic, *Law and Public Order in Space* (New Haven 1963); McDougal, Laswell and James C. Miller, *The Interpretation of Agreements and World Public Order: Principles of Content and Procedure* (New Haven 1967). For other books reflecting the Yale approach, see Lasswell and Abraham Kaplan, *Power and Society* (New Haven 1950); Douglas M. Johnston, *The International Law of Fisheries: A Framework for Policy–Oriented Inquiries* (New Haven 1965); B. F. Murty, *The Ideological Instrument of Coercion and World Public Order* (New Haven 1967); W. Michael Reisman, *Nullity and Revision: The Review and Enforcement of International Judgments and Awards* (New Haven 1971).
5. "The realistic function of . . . rules, considered as a whole, is accordingly, not mechanically to dictate specific decision but to guide the attention of decision-makers to significant variable factors in typical recurring contexts of decision, to serve as summary indices to relevant crystallized community expectations,

and, hence, to permit creative and adaptive, instead of arbitrary and irrational, decisions." McDougal, *Law and Minimum World Public Order* (fn. 4), 57.
6. See, e.g., McDougal and Associates, *Studies in World Public Order* (fn. 4), 169–70.
7. Reisman (fn. 4), 4.
8. *Ibid.,* 5.
9. *Ibid.,* 172.
10. McDougal and Associates, *Studies in World Public Order* (fn. 4), 167.
11. For a luminously perceptive critique along these lines see Gidon Gottlieb, "The Conceptual World of the Yale School of International Law," *World Politics,* XXI (October 1968), 108–32.
12. Cf. Thomas Ehrlich, "The Measuring Line of Occasion," *Stanford Journal of International Studies,* 111 (June 1968), p. 27.
13. Cf. Gottlieb (fn. 11), 116: "The principal intellectual weakness in the theory and practice of interpretation recommended by McDougal and his associates is their failure to conceive of legal language in rules and agreements as a device for the guidance of processes of inference leading to choices, decisions, judgments, and the like, rather than as a device for bringing subjective facts to the focus of attention of decision-makers."
14. McDougal and Associates, *Studies in World Public Order* (fn. 4), 170.
15. Cf. Alexis de Tocqueville, *Democracy in America,* P. Bradley, ed. (New York 1945), II,13: "General ideas are no proof of the strength, but rather of the insufficiency of the human intellect; for there are in nature no beings exactly alike, no things precisely identical, no rules indiscriminately and alike applicable to several objects at once. The chief merit of general ideas is that they enable the human mind to pass a rapid judgment on a great many objects at once; but on the other hand, the notions they convey are never other than incomplete, and they always cause the mind to lose as much in accuracy as it gains in comprehensiveness."
16. McDougal and Feliciano, *Law and Minimum World Public Order* (fn. 4), 237n.
17. In this connection, see my critique of McDougal's and Feliciano's interpretation of Article 51 of the U.N. Charter: "Law and War," in Cyril E. Black and Richard A. Falk, eds., *The Future of the International Legal Order,* Vol. III, Conflict Management (Princeton 1971), 36–40.
18. Alternatively, it may evidence belief that a consensus with respect to certain behavior is so solidly rooted and uniform that codification is unnecessary.
19. (Ithaca 1971).

13

The Regime of the Charter

The Historical Context

The idea that a political entity requires some justification, other than the delectations of aggrandizement, for resort to force appears to have made its first Western appearance in pre-Republican Rome.[1] A necessary prelude to the initiation of hostilities was a finding by a special group of priests, the *fetiales,* that a foreign nation had violated its duties toward the Romans.[2] Following this determination, as Professor Nussbaum describes the process,

> the delegate of the *fetiales,* under oath by the Roman gods as to the justice of his assertion, would demand satisfaction of the foreign nation. The oath culminated in self-execration condemning the whole Roman people should the delegate's assertion be wrong. In case the foreign nation wanted time for deliberation, thirty or thirty-three days would be granted. In the days of the Republic, if the period terminated without result, the *fetiales* would certify to the senate the existence of a just cause of war; the ultimate political decision was left with the senate and the people.[3]

This potentially inhibiting procedure was discarded in the mature years of the Republic,[4] but its doctrinal substance was disinterred and clad in Christian vestments by St. Augustine, who found in it an effective means for mediating between the demands of Caesar and Christ. The specific occasion for the doctrine's reappearance in respectable society was a response to continuing concern within the Church over the propriety of Christian participation in military service. St. Augustine concluded that Christian principles allowed participation if the war were just. The primary requisite of justice was a prior injury to which the war was a response.[5]

St. Augustine's conception was elaborated by Thomas Aquinas, whose formulation became the cornerstone of Roman Catholic doctrine on war.

He listed three criteria of justness: (1) that the prince has authorized the war (that there is *auctoritas principis*); (2) that there is a *justa causa,* to wit, that the adverse party deserves to be fought against because of some guilt of his own (*propter aliquam culpam*); (3) that the belligerent is possessed of a *recta intentio,* namely, the intention to promote the good or to avoid evil.[6]

As one would anticipate, the progressive enfeeblement of the just-war doctrine began on the eve of the epoch of national consolidation. Writing in connection with the conflict between the Conquistadors and the American Indians, the Spanish Dominican scholar, Vitoria, distinguished objective and subjective justness, the latter being the result of "invincible ignorance."[7] By blurring the just-war doctrine's pristine clarity, Vitoria appears to augur, however faintly, its eclipse.

While Vitoria was a sign of impending change, Vattel was the confirmation of its occurrence. He did not reject the notion of the just war as a moral doctrine, but, as Wolfgang Friedmann has noted, he swept away its claim to practical relevance by effecting "the decisive break with ... natural law philosophy. [While paying] lip service to natural law [Vattel relegated it] to the unfathomable depths of the inner conscience of a state, while the only international law that counts for practical purposes is derived from the will of the nations whose presumed consent expresses itself in treaties and customs."[8]

If the narrator is concerned solely with the particular doctrinal form wrought by Aquinas, one could describe the subsequent history of the doctrine in terms of a gradual but perceptible decline into desuetude.[9] But the particular form enclosed a Protean idea that reappears in the Nineteenth Century system of law erected by scholarly zeal out of the bits and pieces of theory and state practice that had been accumulating for the two prior centuries.[10]

The fully emergent system contained two parallel bodies of law: a more elaborate one functioning in time of peace; another which became operative following a declaration of war. Aquinas's central criterion, the *justa causa,* played a rather paradoxical and at least partially theoretical role in retarding movement across the line from peace to war, though not necessarily in reducing the incidence of organized violence. International law provided no real obstacles to passage; but there were certain psychological, commercial, and constitutional inhibitions. Moreover, the complex of rights and obligations attendant on the state of war must have seemed largely irrelevant to the short, decisive little struggles with indigenous groups which in the Nineteenth Century were the most common occasion for the employment of force.

Responding to the real needs of the Western states, the "Law of Peace" legitimized recourse to force for such laudable purposes as "reprisal," "self-preservation," "self-defense," "necessity," and "humanitarian intervention."[11] The modest price of this opportunity to employ force and remain quite at peace was compliance with certain criteria and the consequent theoretical subjection of national behavior to external appreciation of its propriety to the extent that other states—most of whom lived in similar glass houses—might have any interest in the legitimacy of behavior outside their own colonial preserve.

The varied justifications for resort to force in time of peace had three broad criteria in common.[12] One was that, before resorting to force, alternative means of settlement had to be exhausted, except where action was required to prevent imminent or continued value destruction. The second criterion was that the quantum of force had to be proportional to the cause. The third requirement was that force could not be employed for sheer aggrandizement; there had to be a *justa causa*.

The ambiguities clustering around the word "proportional" cannot be explored fully here. For purposes of foreshadowing, I will simply call attention to the fact that, on linguistic grounds alone, the term might refer either to the magnitude of the *causa* or the minimum coercion required to achieve satisfaction even if it necessitates inflicting far greater injury than that caused by the precipitating delinquency.

Given the realities of Nineteenth Century practice, it seems fair to say that the definitions of delinquencies were sufficiently vague to provide a legal cloak for any state with the slightest desire to secure one. Lauterpacht's last edition of Oppenheim's prestigious treatise, for instance, refers blandly to "The right of protection over citizens abroad, which a state holds, and which may cause an intervention by right to which the other party is legally bound to submit. And it matters not whether protection of the life, security, *honour,* or property of a citizen abroad is concerned."[13] (Emphasis added.) The term "property" included contract debts of all kinds. Since citizens of the principal powers were likely in that era to be found in every corner of the globe spreading the benefits of commerce or Faith, and since failure to protect their activities (as well as positive interference) was itself an international delinquency, and since their citizens could through purchase of foreign bonds obtain protected contract rights without moving from the benign Western hearthside to rigorous tropical climes, and since, in addition, national bankruptcy was not regarded as a defense to nonpayment, the opportunities for legitimate intervention were not infrequent. And their number was augmented still further by a doctrine of humanitarian intervention[14] that permitted the application of force to protect citizens of other states—who were almost invariably white and Christian—from uncivilized behavior by the target government or its subjects. Examples of this principle in action were the dispatch of troops to China during the Boxer Rebellion and intervention by Great Britain,

France, and Russia in 1827 during the conflict between the Ottoman Empire and its Greek subjects.

As Ian Brownlie notes in his penetrating work, *International Law and the Use of Force by States*, "Modern writers refer to [the various forceful measures short of war] as though they were highly formalized and well defined."[15] In fact, state practice was complacently casual,[16] at least where the target was comparatively weak, as was normally the case. With an abandon seemingly restrained only by the moment's political sensitivities, governments wrapped their coercive policies in established legal terminology or improvised new language which was dutifully added by zealous scholars to the heap of available syntactical alternatives. Despite assiduous efforts to achieve systematic categorization of state practice, the politicians' indifference to the nuance of relationship between fact and doctrine stimulated scholarly cacophony.

Brownlie notes, for instance, that "some works discuss self-preservation and necessity without mentioning a separate category of 'intervention.' In other works and in monographs on intervention there is an untidy enumeration of grounds of intervention which overlaps the customary law developing on hostile measures short of war and does not reserve the term 'intervention' for cases in which no formal state of war is created."[17]

At the base of this open-textured system was the opportunity to leave it whenever its standards inhibited state policy. Surely a system which did not regard war as the fundamental right of every sovereign state would not have tolerated the amplitude of discretionary behavior legitimized by the system's fluid doctrinal references.

Although one may reasonably regard the Nineteenth Century's legal schema for the restraint of armed conflict with a moderate cynicism, it should not obscure recognition of a certain unease on the part of authoritative decision makers about the use of force to aggrandize the state.[18] One minor manifestation of this unease was the gradual acceptance of the doctrine that resort to war, as well as lesser policies of force, without prior efforts to achieve a negotiated settlement of differences, was a "violation of the Law of Nations."[19] An obvious corollary was the necessity of a preexisting conflict requiring resolution. There is little evidence that up to the First World War this was in any sense a substantive limitation. The genesis and equities of the disputed issue were irrelevant. If State A demanded of State B surrender of one-half of B's territory, and B failed to respond with an enthusiastic affirmative, the requisite dispute existed. In practice, however, war or lesser coercive means always were accompanied by appeals to legal or moral rights which had in some way been injured.[20] Here was evidence of residual just-law conceptions, of attitudes which could serve as the springboard to significant legal control of armed conflict.

Widespread condemnation of Britain for its role in the Boer War evidenced more dramatically an intensifying sentiment against the right of might. The Convention respecting the Limitation of the Employment of Force for the Recovery of Contract Debts ("Porter Convention"), adopted at the Second Hague Peace Conference in 1907, may have been a modest obeisance to that sentiment. Its impact was limited, however, by the conditions that the debtor state had to accept arbitration and honor the arbiter's award. Failure of either condition released a party from his no–force commitment.

The uneven but persistent process through which antiwar sentiment grew and achieved rudimentary legal expression during the period extending from the First World War to the conclusion of its successor conflagration and the adoption of the United Nations Charter has received ample treatment in many standard works.[21] Its monuments were the Covenant of the League of Nations, which may be seen as a codification of the emergent customary obligation to exhaust peaceful means of settling disputes before resorting to war,[22] the Treaty of Paris, which supplemented the covenant by precluding resort to war for purposes of national aggrandizement, and the Nuremberg Trials which confirmed the demise of the conception that justifications for resort to war are not susceptible to evaluation by third parties.[23]

Since 1945, debate about armed conflict has occurred almost entirely within the broad normative framework established by the charter. At a minimum, it has largely determined the debaters' vocabulary. The extent to which it has influenced nonverbal behavior is a principal concern of this chapter. An appropriate point of departure would seem to be the relevant charter language examined with an eye to determining the range of behavioral options consistent with its syntax and legislative history.

The Regime of the Charter

Optional Interpretations

The assertion that Paragraph 4 of Article 2 embodies the charter's principal substantive restraint on the use of force seems uncontroversial. For purposes of the subsequent discussion it may be useful to recall its exact language.

> 4. All members shall refrain in their international relations from the threat or use of force against the territorial integrity or political independence of any state, or in any other manner inconsistent with the Purposes of the United Nations.

In the context of debate over the use of force, frequent reference is also made to the Article 51 provision that "nothing in the present Charter shall impair the inherent right of individual or collective self-defense, if an armed attack occurs against a member of the United Nations."

There is substantial scholarly support for the proposition that these provisions in conjunction with the provisions authorizing collective action divide the world of force into three parts: delict, self-defense, and sanction.[24] All acts of force undertaken or authorized by the Security Council fall into the realm of sanction. The unauthorized use of force not required for self-defense may be analogized, in this normative framework, to the private violence against which Aquinas hurled the first of his just-war criteria.

Study of the practice of states and the writings of prestigious publicists makes it difficult to avoid Julius Stone's acid conclusion that the "right of self-defense under general international law is as vague as it is unquestioned."[25] As Ian Brownlie has pointed out, "the doctrine's diffuse character . . . reflects the lack of legal regulation of the use of force in the Nineteenth Century."[26] Even in the decade following adoption of the League Covenant, he notes, "many writers . . . did not introduce the category since it was superfluous if a broad right of self-preservation or right to resort to war as a means of settlement were asserted."[27]

Through the mist of erratic state behavior and varying scholarly assessments, at least one specific requirement can be observed: The precipitating event must consist of a breach of a legal duty owed to the state claiming a right of self-defense. Beyond that point, nothing is wholly clear. Professor Bowett, who has devoted an entire book[28] to the concept's clarification, lists these additional criteria. The injury must not have been consummated. In other words, self-defense must not be "punitive in character"; it is thus distinguishable from reprisal where "the object is to compel the offending state to make reparation for the injury or to return to legality, by avoiding further offenses."[29] The rights being protected must be "essential," the harm to them "irreparable" and "imminent," and there must not be "alternative means of protection."[30] Finally, the reaction to threatened or actual injury must be "proportional."[31]

Proportional to what: the importance of the jeopardized right or the obstacles which hinder its vindication? On that point Professor Bowett is less than limpid. Since the right must, in the first place, be "essential" and Professor Bowett equates "essential" with "the security of the state,"[32] one might assume that proportional means reasonably necessary to vindicate the right, for the security of the state is treated by most people as virtually an absolute value.[33] However, Professor Bowett's initial identification of self-defense with security seems a little misleading when one comes to appreciate the multitudinous rights he associates with it. They include protection of the person and, in appropriate cases, even the property of nationals.[34]

If the only way to protect the property of a citizen is to invade a neighboring state, bombard its cities, and smash its armed forces, would the rule of proportionality preclude resort to force even if the property in question is a valuable oil refinery? The following statement suggests the author's preference for an interpretation of proportionality that would relate it primarily, at least, to the importance of the jeopardized interest:

> The principle of relativity of rights and the notion of proportionality involve a strict adherence to the measure of proportionality which the occasion demands, so that a state may not lightly violate the independence and integrity of another state in defense of its own right to the treatment of its nationals according to established standards.
>
> This would mean in practice that a large-scale naval demonstration or military landing could never be justified as action in the defense of a single national; to undertake such action would be to totally disregard the rights of the territorial state by the disproportionate enforcement of the protecting state. On the other hand the use or threat of force by the protecting state would be justified where the magnitude of the danger of its nationals satisfied the requirement of proportionality, for the relativity of rights would have been properly assessed.[34a]

As a practical matter, protection of nationals and their property will require highly destructive coercion only where the target state resists. Since self-defense is really "privilege"[35] to effect a prima facie violation of the rights of the target state activated by a prior threatened or persisting violation of the actor's rights, efforts to obstruct exercise of the privilege would appear to constitute a distinct, additional delict and one involving the use of force. Hence, even if force must be proportional to the interest threatened, an escalation of force can be justified because an extremely important interest is jeopardized when the armed forces of the state are attacked. If the attacks intensify, the right of the intervening state to intensify its coercive behavior will increase proportionately, and so on *ad infinitum*.

The apparently uniform indifference to the latent complexities of the notion of proportionality is probably explained by the ease with which the privilege to protect nationals and their property was exercised against non-European states by the Western powers. A few Marines or a brief blockade generally would suffice. Today, when any use of force is so much more likely to send ripples of apprehension around the world and when even weak states may resist vigorously the intrusion of the strong, there is bound to be a more studied assessment of the importance of the threatened right.

Some scholars now argue that Paragraph 4 of Article 2 alone, or in conjunction with Article 51, limits legitimate self-defense to defense against an armed attack.[36] It is argued, in other words, either that Paragraph 4 constitutes a preclusion of all force qualified only by a single exception contained in Article 51 or that Article 51 operates to limit the right of self-defense left unimpaired by Paragraph 4. Advocates of this interpretation tend to deny the legitimacy of anticipatory military initiatives even in the face of a presumably imminent attack.[36a] Precisely what behavior constitutes an "armed attack," whether, for example, it includes assistance to guerrillas who are indigenous to the state in which they are operating, is not terribly clear.[37]

Other scholars insist that the term self-defense embraces a greater variety of contexts.[38] Professor Derek Bowett, for instance, appears to argue that an illegal act, regardless of its form, which threatens major security interests of the target state legitimates a forceful response.[39] A variety of techniques are marshaled to avoid the strictures of the "armed attack" reference. All of them begin with the premise that Paragraph 4 does not itself restrict the right of self-defense.[40] This fundamental premise is generally defended on the grounds that a momentous change in international law requires explicit language.[41] It also is argued that the exercise of rights of self-defense cannot by definition threaten the territorial integrity or political independence of any state, or be inconsistent with any of the enumerated "Purposes of the United Nations."[42]

When uttered by scholars urging a broad conception of self-defense, the latter proposition is not terribly persuasive. But even if the right of self-defense were limited to cases of armed attack against the territory of a state, conflict is possible if the right may be exercised preemptively; surely cases where each state believes the other is about to attack are not inconceivable. "Invincible ignorance" can be bilateral, because it may be reciprocally induced.

One may also imagine a scenario in which one state attacks another to promote self-determination or protect human rights. It could be argued, of course, that the promotion of self-determination and the protection of human rights are "Purposes of the United Nations" which are permanently subordinated to the dominant purpose of maintaining international peace and security. Hence, no state can claim to be advancing these "Purposes" when it breaches the peace to promote other interests, for they simply have no legitimate independent existence outside the context of international peace.

This certainly is a possible interpretation. Measured by syntactical practice and the intent of the drafters, it is easily the most plausible construction. Still it is not the only possible one. The Afro-Asian and

Communist states would, I think, deny that force may never be used against colonial regimes or regimes which discriminate openly on the basis of race.[43] The views of representatives of well over half the human race cannot be casually dismissed, even by legal scholars. It seems fair, then, to suggest that even a narrowly defined right of self-defense is not necessarily compatible in every context with territorial integrity, political independence, and all "Purposes of the Charter" unrelated to those values. When one accepts broader definitions, when self-defense is, for instance, extended to embrace property interests,[44] the possibility of actual conflict between the right of self-defense and, for example, political independence is evident. With virtual unanimity, the General Assembly has recognized a nation's control over its natural resources to be a fundamental right.[45] But exercise of that right may be seen by a foreign state as a grave threat to its security. Suppose, for instance, that all the African and Arab states expropriated the resident oil companies and declared their intention of withholding oil from France until it severed relations with South Africa. This act might appear to authoritative decision makers in Paris as a threat to the state's security serious enough to justify a forceful response.

In light of the difficulties outlined above, the proposition that self-defense is necessarily compatible with Paragraph 4 seems to fall well short of being a truism, even if one construes the reference to territorial integrity, etc., as limiting the initial flat prohibition: "All members shall refrain in their international relations from the threat or use of force." That construction is itself not inevitable. From the Travaux Preparatoires it appears that the apparently qualifying language was added at the specific request of smaller states laboring to close every verbal loophole through which might slip a threat to their territorial integrity or political independence.[46] Thus we are confronted with the splendid irony of a myopic search for specificity culminating in dangerous ambiguity. Although an ardent advocate of a capacious definition of self-defense, Professor Bowett in his useful study, *Self-Defense in International Law,* concludes flatly that "the introduction of the specific references at San Francisco had not, as its purpose, the qualifying of the obligation."[47] Bowett goes on to adduce considerations of policy for not finding a negative pregnant in the reference to the consequences or objectives of a policy of force: "Secondly, to introduce the subjective element of 'intent' seems anomalous once 'war' had been replaced by the more objective phrase 'threat or use of force.' Moreover, in the initial stages at least, it may be extremely difficult to ascertain the intention of a state, and even the most obvious aggression may be accompanied by statements to show a lack of any such specific intent."[48] Finally, he approvingly quotes Lauterpacht, who argues that "territorial integrity especially where coupled with 'political independence' is synonymous with territorial inviolability."[49]

From this carefully constructed platform of argumentation, Professor Bowett then executes a surprising backflip to the obscurantist *ipse dixit* that "the phrase having been included, it must be given its plain meaning."[50] While appearing to regard obeisance to "plain meaning" as a good in itself, he adds, "Moreover to give it its plain meaning coincides with the limitations on the obligation of nonintervention which traditional international law recognizes."[51] The formal virtue of this result is its congruence with the first argument in favor of a narrow reading of Paragraph 4 mentioned above—the plea against implying surrender of important traditional rights. This might be an acceptable guide to the interpretation of an ordinary international agreement. Its implicit assumptions about the intentions of states are considerably less compelling when applied to what might reasonably be regarded as the Twentieth Century's most important treaty, a treaty which among other things, delegates novel powers to a centralized authority and converts the treatment of colonial peoples into a matter of international concern. Implying, from an agreement embodying hopes for the inauguration of a new and more humane international system, an intention to reduce the range of national discretion, does not seem anomalous.

To this point, we have explored divisions concerning the meaning of Paragraph 4 that exist among those who at least agree that self-defense is the only contemporary legal justification for recourse to force. This view does not command unanimous support. There are those who conclude that additional justifications are and ought to be available. Professor Julius Stone, for example, has argued in favor of taking "seriously" the qualification on Article 2(4)'s prohibitions.[52]

> What it prohibits is not use of force as such, but as used against the "territorial integrity or political independence of any State," or "in any other manner inconsistent with the Purposes of the United Nations." These "purposes" may properly extend beyond Article 1 (devoted to "the Purposes of the United Nations"), to include (*inter alia*) the preambulatory references to the saving of the world from the scourge of war, to fundamental human rights, and maintenance of the conditions assuring justice, respect for the obligations arising from treaties, and general international law. The purposes expressed in Article 1 itself, moreover, embrace not only collective measures against threats to the peace, breaches of the peace and acts of aggression, but also (and coordinately) the bringing about "by peaceful means, and in conformity with the principles of justice and international law, adjustment or settlement" of peace-endangering disputes.
>
> It is, we shall submit, far from impossible to argue that a threat or use of force

employed consistently with these purposes, and not directed against the "territorial integrity or political independence of any state," may be commendable rather than necessarily forbidden by the Charter. Nor is it inconceivable that situations may arise in which attempts to settle disputes by peaceful means may be so delayed, and prospects of success so fantastically remote, that a minimal regard for law and justice in inter-State relations might require the use of force in due time to vindicate these standards, and avoid even more catastrophic resort to force at a later stage.

Sir Eric Beckett, the United Kingdom Agent in the *Corfu Channel Case,* used equivalent language in defending the British mine-sweeping operation in Albanian territorial waters: "Our action ... threatened neither the territorial integrity nor the political independence of Albania. Albania suffered thereby neither territorial loss nor any part of its political independence."[53]

Neither those like Dr. Bowett, who recognize self-defense as the only justification for recourse to force but interpret it broadly, nor men like Professor Stone, who would accept additional justifications, appear to regard the Article 51 reference to "armed attack" as a serious objection to their respective interpretations of the Charter. Professor McDougal and Dr. Feliciano, who have the most developed and persuasive set of arguments on this point, begin by disparaging the notion that a "word formula can have, apart from context, any single 'clear and unambiguous' or 'popular, natural and ordinary' meaning that predetermines decision in infinitely varying particular controversies."[54] But just in case anyone is witless enough to impute "some mystical preexistent, reified meaning"[55] to words, they pause to note that Article 51 does not say "if, *and only if,* an armed attack occurs."[56] (Emphasis added.)

They point also to the absence in the provision's "legislative history" of any evidence of an intent to narrow the scope of self-defense.[57] Like the qualifying language in Paragraph 4, Article 51 appears not as one carefully placed arch in a grand architectural design, but a clumsy ad hoc response to the special concerns of a limited constituency, in this case the Pan-American states—and, to a much lesser degree, the Arab League states. They apparently feared that the veto power might be employed to block regional measures of collective self-defense.[58] This much about the origins of Article 51 is clear. What is wholly obscure is the motive which prompted inclusion of the phrase "armed attack." Whatever the motive for its employment, it stands there, solid and sphinx-like, demanding (particularly from those who believe that language has a residuum of denotation that cannot be avoided by contextual fact-grabbing) the attribution to it of operational significance. In the end, McDougal and Feliciano eschew that task, preferring to treat the phrase as accidental in origin and functionally nonexistent, a form of words without substance.

Professor Stone, who shares their desire to preserve inviolate the customary-law conception of self-defense, tries a different approach. He concludes that:

> In reserving a license limited to the case of "armed attack against a Member" the draftsmen were delimiting the reserved powers of Members as against United Nations organs. For other purposes, for instance where the Security Council is not acting, the broader license of self-defense and self-redress under customary international law must surely continue to exist so far as the positive prohibitions of the Charter do not exclude it. Article 51 itself, in reserving as against the Security Council's powers a narrow range of self-defense, can surely not have destroyed the broader area of the license of self-defense and self-redress where the Security Council is not acting, and there is no inconsistency with the purposes of the United Nations.[59]

No one is likely to attribute the varying interpretations of Article 51 and Paragraph 4 primarily to different methods and capacities for exegesis. There is nothing cynical in the judgment that they reflect major differences in value preferences or in calculations of the efficacy of alternative strategies for promoting values. Scholars and elite decision makers openly concede this by invariably citing policy-rooted justifications for preferring one construction over another. There are, of course, times when policy preference degrades law by stretching language to the point of inelasticity and ignoring or distorting legislative history. But within the bounds established by the raw data that the interpreter processes, the rejection of policy guidance would be an act of existential absurdity.

Notes

This chapter is excerpted from Cyril E. Black and Richard A. Falk, eds., *The Future of the International Legal Order,* Vol. III Conflict Management, "Law and War" (Princeton 1971).
1. See Arthur Nussbaum, *A Concise History of the Law of Nations* (New York 1947), 16–17.
2. Ibid.
3. Ibid.
4. Ibid.
5. Ibid., 40–41.
6. Ibid., 42.
7. Ibid., 61. Professor Nussbaum disparages the distinction as a contribution to juristic theory "which must by all means keep asunder the objective criterion of good faith." This cursory dismissal of the distinction's utility may be unwarranted. As Professor Nussbaum himself points out, the distinction was prof-

fered in the course of an analysis of the moral situation at the end of a war when the victor is judging his adversary. A differential response at that point to an objective delinquency committed in good faith would be analogous to a not uncommon domestic law distinction between a tortfeasor and a criminal. "Invincible ignorance" might be analogized to that degree of negligence which requires compensation but does not elicit criminal sanctions. It would seem that this kind of distinction could facilitate termination of conflict through compromise and the restoration of amity. If prospectively different severities of post-defeat deprivations were likely to influence the calculations of potential aggressors, the proposed distinction might weaken the just-war doctrine's prophylactic value in that it creates the opportunity to prove good faith and thus win the lesser punishment (for example, money damages imposed on the defeated state as distinguished from physical sanctions imposed on its leaders). But the underlying assumption that men would initiate wars even if they regarded the risk of defeat to be substantial enough to require a careful weighing of its personal consequences would appear on historical grounds rather doubtful. At least I know of no evidence that the precedent of allied efforts after World War I to extradite the Kaiser for trial ever engaged the concerned attention of Hitler, Mussolini, or their Japanese counterparts.

8. Wolfgang Friedmann, *The Changing Structure of International Law* (New York 1967), 76.
9. See Myres McDougal and Florentino Feliciano, *Law and Minimum World Public Order* (New Haven 1961), 131–35.
10. See Hersh Lauterpacht–Lassa Oppenheim, *International Law,* 8th Ed., Vol. II (London 1955), 177–78, and Gerhard von Glahn, *Law Among Nations* (New York 1965), p. 562.
11. See generally Ian Brownlie, *International Law and the Use of Force by States* (Oxford 1963), and Julius Stone, *Legal Controls of International Conflicts* (London 1954)
12. Ibid.
13. Vol. 1, 309.
14. See Brownlie (fn. 11), at 339–42
15. Ibid., 47.
16. Ibid.
17. Ibid., 41
18. Ibid., 47 and Lauterpacht–Oppenheim, II, (fn. 10), 177–78.
19. Ibid., Brownlie, 43 and Lauterpacht–Oppenheim, II, 291.
20. Lauterpacht–Oppenheim, ibid.
21. See, e.g., Brownlie (fn. 11), 55–101, 216–50, and Stone (fn. 11), 165–84.
22. See Stone, same, 175.
23. At Nuremberg, Professor Jahrreiss for the defense argued that "every state is sole judge of whether in a given case it is waging a war of self–defense." (Trial of Major War Criminals, Nuremberg 1984, Vol. XVII 469.) When it was alleged specifically that the invasion of Norway was an act of self–defense, the tribunal treated this as raising a question of fact and concluded that the criterion of immediate necessity was not satisfied. *American Journal of International Law,* 431 (1947), 206.
24. See, e.g, McDougal and Feliciano, (fn. 9) 126; Lauterpacht–Oppenehim, II (fn.3), 154; George Scelle, "Quelques Reflexions sur l'Abolition de la Compétence de Guerre," *Revue Generale de Droit International Public,* LVIII (1954),

5, 13, quoted in Julius Stone, *Aggression and World Order* (Berkeley 1958), 5. See also Article 2(i) of the Draft Code of Offenses against the Peace and Security of Mankind, Report of the International Law Commission, Third Sess. (1951), U.N. Doc. A/1858. Cf. Bowett (fn. 7) 11–13. But see Stone (fn. 43). In addition, there is, of course, the theoretical possibility of military action against "enemy states" (the World War II Axis powers and their allies) under Articles 53(1) or 107 of the Charter, or joint action of the five permanent members of the Security Council under Article 106. Expectations about the possibility of such action would appear to be very low, so low that the relevant provisions might reasonably be characterized as the charter analogue of the vermiform appendix.

25. Stone, (fn. 11) 243.
26. Brownlie, (fn. 11) 251.
27. Ibid., 231.
28. Derek Bowett, *Self-Defense in International Law* (Manchester 1958).
29. Ibid., 11–12.
30. Ibid., 11.
31. Ibid., 24.
32. Ibid., 101.
33. See William D. Coplin, "International Law and Assumptions about the State System," *World Politics* XVII (July 1965), 615, 633.
34. Bowett, 104. "In conclusion, therefore, it is submitted that, in the absence of international guarantees of the protection of the lives and the property of aliens, the state may exercise its right of self-defense to protect the lives, and in exceptional cases the property, of its subjects. For, '. . . the price of inviolability of any territory is the maintenance of justice therein. Accordingly, when the price is not paid in relation to foreign life and property, the landing of forces for their protection is to be anticipated,'" quoting Charles C. Hyde, *International Law*, 1 (New York 1945), 649. Before reaching this conclusion, Dr. Bowett's argument undergoes certain modulations which left this reader breathless as he attempted to determine Dr. Bowett's precise position. Cf. 94, 98, 101, 103.
34a. Ibid. 94.
35. See, e.g., Rosalyn Higgins, *The Development of International Law through the Political Organs of the United Nations* (London 1963), 198–99 and Sir Humphrey Waldock, "The regulation of the Use of Force by Individual States in International Law," *Hague Recueil*, LXXXI (1952), 455–63. For the distinction between a "privilege" and a "right," see generally Wesley Hohfeld, *Fundamental Legal Conceptions* (New Haven 1963).
36. See Louis Henkin, "Force, Intervention and Neutrality in Contemporary International Law," *Proceedings of the American Society of International Law*, 1963, 147, 149, 165; Phillip Jessup, *A Modern Law of Nations* (New York 1948) 166; Hans Kelsen, *The Law of the United Nations* (New York 1950), 797–98; Josef Kunz, "Individual and Collective Self-Defense in Article 51 of the Charter of the United Nations," *American Journal of International Law*, 41 (October, 1947), 872, 878; Dr. Djura Nincie, in Georg Schwarzenberger, "Report on Some Aspects of the Principle of Self-Defense in the Charter of the United Nations and the Topics Covered by the Dubrovnic Resolution," (International Law Association 1958), 617; Lauterpacht-Oppenheim, II, 16; cf. Stone, (fn. 24), 44. But cf. Stone (fn. 11), 43–44.
36a. See, e.g., Jessup, *ibid.;* Kelsen, ibid., 797; Kunz, ibid.; Niñcié, ibid.; Lauterpacht-Oppenheim, II, same. But see Stone (fn. 11) n.8.

37. See the discussion in Brownlie, (fn. 11) 278–79.
38. See Bowett (fn. 28) 24–25; Leland Goodrich and Edvard Hambro, *Charter of the United Nations* (Boston 1949), 107; McDougal and Feliciano (fn. 9) 232–41; Waldock (fn. 35) 445, 498.
39. Bowett, ibid., 20, 24, 101.
40. There is substantial reliance on the fact that Charter drafting Committee 1/I stated in its report that the "use of arms in legitimate self-defense remains admitted and unimpaired." Report of Rapporteur of Committee 1 to Commission I, as adopted by Committee 1/I, U.N.C.I.O. Vol. VI, 446, 459. The report was approved by both Commission I and the Plenary Conference. See Verbatim Minutes of Fifth meeting of Commission I, U.N.C.I.O., Vol. VI, 202, 204; Report of Rapporteur of Commission I to Plenary Session, same, 245, 247. For approval of Report by Plenary Conference, see Verbatim Minutes of the Ninth Plenary Session, 1 same, 612, 620.
41. See, e.g., Bowett, (fn. 28), 188.
42. Ibid., 185–86.
43. See Richard Falk, *Legal Order in a Violent World* (Princeton 1968), 111–13. In the deliberations of the Special Committee established by the General Assembly (G.A. Res. 1966 [XVIII]) to study and report on the "Principles of International Law Concerning Friendly Relations and Co-Operation Among States," both Soviet Bloc and uncommitted Afro–Asian states insisted that the prohibition of the use of force was not to affect "self-defense of nations against colonial domination in the exercise of the right to self-determination." (Czechoslovakian Proposal, Doc. A/AC, 119/L.6; Report of Special Committee, Doc. A/5746, p. 19) See Edward McWhinney, "The 'New' Countries and the 'New' International Law: The United Nations Special Conference on Friendly Relations and Co-operation Among States,"*American Journal of International Law,* 60 (January 1966), 12. In defending India's occupation of Goa, the Indian spokesman at the Security Council characterized Portugal's 300–year presence on the Asian subcontinent as a continuing aggression. The Portuguese effort to obtain Security Council action was blocked by the Soviet Union, which was joined in opposition by Ceylon, Liberia, and the United Arab Republic. See SCOR, 918–919th Meetings, December 18–19, 1961. The incident is ably discussed in Richard A. Falk, *The New States and International Legal Order* (Leyden 1966), 53–57.
44. See, e.g., the statement of the Lord Chancellor and principal Law Officer of the Crown, Viscount Kilmuir, during the Suez crisis. *Parliamentary Debates, House of Lords,* Vol. 199, Col. 139, November 1, 1956. See also Bowett (fn. 28), 103.
45. Resolution on Permanent Sovereignty Over Natural Resources, U.N. Doc. A/PV. 1193, December 14, 1962. The resolution both affirmed the rights of all states "freely to dispose of their natural wealth and resources" and required, in case of expropriation, "appropriate compensation, in accordance with the rules in force in the [expropriating] state ... and in accordance with international law." Whether exercise of the right is dependent on fulfillment of the obligation and the nature of the obligation imposed by international law were issues left unresolved.
46. U.N.C.I.O., Vol. VI, 69, 346, 557, 720. See Goodrich and Hambro (fn. 39), 103.
47. Bowett (fn. 28), 151.
48. Ibid.

49. Ibid., 152.
50. Ibid.
51. Ibid. For a persuasive account of the uncertainty of traditional international law in this connection, see Brownlie (fn. 11), 231ff.
52. Stone (fn. 24), 43.
53. *I.C.J. Pleadings,* Vol. III, 295-96.
54. Fn. 9, 234.
55. Ibid.
56. Ibid., 237n.
57. Ibid., 235.
58. See U.N.C.I.O., Vol. XII, (680-82); same, Vol. XI, 52-59. See also Bowett (fn. 28), 182-84; Goodrich and Hambro (fn. 39), 297-99.
59. Stone (fn-24), 43-44.

14

On Foreign Intervention in Civil Strife

The Old Law

During the Nineteenth Century, there developed a standard conception of civil armed conflict as being divided into three principal phases: rebellion, belligerency, and, in the case of wars of secession, independence.[1] In phase 1, the antigovernment forces had no international status. The incumbent possessed all of its preconflict rights and obligations as the sole representative of the nation.

At the onset of phase 2, a distinct set of international rules wheeled into place. The rebels vaulted from the status of nonpersons into a position of equality with the incumbents. Foreign governments could not aid either side without being transformed into co-belligerents. If the rebel objective were secession, this phase would last until the secessionists were finally overwhelmed or the incumbents had, in fact if not in form, surrendered hope of maintaining the territorial integrity of the state. The minimum requirements for achieving belligerency were generally acknowledged to be

> the existence of a civil war beyond the scope of a mere local revolt (existence of a 'state of general hostilities'); occupation of a substantial part of the national territory by the rebels, together with the existence of a degree of orderly and effective administration by that group in the areas under its control; observance of the rules of war by the rebel forces, acting under the command of some responsible and ascertainable authority.[2]

This three-phase system gradually became what might be called a three-and-one-half-phase normative order when "insurgency," a twilight zone between rebellion and belligerency, won acceptance. The insurgent force was a party to an internal conflict whom you did not treat as an equal but with whom you were compelled to treat usually because it controlled territory in which you had interests—commercial, financial, and so on—requiring protection.

Although unequal in law to belligerents, insurgents apparently had to cross the same factual threshold. What left them wallowing in the no-man's land of insurgency was, in the view of many scholars, nothing other than the unbridled discretion of incumbents and foreign governments to withhold recognition of belligerency.[3] This was not a uniform view. Its obvious potential for mischief and misunderstanding drove even so cautious a scholar as Lauterpacht to insist on a legal obligation to recognize belligerency once its factual predicate was satisfied.[4] But, although not uniform, it had sufficient support to guarantee its availability in a decentralized legal system as an optional form of state behavior.

A commonplace of contemporary Anglo-American writing on the international law of internal war is the casual announcement that under the "traditional view," foreign governments had the option of assisting a regime attempting to suppress armed dissidents or of remaining neutral, but were precluded from assisting antigovernment forces.[5] Some distinguished treatise is generally cited in support of this proposition. There is nothing politically tendentious about this formulation of pre-Charter law; it appears in the works of scholars with markedly different political preferences.

Any assertions about Nineteenth or early Twentieth Century state practice involving the employment of force must be accompanied by at least a few shreds of doubt. To begin with, consistency either in behavior or in its justifications was not accorded a notably high priority. With an abandon seemingly restrained only by the moment's political sensitivity, governments wrapped their coercive policies in established legal terminology or improvised new language, which was dutifully added by zealous scholars to the heap of available syntactical alternatives.[6] The spongy character of behavior and doctrine was the natural product of an international system that regarded recourse to force as a fundamental right of the sovereign state.

A second reason for a mild tincture of doubt inheres in the fact that, even among scholars, there was dissent from the proposition that direct military intervention on behalf of incumbents was permissible. Writing shortly after the First World War, William Hall observed that

> [If intervention is] directed against rebels, the fact that it has been necessary to call in foreign help is enough to show that the issue of the conflict would without it be uncertain, and consequently that there is a doubt as to which side will ultimately establish itself as the legal representative of the State. If again, intervention is based upon an opinion as to the merits of the question at issue, the intervening State takes upon itself to pass judgment on a matter

which, having nothing to do with the relations of States, must be regarded as being for legal purposes beyond the range of its vision.[7]

I have never seen it demonstrated that this was in fact a minority view among scholars.

A third reason for doubt is the behavior of states; it appears to have corresponded only episodically with the prescription. During periods or, regardless of period, in settings where ideological passions were inflamed, the distinction between incumbent and insurgent often eluded the concern of the great powers.

In 1821, following successful revolutions against Royal absolutism in Spain and Naples, French and Austrian troops, respectively, dispatched under the aegis of the Holy Alliance, intervened to restore the eager monarchs to their full prerogatives.[8] In retrospect, these would seem to be *a fortiori* cases under the traditional rule in that rebellion (counter-revolution) was merely latent, the former absolute monarchs having ceased prior to the intervention to dispose of effective armed force. Of course, to the Holy Alliance with its *"L'Etat, c'est le roi"* view of the world, these were not cases of intervention against incumbents because legitimate authority was immutably associated with the monarchs whose wings had been clipped.

In 1848, animated by the same ideological passions, the Prussian army launched itself into Baden to crush the incipient Republic and a Russian army stormed into Hungary to the ironic end of maintaining the Austro-Hungarian Monarchy.[9]

A comparable contempt for ideologically neutral standards is evident in the wake of the Russian Revolution. The first sign was the abortive allied intervention in Russia itself, which began in 1917 and bumbled on with gradually diminishing conviction until 1920.[10] It was admittedly possible to rationalize that intervention on the grounds that during the period 1917–1920 there were still sufficiently powerful centers of resistance within Russia to deprive the Bolshevik regime of impeccable incumbency credentials. As late as July 1919, Lloyd George believed that the major surviving White Army under the command of General Denikin had a fair chance of consolidating its control over the bulk of Southern Russia.[11] Nor was Denikin the only threat. By October, the White General Ydenich was battering on the outskirts of Petrograd (supported by the British Navy).[12] In the middle of the month, Lenin proposed abandoning the city and gathering all available strength around Moscow; he even envisaged the possibility of giving up Moscow and withdrawing to the Urals.[13]

These facts must be weighed against Soviet control of the historic heartland of Russia, its capital city, and the bulk of its industry, as well as the Bolshevik government's capacity, evidenced by the Treaty of Brest–Litovsk, to enter into international agreements. They must also be weighed against the regime's coherent administration and political programme and its demonstrated ability to maintain itself without external assistance in the face of substantial foreign intervention. Compared, for example, with the rag–tag outfit that seized Pnom Penh in Prince Sinanouk's absence, was immediately recognized by a horde of states, and seated at the United Nations without any persuasive evidence that its writ ran far beyond the Capital's suburbs, Bolshevik incumbency seems incontestable.

However one may judge the merits of the Russian case, it certainly presaged subsequent acts of a less ambiguous character that commenced with Hitler's accession to power. Covert assistance flowing out of Germany to Nazi parties in central and southeastern Europe culminated in the Italo–German joint venture that carried the Fascist insurgents under General Franco to victory over a government enjoying universal recognition at the outbreak of the Civil War.[14]

A second group of delinquent precedents was established during the prolonged decomposition of the Ottoman Empire. Throughout the late Eighteenth and Nineteenth Centuries, the European Powers, following an erratic course charted by the felt imperatives of national interest, lent varying degrees of encouragement and assistance to Christian dissidents. The first notable case was the Greek struggle for independence which, but for the fitful interventions of the British, French, and Russians, might well have been aborted.[15] Evidence of serious normative indeterminacy or of sheer indifference to generalized prescription could be inferred from the wide oscillations between resolute neutrality and direct military aid that marked British behavior during the twelve savage years in which the conflict dragged on.

The Turks were the primary but not quite the only incumbent to experience intervention on behalf of secessionists. In the 1830s, the Concert of Europe sanctioned Belgium's separation from the Netherlands. And in 1898, the United States intervened decisively in the Cuban revolt against Spanish rule.

To be sure, the traditional view is not restricted to the cloistered world of scholarship. Dr. Rosalyn Higgins cites as one clear precedent the justification announced by the United States Department of State for its decision during the 1930s revolution in Brazil to prohibit the shipment of all arms to that country except to the government:

> Until belligerency is recognized, and the duty of neutrality arises, all the humane predispositions towards stability of government, the preservation of international amity, and the protection of established intercourse between nations are in favor of the Existing Government.[16]

The department's views were consistent with an already well-established United States reading of its obligations under international law not to permit military expeditions to leave its territory to aid insurgents, a position affirmed by the United States Supreme Court in the feverish national atmosphere of 1896.[17] Comparable British views were codified in the Foreign Enlistments Act under which the British Cabinet decided in 1825 to prosecute Lord Cochrane, ostensibly for leading an expedition in aid of the Brazilian War of Independence, the real motive being to prevent his organizing a naval force to aid the Greeks.[18]

Foreign reaction to the American Civil War lends support only to one arm of the traditional view, the proposition that it is impermissible to assist rebels. Despite considerable pro-Southern sentiment in British ruling circles, the British Government sought with partial success to prevent delivery to the Confederacy of warships under construction in British shipyards.[19] While denying connivance in the escape of the *Alabama* which scourged Northern commerce during the last two years of the war, the government conceded an obligation actively to prevent use of its territories for purposes of military assistance even to rebels who had achieved the status of belligerency.[20] France, the other country in which the Confederacy had contracted for ship construction, took an equivalent position.[21]

The other arm of the traditional view—a discretion to support the incumbents—was wholly untested, first because the North, being endowed with adequate resources for the equipage of its armed forces, apparently sought no material assistance, and, second, because the political cohesion of the Southern states and their initial military superiority, coupled with Lincoln's promulgation of a formal blockade (an action legitimate only during a state of belligerency), clearly justified recognition of rebel belligerency with attendant declaration of neutrality, the tack chosen by the great majority of foreign states led by Britain and France.[22]

While failing to resolve uncertainty about the putative rights of foreign governments to assist in the suppression of rebels and insurgents, the Civil War was clearly instructive in two respects: First, the diplomatic correspondence and other records confirm that the governments of all the European Powers actually thought of themselves as functioning within a normative universe, the restraints of which merited observance;[23] second, the threats and indignation which ricocheted back and forth across the Atlantic and are preserved in those records confirm the difficulty of achieving agreement on the application of restraints that vary with conditions subject to a largely discretionary appreciation.[24] Although the South satisfied twice over the factual conditions of belligerency, Lincoln's Secretary of State objected stridently to Europe's recognition of that status.[25] And if there were no obligation to recognize belligerency—contrary to the position espoused by the United States during the Revolutionary War in complaining about Danish nonrecognition[26]—Secretary of State Stanton's imputation of hostility to the recognizing states would have been reasonable but for the North's own implied recognition in announcing the blockade.

Adversary appraisal of the propriety of recognizing belligerency was, then, one source of international discord built into a normative framework which gave important, albeit not entirely ambiguous, advantages to an incumbent as long as it could block the passage to belligerency. The post-Napoleonic interventions in Naples and Spain expose a second opportunity for adversary appreciation of the factual predicate for the application of substantive rules. The problem of identifying the true incumbent was theoretically manageable as long as there was a consensus about the conclusions to be drawn from an agreed set of facts. But if the facts were dominated by competing theories of legitimacy, when legitimacy became a question of subjective preference rather than concrete achievements, then the entire system was politicized. Undisputed substantive rules were left floating in a jurisdictional void.

During the Spanish Civil War, this ever-latent state of affairs achieved full realization. At the outset of the struggle, Hitler and Mussolini recognized the ideologically congenial regime of General Franco as the sole legitimate government of Spain and proceeded to assist it with ample war material and powerful military units.[27]

Mexico, on the other hand, adhering throughout the conflict to the view that Franco was a mere insurgent, lent diplomatic support to the Republicans.[28] The Soviet Union sent war material openly and personnel covertly.[29] A group of European States, led by the nervous governments of Great Britain and France, found insufficient latitude in any of the traditional doctrines to satisfy their political needs. Unwilling to recognize a state of belligerency yet determined to avoid involvement, they proclaimed neutrality while denying to either Spanish faction the traditional belligerent right to intercept vessels on the high seas and search for contraband.[30] Thus, the period 1936 to 1939 was the nadir of the traditional international law of civil armed conflict.

No one, I am sure, would suggest that this was a result of architectural deficiencies in that normative structure. International law could stabilize an equilibrium only as long as all major parties accepted the idea of equilibrium. Once it was rejected, no legal structure, however elegant, could by itself hold the parts in a coherent order.

Notes

1. See, e.g., Lauterpacht, *Oppenheim's International Law,* Vol. II, 1952, pp. 248, 253.

2. Ibid., p. 249. See also Van Glahn, *Law Among Nations,* 2nd ed., 171, p. 551.
3. See, e.g., Hall, *International Law,* 3rd ed., 1890, p. 34, and Padelford, *International Law and Diplomacy in the Spanish Civil War,* 1939, p. 8.
4. Lauterpacht, Vol. II, *op. cit.,* p. 250.
5. Ibid., p. 660.
6. For a valuable synoptic view of the process, see generally Brownlie, *International Law and the Use of Force by Staes,* 1963.
7. Hall, *International Law,* 1924, p. 346.
8. Palmer, *A History of the Modern World,* 1954, pp. 460–462.
9. Whitridge, *Men in Crisis: The Revolutions of 1848, 1949,* pp. 277–278 and 318.
10. See generally, Silverlight, *The Victors' Dilemma,* 1970.
11. Ibid., p. 263.
12. Ibid., p. 289.
13. Ibid.
14. Thomas and Thomas, "International Legal Aspects of the Civil War in Spain, 1936–39", in Falk. ed., *The International Law of Civil War* 1971, pp. 143, 146–148.
15. See generally Dakin, *The Greek War of Independence 1821–33,* 1973.
16. "Internal War and International Law," in Black and Falk, eds., *The Future of the International Legal Order,* Vol. III, 1971, p. 98.
17. *The Three Friends,* 166 U.S. 1 (1896).
18. Dakin, op. cit., p. 170.
19. Wright, "The American Civil War," in The International Law of Civil War, op. cit., p. 87.
20. Ibid., p. 81; cf. pp. 86 and 88.
21. Ibid., p. 88, fn. 58.
22. Ibid., p. 82.
23. Ibid., especially pp. 85–94.
24. Ibid.
25. Ibid., p. 85.
26. Moore, *A Digest of International Law,* Vol. I, 1906, p. 168.
27. Thomas and Thomas, op. cit., pp. 160, 164–165. Direct military intervention by Germany actually preceded recognition. See p. 165.
28. Ibid., pp. 161–163.
29. Ibid., pp. 118–120.
30. Ibid., pp. 144–145.

15

The Dominican Invasion and the Cuban Missile Crisis

Treating the Dominican affair as just another case of intervention in defense of nationals[1] on the Nineteenth Century pattern does violence both to the event's subsequently revealed factual and normative complexity and to its larger context. Despite official expression of concern for the safety of nationals,[2] the assessments of nongovernmental authorities, including eye witnesses,[3] coupled with public statements emerging at various times from policy-making levels of the United States government in defense of United States behavior as a response to Communist infiltration,[4] as well as the unabashed confessions of President Lyndon Johnson's special representative, John Bartlow Martin,[5] have convinced this writer that the defense-of-nationals justification was only slightly less flimsy here than it was at Suez.

A second justification—prevention of the fratricidal slaughter of Dominicans,[6] with its aura of transcendence of ordinary considerations of national interest—also is somewhat reminiscent of the factually shabby Anglo-French claim to be acting as an arm of the international community to assure free passage through the Suez Canal. One is hard put to recall a pronounced concern for slaughter in the Caribbean unless one's own citizens were threatened or Cold War perspectives were engaged. It is possible, for instance, to cite relative indifference to the sustained barbarities of the Trujillo regime, including the massacre of thousands of Haitians.

The Dominican intervention bears a more credible resemblance to the Soviet invasion of Hungary. In both cases, great power intervention determined the outcome of violent domestic struggles for political control. Both intervening powers made justificatory reference to traditional legal doctrine: In the United States case, protection of nationals; in the Soviet case, the request of an established government for assistance.[7] Both responded to allegations of interference in domestic affairs and self-determination processes with countercharges of foreign support or direction for the groups whose success they sought to preclude. These are arresting similarities, yet the Soviet Union and not the United States was condemned by the United Nations General Assembly.[8]

The troubling question is whether the discriminatory reaction of the United Nations can be justified in terms of criteria susceptible to universal application or whether it evidences breakdown of the notion of a universal legal order.

The case for discrimination on neutral juridical grounds might rely on the willingness of the United States, in contradistinction to the Soviet Union, to permit general elections under the gaze of impartial observers.[9] While I believe that the elections were not and, indeed, could not have been impartial when United States forces were still the effective operating authority in the country and the United States government was resting on its claim that one of the contestants was under communist influence, nevertheless victory for the Boschites, though unlikely, seemed possible.[10] If this is true, then the General Assembly could not with equal assurance condemn the United States, as it condemned the Soviet Union, for imposing a regime by "armed intervention."[11]

A related basis for distinguishing the cases is United States acceptance of a United Nations observer in the Republic.[12] United Nations representatives were denied access to Hungary.[13]

A further distinction between the cases was the absence in the Dominican Republic of an effective government. At the time of the Russian attack in Hungary, Imre Nagy and his colleagues were in control of the entire country and were supported by the regular armed forces. The self-determination process had come to rest. Although some reports indicate that the Dominican right-wing military group was on the point of collapse before United States intervention,[14] this has never been established conclusively.

A final possible distinction could rest on the implication of *ex post facto* O.A.S. ratification of United States action, arising from the organization's willingness to assume responsibility for the occupation force.[15] The argument would be that the Dominican strife was a matter "relating to the maintenance of international peace and security," that it was "appropriate for regional action," and that such action was "consistent with the Purposes and Principles of the United Nations" in that it was designed to minimize destruction and promote self-determination.[16]

Allegations that the enterprise violated Article 53's prohibition of "enforcement action . . . without the authorization of the Security Council" have encountered the following responses: That "enforcement action" refers to regional action against an established government or it refers to compulsory collective action as distinguished from merely recommended behavior or, finally, that the silence of the Security Council can be construed as assent.[17] If the latter argument is applied to the case of silence induced by veto of the concerned great power, it emerges as a transparent assertion of great power freedom from charter norms and hence its claim to juridical significance can be dismissed with contempt. On the other hand, if a Security Council Resolution under Chapter VI—and thus not subject to veto by "a party to [the] dispute"—recommending nonintervention is deemed a denial of authorization, the acquiescence argument may aspire to a modest respectability, although it hovers on the outer fringe of the syntactically plausible and, as a matter of policy, encourages decentralized appreciation of issues of war and peace, even where they have transregional implications.

A similar tendency can be seen in the alternative juridical implication that might be drawn from the Dominican affair if it is seen not in isolation but as part of the continuing pattern of behavior by the United States in the Western Hemisphere. On the control side, one can point to Guatemala and the Bay of Pigs, both cases where United States involvement was inconsistent with the views of its own governing elite that aid to rebel expeditions violates international law.[18] The sense of an emerging pattern is strengthened by undenied allegations of covert United States involvement in British Guiana to prevent the electoral success of Cheddi Jagan's left–wing party[19] and in Bolivia to assist in antiguerrilla operations.[20] On the authority side, one can point principally to the Punta del Este Resolution,[21] which may be construed as a declaration of the inherent illegitimacy of Western Hemisphere regimes that espouse Marxist–Leninist principles of domestic public order. In this data one might discern an emerging regional norm allowing intervention pursuant to OAS constitutional procedures, and possibly unilaterally as well, for the purpose of preventing the creation of communist regimes or of eliminating those already established. If confirmed by future events, it would constitute the Western Hemisphere's analogue to the Brezhnev Doctrine, enunciated after the occupation of Czechoslovakia, which in effect declares that the national sovereignty of Socialist states is conditioned on governance by ideologically sanitized regimes.[22] While the Soviet claim has been rejected explicitly by two communist governments within Eastern Europe[23] and by a substantial number of Communist parties,[24] United States reaction has been restrained[25] and the United Nations accordingly acquiescent.

Neither the explicit Soviet claim nor its more ambiguous United States counterpart seems reconcilable with the prevailing perceptions of the legal order established by the United Nations Charter. The keystone of that perceived order is the sovereign equality of states and the corollary inviolability of their respective authority structures, except in those instances where the Security Council finds a threat to the peace, as it has done in the case of Southern Rhodesia.[26] The charter is seen, in other words, as an effort to centralize peacekeeping and restrain "private violence." Regional organization plays a supplementary role in this scheme.

At their narrowest, explicit Soviet and muted United States assertions of an interventionary privilege in their respective regions constitute claims to treat certain domestic political phenomena as threats to their national security, thus activating the privilege to engage in normally proscribed behavior, whether under the rubric of self-defense, or some less conventional fig leaf. Although each power's claim is phrased in terms that implicitly reject reciprocal application, in the context of events, including a low Soviet profile in the Western Hemisphere since the missile crisis, they may be construed as reflections of an emerging pattern of reciprocity, a kind of normative regime specialized to the self-defined requirements of the superpowers. Their toleration of the regional renegades—Yugoslavia and Cuba, respectively—may reflect a tacit agreement against retroactive enforcement of their interventionary doctrines or rational assessments of the costs of occupying countries that appear to possess the will and capacity to offer substantial resistance.

United States reaction to the emplacement of Soviet missiles in Cuba would seem to be an *a fortiori* application of the norm, as well as confirmation of its operative force. The efforts to drape it with the venerable mantle of self-defense, without radical alteration of the concept, encounter imposing obstructions. They require, of course, repudiation of the view that an actual or imminent armed attack is a necessary precondition for legitimate recourse to force or the threat of force. Descriptions of Soviet behavior as preparation for an armed attack[27] are wantonly unconvincing because they require imputation of psychotic, suicidal tendencies to the Soviet leadership. Secretary of Defense McNamara pointed out during the secret discussions that led to the quarantine that the missile buildup in Cuba did not give the Soviets anything resembling a first-strike capability.[28] Indeed, it could easily have been construed as a desperate defensive response to the missile gap, which exposed the Soviet Union to the risk of an American first strike.[29] Authoritative and semiauthoritative accounts of the crisis agree that the decision to act was based on concern for the broad political and psychological consequences, both in the international arena and within the United States, of the Soviet gambit.[30]

It has been argued, sometimes with more noise than reason, that, if nothing else, the Soviet move threatened the stable balance of power.[31] The factual predicate is doubtful. Given the dimensions of the missile gap, which became apparent after Kennedy's election, any possible impact of the missile buildup would have been in the direction of *creating* nuclear equilibrium between the superpowers.[32] It is arguable, however, that the creation of nuclear equilibrium might eventually have encouraged the Soviet Union to new adventures in areas such as Berlin, where it enjoys conventional superiority. Speculations concerning Soviet reaction to the creation of a true nuclear standoff are inevitably guided by underlying assumptions about the essential thrust of Soviet foreign policy: Those who see the Soviet Union as an aggressive, expanding power, and view the Cold War as a mere reflection of those characteristics, naturally read the emplacement of missiles in Cuba as a prelude to intensified coercive behavior.[33] But even if the postulation of disequilibrating consequences were true, they have no juridical significance if self–defense is the only justification for unilateral recourse to force, unless the criterion of imminent and irremediable injury to specific interests is rejected.

Perhaps it is just such a rejection that the impartial empiricist should record. From the tremors in Czechoslovakia and Cuba, followed by little more than token opposition in the former case and large–scale support for the party defending his sphere in the latter, one might infer a change of state for self–defense from a solid cluster of criteria to a fluid prescription for maintenance of the prevailing relationship of force. Such an inference would, however, seem to require at least one important qualification. Where the behavior (other than preparation for an imminent attack) that threatens the existing relationship of force occurs within the territorial confines of one of the belligerently juxtaposed states—for example, by a dramatic increase in the defense budget—efforts to abort the development by threats of force would be precedent–shattering and presumably would be regarded as impermissible.

Looking ahead, a possible exception to that qualification would be the case where a change in domestic behavior violated treaty obligations relating to arms control or disarmament. In its first report, issued in 1946, the United Nations Atomic Energy Commission suggested that if the members concluded an atomic arms control treaty, "a violation might be of so grave a character as to give rise to the inherent right of self–defense recognized in Article 51."[34] The limited Test Ban and the Nonproliferation Treaty have vastly increased the probability of such a contingency. And this would be true of any other significant arms control or disarmament agreements that may be negotiated. Such agreements are likely to create powerful expectations of an intensely coercive response to major violations.

Recourse to force in case of a violation of an important arms control or disarmament treaty could be justified as self–defense without severely straining the term's traditional connotations. One could reasonably presume that no state would violate such a treaty unless it anticipated important military gains and intended to exploit them to achieve major value reallocations. Since violation inevitably would be covert, once discovered it would be difficult to determine quickly how long violations had been occurring and hence how great an advantage had been secured. Under those circumstances, the requirements of an apparent need to act immediately for the protection of essential values would appear to be satisfied.

While the decline of a rigorous conception of self–defense is a conceivable inference from contemporary behavior, the alternative inferences of a merely regional relaxation of criteria or of the evolution of special criteria governing relations between the polar powers seems more in accord with both control and claiming behavior. President Kennedy's decision in the missile crisis, reportedly based in substantial measure on concern for the precedential implications of a self–defense claim,[35] to rely on regional processes and norms for defense of the quarantine rather than Article 51 of the charter may evidence a desire to restrain the tendency to return to uninhibited unilateral appreciation of the need for recourse to force. The international community's reaction to Israel's initiation of hostilities in 1956 may also be interpreted as evidence that a rigorous conception of self–defense still enjoys wide support.

Notes

1. On April 30, 1965, President Johnson announced: "For two days American forces have been in Santo Domingo in an effort to protect the lives of Americans and nationals of other countries in the face of increasing violence and disorder." *New York Times,* May 1, 1965, p. 6, col. 4.
2. See President Johnson's statement in the *Department of State Bulletin,* LIII (July 5, 1965), 20.
3. See. e.g., Theodore Draper, "The Dominican Crisis," *Commentary,* XL (December 1965), 33–68; Philip Geyelin, *Lyndon B. Johnson and the World* (New York 1966); Tad Szulc, *Dominican Diary* (New York 1965). Geyelin and Szulc had access to cables that passed between Washington and the embassy in Santo Domingo.
4. On May 2, eight days after the beginning of the revolution, President Johnson publicly declared that the revolution had taken a "tragic turn. What began as a popular democratic revolution that was committed to democracy and social justice moved into the hands of a band of Communist conspirators." Quoted in Draper (fn. 3), 42.
5. In his book, *Overtaken by Events: The Dominican Crisis from the Fall of Trujillo to Civil War* (New York 1966), Martin quotes Ambassador Bennett to the effect that President Johnson asked for a written request from the military junta for U.S. military intervention, citing the danger to lives and property in order to provide the "juridical basis" of the action. (657).
6. See Leonard Meeker, "The Dominican Situation in the Perspective of International Law," *Department of State Bulletin,* LIII (July 12, 1965). 60, 62.

7. See, e.g., statement of the Soviet delegate (GAOR and Emergency Special Sess., 564th Mtg.)
8. Res. 1004 (ES-II), November 4, 1956.
9. See Richard Barnet, *Intervention and Revolution* (New York 1968), p. 178.
10. With the assistance of U.S. forces, the military junta eventually destroyed the Boschite military capability. Barnet, same 9, 175. Hence, in the months immediately proceeding the election, the right-wing military group was the only indigenous public order authority, a de facto position it employed to intimidate the opposition. Juan Bosch was so fearful of his personal safety that he never left his residence during the campaign. In addition, the United States government, openly anti-Bosch, poured aid funds into the country. Indeed, in the year following the revolution, the Dominican Republic received almost 300 per cent more aid per capita than any other country in Latin America. See Barnet, ibid., 173-78.
11. See Res. 1133 (II), September 14, 1957.
12. See *New York Times,* May 15, 1965, p. 1, col. 5 and ibid., May 16, 1965, p. 62, cols. 4, 6, and 7; U.N. Docs. Nos. S/6365, S/6369, 1965; U.N. Doc. No. S/6358, 1965.
13. See *New York Times,* November 13, 1956, p. 1, col. 8.
14. See, e.g., Barnet (fn. 9) 170-71, and Juan de Onis in the *New York Times,* November 5, 1969, p. 8.
15. But see Richard Bohan, "The Dominican Case: Unilateral Intervention," *American Journal of International Law,* 60 (October 1966), 809, 811-12.
16. Art. 52, Par. 1 of the Charter of the United Nations. Cf. Meeker (fn. 6), 61-62. With a dauntless indifference to United Nations Charter obligations, Dr. Charles G. Fenwick has proclaimed that: "Had the Meeting of Consultation [of O.A.S.] been willing to justify its action on the ground of a *possible* take-over of the pro-Bosch rebels by Communist elements, *there would have been no legal basis of criticism,* assuming ... that there was *reasonable* evidence of the fact. For the resolution taken [sic] at Caracas in 1954, clearly covered such a situation." (Emphasis added.) *American Journal of International Law,* 60 (January 1966), 64, 66. Dr. Fenwick also argued that the United States could have acted alone to assure rebel failure on the grounds that prior experience with the Communist government of Cuba would justify "intervention in self-defense." Ibid., p. 65. In light of the balanced concern for relevant juridical data manifested by Dr. Fenwick, Richard Bohan's suggestion that Fenwick's piece "shows ... the possibilities for the misuse of international law as an instrument for the self-righteous justification of illegal acts" does not seem unfair (fn. 14), 809.
17. See, e.g., statements of the United States representative to the Security Council, U.N.S.C. *Official Records,* 20th year 1220th Mtg. 17 (S/PV. 1220) 1965; same, 1219th Mtg. 5 (S/PV. 1219), 1965. And see Abram Chayes, "Law and the Quarantine of Cuba," *Foreign Affairs* (April 1965), 556. After the Cuban quarantine, the State Department Legal Advisor, Leonard Meeker, seemed to intimate that, in the view of the United States, authorization simply is no longer necessary. "Defensive Quarantine and the Law," *American Journal of International Law,* 57 (July 1963), 515, 522.
18. This view is implicit in the government's contention that North Vietnam's support of the Vietcong constituted an "armed attack" against the Saigon regime. See the Memorandum of the State Department on "The Legality of U.S. Participation in the Defense of Vietnam," submitted to the Senate Com-

mittee on Foreign Relations on March 8, 1966, reprinted in Richard A. Falk, ed., *The Vietnam War and International Law* (Princeton 1968), 583.
19. See Barnet (fn. 9), 240–43, and sources cited there.
20. See *New York Times:* September 11, 1967, p. 13; January 5, 1968, p. 18; August 18, 1968, p. 1; August 19, 1968; p. 8.
21. "The principles of communism are incompatible with the principles of the Inter-American system ... [and] adherence by any member of the Organization of American States to Marxism-Leninism is incompatible with the inter-American system and the alignment of such a government with the communist block breaks the unity and solidarity of the hemisphere ... [The] member states [are therefore urged] to take those steps that they may consider appropriate for their individual or collective self-defense, and to cooperate, as may be necessary or desirable, to strengthen their capacity to counteract threats or acts of aggression, subversion, or other dangers to peace and security resulting from the continued intervention in this hemisphere of Sino-Soviet powers, in accordance with the obligations established in treaties and agreements such as the Charter of the Organization of American States and the Inter-American Treaty of Reciprocal Assistance." *State Department Bulletin* (February 19, 1962), 278. See also the declaration of the Caracas Inter-American Conference of 1954 (which was motivated by U.S. concern with the Arbenz government in Guatemala). Documents in *American Foreign Relations 1954* (1955), 412.
22. The "Doctrine" is actually a composite of a number of pronouncements: See statement of Ambassador Malik addressing the Security Council, U.N. Doc. S/PV. 1441, August 21, 1968, 48–50; *Pravda* editorial, translation by the Soviet Press Agency reprinted in the *New York Times,* September 27, 1968, p. 3; statement of Foreign Minister Gromyko to the U.N. General Assembly, U.N. Doc. A/PV. 1679, October 3, 1968, 26, 30–31.
23. Rumania and Yugoslavia.
24. See *New York Times,* August 22, 1968, p. 18; September 27, 1968, p.3; October 22, 1968, p.11.
25. Conceptions of restraint assume meaning, of course, only within a specific context of expectations and possibilities. One certainly might argue that United States behavior should not be characterized as acquiescent. Washington did go beyond purely verbal condemnation. There were N.A.T.O. meetings and announcements of plans to bolster N.A.T.O.'s military capabilities. The White House's planned announcement of an agreement to enter into missile limitation talks with the Soviet Union was postponed. Under-Secretary of State Katzenbach was dispatched to Belgrade with assurances of support (assurances that did not appear to commit the United States to any concrete action in case of Soviet intervention). And Rumania, the only Warsaw Pact nonparticipant in the invasion, was rewarded with new agreements relating to the peaceful uses of atomic energy and cultural exchanges, while prospective agreements with the other Pact states were placed in the freezer. (See Andrew J. Pierre, "Implications of the Western response to the Soviet Intervention in Czechoslovakia," paper delivered at the Conference on "The Impact of the Czechoslovak Events on Current International Relations," Center for International Studies, New York University, December 6, 1968.) But there is no evidence of which I am aware that either the United States or the Soviet Union regarded these moves as more than formal gestures, largely occasioned by the requirements of domestic and N.A.T.O. politics. They were not costly either to Washington or Moscow. The

latter capital did not treat them as provocative or threatening. They seemed to fall well within the ambit of a relatively unconcerned expectation concerning the probable Western response.

26. S.C. Res. 232, December 16, 1966 and S.C. Res. 221, April 9, 1966.
27. See, e.g., Charles Fenwick, "The Quarantine Against Cuba: Legal or Illegal?" *American Journal of International Law,* 57 (July 1963), 588, 589-9.
28. See Roger Hilsman, *To Move a Nation* (Garden City 1967), p. 201.
29. Ibid. See also speech delivered by Deputy Secretary of Defense Roswell Gilpatrick on October 21, 1961, quoted in Elie Abel, *The Missile Crisis* (New York 1966), 36.
30. See Abel, same, 50; Arthur Schlesinger, Jr., *A Thousand Days* (Boston 1965), 803.
31. See, e.g., Myres McDougal, "The Soviet-Cuban Quarantine and Self-Defense," *American Journal of International Law,* 53 (July 1963), 597, 601.
32. See source cited at footnote 28.
33. See McDougal (fn. 31), 601-02. In his review of *Law and Minimum World Public Order,* Richard Falk suggests that

> McDougal and Feliciano apparently accept without question (or at least they do not disclose any questioning) the image of the Cold War put forward by Robert Strausz-Hupé and others in *Protracted Conflict,* New York, Harper and Brothers, 1959; see, e.g., p. 279, passim. I find this image to be an unacceptably self-serving interpretation of the Cold War that overrigidifies "the enemy" and is *too clear* about his objectives. See note 57, pp. 86-7n.

Unfortunately, a not altogether dissimilar perspective may be found in Professor Falk's early writing. See, for example, the following ominous reference: "The Caracas Declaration of Solidarity is but an illustration of a coherent worldwide policy pursued by the United States since the close of World War II. It has, by necessity, manifested the interventionary character inevitable *in a world stalked by a potent aggressor."* (Emphasis added) Ibid., p. 178. On the other hand, the guiding conception of world affairs manifested in such prose is balanced, to some degree at least, by insights such as the following: "As well as the Dulles version of the overthrow of Arbenz—patriots arose in Guatemala to challenge the communist leadership—there are those who regard the revolution as an interventionary joint venture between the United Fruit Company and Ambassador Peurifoy." Ibid., 177.

For interpretation of Soviet behavior at variance with the one urged by Strausz-Hupe and company, see, *inter alia,* Gar Alperovitz, *Atomic Diplomacy: Hiroshima and Potsdam* (New York 1965); David Dallin, *Soviet Foreign Policy After Stalin* (New York 1961); D. F. Fleming, *The Cold War and Its Origins,* Vols. I and II (Garden City, 1961); Louis Halle, *The Origins of the Cold War* (New York 1967); David Horowitz, *The Free World Colossus* (New York 1965); Marshall D. Shulman, *Stalin's Foreign Policy Reappraised* (New York 1963). See also, Arthur Schlesinger, "The Origins of the Cold War," *Foreign Affairs,* XLVI (October 1967).

34. U.N. Doc. AEC/18/Rev. 1, 24.
35. See Abel (fn. 29) 155.

16

Nicaragua 1981–?

Lawyers and laymen alike speak of the rule of law in reverential tones. Those of us who have investigated societies where it either has never existed or has collapsed recognize with a peculiar intensity the appropriateness of the tone. When law becomes the whim of the leader or the high command, however initially benign or well–intentioned, we are in the jungle where terror will eventually become a natural state.

As long as we are speaking only of domestic society, no one is likely to dispute this proposition, although some might say that even commencement speakers have an obligation to rise above the level of cliche. But when we turn to the society of nations, consensus dissolves. Not only the laity, but lawyers as well often disparage the very claim that the relations of states are governed by law. And among those who concede that some lawlike process operates on the international plane are many who deny its relevance in cases engaging important or at least allegedly important national interests.

This perceptual separation of the domestic and international realms is evidenced today in the debate over American foreign policy in Central America. It is conducted almost exclusively in the idiom of morality and national interest. Even when law is invoked, it normally appears either as a throwaway argument, the sort you use before a court when you find you have five minutes left in your allotted time and nothing much left to say, or as unanalyzed and unexplained *ipse dixit,* a mere verbal club.

I suspect that a principal reason, other than ignorance, for failing to use law as a means for orienting ourselves toward this country's Central American policy is a sense that the law is somehow detached from moral and strategic concerns and is, therefore, an insufficient basis for determining where we as individuals ought to stand. Ironically, those most indifferent to the legal position of the parties often are the quickest to employ terms like "aggression," which, when detached from the world of law, have the same rational force as a punch in the nose. Whether we like it or not, legal concepts—i.e., concepts that have evolved from the claiming behavior of states—have insinuated themselves into our minds, our hearts, and our words, just as our deepest values and most profound interests have inevitably shaped the evolution of those concepts.

Precisely because international law reflects the consensus of the parties it governs, rather than being a body of coercive norms imposed by one or a handful of people who may or may not reflect the will of the governed, it must embody shared moral values and strategic interests. To ignore it, therefore, is to ignore the rules and procedures deemed by all states to be essential to their collective interest in survival.

In any legal system, law provides continuity. In that sense, if no other, it tends to protect the interests of those with a stake in the status quo and to frustrate revolutionaries, that is, those who wish to manage a sharp break with prevailing conditions. It would seem to follow, then, that the United States, as the richest, most powerful, and most influential state, has a particular interest in upholding the rule of international law. And that is sufficient reason for a patriot, committed to advancing our national interests, to feel concern about the decision of the present administration to reject the jurisdiction of the International Court of Justice in the case brought against us by the government of Nicaragua. Concern about this unilateral denial of jurisdiction is shared both by those who believe that the court erred in finding that it had jurisdiction and that, in any event, the United States has a winning case on the merits and those who think the Court's finding was reasonable and that the United States was likely to lose on the merits.

After all, one of the general principles of law at least in the West is that a court has the power to determine its jurisdiction. Of course, if in the instant case there were evidence that the Court had been corrupted or coerced, one would feel differently. In fact, even the most fervent advocates of the administration's position have suggested nothing of the kind.

This happy occasion is hardly the appropriate moment to offer a full-scale analysis of the procedural and substantive issues implicated in the Nicaraguan case. On the other hand, I assume I was not invited to mumble the usual commencement bromides about the charming, frolicsome world of the law that breathlessly awaits your arrival so that you can join in the game of fun and profits, not that I have anything against either. So, at the risk of saying either too much or not enough, of being either boring or superficial, I am going to sketch the most portentous issues this case has managed to raise.

One is the issue of justiciability. The United States argued, before withdrawing from the case, that the Central American conflict was essentially a political question and hence beyond the jurisdiction of the World Court.

The Court, including its distinguished Western members, rejected that contention, in my judgment rightly. The fundamental constitutional document of the contemporary international system is the United Nations Charter. I think it hard to disagree with the proposition that the principal purpose of the charter, of the norms it announced and the institutions it established, was regulating and limiting the use of force. The charter speaks directly to the issue of when force may legitimately be employed, namely in self–defense and, conversely, never in ways that threaten the political independence and territorial integrity of any state.

The Nicaraguan claim rests directly on an alleged violation of the charter. The Court's jurisdiction extends to cases arising out of treaties—the Charter is, of course a treaty—and since it was established coincident with the establishment of the United Nations and interrelates functionally with that institution, one may reasonably assume that the Founding Fathers regarded it as one of the linchpins of the new system. Since the overriding purpose of the new system, as I have already pointed out, was restraining the use of force in international relations, it would seem that if the Court were to have jurisdiction over any issue, it would be that one.

The United States position, as I understand it, is that, while the Court may be authorized to consider disputes before they erupt into armed conflict, once conflict has broken out, only the Security Council has jurisdiction. There is force to that argument, if the council is indeed functioning. But it plainly was not functioning at the time the United States challenged the Court's jurisdiction, in part because, by an earlier veto, the United States had indicated that it would not tolerate Security Council review of its actions against the Nicaraguan government. For the United States to invoke the putatively exclusive jurisdiction of the council after having disabled the council is, to say the least, amusing.

I turn now to where the Court will itself soon go, to the merits. As Counsel for the State Department, I would argue roughly as follows. The government of Nicaragua is in some measure aiding an armed rebellion against the recognized government of El Salvador. Since the rebels have not been recognized explicitly by any government, including the government of Nicaragua, as a movement equivalent in legitimacy to the Duarte regime, other states are not entitled under international law to aid them, just as all states are entitled to aid Duarte and his colleagues. Thus, Nicaragua cannot justify its behavior on the grounds that it is responding to prior illegal acts by the United States and other countries, such acts being the military assistance extended to the Duarte government. Unless and until the rebels are widely recognized as belligerents and the conflict as a classic civil war, aid to the rebels is an act of aggression. Within the terms of the

U.N. Charter, it is an armed attack entitling the friends of El Salvador to join it in acts of collective self–defense.

As part of the self–defense effort the United States has organized, armed, and supplemented opposition forces in Nicaragua, the so–called contras. Aid to the contras being in pursuit of Salvadoran security, it is legitimate as long as it complies with the classic principles of proportionality and exhaustion. Our response is clearly proportional to the delinquency, since that delinquency is properly defined as collusion in a sustained, powerful, and comprehensive effort to overthrow a legitimate government. We have, moreover, resorted to force only after failing through negotiations, threats and economic inducements to terminate the violation of Salvadoran sovereignty. To be sure, negotiations are episodically renewed. Their renewal is a sign of our good faith. But so far, they have proved fruitless because the Nicaraguan government is intransigently committed to a revolution without frontiers.

There, in essence, is the U.S. case. It is sufficiently respectable that a lawyer could present it without embarrassment. But in the end it fails to persuade me either as an application of existing international law or as an implicit claim about what the law ought to allow. Both considerations of policy and canons of construction cast doubt on the claim that virtually any level and kind of assistance to rebels allows other states to treat such assistance as the legal equivalent of an armed attack. Since aid to rebels is such a persistent feature of the contemporary state system with its porous borders and transnational sympathies, is it reasonable to construe a charter, designed above all to limit conflict, to authorize states to expand an essentially domestic conflict into an international one? Except in cases where cross–border aid is an important if not essential element in triggering or sustaining rebellion against duly constituted authorities, I think the answer must be "No."

Of course, the Reagan administration has alleged that Nicaraguan aid *is* essential for maintaining the Salvadoran opposition as a serious threat to the Duarte Government. But despite plausible claims by U.S. intelligence that it can determine when a toilet flushes in Managua, the evidence adduced by the administration to substantiate its allegations about the levels of Nicaraguan aid has been meager, insufficient to impress even the reporters of the *Wall Street Journal,* a newspaper not known for its leftist inclinations. This is, nevertheless, a question of fact that could have been presented to the World Court. The argument that we would have been hopelessly constrained by the need to protect intelligence sources is not wholly convincing, because most of the sources are doubtless technological in character rather than human and much of the technology of intelligence gathering is practically in the public domain. Furthermore, we would not have had to expose every grain of evidence to make our case. Surely, if Nicaraguan aid levels are as high as the administration implies, there ought to be a rich cornucopia of evidence from which we could draw sufficient nuggets to satisfy any reasonable evidential burden.

Be that as it may, the more serious objection to the administration's legal position is its claim to have exhausted measures short of force. That claim would be persuasive if we were offering to terminate aid to the contras in exchange for verifiable guarantees from the Sandinistas to terminate all forms of aid to the Salvadoran opposition. Under existing international law, that is all we have a right to demand. In an effort to circumvent this difficulty, the administration has sometimes alleged that the only secure guarantee of compliance would be the existence of a totally open political system in Nicaragua. For moral reasons, I would love to see such a system flourishing in that sad country. But the claimed connection between verification, on the one hand, and free press and an effective political opposition on the other is far too speculative to sustain the administration's legal argument. Exposés long after the fact have demonstrated the capacity of democratic governments like our own or those of Western Europe to carry out extensive intelligence operations in secrecy and in peacetime. But for the Watergate burglary, for instance, even today we would probably know nothing about the assassination plots and other operations conducted by the Central Intelligence Agency. Conversely, despite its restraints on the press and other deviations from the democratic model, Nicaragua, because of its position, is a porous and penetrable place and will remain so even if its government takes a still more authoritarian turn.

For at least two years, Managua has been sending signals indicating its readiness to trade revolutionary fraternity throughout Central America for U.S. tolerance of the revolution in Nicaragua. Contemporary international law requires the United States to test the bona fides of that offer. By upping the ante, by demanding power sharing in Managua (which may be a mere preliminary to an effort to eliminate the Sandinistas altogether), the United States has stepped outside the domain of legal justification as well as estranging itself from the Contadora powers.

Can it nevertheless be argued that the United States is acting in a manner consistent with the nature of a decentralized legal system where new law can be made only by pushing hard against the boundaries of the old law? That would depend, I take it, on whether U.S. behavior can be framed in terms of principles we are prepared to allow others to use as justifications. Particularly in the past year or two, the President has implied that producing democracy in Nicaragua is an end in itself justifying the use of force. Like Mario Vargas Llosa, the eminent Peruvian writer, I find it hard to imagine democracy taking root in the ruins left after a U.S.-orchestrated invasion of Nicaragua. But putting aside the question of plausible connection between the President's ends and the available means, is he in fact claiming that military interventions to create democracies should be treated as exceptions to the general prohibition of aggression?

In a world where most governments are not democratic, such a norm could never win much support and therefore cannot by its nature be anything more than a challenge to the very existence of a system of law among nations. Moreover, it is doubtful, very doubtful, that we as a people are prepared to act on the basis of the norm except where the nondemocratic regime is unfriendly to the United States or one of its allies. If we were prepared to intervene in Guatemala and Paraguay and South Africa, as well as Nicaragua, and remain in occupation the many long years required to construct a democratic system with any hope of surviving our departure, the norm would at least have *moral* allure.

The administration's rhetoric implies another claim that can be given legal form, namely that a certain sort of revolutionary regime is by its nature threatening to its neighbors and they are therefore entitled to eliminate it preemptively. This is, of course, somewhat, and hence disturbingly, analogous to the view the Soviet Union takes of non-Leninist parties of reform in Eastern Europe. In any event, it represents such an extension of the concept of self-defense that the term must become entirely subjective. And so it leads us back to the legal universe before the Second World War, when force was simply the conduct of diplomacy by other means. Being a great, civilized, and essentially satisfied power, our interests are unlikely to be best served by the recreation of a Hobbesian jungle where the rule of law has ceased altogether to restrain violence among states.

I appreciate that many of you may not agree with my analysis. My hope, however, is that you will agree that approaching the conflict in Central America from a legal perspective does help to sharpen the issues and to provide a framework encouraging to the open, informed, and mutually tolerant debate that is the hallmark of a democratic society.

Note

This chapter was originally delivered as an address to the Class of 1985 on the occasion of the University of New Mexico Law School's 36th Commencement.

17

On the Decision of the International Court of Justice in *Nicaragua* v. *United States*

As a recurring feature of the Cold War that has dominated international relations for the past four decades, foreign intervention in civil armed conflicts has focused and inflamed scholarly debate over the content of the relevant legal restraints. Conflict has raged particularly around the following issues: First, what forms and degree of assistance to rebels constitute an armed attack within the meaning of Article 51 of the Charter authorizing individual and collective self–defense? Second, in cases where assistance does not reach the armed–attack threshold, are there any circumstances in which the target state and/or its allies may nevertheless use forceful measures to terminate it?

The case of *Nicaragua v. the United States* presented the International Court of Justice with its first opportunity to confront these issues. If one takes decisions of the Court to be extremely persuasive statements of prevailing law, as I do, then the grounds for legitimate dispute have been sharply narrowed.

On the one hand, the Court concludes that there are circumstances where aid to rebels can be deemed an "armed attack" with all the attendant legal consequences. On the other, it categorically rejects the claim that a state crosses the armed–attack threshold merely by arming the rebels. Nor does it appear that arms plus advice and sanctuary for rebel leaders suffice to transform illegal intervention into an armed attack. What will suffice, if I understand the court correctly, is a level of collaboration exemplified by the Bay of Pigs, that is, where the rebels are organized, trained, armed, and then launched by their patron in an assault of such dimension that, if it were carried out by the patron state's own armed forces, there would unquestionably be an armed attack. Presumably (although the Court did not have to address this case), the dimension can be measured over time; in other words, multiple infiltration by small units ultimately could equal a single mass border crossing.

Infiltration into South Vietnam of Vietcong units from the North would seem to have satisfied the Court's standards, as does our relationship with the Nicaraguan contras. Nicaraguan assistance to the rebels in El Salvador, even if one accepts the U.S. government's broadest claims concerning its dimensions, does not.

With respect to the second issue, the Court seems to distinguish between an individual state's response to an illegal intervention in its affairs and the response of a third party on its behalf. If I understand the Court correctly, the former may retaliate by means short of an armed attack that, in addition, comply with the tests of necessity and proportionality. It follows, then, that El Salvador, the party aggrieved by Nicaragua's assistance to its rebels, but not the United States, is justified in providing arms to the contras, unless Nicaragua has ceased aiding its rebels or it appears reasonably likely that an end to such assistance could be achieved through negotiations. What is not entirely clear, however, is whether the Court intended to prohibit a third party, such as the United States, from sending arms to El Salvador on the condition that they be transshipped to the contras. Presumably, the mere knowledge of Salvador's intention to share U.S. military aid with the contras would not render such aid illegitimate.

While this is not an inevitable interpretation of contemporary international law, in my judgment it is the one that most effectively reconciles the international system's preeminent interests: conflict containment and national sovereignty (expressed in terms of territorial integrity and political independence). Since aid to rebels is a ubiquitous feature of the contemporary state system with its many porous borders, authoritarian and narrowly based governments, sectarian strife and transnational sympathies, anything other than a high and conspicuous threshold between an armed attack justifying the exercise of self-defense and lesser forms of intervention, particularly forms that transiently threaten freedom of choice but not the long-term territorial integrity or political independence of the state, would invite internationalization of essentially civil conflicts. Of course U.S.–Soviet competition enhances the prospect and gravely aggravates the potential consequences of civil conflicts spilling across national boundaries. By distinguishing between individual and collective response to illegal intervention, the Court seeks to reduce the risk of direct involvement by a superpower, presumably on the plausible assumption that, because of their concern with "credibility" on a global basis, the great powers tend to impute cosmic significance to minor conflicts.

But rather than being the system's summit value, war avoidance enjoys at best a standoff with national sovereignty. The charter is not a mandate for pacifism. It recognizes an inherent right of self-defense. Hence, the Court could not reasonably hold that aid to rebels can never serve as the equivalent of an armed attack. For in that event, one state could with legal impunity eliminate another as an independent political actor through the medium of a mercenary army recruited from the citizens of the target state.

One obstacle to this stratagem for subverting another state's independence is the still unchallenged right of a third power to aid a recognized government within its territory. But not every vulnerable state may have a white knight willing to provide large-scale assistance. Moreover, even where one is available, inability to attack the rebel base will in some cases promise a more prolonged and costly involvement. Thus, the knight will have additional incentive to remain in his castle or to return to it before the damsel is secure.

It is as difficult to generalize about the impact of foreign assistance on rebellions as it is to generalize about rebellions. Nevertheless, I think one can say with little fear of contradiction that most subversive movements fail with or without some measure of external aid. Through their control of the bureaucracy and the national communications network, of the principal cities and ports, of the security forces and financial reserves and jobs, and through their ready access to the international arms market, established governments begin with immense advantages. A few manage by virtue of extraordinary ineptitude and avarice to activate a broad, multi-class opposition that eats away at their human base until the superstructure finally topples.

In a world drowning in arms available with no questions asked to anyone with ready cash, few rebels are critically dependent on foreign patrons, at least before they have multiplied to the point where, properly armed, they can engage government forces in large-unit combat. Writers eager to justify treating aid to rebels as the equivalent of an armed attack tend wildly to exaggerate the costs of counterinsurgency. Their favorite cliché is that guerrillas win if they do not lose; in other words, that the government must utterly annihilate its opponents or face eventual defeat. This is one cliché that lacks the simple dignity of truth. If the bulk of a nation's human and material resources are in areas inhospitable to guerrilla operations, governments can survive indefinitely without eradicating the rebels, can even prosper (like the government of Thailand, for instance) while guerrillas wither in the bush.

If, as I believe, the availability of arms and advice from a foreign patron is an insufficient condition for the outbreak of an authentically indigenous rebellion, much less its development into a force capable of replacing the recognized government, then it seems fair to conclude that in prohibiting third-party retaliation against the rebels' arms supplier, the Court has not, in the process of restricting legal justifications for cross-border escalation of civil strife, radically discounted the value of political independence. From one perspective, the decision can be seen even to enhance its value, depending on whether or not one regards a recognized government as the exclusive repository of national sovereignty.

In the colonial context and in the name of national self-determination, the U.N. has gone behind the political institutions established by metropolitan governments to locate sovereignty in the people of the territory. There is, therefore, some precedent at the global level for regarding people, not governments, as the ultimate locus of sovereignty. One regional precedent pointing in the same direction was the resolution of the OAS Organ of Consultation calling for the resignation of Anastasio Somoza in the light of overwhelming popular opposition to the continuance of his reign. On this view of sovereignty's source and on the assumption that rebellions rarely succeed unless the rebels enjoy very broad popular support vis-à-vis the incumbents, a decision adding yet another weapon to the incumbent's vast armory of advantages would have undermined political independence properly conceived.

My assumption about the normal prerequisite for a successful rebellion is least plausible where a foreign patron does not serve merely as rebellion's armorer and advisor, but rather plays a role in its creation, organization, financing and training and in its tactical and strategic direction. Because there have been cases where foreign patronage was essential for the emergence of large-scale insurgency threatening the survival of the established political authorities, immunization of the patron from retaliation under all circumstances could not have been squared with the indisputably powerful claims of national autonomy. The Court has drawn as bright a line as the conflicting values permit and it has drawn it in the right place.

Because of the Court's position on the basic legal issues, and because those issues have been relentlessly contested in every sort of forum and scholarly journal, the refusal of the United States to defend its position on the merits in no way undermines the force of the Court's conclusions. As I pointed out above, given the Court's statement of the law, U.S. aid to the contras would be culpable, even if one accepted at face value the administration's most extravagant claims about Nicaraguan aid to Salvador's insurgents.

Since, on the basis of its past performances, no one could have confidently anticipated the court's laudable but bold resolution of such fundamental legal issues, I think we need to look elsewhere, though not far, for an explanation of the administration's decision to cut and run. The fact is that the administration was bound to lose however the Court ruled on the question of whether arming rebels triggered rights to the exercise of collective self-defense. For recourse to force would in any event remain subject to the condition that nonviolent remedies have been exhausted.

For several years, the comandantes in Managua have been signaling their readiness to trade the option of aiding entrepreneurs of revolution elsewhere in Central America for U.S. tolerance of Nicaragua's revolution, such as it is. Undisputed legal norms require Washington to test the bona fides of that offer. By upping the ante, by demanding power sharing in Managua (possibly as a ploy for eliminating the Sandinistas altogether), the United States has stepped outside the bounds of possible legal justification. As for the moral dimension of policy, like that impeccable Latin democrat, Mario Vargas Llosa, I find it hard to envision democracy taking root amidst the ruins and the White Terror that would follow a U.S.-powered occupation of Nicaragua's cities by the contra armed forces. If the past is prologue, we should anticipate ending up not with a second Costa Rica, but rather with another Guatemala of the past three decades: Murder Incorporated with a flag.

Note

This chapter was originally published as a comment in the *American Journal of International Law,* January 1987. Reprinted with permission.

PART IV
THE UNITED STATES IN CENTRAL AMERICA: COSA NOSTRA

18

Central American Realities

I

I will not begin by indulging the amiable cliché about your unenviable task. By definition, public men aspire to serve the nation by clarifying and prescribing policy. So do most academics.

To call your task enviable is not to disparage its difficulties. Both the President and most of his critics have announced goals for the United States in Central America that are very difficult to reconcile. Indeed, as I wrote recently in the journal *Foreign Policy*, if democracy, human rights, economic development, and security objectives can be reconciled at all, it is only through yet more intensive intervention in the region's affairs, "for ends uncongenial to conservatives, by means unsettling to liberals, and at a cost disproportionate to any conventional conception of the national interest." The enormous obstacles to reconciliation stem directly from the political, social, and economic realities of Central America.

Before trying to sketch those realities and to suggest their implications for national policy, I probably owe you a mercifully brief autobiographical note, which will suggest the values and experiences in which my analysis is rooted. Nominated originally by the Ford administration and renominated four years later by its Democratic successor, I have twice been elected by the Member States of the OAS to the Inter-American Commission on Human Rights. From 1980 to 1982, I served as the commission's president, the first North American to be selected by his colleagues for that post. The commission consists of seven people, usually lawyers with a background in public service and/or academic life, who are morally and legally obligated to promote and enforce the human rights codified in relevant treaties and declarations, and to do so completely independently of the governments of which they are citizens.

I am not telling tales out of school when I say quite frankly that in the eight years I have served, the commission has represented a broad swathe of the hemispheric political spectrum extending from the Right to center–Left, a space as wide as that which separates the right and left wings of the Republican and Democratic Parties in this country. Despite our ideological differences, we have consistently achieved consensus about the situation of human rights in the many countries we have examined. In the course of the commission's work, I have visited Guatemala, El Salvador, and Nicaragua; three times in the latter case. I also have been in Costa Rica several times on human rights matters. The present Foreign Minister of Costa Rica, Fernando Volio, was my colleague on the commission from 1976 to 1979, and the Foreign Minister of Honduras, Dr. Edgardo Paz Barnica, was for a number of years a lawyer on our staff.

II

What are the principal characteristics of the political institutions and practices of the Central American countries?

At least until the overthrow of the Somoza regime in Nicaragua, one could usefully divide them into two categories: Costa Rica and the rest. Costa Rica was and remains an authentic political democracy. That democracy coincides with three other societal characteristics: the absence of a highly concentrated pattern of land ownership; the absence of an institutionalized officer corps; and ethnically a rather homogeneous population. Since other countries with comparatively homogeneous populations—most notably Argentina—have not yet managed to produce a democratic political culture, I am inclined to discount, albeit not to exclude, that factor as an explanation of Costa Rica's achievements. The other two factors are in conjunction unique not only for Central America but for the whole of Latin America. Even individually they are remarkable.

The dispersion of land ownership can be traced back to the Colonial period. The elimination of the officer corps is a more recent phenomenon. In 1948, when political adventurers tried to set aside constitutional and electoral restraints by calling in the country's small armed forces, Pepe Figueras led a coalition of citizen–soldiers to military victory. They then consolidated civilian rule by choosing not to replace the officer corps. They recognized that, as they lived under the shadow of the United States, they lived as well under its protection from external attack. They recognized, in other words, that historically the only real function for armed forces in Central America has been to foster social mobility for middle–class lads with a taste for violence and to repress challenges to the distribution of wealth and power. Since there already existed in Costa Rica a rather broad consensus that the distribution of values was not conspicuously unjust and since Figueres and his colleagues were determined to use the political process to promote consensus-building social justice, an officer corps represented to them a cluster of vices without compensating virtues.

Costa Rica has a constabulary; but it is small, lightly armed, and its most senior officers are nonprofessional, political appointees who only expect to serve during the term of the president who appoints them.

I don't want to idealize this country, which is, after all, run by men, not angels. There is poverty despite welfare programs unusually broad for a country at its per capita income level. There appears to be neglect of, if not outright discrimination against, the Black minority that lives on the Atlantic Coast. I am not blind to blemishes, but after a decade lifting rocks in various Latin American countries to see what's crawling around underneath, I cannot help being deeply impressed by the civility, the tolerance, the commitment to majoritarian democracy and the fair application of the law and the aspiration to social justice that characterize Costa Rican political elites.

Through bad management and bad luck, the country has been hard hit by the global recession. Some have criticized its politicians for spending profligately to provide a very modest measure of economic security for its middle and lower classes, as if political elites should be punitively singled out for such atypical concern. Well, Costa Rica's financial condition is doubtless grave. But we find the same illness in countries whose leaders could never be accused of undue concern for the impact of their policies on ordinary people.

We have discovered how hard it is to build democracy in the Third World. Here is one that has built itself. If there is a scintilla of truth to our claimed passion for the spread of this political species, then we should do what is necessary to help Costa Rica through this difficult period.

III

I turn now to Nicaragua, El Salvador, and Guatemala. Before the fall of Somoza, they had every ugly feature so notably absent from Costa Rica: brutal and parasitic armed forces; heavy concentration of land ownership and, for that matter, all other forms of wealth and status; and corresponding political institutions and processes that hid the substance of tyranny behind the thin, mocking forms of constitutional democracy. While sharing those primal characteristics, they differed in some consequential ways.

If El Salvador was the country of the fourteen families, Nicaragua was the country of only one. The Somoza family's acquisitive passions achieved their apogee in the person of Anastasio, whose achievements gave new meaning to the term kleptocracy, that is, government as theft. It appears that the opportunities for profit created by the disastrous earthquake of 1972, which practically wiped out the city of Managua, turned mere passion into mania. Of the tens of millions of dollars poured into the country by public and private philanthropies, few seem to have contributed to reconstruction. Arriving in Managua for the first time, I had to be reassured that I had arrived in Managua rather than the shattered remains of an extinct civilization grouped around the Intercontinental Hotel. It is estimated that by the time he resigned and fled the country, Somoza controlled entities producing 25% of the gross national product. Of course, any such estimate would not take into account the thin line between the national and the family budget.

During most of the Somoza family's 47-year rule, the country's business, land-holding, and professional classes had either collaborated with the regime or formed a tolerated, conspicuously ineffectual opposition, which, by participating in elections and serving in the National Congress, lent some credibility to what was in fact an electoral farce. But as Somoza's galloping greed discouraged foreign investment, distorted the economy (which nevertheless continued to grow), and progressively concentrated in his hands capital assets and investment opportunities, the bulk of these classes united behind Pedro Chamorro, who had for years been Somoza's most courageous, effective and consistent opponent. By the time Chamorro's assassination lit this tinder, the regime had been reduced to the family, its civilian retainers, and the National Guard. The guard was nothing more than a private army owing allegiance not to the abstraction of the state but to Somoza himself. Nicaragua was in effect a country occupied by a kind of Cosa Nostra. And the rising sparked by Chamorro's death was nothing less than that rarest of phenomena, an authentic multi-class rebellion against a nominally indigenous group seen to be as alien as a foreign army of occupation.

Since the revolution, the commission has, at the invitation of the government of Nicaragua, conducted two "observations *in loco.*" The first, carried out almost exactly one year after Somoza's departure, led to a report presented to the 1982 General Assembly of the OAS. It dealt with all aspects of the postrevolutionary condition of human rights.

In June of 1982, I was a member of a subcommission that made a second visit, this time focused on the situation of the Miskito Indians. The report stemming from this last visit and a related one carried out in Honduras at the main refugee camp is still confidential because in the interim, at the request of the Nicaraguan government, the commission has been trying to arrange a friendly settlement of the complaints made against the government by various Miskitos.

I will be happy to answer questions about my observations of human rights conditions if you deem them relevant to your inquiries. Of course, I think they are. But since the time for this initial presentation is limited and since I anticipate some of you will wish to pursue the human rights question, let me refer briefly to several aspects of the Nicaraguan situation that you might not elicit through questions and that are clearly relevant to the optimal shape of U.S. policy toward this country.

First, I have been told, not only by high officials of the present government but also by members of the credible opposition, that the Sandinistas do wish to preserve a private sector. They grudgingly recognize the need for its managerial and entrepreneurial skills. What, it seems to me, they have not worked out in their own minds is how to maintain an effective private sector while attempting to deny it political influence. The recent history of Brazil and Chile demonstrate, if demonstration were needed, that a vigorous private sector can coexist very cheerfully with harsh authoritarian government. But those governments did not have among their central political projects the promotion of equality and mass welfare and the political isolation of what the Sandinistas would call the "bourgeois classes."

Second, the Sandinista leadership is for the most part insular and inexperienced. These are generally quite young men and women with little direct knowledge of the world beyond Central America. For them, the United States is personified by generations of U.S. ambassadors who hobnobbed with Somoza and of U.S. officers who provided technical assistance to Somoza's goons. Conversely, they have a romantically colored view of the Soviet Union and Cuba.

But, *third,* despite being at the outset besotted with a naive, Marxist conception of the universe and despite their provincialism, not always untainted by arrogance, they apparently have begun to discover the complexity not only of the outer world, but of their native land. For instance, they apparently have stopped seeing the United States as a monolith driven by a Procrustean passion to shape every nation into a cog in a single vast capitalist machine.

They also have begun to learn that Nicaragua is not Cuba. In Cuba at the time of Castro's accession, landless laborers on the sugar estates were numerically predominant in the countryside. Castro could win their support without setting them up as successful, independent farmers. In Nicaragua, however, even peasants who worked on estates usually had a little land. After the revolution they hoped for more. Driven by ideology alone, determined not to produce what they saw as a Kulak class of comfortable, organized, and politically potent farmers, the Sandinista leadership refused to solve the minifundia problem. And it added injured pocketbooks to crippled hopes by suppressing the price of food produced by small farmers for Nicaragua's urban markets. As a result, the wealthy ex–Somocistas in

Key Biscayne and the ex-Guardia officers who run the "contras" have been able to recruit cannon fodder from among the peasantry, particularly in certain parts of the country. Of course, the great majority are not involved in the fighting. But like all similarly circumstanced farmers, they fight back by cutting back production. Momentum for a family-farm-oriented land reform program finally seems to be building within the Sandinista leadership. Probably from its perspective this is only a tactical step. But such a tactical step will create powerful obstacles to the later socialization of agriculture. My primary point, however, is that ideological hallucination is yielding in various areas to the educative force of experience. One can strike pragmatic interstate deals with pragmatists. With fanatics there is less hope.

Fourth, at least as of the time of my last visit and (according to my sources) even today in the midst of war, the country itself still is very accessible, almost transparent, and its political, social, and economic institutions still in flux.

Fifth, it clearly is the intention of the Sandinista government to educate and mobilize into heightened political awareness and permanent political participation the great mass of the population which, until the assassination of Pedro Chamorro, was essentially passive, excluded and miserably poor. The Sandinistas presumably assume that in doing so they will facilitate perpetuation of their regime. My own assessment is that a mobilized, politically aware population will not for long submit to government by junta, even a junta which enjoys the glamour of military victory and employs egalitarian rhetoric.

This is a Catholic country; and it is a country with only a very small cadre of ideologically committed activists. And even within the cadre one senses considerable disparity in political vision as well as competing ambitions. And it is a cadre without the resources or the skills required to make a centrally planned and managed and autarkic economy function. The need to relate to the international economy, to export to and import from capitalist countries and to encourage investment, will reinforce domestic pressures for a more pluralistic regime. But for the time being, these forces cutting against the sustained centralization of power are offset by the regime's ability to invoke national pride and intense fear of the old National Guard officers who dominate the military force we have armed, paid, and organized to oppose the Sandinista government. Paradoxically, the economic sanctions organized by the Reagan administration also play into the hands of the most extreme Sandinistas; for they deprive the economy of almost all essential goods other than the ones the regime itself controls, and help it justify that control. Obviously monopoly control of food and heat-ing oil and other necessities facilitates the regime's efforts to mobilize people into the militia and the civilian mass organizations.

I think that one root of present policy is a theologically pessimistic assumption about the natural course of left-wing revolutionary regimes, in particular about their ability to perpetuate themselves without evolving into more participatory political orders. In light of the many paths left-wing authoritarian regimes have followed after their birth, I believe that assumption is unwarranted.

IV

If one is interested in examples of stable, authoritarian rule, one need only take the brief boat trip across the narrow gulf of Fonseca to El Salvador, where a political and social order established several centuries earlier during the Colonial era remained essentially unchanged until 1979, when a coup d'etat organized by younger officers offered the first promise of serious reform. Independence from Spain had simply meant that the handful of land-owning families could rule undisturbed by Spanish bureaucrats and had to use a home-grown army rather than Spanish troops as their instrument for repressing and disciplining the peasant masses.

As the World Bank has noted, among the several great pools of poverty in the world, Latin America is distinguished by its intense concentration of land holding. But even in an area where concentration is the norm, El Salvador's concentration was remarkable.

You know, of course, that the officers who led the 1979 coup, having co-opted leading members of the democratic political opposition to the new government, announced a sweeping land reform. This remarkable break with the past occurred precisely three months after the collapse of the Nicaraguan National Guard and was timed to coincide with the release of our commission's Report on Human Rights in El Salvador, a report known by the El Salvadoran armed forces to be extremely critical. Our earlier report on the Somoza regime had, according to Somoza himself, been one of the factors leading him to conclude that his regime was doomed. Aside from this circumstantial evidence, my conversations with civilians who participated in the post-coup government confirm that the dominating force behind the coup was not moral regeneration through divine intervention; it was fear—fear that what had happened in Nicaragua could happen in El Salvador: If the United States were passive, the armed forces could be defeated by rebels enjoying broad support.

The land reform, together with the nationalization of finance and exporting companies, was designed to win the approval of the United States, to appease peasant hostility and to break the political power of an oligarchy rigidly hostile to social reform. But all of these steps were designed ultimately to preserve the military as an institution, a self-perpetuating, autonomous force, a state within the state. Inside the armed forces there may have been, perhaps there still are, a few idealists. As a rule, however, idealists would not be much attracted to an institution that had stolen the prior two presidential elections, massacred unarmed supporters of the defrauded candidates, and was the notoriously corrupt instrument of a tiny oligarchy.

What has become evident in the disillusioning years since 1979 is that the principal division within the armed forces was between those who believed that they could best survive through reform and those who believed that massacre, a time-tested means, would suffice. For me, the most significant fact about the post-1979 years is that the diminished momentum of social reform coincides almost perfectly with the election of the Reagan administration, which, even before it assumed office, had already sent messages throughout Latin America that it was unconditionally committed to the defense of all right-wing regimes. The fundamental dilemma of policy in El Salvador, or, for that matter, in Guatemala, is how can we hope to reform systems of power that seem responsive only to the threat of their destruction, when we begin by guaranteeing their survival.

The only semblance of a theory I have heard consistently articulated is that by training the officer corps our own officers will somehow inculcate them with democratic values. If public, pundits and politicians were not so amnesiac in this country, the collective response to this assertion would be a yawn of déjà vu. In the early days of the Kennedy administration, I was responsible for the presentation of the military assistance program to Congress. Those were the days of the Alliance for Progress, with its theme of providing a shield behind which, under our prodding, the Latin governments would somehow reform themselves. One point I wrote regularly into the presentation books for Latin America was the tremendous capacity we enjoyed for imparting democratic values to decidedly undemocratic military officers.

Did I have a theory about how this might occur? Had I even bothered to investigate which U.S. officers with what sorts of ideas and using what means were carrying out this training? Of course not. It was just a pious slogan, a fact I don't think I quite appreciated at the time.

Since then, I have had occasion to talk with Latin graduates of our training schools and with U.S. military men who know something about the programs. And I can assure you, that the inculcation of democratic values does not rank high on the list of training priorities. On the contrary, programs, to the extent they have an ideological content, reinforce the view instinct in Latin security forces that the Communists are everywhere, insinuating their way into every social institution, concealing themselves as reformists. And the military is therefore encouraged to develop total responses. National security becomes a fig leaf for military efforts to dominate or destroy every institution threatening the status quo.

Would anything change if you sent me down to give lectures on human rights and democracy? Only on the implicit theory that these chaps we are training are fools who do not know what is in their interest. If only they were more professional, if only they were *au courant* with modern methods of interrogation and sophisticated rules of engagement, I've heard it said, they would stop busting the skulls of babies, raping their mothers, and castrating before garroting their fathers.

What an arrogant and cheap delusion. Most of the Latin American military men (not to mention right–wing civilians) I have spoken to in countries where violations of human rights are epidemic are perfectly rational people led by experience to conclude that as their own objectives become progressively incongruent with the demands of an increasingly mobilized civilian population, ever more extreme forms of intimidation are required to maintain the essentials of the status quo, above all to maintain the dominant role of the armed forces and of the agro–industrial oligarchy on which they rely to make the economy work.

Another conceivable theory justifying U.S. assistance to armies dedicated to their own hegemonic role is that somehow, someday, if economic growth persists and the middle class expands, Central American states will duplicate the experience of Northern Europe and North America in producing welfare democracies and armies subject to civilian control. This is a very pretty idea. It could happen, but not unless these societies first undergo changes that go to the institutional roots of the status quo. In brief, I propose that producing reasonably just, stable, and democratic systems in El Salvador, Guatemala, and Honduras too requires changing basic institutions. Those changes, including the reduction and transformation of the armed forces, in that they constitute changes in bedrock features of those societies, are literally "radical." If they were to occur, then after the event one would say: "These countries have experienced a revolution." I see no signs that the United States is prepared to manage it.

I imagine that some of you, citing cases like Peru in the late 1960s, Turkey in the era of Ataturk, and even Egypt's Nasser, might wonder why such nationalist reformers have not emerged as dominant military leaders in Central America. Paradoxically, the one clear case of such a phenomenon occurred in a country that in the past 30 years has become a synonym for state terror in the service of the status quo. I refer, of course, to Guatemala. Even conservative, circumspect Latin diplomats and lawyers and politicians privately describe the *typical* Guatemalan officer and his civilian political allies as "savages," men with an unparalleled instinct for butchery. The extent of that butchery—indiscriminate murder and unspeakable torture of professors, priests, students, labor leaders, politicians, or anyone who questioned the existing order is recounted in a report of the Inter-American Commission covering the Lucas era. A report on the Rios Montt period will be published shortly. No doubt there will be a third, since as awful as was the behavior of the armed forces during Rios Montt's ascendancy, he nevertheless took a few hesitant steps in the direction of institutional change. Now he has been replaced by officers who are the old companions of General Lucas and in many cases tied to the pro-Fascist parties of the political Right.

Where are the reformers in Guatemala? They emerged in the early 1940s. A reformist faction in the armed forces backed the distinguished civilian leader, Juan José Arévalo. He served a presidential term, initiated reforms in land tenure and the conditions of rural labor, and was succeeded by a military officer, Jacobo Arbenz. The single largest land owner in the country was United Fruit. Its old lawyer, John Foster Dulles, by now Secretary of State, cynically or otherwise accepted United Fruit's charge that Arbenz was a Communist and set about organizing his overthrow. The CIA coordinated the successful effort. It led in turn to a purge of reformist officers who had backed Arbenz. A second purge occurred in 1960, when cadets and some younger officers, their nationalism inflamed by the use of Guatemalan soil by the CIA for training the force that would soon invade Cuba, staged a coup. And that coup might well have succeeded if the rebels had not been bombed and strafed by planes flown by Cuban participants in the forces undergoing training. Officers who survived were purged. Some, including two outstanding men trained by the United States, went into the hills and formed the first guerrilla movement. Aided by us, the government launched the first of its counterinsurgency campaigns using the time-honored tactics of massacring the peasant population in the areas of guerrilla operations. In Guatemala, the more things change, the more they remain the same.

The situation in Guatemala underscores the pernicious illusion that elections equal democracy and legitimacy. Elections are, of course, a necessary condition of democratic government; but even the meagerest experience in Central and, for that matter, South America reveals that they are by themselves insufficient. One of the reasons my commission has consistently rejected invitations to observe elections is our realization that we could do little more than assure that the ballots were counted accurately. Yet we know that in the social, economic, and political conditions obtaining in many countries, the ways of fixing the outcome of elections are as diverse as any other product of the human imagination.

Let me conclude with a word on Honduras, a country whose evolution illustrates the tragic consequences of the policies we are pursuing in the name of democracy. On the one hand, Honduras is by far the most underdeveloped country in Central America. When I last looked its per capita income was the lowest in the Caribbean Basin, with the exception of Haiti. It was also widely perceived as the country for which the term "Banana Republic" was conceived; not only or even primarily because of its dependence on this export crop, but rather because of its passive, almost sycophantic, relationship with U.S. interests controlling the growth and export of bananas.

On the other hand, by comparison with their counterparts in El Salvador, Guatemala, and Somoza's Nicaragua, the Honduran military seemed benign. It tolerated the development of trade unions among its very small working class and of peasant unions as well. It at least dialogued with representatives of the poorer classes. It did not treat every effort to organize the lower classes as a threat to be liquidated forthwith. It even began a trickle of land reform. And in the wake of revelations that the successor to United Fruit had bribed the then president, a general, to avoid the export tax on bananas, a group of younger officers forced the thief's resignation and quickened the pace of reform.

Prodded by the middle class and the trade unions, and pushed as well by the Carter administration, the armed forces finally resolved to restore civilian government. Full–fledged democracy was a bit much for them to swallow. They manipulated the party registration laws to hamstring the Christian Democratic Party, since they regarded it as too reformist and uncontrollable. And they allowed the liberal candidate, Roberto Suazo Cordoba, to assume office only after he had agreed not to exercise his constitutional power to replace officers whose commitment to civilian rule was doubtful. Nevertheless, our commission and everyone else in the hemisphere who welcomes the spread of democracy felt a surge of optimism about the future of Honduras.

Optimism was transient. It is now evident that most important policy decisions in Honduran society—decisions about the budget, about foreign and defense policy—are subject to veto by the military when it does not simply dictate them. The civilian regime is only a little more than a facade. When you take a country with a long tradition of profound psychological dependence on the United States, a country without any tradition of military subordination to civilian rule, a country with a small middle class and a still essentially passive peasantry; a country that is miserably poor; when the United States takes such a country and pours resources directly into the hands of senior military officers, the United States is gutting the promise of civilian rule. It is doing more than that. Civilian government and the brief flowering of hope created a will to resist de facto military rule. Officers enthusiastically complicit in the process by means of which Honduras has become a U.S. base for open and clandestine military operations, together with Right-Wing business interests and, it is reported, local representatives of the Moonies, have attempted to suppress critics. There have been beatings and some disappearances. The society is polarizing. Soon not even the fragile tradition of dialogue will remain to commemorate a once hopeful experiment.

I have not painted a pretty picture. What else could I do, being wedded as I am to the ethics of candor.

V

It is fashionable in some circles to blame external forces for Central America's convulsions. External forces have played an important role; but the main external force is not military and communist; it is economic and capitalist. During the two decades ending in the late 1970s, ripples from the dynamic centers of world capitalism coursed through Central America, helping the region's states experience a novel period of sustained high growth. While a good deal of the resulting wealth passed through Central America like a dose of salts ending up in Miami, Geneva, and other developing areas, growth did, nevertheless, expand the middle and industrial working classes. While it vastly increased the wealth of a few and modestly enhanced the income of a considerably larger number, its net effect on the poorer classes—60% to 80% percent of the population in Guatemala, Nicaragua, Honduras, and El Salvador—varied from marginal enhancement to absolute deprivation. Rapid growth meant inflation, which is disastrous for those without the means and leverage to keep ahead of price increases. And rapid growth encouraged the rationalization of agricultural enterprise through the substitution of machinery and wage labor for tenant farmers. When the appetite for profit maximization penetrates less developed areas, it leads also to extralegal land seizures by officers and oligarchs in control of the state machinery.

As it displaces peasants and mutilates their time-honored expectations, and as it expands the middle classes in countries where officers and oligarchs treat their own perquisites as if they were holy relics, growth generates revolutionary pressure. If this is disturbing to persons ready to sacrifice every American ideal on the altar of stability, it should be good news for those who welcome the proliferation of democracies. For what growth has accomplished in conjunction with the spread of the idea of human rights, thanks in part to the efforts of the Catholic Church, is to create the class and ideological materials requisite for building democracy. But it cannot be built by reinforcing the men and the institutions consecrated to channeling change within obsolete and antidemocratic forms. It can be built only by fracturing the old order of things. To fracture it, we must present its defenders with the alternatives of change and defeat. The authoritarian Left is our principal lever against the authoritarian Right.

As I have argued elsewhere, traditionally conceived national security interests do not require our involvement in Central America's civil wars. Our military, economic, and political weight enables us to impose a pax Finlandia on Nicaragua and any other Marxist regimes which may emerge. Traditional notions of security require only that such regimes deny military facilities of any kind to extracontinental powers and do not invade their neighbors. However, if for idealistic reasons we wish to do more than national security requires, then we must act like a great power.

The place to begin is with language itself. As we use it today, "nonintervention" means *intervention to guarantee the survival of an obsolete class of rulers.* As building blocks for democracy, the armed forces of El Salvador, Guatemala, and Honduras are about as adequate as their Polish counterpart. As long as we deceive ourselves with this sort of newspeak, we will neither build democracy nor purchase security at a rational cost.

Note

This chapter originated as a statement presented to the National Bipartisan Commission on Central America, September 19, 1983.

19

Manage the Revolution?

In his July 18, 1983, speech to the International Longshoremen's Association outlining U.S. policy for Central America, President Ronald Reagan appealed for consensus, presumably between his liberal critics and conservative enthusiasts. Yet liberal and conservative rhetoric already implies agreement on the fundamental goals of U.S. policy toward the region. The real problem is that the objectives both groups nominally support in Central America are mutually inconsistent, given the current form and level of U.S. involvement. And the only way to reconcile them is through yet more massive intervention in Central American affairs, particularly in El Salvador, for ends uncongenial to conservatives, by means unsettling to liberals, and at a cost disproportionate to any conventional conception of the national interest.

Purporting to speak as liberals, the editors of *The New Republic* say: "It is difficult to quarrel with a plan to 'support democracy, human rights, and freedom, economic development, the security of the region's threatened nations [and] dialogue and negotiations.'" The problem, they conclude, lies not in Reagan's words but in his deeds, including "the firing of Thomas Enders and Deane Hinton, officials who support the telling of the full truth in Central America." Yet the very statement of aims that *The New Republic* applauds is itself a denial of the truth, as well as an unintended promise that consensus will never be achieved.

The claim that the region's nations are threatened is deceptive. No matter who wins in El Salvador, Guatemala, or, for that matter, Nicaragua, each nation will survive as a state no less independent than most of its other Third World peers. None will turn into Afghanistans, much less Latvias. Nor, in the event of rightist victories, is Congress likely to incorporate them into the federal union.

Civil wars, not invasions, convulse Central America. Each side receives external assistance. Even taking at face value the most extravagant administration claims about Cuban assistance, U.S. levels of material support dwarf it. But if levels of assistance cannot be employed as proxies for illegal invasion, the only distinction remaining to support the President's claim about the threat to the region is one that emphasizes the character of those who receive outside aid. Implicit in the Reagan administration's view of El Salvador is the proposition that aid to the recognized government is qualitatively different from aid to its opponents: Only the latter threatens the "nation."

For well over a century, this distinction has generally prevailed in international legal theory and in state practice as well, although it has never been free of critics. In particular cases, dispute has swirled around the identity of the legitimate government. Normally, however, the mantle of legitimacy has been worn by any faction able to achieve and sustain effective control of the national capital, except possibly in cases such as Cambodia and Afghanistan, where the initial seizure of power as well as its retention depended on massive foreign intervention.

This traditional discrimination in favor of the once-recognized government allowed such regimes to retain their auras of legitimacy even if, after having achieved power more or less independently, they survived only through the support of a foreign army. The traditional rationale stemmed naturally from the once-unchallenged assumption, in part functional and in part metaphysical, that sovereignty was an indivisible attribute that had to be situated somewhere—before the Eighteenth Century, for example, in an absolute monarch, the sovereign.

As sovereignty was indivisible for international legal purposes, so was the nation and its governing regime, the latter being simply the organ of the former, which was authorized to speak for it in international affairs. If the cluster of transient power holders in the capital is regarded as the nation, then it follows logically that aid to its opponents is a kind of aggression.

Since international law is nothing more than the consensus of governing elites, the enduring charms of this conception are unremarkable. But in attempting to rally support for his policies, Reagan has used not only the dry language of legal rectitude but also the stirring metaphors of morality, the morality of liberalism, which roots legitimate rule in popular consent. Only where that consent is manifest have liberals been prepared to equate the regime and the nation. This conception of legitimacy has monopolized American popular sentiment right across the political spectrum. Conservatives such as President William McKinley and liberals such as President John Kennedy alike have invoked it to justify their foreign adventures.

Incompatible Rationales

The legal and liberal conceptions of legitimacy employed by Reagan with the apparent agreement even of many of his harshest congressional critics serve badly as justifications for U.S. policy in Central America. The conceptions serve badly, first, because they are conceptually incompatible. The United States cannot have it both ways. If the only legitimate governments are those with an electoral mandate, then, even under the administration's version of reality, the government of Guatemala, one of the countries on the President's list of threatened states, was patently illegitimate at the time he spoke. And it would therefore follow that aid to its local opponents was not.

The conceptions also serve badly because in prior dealings with Latin America the United States has applied these norms selectively, imposing on its hemispheric neighbors through covert actions or actual invasions what former Under Secretary of State George Ball recently called "a reverse Brezhnev doctrine." Hence, the current U.S. insistence on the merits of such rationales is unpersuasive to many liberals and to almost all social democrats in Latin America and in Western Europe, presumably natural U.S. allies. A new President might begin with an almost–clean slate by repudiating his predecessors. But this administration shows no inclination to distance itself, on the one hand from the 1961 Bay of Pigs or the 1965 Dominican Republic invasions—which cannot be reconciled with the legal norm–or, on the other hand, from the coup managed by the Central Intelligence Agency against an elected Guatemalan government in 1954 and U.S. encouragement of a coup against the lawfully elected government of Chile in 1970—actions irreconcilable with either norm.

The third vice displayed by these conceptions is their incompatibility with a settlement of the Central American crisis on terms consistent with the humane and democratic values of U.S. allies and, more important, of U.S. citizens. For how can anyone who believes that the Salvadoran government under its current leadership represents that country's sole repository of legal and moral legitimacy pressure El Salvador to negotiate anything other than the terms of rebel surrender? Yet the fact remains that negotiations are a necessary first step, not only toward ending the slaughter but also toward establishing in that country for the first time a minimally just society and minimally democratic government.

That negotiations are a precondition implies a fourth and terminal vice, namely, that not even the moral norm is applicable to El Salvador. The Reagan administration surpasses its recent predecessors in at least one respect: myth making. And none seems to have so effectively insinuated itself into congressional and public consciousness as the myth that the present government of El Salvador is democratic.[1] Barely questioned or analyzed by either its authors or its audience, it has acquired the status of received truth on both sides of the partisan aisle.

In an interview with *The New York Times*, House Majority Whip Thomas Foley (D.–Washington) declared emphatically that a Democratic President would be "no more willing than Mr. Reagan to allow the fall of democratic governments." He made the point squarely in the context of questions about U.S. policy toward El Salvador. The same unreflective attribution of democracy to El Salvador occurred during a debate over covert aid to the anti–Sandinista Nicaraguan rebels known as *contras*. Representative Jim Leach (R.–Iowa), otherwise critical of U.S. policy, denounced "U.S. actions against Nicaragua because they undercut the moral imprimatur upon which U.S. policy in El Salvador is based." He opposed those in El Salvador "who are armed and financed from abroad and who would shoot their way into power."

How, one wonders, does Leach think the present government arrived there? "Government" refers, of course, not to that chamber of winds in San Salvador known as the Constituent Assembly but to the persons who possess effective power and determine without appeal or restraint the identity of the country's civilian officials—bureaucrats and ministers alike—and the policies that will be implemented. "Government" refers, of course, to the senior officers of El Salvador's armed forces.

"We'd be asking too much," Vice President George Bush recently warned the inaugural session of a new international organization of center-right political parties, "if every democracy reached the degree of perfection of the U.S. or European democracies." Solecisms aside, the Vice President may not be the most astute guide to the locations of democratic governments. He is, after all, the man who congratulated President Ferdinand Marcos on the quality of democracy in the Philippines, a compliment doubtless as astonishing to Marcos as to his frequently jailed opponents.

Be that as it may, Bush has made a valid point, even if only by chance. There are degrees of perfection. There also are thresholds below which democratic forms thinly mask an authoritarian substance.

The only possible basis for characterizing El Salvador's government as a democracy is the election of March 28, 1982. Elections are a necessary but insufficient condition of a democratic government. Cuba, for example, has begun to hold elections in which the electorate has a small measure of choice among the carefully screened candidates. The political bodies filled by these elections actually may exercise some influence on certain issues, such as the timing of refuse collection. While this process may not be entirely sterile, no one confuses it with government by popular consent because, as long as the armed forces, the intelligence agencies, and the revolutionary cadres remain loyal to Premier Fidel Castro, he and his inner circle will continue to hold the real power in Cuba.

In the Cuban case, the explicit parameters of the electoral process and the popular assemblies underline the well-known reality of authoritarian government. Regimes can, however, achieve the same results behind a fully democratic facade. During the ascendancy of General Romeo Lucas Garcia, the Constitution of Guatemala guaranteed elections and those rights of association and speech needed to transform political conflict into authentic electoral competition. Indeed, the constitution guaranteed in theory every political and civil right. What it did not guarantee in practice was the right to life. Thus when Alberto Fuentes Mohr, the distinguished former foreign minister, exercised his constitutional right to register a new political party, the constitution did not prevent death squads from murdering him. By organizing, conniving, or acquiescing in the murder of any person foolish enough to exercise his or her rights, Lucas and his colleagues maintained all the forms of democracy, while sacrificing only its substance.

The consequences of that sacrifice will be felt for years. Mass murder has decimated not only the reformist political parties but also universities, bar associations, trade unions, peasant cooperatives, the grassroots organizations of the Roman Catholic Church, and other institutions, leaving the political field open primarily to parties of the extreme Right, the electoral manifestation of different fragments of the civil-military coalition that has governed the country since 1954.

In the case of Guatemala, even the Reagan administration seems willing to pierce the democratic veil and concede that Guatemala under Lucas was not a democracy. Washington welcomed the authoritarian government of General Efrain Rios Montt, which fell in August 1983, as an improvement justifying a renewal of suspended military aid.

The situation in El Salvador is essentially identical. The Lucas government came to power in an election that by Guatemalan standards may have been relatively uncorrupted. And recent Guatemalan governments have exterminated parties of the Left. In El Salvador, the real governing authority, the armed forces high command, is simply unelected. And these authorities have used torture and execution to drive the parties of the Left underground. The only possible distinctions between the two countries are the large percentage of the population that turned out for the last Salvadoran election and, as far as foreign observers could tell, the freedom from intimidation at the polls plus a procedure for counting the ballots that offered some guarantee of accuracy. It cannot be assumed, however, that these elements give the government of El Salvador what *Time* magazine casually referred to as "indisputable legitimacy."

Manipulating Elections

Any reasonable analyst would proceed from the historically verified assumption that elections conducted by an authoritarian regime, particularly in the course of a civil war, will produce whatever result the regime prefers, necessarily one that demonstrates its legitimacy. The variety of methods for achieving desired results is limited only by the human imagination.

If anything, civil wars heighten the capacity of incumbents to manipulate results: Troops are on alert, numerous, and widely deployed; such constitutional rights as people may enjoy in times of peace are in some degree suspended; military tribunals or simply field officers displace the jurisdiction of civilian courts in all spheres deemed relevant to national security; the use of force becomes commonplace and is rarely, if ever, investigated; under the best of circumstances, excesses are presumed normal, collective punishment of civilians is commonplace, and the media are under strict control.

As long as the French government clung to Algeria, it had no difficulty producing electoral results consistent with the dictum "Algérie francaise." But as soon as then President Charles de Gaulle negotiated a settlement implying France's wish to depart, the great majority voted for independence. The same phenomenon occurred in Zimbabwe-Rhodesia with strikingly different results in the elections before and after the British government assumed responsibility for the electoral process and its outcome. In El Salvador's 1982 election, voters could choose between a center party, the collaborating faction of the Christian Democratic party, and several right-wing parties associated with one or another faction of the armed forces.

Despite corruption and inefficiency, the incumbent armed forces in any civil war have a tremendous advantage over their opponents by virtue of their control of the main cities and communication links to the exterior, the national armories, and the society's taxation mechanism. Even in cases where they have ultimately lost the military struggle, incumbents have been able to dominate major population centers virtually until the moment of total collapse. Control, however, reflects the advantages just enumerated, which are peculiarly heightened in Central American conflicts by U.S. aid. Control does not necessarily reflect popular support. Thus, in El Salvador there existed no sizable area where leftist politicians could have canvassed the electorate beneath the guerrillas' protective guns. Indeed, under the circumstances that prevailed in El Salvador, leftist participation would have been suicidal. The same circumstances prevail today.

The fact remains, however, that, despite being deprived of a wide range of choice and despite threats from several if not all the guerrilla coalition's five factions, about 74% of El Salvador's eligible voters turned out and cast valid ballots. Why don't those facts add up to a popular mandate for the parties, the successful candidates, and indeed for the whole political system? The legitimacy of elections, after all, is a function of the perceptions of the electorate. Wouldn't a majority of voters have stayed home or cast blank ballots if they believed that the absence of the Left deprived them of any real choice? Of course they might have. But given their experiences, abstention would have been an act of wild bravado: The risks would have been severe and the potential payoff doubtful.

The armed forces and their paramilitary appendages were eminently capable of identifying those who did not vote. Failure to vote would have amounted to declaring sympathy for the guerrillas, that is, expressing a death wish. Casting a blank ballot or one inconsistent with the preferences of the officer in charge of local districts or barrios would have been equally perilous. Most foreign skeptics rejected their invitations to observe the voting. Most of the observers who accepted were disposed to believe in the legitimacy of the elections and were persuaded that ballots were secret. If mistaken, they had nothing to lose but their self-esteem. Salvadorans, having rather more material interests at stake, no doubt employed a more demanding calculation of risk. In an election conducted under the patronage of and manifestly important to the country's armed forces, no modestly prudent Salvadoran could have trusted his life to technical guarantees. Moreover, even if voters were confident that individual choices could not be identified, the inhabitants of an urban barrio or a village would nevertheless have been inclined to vote in accordance with the declared preference of a local commander who could easily identify their collective political preferences. Discrimination in reprisal is not the hallmark of the Salvadoran armed forces.

Voters in El Salvador had nothing tangible to balance against these terrible risks. Regardless of how they voted, after the election effective power would continue to flow out of the barracks door. This fact alone qualitatively distinguishes the El Salvadoran election from the Zimbabwean contest won by Robert Mugabe. And it will distinguish and deform all future elections unless and until the strangling grip of El Salvador's armed forces is broken. Yet these are the very forces that are being strengthened by the Reagan administration for the declared end of building democracy in El Salvador. One might as well have sent efficiency experts to Al Capone for the purpose of improving municipal government in Cicero, Illinois.

The Unity of the Military

Two years and twenty thousand–odd deaths ago, Leonel Gomez, once deputy director of the land–reform program invoked by Reagan as a sign of U.S. commitment to humane reform, dissected the nature of political power in El Salvador.[2] He described how peer groups formed by upwardly mobile, middle class youths in the country's lone military academy construct coalitions to divide up the spoils of corrupt service to the country. The various forces commanded by this stream of graduates have traditionally concentrated on two activities: enriching officers and maintaining order for the unusually narrow and extraordinarily wealthy national oligarchy. Before the coup of 1979, the two functions were perfectly symbiotic. After a brief separation the ends are being reknit.

Corruption may not rot the entire officer corps. The Carter administration's policy rested on the belief that the corps included men who wanted to transform this Cosa Nostra into a real national army serving all classes and who understood that transforming the army required transforming the society into one with a more just distribution of wealth and power. A sense of disgust with the endemic corruption of senior officers and with the brutal mission of repression led by those officers on behalf of their oligarchical paymasters seems to have been one factor behind the coup against General Carlos Humberto Romero's government in 1979 and the brief burst of reformist energy that immediately ensued. But baser considerations influenced their thinking as well—notably the intense fear generated among idealists and thugs alike by the dramatic collapse of another brutal and corrupt military establishment, the Nicaraguan National Guard.

Fear and idealism fueled a chain reaction culminating in a brief flurry of reform. Reform served two central purposes in a shrewd strategy for preventing revolution. In addition to reducing the flow of recruits to the guerrillas, it would reverse the regime's growing isolation within the hemisphere. Popular opposition alone had not toppled Nicaraguan dictator Anastasio Somoza Debayle. Through sheer firepower and a monstrous will to employ it, he probably would have survived if his neighbors, particularly Costa Rica and Panama, had continued their normal policy of noninterference rather than aiding the rebels and if the United States had remained at least a psychological prop to the tyrant.

Subsequent events confirm the signal importance of fear in the mix of factors leading to the 1979 coup in El Salvador. As the U.S. commitment has intensified, the concern within the officer corps about U.S. support has declined and the momentum of reform has correspondingly decelerated. The reform campaign has yielded to the blandishments of a regrouped oligarchy—with much of its treasury safely ensconced in Miami—and to the individual officer's immensely powerful, ingrained commitment to the institutional unity of the military. Preserving this unity is flatly incompatible with rooting out either corruption or brutality. The price of unity is tolerance of both.

The resulting dilemma for declared U.S. objectives is one that neither the President's men nor his unwitting supporters nor even the social democratic heart of the Democratic Party have been willing to grasp. The first evade with abstraction. In his confirmation hearing before the Senate Foreign Relations Committee, Langhorne Motley, the President's choice to replace Enders as head of the State Department's Latin American Bureau, cautioned: "It is true that democracy can be slow in achieving results, sometimes frustratingly so. . . . But surely we have the patience to help our neighbors shield themselves from Communism and build democratic institutions." In addition to offering no evidence that an authentic democracy is frustratingly slow to produce reforms, he offered no theory explaining how these institutions could be built by means of a flow of arms to the Salvadoran armed forces.

Both supporters and opponents of the President's policies perform marvels of internal contradiction. Thus, in a lead editorial on the "Central American Wars," *The New Republic* first incisively observed: "The real political requirement of . . . any right and realistic American policy . . . is the final surrender of the Salvadoran security forces, and of the odious oligarchical interests they serve, in the interest of the democratic development of the country." But in light of this insight, the magazine recommended: "Military assistance should be modest, though not too modest to produce results in the field, and it should not be unconditional." In the end, this formula is just as evasive as the administration's reasoning; the evasion simply occurs at a later point in the argument. For the brutal question remains: Why should the Salvadoran security forces be intimidated by aid conditions if the very congressmen who imposed them, not to mention the President theoretically obligated to administer them, simultaneously affirm their determination to prevent a rebel victory?

Demanding the whole truth from the President, many liberals tender half-truths themselves. They rightly argue that El Salvador will remain a valley of death until the oligarchy and the security forces surrender. But liberals shrink from admitting, first, that such a surrender would constitute revolution, the overturn of the old order, and, second, that the only present instruments of revolution are the guerrillas.

The same schizophrenia haunts the liberal reaction to U.S. policy toward Nicaragua. Liberals would extend guarantees of security to the Nicaraguans in exchange for Nicaraguan commitments to end the "export of revolution." Talk of exporting revolutions—as opposed to coups d'état—is Orwellian "Newspeak." As Cuban revolutionary Che Guevara discovered in Bolivia at the moment of his death, revolution cannot be exported. Revolutions begin when a critical mass of locals becomes angry and desperate and hopeful and brave enough to take up the gun. In Latin America, many of those who have reached the point where furious despair transmutes into hope are Marxists.

One reason for this fact is that Cuba opens the doors of its schools, its treasury, and its armory to young and tough idealists. Young, middle-class men who are merely tough can find power and distinction in the security forces. Another reason is that Marxism offers a neat and comprehensive explanation both for the tyranny under which they live and for the symbiotic links between their tyrants and local representatives of the United States: Diplomats, military attachés, Green Berets, and investors. The impact of witnessing daily the collaboration between local soldiers and oligarchs on the one hand, and U.S. businessmen and representatives on the other, is heightened by the undeniable fact that, for all its democratic rhetoric, never in its entire modern history has the United States supported a revolution against tyrannies of the Right.

Speaking of exporting revolution is simply a biased and false way of describing military assistance to rebels seeking power and social transformation. It is true that Marxist dogma, a provincial outlook, and an often justified contempt for sham democracy—the only version many have ever known—coupled with Cuban aid and U.S. hostility, blind many rebels to the corrupting consequences of a revolutionary transfer rather than dispersion of power.

However, Marxist-educated, Cuban-aided rebels hold no monopoly on the tendency to build a new authoritarianism on the ruins of the old. Neither Karl Marx nor Cuba made the Ayatollah Ruhollah Khomeini's revolution. The tendency is immanent in every successful revolution unmediated by external forces that are committed to a democratic outcome. It is immanent because democracy grows not from an act of will but from the fact of shared and balanced power leavened by the experience of cooperation. Most revolutions are organized by a small core of daring souls. Bonded by danger and privation and prone to moral arrogance in reaction to widespread popular passivity and sporadic popular collusion with the old order, the revolutionary elite attains victory in a spirit of moral triumph and finds itself in possession of overwhelming power. Hence, the dilemma of honest liberals: Democratic reform in El Salvador requires revolution; but the forces of revolution, though they are committed to reform, are unlikely to make it democratic.

From this dilemma there is only one even plausible exit. If the United

States wants democracy at any price, then the United States must manage the revolution. Managing a revolution in El Salvador will not create a precedent for managing one wherever vast wealth grins at immense poverty. Many countries plagued by comparable injustice lie outside the reach of U.S. power. In others, governments manage to retain the signs of legitimacy—for example, authentic competitive elections—despite their failure to address the question of mass misery. In yet a third cluster of states, injustice has failed to generate an effective opposition.

The case against imposing revolution in a nonrevolutionary setting is powerful and usually irrefutable. Revolutions such as the one in El Salvador, having been ignited by internal combustion, are distinguishable on that ground alone. Their Caribbean Basin location distinguishes them on another ground. Having played for so long a decisive role in the political, economic, and cultural life of this area, the United States cannot help but affect the outcome of local revolutions, whether it intervenes or acquiesces in the outcome. Nonintervention is not possible. Choice is the fate of the United States.

By dogmatically pursuing this illusory option in Nicaragua, by refusing to force Somoza from office as part of a negotiated settlement, former President Jimmy Carter dissipated a potentially great triumph for human rights. Somoza was unmoved by hints. All his experiences and intimate connections with the United States convinced him that any administration facing a choice between a friendly tyrant, no matter how vicious, and a military triumph by the Left would rescue the former. And so Somoza hung on, pretending to negotiate, butchering more of his people, and liquidating his holdings until, finally, with the country in ruins, the Carter administration unequivocally committed itself to his removal. Somoza and his high command soon fled and the Sandinistas moved into the vacuum.

Neither individual nor collective tyrants yield power for the sake of abstractions like the nation. The nation is simply the carcass off which they feed. Having lived by force, it is to force alone they will yield. In El Salvador, the armed forces will yield only when the United States confronts them with the prospect of defeat. Of course, they will tolerate elections. They will tolerate any measures that leave effective power in their hands.

U.S. Occupation?

Yet alternatives to these tyrants exist. Under one option, the United States would use its overwhelming military strength to occupy El Salvador for as long as it takes to build democratic institutions. This policy would involve disarming the security forces and gradually reconstituting a sanitized, miniaturized and lightly armed constabulary like the one Costa Rican democrats established after routing their own army in 1948. Guerrillas willing to lay down their arms would be eligible to join the new force. Guerrillas also would be eligible to serve in public administration positions and to seek election to a new constituent assembly, which would draft a constitution. This policy could be called the Japan option. Having successfully implanted democratic institutions in enemy territory after 1945, Americans have every reason to regard El Salvador as an *a fortiori* case.

El Salvador is not, like Zaire or Haiti, a disorganized and disoriented sea of misery. Despite a long history of vicious harassment by the security forces and unofficial death squads, trade unions, *campesino* (peasant) organizations, Catholic lay groups, and other institutions have organized and endured with the encouragement and aid of the Roman Catholic Church. And there are politicians on both sides of the present divide, such as former President Jose Napoleon Durate and his running mate in the 1972 election, Guillermo Ungo, whose courage, integrity, and commitment to pluralism seem beyond question. In Japan, the United States built in a vacuum. In El Salvador, the builders are already there. All they require is someone to give them a chance.

If the Reagan administration had a credible commitment to democracy and reform, it might be able to rally broad domestic support for occupation. The policy could be presented as an alternative to the present strategy of tying U.S. honor to a foreign military establishment with a long and consistent record of contempt for democracy and human rights—an establishment that for those reasons and because of its hopeless inefficiency may in any event lose.[3] A credible U.S. administration might use this policy to win the support of allied and nonaligned states. An administration that sends its United Nations ambassador on periodic tours of dictatorships with which she seeks, in her own words, "pleasant" relations lacks the requisite credibility.

Nor is there much hope for change, since the President does not seem even to understand the problem. If he did, he would hardly have selected as his first roving peacemaker in Central America former Senator Richard Stone (D.–Florida), whose best known tie to the region is prior service as a public relations agent for Guatemala's ineffable Lucas regime.

In short, an occupation carried out by this right–wing administration is certain to backfire in allied states where Reagan's policies have already left a heavy deposit of emotional anti–Americanism. For that reason, and also because of the relatively great material costs of an occupation, the unambiguous break it would constitute with U.S. foreign policy conventions, the impossibility of distinguishing it legally from Soviet invasions of Hungary, Czechoslovakia, and Afghanistan, and finally, because of its unacceptability to pro-reform Latin American states such as Mexico, Columbia, Panama, and Venezuela, a more indirect approach is clearly preferable.

This lower-profile policy would require a declaration by the administration conceding that real power remains in the hands of the Salvadorean armed forces that have finally demonstrated they will not reform as long as they enjoy U.S. economic and military support. The statement would go on to express confidence in the commitments to democracy of some elements of both the Salvadoran military and the guerrilla forces, and to urge these elements to unite to form a new political-military movement that would purge the military and the guerrillas of butchers, complete the three phases of the land-reform program, and create conditions for the establishment of constitutional democracy. The United States would pledge military assistance to an emergent third force, including, if necessary, air cover and logistical support, and large-scale financial aid. The statement would reaffirm Washington's immovable opposition both to the status quo and to its replacement by a new authoritarianism in Marxist clothing. It would call upon both armed forces to agree to a cease-fire and to begin withdrawing to barracks and base camps. To that end, the United States would announce an immediate suspension of aid. But it also would warn the guerrillas that any attempt to exploit such a withdrawal would be met by direct U.S. military intervention.

Washington would circulate a draft of this statement to its West European allies and to democratic regimes in Latin America. While confirming that its stated objectives are immutable, the United States would declare its willingness to compromise on details and would urge these states to turn this initially unilateral initiative into a collective venture. Washington would announce that, while the United States was prepared to live with the consequences of unilateral action, it shared their natural concern over establishing a significant precedent.

Whatever the reaction of its allies, the United States might then invite Cuba to participate in the effort to bring the antagonists to the negotiating table. Washington would assure Havana of U.S. readiness to tolerate whatever foreign policy a democratic El Salvador decides to follow. This offer would effectively force Cuba to choose between using its influence with the guerrillas to draw them into negotiations and raging futilely from the sidelines while the United States managed an epochal change in Central American autocracy and transformed its own image as a guarantor of plutocratic tyrannies.

After a brief period of consultation with allies and other interested parties, Washington would publish a "white paper" and initiate discussions with the various Salvadoran factions. A possible but by no means certain result of this demarche would be a splintering of both the guerrilla and antiguerrilla coalitions and the emergence of politicians and soldiers on both sides willing to work toward the new El Salvador outlined in the U.S. draft.

The first task for the negotiators would be creating a provisional government. Since the negotiators would almost surely not represent all of the armed bands in the country and would, moreover, distrust one another, they would undoubtedly seek not only military aid from sponsoring countries but also a peacekeeping force to guarantee their security from each other and from those groups that refused to participate. If the persons designated by the negotiators as the legitimate government of El Salvador were seen to control a substantial portion of men in arms and national territory, the United States and other sympathetic countries could first recognize this new government and then accede to its request without patently violating international law.

Hating these goals, the right wing in Latin America and its North American supporters will damn this scenario as intervention. Mistrustful of its means, some on the Left also will invoke that epithet. By any name, it is the only way to bridge their respective objectives. It assimilates the Right's insistence on U.S. security interests in El Salvador, while promoting the political values of the Left.

Put differently, rightists are fond of arguing that a great power that refuses to impose its will on small states ceases thereby to be a great power. But the United States is not simply a great power; it is also a liberal democracy. Presidents must use American power for ends compatible with this country's libertarian ethos or risk evading the political constraints that will otherwise inhibit executive privilege. The United States doubtless has the power to ram a dressed-up status quo down the throats of the Salvadoran people and can prove that their sacrifice has been in vain. But Reagan will, I believe, find only a minority of Americans who will consider this an example of greatness. Moreover, those liberals and moderates who honor U.S. values and have the wit to appreciate the truth about Salvadoran society will never swallow an administration policy that represents in its most debased form the assertion of power without the assumption of responsibility.

For all its vices, direct imperialism as practiced by the British in the Nineteenth and Twentieth Centuries built roads, spread education and health, delivered the mail, established a civil service, maintained peace, and applied the law—albeit law that was often unjust—with a fair degree of impartiality. The positive side of British imperialism for a time made it appear morally compatible with the liberal values that were progressively penetrating Great Britain's own political system. Good works were a ticket to legitimacy. But they were an expensive one. And as it gradually became apparent to people who could do their sums that the burden of doing good outweighed the benefits of rule, the national taste for empire began to wane.

Being both liberal and good at sums, Americans never acquired much of a taste for genuine imperialism. To be sure, the United States has frequently intervened in the affairs of smaller countries, sometimes violently, often decisively. Until Vietnam, however, the country succeeded rather well at containing any incipient sensation of guilt. Like the British, the Americans held guilt at bay by discovering or inventing beneficial consequences for the populations in countries where the United States worked its will. Unlike the British, the Americans also drew moral balm from their determination to treat any intervention as transient and superficial. The United States assured the world and itself that Americans would stay as briefly as possible and would manage no fundamental change in the status quo. What it declined to recognize was that the reinforcement of a crumbling status quo can have consequences no less profound and often more terrible than actions that accelerate the pace of change.

When governments pursue ends incompatible with the deeply felt needs and preferences of their subjects, sooner or later these regimes will employ terror, because nothing else can overcome popular opposition. The degree of terror will be determined not by the government's ideology, but rather by the fit between its political projects and social reality. The worse the fit, the greater the requisite terror.

In Central America, social forces released from old bonds by all the powerful solvents of modern times—population pressure, economic growth, transnational companies and markets, urbanization, egalitarian ideas—press against a semifeudal order. The United States can continue shipping guns and advisors to the besieged oligarchs and officers and thus, at great cost to the population of these ravaged countries, temporarily maintain the status quo. Or the United States can assume responsibility and, possibly at great cost to itself, assist popular majorities in establishing new political and social forms.

The Finland Option

There is, of course, a third, far less expensive alternative—a diplomatic arrangement employed through recorded history by great powers where their principal interest in another state concerned its foreign policy rather than its resources. This arrangement used to be called a protectorate. Today it is known as Finlandization.

Under this option, Washington would tolerate a wide range of domestic systems within Caribbean Basin states. The United States also would respect their autonomy on international economic issues. What the United States would not tolerate and would openly be prepared to prevent, even by the use of force, would be a military relationship between any of these states and an extrahemispheric power.

Tolerance of revolutionary governments would eliminate their only rational reason for seeking a security relationship with the Soviet bloc. Tolerance backed by a public commitment to block extrahemispheric military ties should suffice to deter even irrational leaders, as well as the Soviet Union, from seeking such ties. Moscow has, after all, displayed great caution since the 1962 Cuban missile crisis about challenging Washington's will in an area where the United States enjoys overwhelming conventional superiority.

The Finland option responds directly and inexpensively to the security concerns rightly or wrongly accepted by Reagan and his democratic critics alike as the fundamental reason for U.S. involvement in El Salvador. If it lacks the moral glamour of managing revolution, it lacks as well the moral stain incurred by galloping after security on the backs of indigenous monsters. The Finland option is realpolitik. As such, it should appeal to conservatives. But it does not, because American conservatism has never accepted Edmund Burke's politics of prudence, caution, and conservation. The U.S. conservative impulse is radical and its judgment twisted by an ideology no less distempered than that of the far Left.

Realpolitik though it is, the Finland option should also appeal to liberals because they are the heirs to a tradition of skeptical induction. Managing revolution is a seductive idea. But nagging questions persist. Can the American political system, uniquely hostile among Western capitalist democracies to state-directed reform and uniquely sensitive to the claims of private property, manage revolution? If security is the only justification for the U.S. El Salvador policy that enjoys substantial public support, when U.S. intervention causes this justification to vanish, won't support vanish as well? And even if, after possibly great trouble and cost, the United States were able to manage a successful transition in El Salvador to a more modern, egalitarian, and pluralist society, what basis would it have established for future policy in the region? Are the American people likely to bear the same burden in other states? Will Americans support renewed intervention if El Salvador falls again into civil war?

Reasonable doubts about the United States' ability and will to manage even one revolution, and anxiety about the precedent this might set provide a moral basis for embracing the Finland option as the lesser evil in Central America. The availability of that option leaves no basis at all for the policies the Reagan administration is now pursuing in the name of democracy and national security.

Notes

This chapter was originally published in *Foreign Policy,* No. 52, Fall 1983.
1. The reader will note that this observation was made before the 1984 election in El Salvador. After that election, the question was (and remains) whether a country ought to be described as "democratic" when its armed forces reserve to themselves the final word on critical issues.
2. Leonel Gomez and Bruce Cameron, "The Current Danger: American Myths," *Foreign Policy* 43 (Summer 1981), p. 75.
3. At the end of 1986 it seems likely that, assuming U.S. aid continues at the current level, the military institution will survive.

20

Liberals and Duarte: Faith Over Reason?

With its hint of desperate hope, its mute appeal to faith over reason, that ancient war cry of New York Mets fans—"You gotta believe!"—mirrors the liberal mind contemplating the presidency of José Napoleon Duarte. Like any passion, this one has the power to convert thought into mush.

Illustrative of both the passion and the mush is a recent[1] lead editorial in the *New York Times*:

> With Mr. Duarte in clear command, El Salvador can count on help without second guessing. But only his stature preserves the American consensus for aid. That is the Duarte difference. May it be a weapon more potent than guns.

Is it possible that through some process of Divine Intervention organized by the Reverend Falwell, *The Times* has arrived at the same position as the Reagan administration, which, since its inception, has been demanding that Congress do just that—stop second-guessing the government of El Salvador so that it can get on with the business of winning the war? One cannot tell whether *The Times* believes that Duarte has already achieved the happy state of being "in clear command." If he is not there yet, by what signs will we know when he has arrived? Why should second-guessing end? Since in the whole history of El Salvador no reformist government has ever achieved more than fleeting control, why assume that the sudden ascension of this one should place its policies beyond criticism or doubt? *The Times* being characteristic, one can say that the principal "Duarte difference" to date is relaxing liberal restraints on the pursuit of military victory in El Salvador.

The liberal's infatuation with Duarte has political, ideological, and moral sources. Its political source is an alloy of conviction and fear. The conviction, which he shares with conservatives, is that the ideology of regimes tends to determine their international alignment and that the alignment of regimes in Central America bears significantly on the global balance of power. For some, significance is a function of geography. For others, it turns on the credibility of American commitments; we have committed ourselves to preserve a non-Marxist government in El Salvador, they argue.

Fused with conviction there is fear, fear of a conservative-inspired indictment for losing another country to communism.

The ideological source of Duarte's appeal is, of course, his electoral "mandate." Treating electoral triumph as the exclusive source of political legitimacy is a classic liberal reflex. The conservative tradition, on the other hand, is considerably more eclectic in this respect, being prepared, for instance, to find legitimacy in a particular class's supposedly superior capacity to govern or in the sheer fact of continuity without serious opposition. As for Marxists, their view of elections as mere box scores recording the outcome of the class struggle is too well known to require elaboration here.

One could question, and advocates of Major d'Aubisson have questioned, the purity of Duarte's victory. Liberals, for all their attachment to the view that a fair count suffices to validate an election, normally will concede that stuffing voting urns and marching electors into voting booths at gun point are not the only means for cooking elections. There seems little doubt that Duarte enjoyed large infusions of American capital as well as the conspicuous blessing of Uncle Sam. But neither of these factors degrades Duarte's achievement.

To the extent funding mattered very much—which in a country the size of El Salvador and in an election between such polarized opponents is arguable—CIA funds are unlikely to have done more than balance d'Aubisson's access to the treasury of the oligarchy. Similarly, U.S. political support simply offset d'Aubisson's base in the more fetid cantonments of the armed forces. It probably constituted the difference, not between victory and defeat for the Christian Democrats, but rather between sham and something resembling a real election. Quite possibly it also meant the difference between Duarte's life or death. Some readers may remember how Archbishop Oscar Romero, a man of greater stature and popular support, fared at the first sign that his survival was not a condition of American aid.

The election's flaws lie elsewhere. One was the *de facto* banning of the Left. Neither condition of its participation—a chance to rebuild its organization in areas under government control and a chance to campaign with a reasonable degree of security—were satisfied.

The Left's preclusion inflicts moral ambiguity on Duarte's victory. If the country had been occupied by a peacekeeping force capable of enforcing the electoral results, the Left, campaigning on behalf of the broad land reform announced in 1980 and thereafter miniaturized by the traditional collusion of officers and oligarchs, might have done well. With peace guaranteed by the occupiers, Duarte could no longer have campaigned as the apostle of peace, in the opinion of many his most powerful theme. And, because of all that has happened to the land reform promulgated by the junta in which he himself participated, for the majority of campesinos, he would have carried an aura of failure on that critical issue. No one thinks that the Left could have won a majority. But under the ideal conditions hypothesized, it might have gotten its candidate into the runoff between the two highest vote-getters. One must admit, however, that those conditions are so far removed from Salvadoran reality that any estimate of the Left's electoral potential cannot be much more than speculation of the wilder sort.

The other flaw in the election tends rather to enhance Duarte's mandate. He won by dominating the capital, not the countryside where one would have expected the Christian Democratic platform of land reform and peace to command powerful support among the peasant masses, in the absence of an alternative to the Left. This discrepancy tends to support the conclusion that electoral activity in the countryside remains subject to crippling coercion in favor of the Right.

To be fair, the Right does have a rural base including both large and medium-sized landowners plus parts of the small commercial class, probably the sort of people who in Victorian England voted at the command of the manor. In addition, the Right can depend on the numerous rabble organized by the military during the 1970s to serve as informers, frighteners and hit men. ORDEN, its acronym when its activities were run out of the office of ex-President Romero, organized the rural riff-raff—the drunks, bullies, and petty hoods who pollute any congested place—into a paramilitary force penetrating the countryside. Theoretically dissolved after the coup of 1979, it remains a functioning organization no doubt able to provide voters, a local polling structure, and a mechanism of intimidation for the parties of the Right, above all d'Aubisson's party, ARENA. But ORDEN could not function effectively in a countryside criss-crossed with regular troops and guerrillas if its button men were not in symbiosis with the traditional guarantors of the rural status quo, the Treasury Police and the National Guard.

Along with conviction, pragmatism, and ideology, moral concerns explain liberalism's embrace of Duarte. Total victory for the Right could be achieved only by an American-aided slaughter, and it could be maintained only by ceaseless repression. A victorious Left is almost certain to extract a terrible vengeance.[2] So great and pervasive are the hatreds generated by fifty years of repression and five of civil war that vengeance might consume not merely the delinquents of the security forces and their paramilitary auxiliaries, but also whole sectors of the upper–middle classes. Nor, having won so awful a struggle, are the guerrillas going to have indigenous incentives to establish a relatively moderate, much less pluralistic regime.

Whatever their faults, both their ideology and their constituency push Christian Democrats toward mild social reform, plural politics, and the rule of law. But they are not masters of their fate. And that is why any optimism among Americans about Duarte's ability to restore peace and establish justice requires the relaxation of critical judgment.

"How many divisions has the Pope?" Stalin is reputed to have asked. Divisions are not everything, but they are much. The Christian Democrats do not have any. Nor in El Salvador do they have anything resembling the Pope's moral authority.

Nothing he subsequently does can quite erase the fact that Duarte and his closest associates remained in the military–dominated juntas that ran the country from 1980 to 1983 while the death squads roamed at will, leaving a trail of corpses. Not only did they remain, and their presence alone eased President Reagan's task of extracting arms from a Congress less inclined to finance slaughter; in addition, they were mostly mute. And when they were not mute, at times they were apologists. As the distinguished journalist Christopher Dickey reported in June 1983, Duarte continually delivered anesthetic messages to the foreign press, assuring it that as a consequence of Christian Democratic participation in the government, "a process of control" over the armed forces was occurring. While he wove visions of civilian rule, the stench of death rose higher.

Being wrong then about the "process" does not guarantee that he is wrong now. But no matter how great our desire to believe in Duarte, since he seeks more than our prayers, since he seeks money and guns, surely before providing them we should demand some semblance of a credible scenario for achieving a just peace.

The scenario sketched during Duarte's presidential campaign looked roughly as follows. By virtue of his electoral mandate, his consequent moral authority, his noble ideals, and his ability to secure economic and military aid, Duarte would establish effective control over the armed forces. Control would produce a climate of security for all those willing to play politics by democratic rules.

Coincidentally, Duarte would press forward and complete the process of economic and social transformation. Since it was despair over ever achieving reform by means of electoral politics which had populated the ranks of the violent Left, neither its social–democratic partners nor its mass base among workers, peasants, and students would have any further reason for remaining out in the cold. Thus isolated, the comandantes would either have to accept amnesty and peaceful political struggle or face liquidation. And the country would live happily ever after.

It is a pretty vision. It is not a very plausible one. To begin with, there remains the officer corps, that tightly knit state within a state long accustomed to ruling, stealing, and killing with impunity. Despite its traditions and temptations, the military institution has, it is true, periodically produced a cluster of officers with a taste for reform. The coup of 1979 was the fifth bid for power by Reformists since the mid-1940s. The governing coalition of conventional officers and economic royalists had quickly liquidated the earlier attempts. In 1979, the reformers were again a distinct minority of the officers corps. They were, moreover, primarily of junior rank. Yet for a moment it appeared that they would drag the institution across the threshold of a new order. This seemed possible because they had working for them a force that in the Salvadoran jungle is far more potent than moral authority or simple justice. They had fear.

Mass unrest twisted through country and city alike. Aided by priests and students and politicians, the popular classes had achieved an unparalleled degree of mobilization. What had happened in Nicaragua, a majority of officers began to believe, could happen in Salvador—a popular rising, backed by well-trained and armed guerrillas and tolerated by the United States—which would sweep away the whole traditional order of things.

Exactly why the weight of influence in the military shifted quickly away from the reformers is a subject bitterly disputed within our own liberal community. One view is that the Carter administration, acting through Ambassador Robert White, threw its own weight against the reformers because it distrusted their willingness to negotiate with the Left. The contrary view is that the administration was not hostile, just insufficiently supportive because of inattention, not indifference.

Between the two theses, the latter seems more persuasive. In the first place, the armed Left was unwilling to negotiate in 1979. Offers were made; it rejected them. Second, given the character of the military institution—its role as a ladder of social mobility, its independence, its innate contempt for civilians and its tradition of respect for the hierarchy of rank—the natural balance of power was on the Right, even without taking into account the corrupting weight of resources the oligarchy could deploy from havens in Biscayne Bay. Moreover, this natural tilt was strengthened by the intransigence of the Left; initially it treated the coup as a breach in the old order through which armed revolutionaries could pour.

In addition, evidence has now emerged suggesting that one or more of the leaders of the reactionary faction within the military had professional links to the CIA. Given the agency's mission in Latin America, its natural tendency to recruit agents with impeccable anti-Leftist credentials, its ease of access to the far Right, and the relatively greater difficulty of corrupting officers with an inclination for reform, collaboration with the intransigent faction may well have occurred. Whenever an issue is on the periphery of presidential concern, as El Salvador was during the crucial period after the coup, ambassadors have difficulty preventing other members of the country team from playing an independent hand. It is therefore possible that, while White was trying to fuel the little engine of reform by emphasizing the conditionality of American aid, the officer corps was receiving a different message from other members of the "Country Team."

In trying to assess Duarte's prospects for neutralizing the hard-core Right within the military, possible ties between them and extremely conservative elements in our own bureaucracy and their allies in the Jesse Helms wing of the Republican Party are not irrelevant. But they are of very minor significance compared with the indisputable fact that, as he seeks to establish control over the armed forces or at least to manage their transformation into an institution respectful of human rights and willing to enforce the writ of a reformist civilian government, Duarte seems in most respects to occupy a weaker position now than at the beginning of the decade, when he failed.

The reformers have been purged. Fear has diminished, in part because the death squads decimated the Left's urban infrastructure, in larger measure because the Reagan administration has deepened the U.S. commitment by declaring El Salvador a supreme test of our will to resist communist expansion, and in part because the American Congress has proven consistently unwilling to enforce the conditions it attached to aid. Furthermore, given the extent of the massacres since 1979, most senior officers must be implicated, whether through acts of commission or omission and cover-up. Hence, they have even stronger reasons to insulate themselves from civilian oversight, since it might someday produce inquiries into prior conduct.

What can Duarte offer as means for climbing these heightened obstacles? His electoral mandate? A more clearly unsullied one in the pivotal election of 1972 lent him such intimidating moral authority that the armed forces beat in his face and threw him across the frontier. Insofar as the collective psyche of the higher officers is concerned, electoral mandates compare unfavorably with well-armed divisions.

Some among the administration's crew of professional optimists have suggested that, although senior officers may not have experienced a moral epiphany, they gradually will be swamped in a sea of American-trained juniors. And thus, in the fullness of time (ex-Ambassador Deane Hinton is reported to have predicted a generation, which is the sort of restrained optimism that leads to unemployment), the armed forces will acquire a higher moral tone.

The morally edifying consequences of exposure to instruction by Americans is a thesis whose basis remains unknown. Such evidence as there is suggests that our training and advice and indoctrination has, on balance, helped to confirm an omnibus hostility to the Left—and hence to advocates of egalitarian reform—and to implant a doctrine of counterinsurgency that, in the name of national security, justifies military penetration into every corner of civil society. It is useful to recall that Latin American officers are not generally dispatched to Harvard for courses in moral philosophy.

As in the past, Duarte's only real weapon is the army's dependence on American aid. The disturbing question for Duarte, as well as for American liberals, is whether so deeply conservative an American administration, one so viscerally hostile to egalitarian reform and so committed to victory in Central American, will empower Duarte by allowing him to dictate the conditions for giving and withholding aid. As the Catholic Church in much of Latin America recognizes a preferential option for the poor, President Reagan seems to feel one for the rich. The pressure of democratic governments in Europe and Lain America and, more importantly, of public and congressional opinion in the United States have inhibited the exercise in Salvador of that preference and of the passion for an unequivocal military victory achieved regardless of the means employed. It survives, nevertheless, straining for full expression and influencing, however subliminally, Washington's game plan.

To liberals, Duarte is the hoped-for instrument of reconciliation and reform in his country. To the forces of the American Right, blessed by the President and led by Ambassador Kirkpatrick and William Casey, he is the best available means for replicating the triumph in Grenada. However disparate their moral, intellectual, and emotional sources, these two visions of Duarte's historical role are not necessarily incompatible. Duarte's own scenario seems to reconcile them by offering both victory and reform.

The high obstacles to reforming the armed forces have already been discussed. A hardly less formidable impediment to reform is the need for cooperation from the private sector. Despite internal divisions, it has rallied fiercely against every reform initiative that has surfaced during the past five decades, even the pallid land reform proposed by President Molina in 1976 as a means of demobilizing the peasantry.

Since the coup of 1979, the leaders of the private sector have maneuvered incessantly to restore the status quo. While there remain differences over tactics—only one segment of the oligarchy is reported to have financed the death squads—as far as I know, not one of the numerous private-sector organizations has openly condemned the terror of the Right, much less endorsed the social and economic reforms or negotiations with the Left. In the words of Enrique Baloyra the leading U.S. academic authority on El Salvador, for the leaders of the private sector, what is at stake

> is not merely ... whether the government should not bend too much in the direction of union demands, spend too much on welfare, link public policymaking to the electoral process, or try to push taxes beyond reasonable limits. The leaders of the reactionary coalition of El Salvador *do not believe in unions or in welfare or in suffrage*.[3]

With the encouragement and active support of the Reagan administration, Duarte has been sending friendly feelers to the entrepreneurial community. If his purpose is reconciling some significant slice of it to his government and its declared ends, he has failed miserably. On every test to date in the Legislative Assembly, a coalition of parties representing the several segments of the private sector have ridden roughshod over Duarte, terminating phase III ("land to the tillers") of the land reform, imposing an ARENA Party leader as attorney general, and in various other ways reaffirming their intransigent hostility to change.

At this point, it is hard to see how Duarte can simultaneously secure the cooperation of the private sector and implement reforms preempting the appeal of revolution. Their collective behavior since 1979 implies that, unlike the armed forces, industrialists, financiers, merchants, and landowners (the functions are often intertwined) have never doubted the efficacy of violence and the disutility of reform.

Perhaps it is not surprising, therefore, that, since assuming the presidency, Duarte appears to have been marginally more successful in relating to officers than oligarchs. Consistent with if not as a consequence of his desires, a number of the officers most frequently identified as death-squad leaders have been relieved of their commands and transferred to less exacting duty, for example attache in Paraguay or student at the Inter-American Defense College. In addition, again at Duarte's request, control of the National and Treasury Police and the National Guard has been centralized under a vice minister of defense mutually acceptable to Duarte and the high command. On the theory, which Duarte apparently accepts, that lower-ranking members of these forces simply free-lanced as death-squad members, this could be a step toward reducing right-wing terror. The high command has also agreed to submit promotion lists to Duarte, and it allegedly accepted his veto of promotion for one junior officer with a particularly poisonous reputation.

On the other hand, Duarte has heeded the pre-election warning that he must not attempt to alter the structure of the military institution. Thus, the Treasury Police still exists. And although its notorious intelligence unit has, in theory, been disbanded, there is no sign that any of its delinquents have been cashiered. So this could be a case like ORDEN, where dissolution is little if anything more than a matter of form.

Leaving the Treasury Police essentially intact is only one of the mix of acts and omissions Duarte has used to ingratiate the armed forces. He has, for instance, announced that the conviction of four enlisted men closes the case of the murdered American nuns. Yet the Tyler Report, which the State Department keeps classified, states flatly that the first thing senior officers did on learning of the killings was to organize a cover-up. One of the officers reportedly involved is the present Minister of Defense, General Eugenio Vides Casanova.

The likelihood of any serious inquiry into the other 30,000 to 40,000 noncombatant deaths attributable to military and paramilitary "operations" looks about equally promising, although the fault is not entirely Duarte's. With the attorney generalship and the Supreme Court already packed with rightists (the Supreme Court in turn appoints all lower-court judges under the constitution drafted by the same rightist coalition), Duarte's only avenue of investigation would be a special commission. Nominally, one has just been established; but it still is not functioning. And without a mandate from the Assembly, it may never begin, even if Duarte wants it to. Unlike President Alfonsin of Argentina, Duarte's concern about the past has not seemed intense.

Vengeance is not the issue. The issue is whether the officer corps shall retain its *de facto* immunity for crimes against the civilian population. As long as it does, the rule of law will not operate in El Salvador.

There is another, more prominent respect in which Duarte's efforts "to consolidate his position" may leave him with one not readily distinguishable from that of his old opponents on the Right. I refer to his hard line against serious negotiations with the Left. His initial move, demanding that the political leaders of the Left first demonstrate the sort of unambiguous control over the guerrillas that he exercises over the military institution, is the height either of cynicism or self-delusion.

His next declaration, issued through a spokesman, that he could not envisage even an electoral role for the Left before 1988, not only repudiates a principal theme of his campaign, but seems little short of a commitment to war *a outrance*. It also distances him from both liberal and centrist opinion throughout the hemisphere typified by the report emanating from the so-called Inter-American Dialogue, a gathering of North and South American notables from the worlds of business, politics, and government, cochaired by Sol Linowitz and Galo Plaza (former president of Ecuador and secretary-general of the OAS) and sponsored by that impeccably establishment venue, The Wilson Center of the Smithsonian Institution. The group's consensus report, *The Americas at a Crossroads,* urges negotiations to begin "at once" (pp. 45-46).

Of course, Duarte's present line could be a mere artifice designed to ease pressure from the Right while he completes the process of establishing control over the armed forces so that he can begin to negotiate. Although I am inclined to be optimistic about Duarte's motives and agnostic about his judgment, I see little credible evidence that the process of control is finally under way. *Deaths and disappearances have fallen dramatically in pacified areas.* The decline dates, however, not from Duarte's inauguration; it dates from the fall of 1983 when the White House, having decided, finally, that the carnage was counterproductive, dispatched personal representatives to order the production line closed. Pressure culminated with a visit from Vice President Bush, who apparently warned an assembly of thirty-one top military leaders that aid really was conditional on good behavior. Since November 1983, when the pressure culminating in Bush's visit crescendoed, each month's total of death-squad killings has been lower than during any preceding month since the slaughter began some four years ago.

This phenomenon confirms two things: First, that when, in his address to the American people on May 9, 1984, Ronald Reagan attributed human rights abuses in El Salvador to "a small, violent right wing [that] are [sic] not part of the government," he was misinformed; second, that pressure from the United States, even when it emanates from a President rhetorically committed to going all the way in El Salvador, remains a potentially decisive force in the politics of that country. As it confirms these realities, it underscores Duarte's dilemmas.

If there were no civil war, there would be no Duarte presidency, because the Right would not need him and he has no divisions of his own. What he has is the key to American aid. As long as that aid seems vital and conditional, Duarte has the power to influence events. But the closer the armed forces approach victory as a result of that aid, the weaker Duarte will become, unless, in the interim, he manages to construct an independent power base and substantially to transform the military institution.

The latter prospect threatens the leaders of the armed forces only somewhat less than defeat by the Left. The former requires a buildup of worker and peasant organizations linked to the Christian Democratic Party. And that in turn requires confrontation with the second most powerful actor on Duarte's side of the civil war, the private sector with its strong ideological links to the Republican Party. If he presses hard on these actors, they may take their risks and topple him. If he does not, if he essentially accepts the social and institutional status quo, then while he may preside over the tranquilization of El Salvador, it will be a tranquility recalling Tacitus's epitaph for an earlier campaign of pacification: "To robbery, butchery, and rapine, they give the lying name of 'government'; they create a desolation and call it peace."

Even if he were collaborating with an American President who shared Christian Democracy's political vision, Duarte's chances of finding a way through his dilemmas would be slim. As it is, liberals have ample reason to hedge their bets.

Notes

1. This essay was written in the fall of 1984.
2. To be fair, the Sandinistas, on the whole, resisted a not wholly dissimilar temptation.
3. "The model of Reactionary Despotism in Central America," in Martin Diskin, ed., *Trouble in our Backyard,* Pantheon 1983, p.112; for more detail and historical perspective, see Baloyra's *El Salvador in Transition,* (U. of North Carolina, 1982).

21

At Sea in Central America: Can We Negotiate Our Way to Shore?

Negotiations can serve either to promote compromise or to confirm defeat. This deep ambiguity allows President Ronald Reagan to claim without mendacity that, no less than the critics of his policies in Central America, he favors negotiations. For clearly he is prepared at any time to negotiate the surrender of the Sandinista Government and the Salvadoran opposition. These ends being nonnegotiable, at the moment, the President must pursue them through other means.

The administration's compulsion to batter chosen opponents into submission is a sad spectacle because it augurs further suffering for the people of Central America, already mutilated by a terrible history, in which the United States has played a conspicuous part. This compulsion is also paradoxical. Normally, self-interest is the force that drives the leaders of one state to impose agony on the people of another. In this instance, any rational definition of self-interest dictates a policy of compromise.

A second paradox springs from the President's claim to be animated not merely by a parochial conception of national interest, but also by concern for the men, women, and children of Nicaragua, El Salvador, and the other countries being sucked into the vortex of regional war. When enumerating his objectives, President Reagan speaks of human rights and democracy in the same breath that invokes threats to U.S. security. Yet, the only possible means of reconciling the humane with the strategic is through the very compromises this administration now seems to eschew—compromises that its own policies may have made possible.

There lies the final and most bitter paradox, that of a President, blinded by ideology, who will not reap what he helped sow. Three years ago, the Left in El Salvador envisioned an absolute military victory. In that triumphal spirit it rejected negotiations. Now the Left pursues them. Three years ago, the Sandinista comandantes apparently envisioned Nicaragua as the asylum, command point, and entrepôt of an isthmus-wide revolution. Now they seem eager to negotiate pacts of mutual tolerance with their neighbors. Both the Sandinistas and the Salvadoran Left appear, therefore, to have arrived at a point of convergence with U.S. objectives announced by President Carter and at least nominally adopted by his successor. However, as revolutionary forces have reduced their appetite, ours apparently has grown.

Nicaragua

The Reagan administration originally justified military aid to opponents of the Sandinista regime, the so-called contras, as a means of cutting off the arms supply to the Salvadoran guerrillas. In this connection, the administration urged the notion of symmetry. Such aid would help the enemies of the Managua government as long as that government helped the enemies of our "friends" in San Salvador. But now, having dined on the first course of its campaign to make Managua more pliable, and having found the eating good, the administration apparently wants the Sandinistas to serve up something more than an enforceable commitment to neutrality. And that something is themselves.

In April 1983, then Assistant Secretary of State Thomas Enders told the Senate Foreign Relations Committee:

> Central American democrats . . . are particularly clear on the need for democratization [in the region]. Only in this way could they be confident they will not have to face sometime in the future an aggressive neighbor unconstrained by the limits democracy imposes.[1]

Three months later, a senior U.S. diplomat based in Central America informed Christopher Dickey of *The Washington Post* that issues other than the questions of aid to the insurgents in El Salvador probably could not be negotiated successfully with the Sandinistas until they changed their approach to government. He added:

> It is now considered that the only way they can be trusted to keep an agreement is to have the type of government which would force them to do so or make it a public issue.[2]

The administration dispelled any lingering doubts about its objectives when it brushed aside the package of proposals presented by the Nicaraguan government on October 20, 1983.[3] Unlike proposals of a more general character, which Managua had made in 1982, the 1983 package included detailed provisions designed to assuage Washington's anxieties concerning aid to possible revolutionary movements and Soviet or Cuban use of military facilities in Nicaragua. Pursuant to the proposed treaty with the United States, Nicaragua would pledge that "it will not permit [its territory] to be utilized to affect or to threaten the security of the United States or to attack any other state."[4]

Nicaraguan Foreign Minister Miguel d'Escoto said the agreements required his country to dismantle any command and control facilities on Nicaraguan soil that might exist for use by Salvadoran guerrilla groups to coordinate the movement of their forces inside El Salvador and to arrange for supply shipments.[5] More significant than these verbal commitments is the Nicaraguan government's declared willingness to allow on-site observation as a means of policing compliance.

To be sure, the draft treaty in this package, directed specifically to the conflict in El Salvador, treats the regime and its opponents as equals and even-handedly prohibits aid to both.[6] If, as some informed observers believe,[7] the Salvadoran security forces would disintegrate without constant infusions of U.S. aid (even if the guerrillas were also cut off from external suppliers), the treaty in its present form is unsatisfactory. But it would be an odd diplomacy indeed if a country initiated negotiations by conceding all its opposite number's demands. So the inclusion of reciprocal restraints in what the Nicaraguan government simply calls a basis for negotiations does not satisfactorily explain their back-of-the-hand reception in Washington, particularly in light of the administration's formal insistence on the significance of external aid to the guerrillas.

The administration's refusal either to accept the proposals as a basis for negotiation or to table any alternative negotiating package reinforces the impression that Washington seeks to alter the Nicaraguan regime itself rather than its external policies.

On their face, demands for the democratization of Nicaraguan politics are not equivalent to proposals for a unilateral suicide pact. The statements quoted above could be interpreted as envisioning continued Sandinista preeminence coincident with an institutionalized and secure opposition. One feels, nevertheless, that, to the extent the Reagan administration has anything very specific in mind, it must be more than that. If the United States is demanding democratization merely to secure monitors of Sandinista compliance with a no-export-of-revolution agreement, the demand seems gratuitous. It seems gratuitous, first, because the administration's indictment of Nicaraguan aid to the Salvadoran rebels rests on its claimed capability to monitor Managua's behavior. Second, although the opposition is harassed and censored, the country remains so porous that there is little that happens there that is not quickly and widely known both within and beyond its frontiers.

If a secure political opposition cannot heighten the already high risk of exposure—should the Sandinistas violate a nonintervention commitment—surely something more than exposure is at stake. Must the opposition have a permanent veto on the government's foreign policy in order to mitigate Washington's distrust? That would be a curious constitutional provision, one with little or no parallel in the known world. Even if such a provision existed on paper, would it deter a regime willing to risk exposure and consequent retaliation from the United States? As a practical matter, the only consistently effective domestic political restraint is the threat of electoral defeat. So Washington's linkage of democratization and nonintervention logically implies an opposition that, by means of exposure, can hope to win an election and replace the Sandinista government.

Sandinista acceptance of a competitive political system would not be suicidal. The comandantes still appear to enjoy support, particularly among younger Nicaraguans. A government wholly reliant on the terror its security forces could impose would not distribute arms rather broadly among the civil population, as the government in Managua has done. This support has survived conflict with the Catholic Church, economic privation, and betrayal of the original commitment to nonalignment in international affairs. In opening the political system the Sandinistas would concomitantly reduce their electoral liabilities, because the decision to open would be taken as part of a larger decision to pursue reconciliation with the democratic opposition. To achieve reconciliation, the government in Managua would have to lift restrictions on free press, association and speech, to offer attractive concessions to the Miskito and other minorities and initiate the institutional separation of the Sandinista Party and the state, including its armed forces.

These steps, plus the removal of U.S. economic sanctions, could create the climate of confidence essential to reverse the outflow of capital and managerial talent, and might thus fuel economic growth. Once unencumbered by a shrinking economy and perceived responsibility for every objectionable act and omission of public policy, the comandantes—with their far-flung organization, populist program, newspaper, and residual mystique as military leaders of the national revolution—would represent a powerful electoral force, if they remained united. The Sandinistas' potential ability to win an electoral competition makes the U.S. demand for democratization something less, at least in form, than insistence that the comandantes self-destruct.

With the Reagan administration dangling the seductive image of an emergent social democracy in Nicaragua, moderates and liberals have found it difficult to unite in opposition to the President's actual policies. Americans who cheered the Nicaraguan revolution have felt betrayed by the subsequent course of events, rather as if they were personally responsible for the overthrow of Anastasio Somoza. President Reagan has played on that feeling, even claiming ignorantly that the Sandinistas had violated a kind of legal commitment to the installation of multiparty democracy.

The truth, of course, is that the United States contributed to the revolution only by doing nothing decisive to block it. A faction within the Carter administration did urge positive steps to force Somoza out; but it lost every battle. With characteristic amnesia, many Americans have forgotten the Carter administration's determined effort, initiated at the first sign of Somoza's weakness, to assemble an anti-Sandinista coalition, including the civilian apparatus of the Somoza regime, with a "sanitized" National Guard as its chopping edge. That effort could only have produced war without end to defend *Somocismo* without Somoza.

Whether wise or foolish, moral or squalid, the Carter administration's actual behavior during Somoza's last year can hardly be squared with the proposition that, in consideration of U.S. aid in defanging Somoza, the Sandinistas assumed an obligation to institutionalize democracy.

Of course the United States should have deployed its political and economic resources to accelerate Nicaragua's transformation. If it had, several tens of thousands of people now dead would be alive. Today, Nicaragua would probably be governed by a coalition, including the Sandinistas, committed to nonalignment in foreign affairs and, domestically, to reform within a capitalist framework.[8]

I rake over the past only because its coals still burn among us.

Naturally, Americans committed to the promotion of democratic values everywhere in the hemisphere should complain about authoritarian rule in Nicaragua. We would therefore be right to support the administration's policies if there were still a credible basis for believing that, at reasonable cost to our national interest and the people of Nicaragua, these policies were likely to promote a democratic outcome. Today, such a belief must rest on faith alone.

Had the promotion of human rights been its main concern, the administration's strategy—organizing a military force to challenge the Sandinista government and threatening direct military intervention—would from the outset have seemed a wild gamble. For such a strategy could succeed only if the comandantes responded to the military challenge by offering their opponents a nonviolent route to power. Yet historical experience suggests that military threats create an environment peculiarly inclement for political participation or any other kind of human right. As administration ideologues have been quick to point out when defending the delinquencies of right-wing regimes, subversion aggravates the endemic paranoia of authoritarian leaders, leading them to impose a tighter grip on society. Whatever capacity they once had for distinguishing dissent from treason rapidly atrophies. By driving moderates underground, where they join the violent opposition, the crackdown further polarizes society, eroding conditions necessary for a politics of accommodation.

Nicaragua's government is conditioned by history and ideology to view the United States as an irreconcilably hostile power regardless of who occupies the Oval Office. Its occupation by a leader of the American Right naturally strengthens the belief that the United States will try to liquidate any government of the Left in the Western Hemisphere, even an elected one. Opposition movements tied politically and militarily to the United States will be seen as means to U.S. ends and, hence, irreconcilable. Thus, from this perspective, concessions are not only useless, but dangerous. Concessions imply recognition of opponents as a substantial political force, a legitimate claimant to rights of participation in the national political order. Once endowed with such legitimacy, a movement is better positioned to invite intervention on its behalf, since intervention by invitation of a substantial, indigenous actor is less quickly characterized as aggression. The strategic dilemma, then, is that the added leverage any opposition group acquires against the Nicaraguan regime by virtue of U.S. support is offset by the tendency of that support to convince the regime of the disutility of compromise.

Although moved by quite different ends, the administration's policy of concentrating support on (indeed largely creating) the Honduran–based opposition group, the Democratic National Front (FDN), with its conspicuous ties to the Somoza order, has somewhat eased this dilemma in that it gives the progressive opposition grouped around Eden Pastora and Alfonso Robelo leverage without the taint of the American connection. As a stratagem for promoting democracy in Nicaragua, it seems inspired. The Sandinista government's prudent response would have been to seek reconciliation with Pastora's group, the Democratic Revolutionary Alliance (ARDE) and the establishment of a Popular Front Government.

Among its many virtues, power sharing in Managua would turn the edge of the U.S. argument for symmetry in dealing with El Salvador and Nicaragua. I once concluded a private talk with Interior Minister Tomás Borge and Daniel Ortega (before he became President) with the warning: "Remember, you have an opportunity to make a unique contribution to fascism in Latin America. To guarantee its ascendancy, to doom hope for reform, all you have to do is force this national revolution into an authoritarian mold."

The obverse also remains true: the successful emergence in Nicaragua of a political order as committed to freedom as it is to reform would shake the very foundations of neighboring authoritarian states. In this historical moment, the force of example is greater than the example of force. Believing as they do in the efficacy of raw power, President Reagan and his aides probably are constitutionally disabled from envisioning the ripple effect of a democracy in Nicaragua. Unfortunately, the Sandinistas seem to suffer equally from lack of imagination.

By not being consciously pursued, the strategy has had its best possible test. The Sandinistas know that Washington has not been seeking to induce reconciliation with ARDE and a consequent social democracy in Nicaragua. They believe that Reagan seeks not to reform but rather to destroy their regime. They take his threats seriously and are prepared therefore to make concessions; but not concessions concerning the distribution of government offices that would amount to an immediate sharing of power. The United States has now done almost everything but invade. It has failed to pry open the regime. One can conclude that military pressure will not bring democracy to Nicaragua.[9]

The democratic promise of present policy being slight, the United States should try one less costly in the currency both of human rights and national interests and which, coincidentally, is more likely to succeed.

A first objection to current policy is that it kills people and promises to kill many more. Although the contras seem unable to pose a serious challenge to the Sandinistas, they have managed to kill several thousand supporters and employees of the government and doubtless have suffered substantial casualties of their own. We are not doing the killing ourselves. But without U.S. financial support and training, and without the hope of an ultimate ride to victory on the back of a U.S. invasion force, and without the U.S. guarantee of Honduras' security, which in turn produces a Honduran sanctuary, the contras would soon be reduced to the level of a nuisance.

A second objection is the effect of current policy on the democratic prospects elsewhere in Central America, particularly Honduras. In the course of turning that country into an American base for operations against the Sandinistas, the United States has succeeded in polarizing Honduran politics and strengthening the hand of the most authoritarian elements in the armed forces. A society comparatively free of extreme human rights violence is increasingly marked by goon–squad operations on the Right and incipient recourse to armed subversion on the Left. U.S. pressure on the armed forces and the civilian Right helped to extract the commitment to electoral politics that is now unraveling. The United States will not restore that pressure as long as Honduras is a useful tool for harassing Nicaragua.

A third objection is the policy's capacity to distract both Congress and the executive branch from intrinsically more important issues.[10]

A fourth risk is igniting and then sucking the United States into a regional war. The Honduran armed forces, made cocky by U.S. backing and eager to take on Nicaragua, might arrange some extreme provocation—for example, crossing the border on the pretext of a prior Nicaraguan incursion, then invoking U.S. guarantees. Or Honduran and contra troops, possibly reinforced by Guatemalan and Salvadoran units, might drive into Nicaragua, set up a provisional government, secure recognition from the conspiring regimes and then, when threatened with destruction by Nicaraguan armed forces, launch an appeal our right-wing President might find hard to resist.

A fifth objection is the policy's power to reinforce the image of the United States, so current among the educated youth of Latin America, as the implacable foe of social change, an image that helped shape the mentality of the young men and women who now govern Nicaragua. An administration seeking pleasant relations with every right-wing gunman in the hemisphere is simply unconvincing when it claims to be struggling for democracy in Central America.

A final objection to continuation of the present policy is the availability of an alternative more likely to produce the desired result. The Sandinistas have established nothing like totalitarian control over Nicaragua, not because of U.S. opposition but rather because of the nature of Nicaraguan society and, possibly, of their own movement.

The great mass of the population is Catholic and socially conservative. As opponents of Somoza during the national rising, the church hierarchy avoided any taint from the old order. On the contrary, the church enjoys the prestige of participation in the liberation struggle. Within the Sandinista movement itself, Catholics, including priests, play a substantial role. They may be hostile to the hierarchy; they may believe in a socialized economy, but it is highly unlikely they would support an attack on the church as such. Whatever their ideology and ambitions, the comandantes have no hope of eliminating this powerful institutional expression of pluralistic values.

Geographic position is an additional obstacle to the perpetuation of rigid, authoritarian rule. Nicaragua, like all of the Caribbean Basin, is inevitably subject to the magnetic force of American culture, as it is doomed to dependence on American markets. The country has neither the size nor the resources nor the trained cadres to run an autarkic economic system. Furthermore, the Soviet Union has indicated plainly that it is not prepared to assume responsibility for yet another welfare case. This factor in itself distinguishes the Cuban precedent. By withdrawing the military threat, Washington would itself establish a second decisive distinction. Then, unlike Castro, the Sandinistas could not portray themselves as nationalist heroes facing down the regional Goliath. In this respect, current U.S. policy plays into Sandinista hands, creating a drama in which they can star.

The country's cultural and institutional heritage, together with its geographic position and economic necessities, will exert continuing and ultimately effective pressures for a plural political order, even if the United States is passive. Ending the U.S. military threat to the Sandinista regime does not, however, entail passivity. We could continue to deploy economic sanctions and incentives. The Sandinistas need access to American capital and markets, as well as private sector confidence, in order to deliver promised economic and social progress. A conservative President is peculiarly well-positioned to extract from Congress the kind and quantity of economic carrots capable of influencing political developments in Nicaragua. Economic cooperation conditioned neither on Nicaragua's openness to U.S. investors nor on Chicago School economics, but rather on its respect for human rights, including the right to participate in government, will augment the internal forces advocating democratic reform. If not tied to conservative theology, U.S. efforts are more likely to attract reinforcing action from democratic governments in Europe and Latin America.

Such a policy does not promise immediate results and cannot guarantee success. For the American Right, it will never have the charm of military force with its false promises of decisive consequences. American forces thinly veiled by the contras could, if committed in large number, successfully invade Nicaragua and occupy its major cities. They could not, in the foreseeable future, pacify either the urban barrios or the countryside. Instead, the United States would incur costs out of proportion even to the most demented conception of the national interest and extract an unspeakable toll on human rights. The Sandinistas clearly have a substantial social base. In case of invasion, nationalists, including some present opponents of the regime, might join in defending the country.[11] Faced with determined resistance, the United States would use its vast fire power. What sort of democracy could be fabricated amidst the blood-soaked ruins?

Though it has not succeeded in producing democracy in Nicaragua, administration policy apparently has convinced the Nicaraguan government of the need to allay U.S. security concerns. Now is the time to negotiate the sort of compromise settlement former Assistant Secretary of State Thomas Enders apparently offered the Sandinistas early in the Reagan era, before our appetite grew.[12] Managua would agree to neutralize itself: no military relations with Cuba or the Soviet Union; no assistance to Central American rebels; no army out of proportion to the forces of its neighbors. After agreeing to respect Nicaragua's neutral status, the United

States would have to terminate support for the contras,[13] withdraw troops from and vastly reduce military aid to Honduras, and encourage Honduran participation in the neutralization negotiations. Such an agreement is, in essence, what the Contadora States (Panama, Mexico, Columbia, Venezuela) have tried to achieve. Negotiations would be carried out under their auspices and would include all the Central American States and the United States. In light of Cuba's declared sympathy for the Contadora framework, and the utility of obtaining its formal commitment to the terms of any settlement, Cuba should be invited to participate.[14]

Since, at the urging of the Contadora group, democratization has already been accepted by all the Central American States as one of the bases for a settlement, it should be an issue in the negotiations. As things stand now, a precise enumeration of steps for converting that principle into practice probably cannot be obtained. However, the principle itself should be incorporated in the ultimate substantive agreements, as a latent benchmark of legitimacy. Furthermore, the United States should urge that the agreements include a commitment from Managua to amnesty all members of the opposition not guilty of atrocities committed during the Somoza period or war crimes during the current conflict, and willing to renounce the use of force. Finally, all parties to the agreements should agree to strengthen existing protections and guarantees for human rights in their respective countries, including the right to free expression of political views.

El Salvador

The political and psychological pressures on Nicaragua to negotiate a specific program for opening its politics would be far greater if the United States were correspondingly prepared to press the virtues of political accommodation on its Salvadoran clients. The United States has, however, ample other reasons for doing that.

Yet, despite its theoretical preference for nonlethal politics, despite its inability to build clients into a force clearly able to win without endless U.S. aid, despite the resultant drain on the energy and cohesion of the U.S. decision making community and despite the subtle but real damage to its image among West Europeans, the administration continues to pursue a military solution. No one can honestly doubt the proposition that the only thing President Reagan wishes to negotiate in El Salvador is the surrender of the Left.

With the rumored exception of a brief hesitation during the watch of Thomas Enders at the State Department, the administration has been fiercely consistent and almost frank. Before assuming office, a future architect of the administration's Central American policies, Jeane Kirkpatrick, responding to a question about how the conflict could end, snapped: "They could give up."[15] Three years later, Under Secretary of Defense Fred Iklé echoed Mrs. Kirkpatrick when he announced:

> We do not seek a military defeat of our friends. We do not seek a military stalemate. We seek victory for the forces of democracy. And that victory has two components [one of which is] defeating militarily those organized forces of violence that refuse to accept the democratic will of the people.[16]

In the same spirit, Richard Stone, while serving as President Reagan's Central American negotiator, continuously emphasized that the only negotiable issue is how the Left's participation in the elections run by the present government could be facilitated.[17]

Participation in elections conducted under the tender auspices of the Salvadoran armed forces is tantamount to surrender not only for those opposition members who aspire to total power, but also for those, like Guillermo Ungo and Ruben Zamora, with unimpeachable democratic credentials. One normally thinks of elections as deciding who shall govern— that is, who shall make all basic policy decisions and control the state's monopoly of legitimate violence. In El Salvador, however, any foreseeable election could bear the weight of that meaning only if one or both of the following conditions were previously satisfied: either (a) the Salvadoran armed forces must have been transformed into an institution actually subject to civilian control or (b) its pre- and post-election behavior must be guaranteed by a superior external force. In the absence of either condition, the election is unlikely to reflect a reasonably informed and uncoerced popular choice. And, even in the remarkable event that the election was not corrupted, it nevertheless would fail in its nominal purpose of determining who shall rule.

"The civilians are not yet the ones that control the situation here," Rey Prendes, leader of the centrist Christian Democrat caucus in the Constituent Assembly has said. "The army still has tremendous power in this country, political power, and in the end the army makes the decision."[18] Since this has been true for at least half a century, what reason is there to believe it will be less true after another election? To be sure, if the Right were to win, its policies would so closely coincide with those of the armed forces' senior officers, purged since 1979 of their more enlightened elements, that the question of who rules probably would not arise. But in the event of victory by a center-Left coalition, the question would be unavoidable, and I know no one who believes it would be resolved in favor of the new government.

The very certainty that the armed forces as presently constituted would not tolerate a government to the left of center would taint the election itself. The armed forces and their paramilitary auxiliaries may not be able to identify the preferences of individual voters, but electoral tabulations will reveal the voting tendencies of villages and neighborhoods. In a country with a grand tradition of collective punishment for challenging the preferences of oligarchs and officers, only the very brave and very foolish would vote for parties certain to lose even if they won.

The Reagan administration has insisted that the Left's demand for power sharing in advance of elections constitutes a rejection of democratic processes. The FDR/FMLN's offer for "peace talks among all interested parties," delivered by Foreign Minister Casteñeda of Mexico to the then Secretary of State Alexander Haig on March 6, 1982, envisioned negotiations of "a transitional government" to be followed "within six months" by a ratification plebiscite; and thereafter by municipal and then general elections.[19] The administration claims that power sharing somehow would violate the purity of Salvadoran democracy. Since the Left was effectively excluded from the last election, since that election was conducted by the armed forces in conditions of civil war, and since, in any event, power remains with the armed forces, El Salvador is not presently a democracy and therefore the claim is spurious.[20] As long as the sharing is provisional, it no more ravages democratic theory than the decision of a ruling parliamentary coalition to alter its policies or enhance its strength by revising the coalition in favor of hitherto excluded parties. Was British democracy violated when, in the early days of World War II, the Conservative Prime Minister organized a government of national unity by distributing ministries to Labor Party leaders?

Rather than violating democratic values, power sharing is one of the only two routes to authentic democracy in El Salvador. Perhaps it is the only one. An external, election–supervising force could guarantee both an election relatively coercion–free and a transfer of formal power to the victorious coalition. But suppose a right–of–center coalition won? Since its ends would coincide with those of an unreformed army, it would have every incentive to invite the peace force to depart. If, as a condition of participating in elections, the Left has laid down its arms, then that force would represent the only obstacle to restoration of the traditional authoritarian coalition of the civilian and military Right.

The harsh fact is that, in a country so deeply divided over economic and social issues and lacking a tradition of political compromise, pluralism must rest precariously on a balance of power. For the opposition groups to lay down their arms and join the so–called electoral competition is nothing less than surrender. They would lose everything including their lives. But the Left will not be the only loser. To the extent the United States seeks democracy, social justice, and the promotion of human rights in El Salvador, it will have lost all.

If a powerful opposition is the only available instrument for levering reform out of the military, it follows that by pursuing "victory," the United States negates the possibility of a new order in El Salvador, one that could survive without continually trashing human rights.

The administration has refused to acknowledge this dilemma, much less suggest how it proposes to escape it. This denial of reality in part reflects the place of democracy and reform in the hierarchy of administration values. The President's policies clearly suggest that, while democracy is something it would be nice to have, the effort to promote it must be subordinated to the defense of friendly regimes. Given that priority, one might still ask: Why not try to achieve both democracy and, if not a friendly regime, at least a neutral one, particularly if by doing so you may reduce the risk of failure or, to avoid failure, an investment disproportionate to U.S. interests? The short answer, according to a report in *The New York Times* based on interviews with leading actors in the administration, is that "Senior administration officials simply do not believe that civil wars are settled by negotiations."[21] History, *The New York Times* correspondent adds, bears out their skepticism.

A wiser man would have noted that history will bear any conclusion one is determined to assemble from its vast, randomly assorted shards. To make their case, administration officials cite Nicaragua as an example of the perfidy and competence of Marxists in undermining power sharing agreements—an example that ostensibly reduces U.S. options to "gutting it out" or "cutting and running." But all Nicaragua confirms is that agreements unsupported by an effective network of sanctions and incentives are unlikely to restrain anyone. Curiously, almost no one cites cases, such as the first post–war Gaullist government in France, where Marxist parties failed to convert power sharing into dominant power.

The top leadership of the Salvadoran guerrilla groups inevitably will have an instrumental view of democracy and of any settlement agreement. This view, however, is not peculiar to radicals. When a democratic process is seen to threaten important interests, persons who feel threatened suddenly discover values more important than the process and the constitution that embodies it. Neither the United Nations Charter nor the Charter of the Organization of American States (OAS), with their unequivocal prohibitions of intervention, restrained an impeccable conservative, Henry Kissinger, from conspiring with fascists seeking to prevent Salvador Allende's coalition from assuming power in Chile.[22] Under the right circumstances, then, quite varied sorts of people are able to place substantive ends above democratic means.

There is, nevertheless, a conspicuous difference between persons with a powerful commitment to democracy and persons who, given their choice, prefer authoritarian politics. A preference for authoritarian politics can stem from the cold calculation that, in a particular historical setting, it is more likely to produce leaders and policies compatible with your interests. A very small, inbred oligarchy controlling most of the nation's wealth does not expect to sustain control through fair electoral competition. So it goes knocking on the barracks door to exchange gratuities for protection. Or, as in the Soviet Union, it equates criticism of the system of privileges with psychosis. Alternatively, the preference can spring from a theological passion for realizing in society a particular set of values. One of democracy's essential features is a tolerance even of behavior powerful constituencies deem abominable. The preference is also found among those who regard democracy as an illusion concealing the reality of minority control.

While neither the officers and oligarchs of El Salvador nor its guerrilla leaders have a democratic vocation, the latter are more apt to find democracy consistent with their values and interests. Why? Because social mobilization over the past two decades has heightened political consciousness among peasants and workers. Free of coercion, they are likely to give the parties of the Left a mandate to continue and deepen the reforms initiated after the 1979 coup. Marxism in Latin America emerges from specific social conditions, not simply as a fire in the minds of ideologues. It has claimed adherents by providing an explanation of and a diagram for altering social hierarchies inherited from the precapitalist era and rigidly defended often with extreme violence and frequently concealed behind democratic forms. That being the case, the demonstrated ability to establish a more egalitarian society through democratic means could affect the outlook of the guerrilla Left.

Transition via power sharing to democracy in El Salvador need not, however, rely on the possibility of such an epiphany. In the Nicaraguan case, the disintegration of the National Guard eliminated the internal balance of power and it was not replaced by external guarantees. Unlike the Nicaraguan case, power sharing in El Salvador would rest on an internal balance of power between army and guerrillas guaranteed by foreign forces. Furthermore, the conditions for transforming an armed truce into a plural political order are more favorable in some respects than those that existed in Nicaragua at the end of the Somoza era. Salvador has a larger middle class, better organized peasants and workers, a more developed party structure, and political leaders on both sides of the present divide with an unimpeachable commitment to democracy. El Salvador also has a history of collaboration, symbolized by the fact that Napoleon Duarte, the dominant Christian Democrat, and Guillermo Ungo, leader of the political wing of the opposition, were running mates in the 1972 presidential elections in a coalition with the Communist Party. Cynics accuse American liberals of searching mindlessly for a political middle in countries where there are only extremes. Such hopeless countries exist. It just so happens that El Salvador is not one of them.

The fundamental dilemma for U.S. policy remains: How to reform a system of power that seems responsive only to the threat of its destruction, when we begin by guaranteeing its survival? To exit from this dilemma, we must change and condition the guarantee. We must change it because democracy cannot sustain itself alongside a standing army led by a self-perpetuating officer corps hostile to the very idea of civilian control. We can guarantee the physical survival of officers. We can guarantee pensions. And we can guarantee an opportunity to compete for positions in the miniaturized constabulary subject to civilian control that democratic politicians, following the Costa Rican model, would almost surely prefer. But those guarantees must be conditioned on the military institution's support for negotiations directed toward establishing a regime able to manage the transition to democracy. And it must be clear that if the conditions are not satisfied by a stated time, Washington will forthwith suspend all military and economic aid, withdraw its advisors, and discourage any other states from continuing to assist the Salvadoran armed forces.

To sharpen the alternatives for all interested parties and to rally support among democratic elements inside and outside the country, Washington would initiate this fundamental policy shift toward compromise with a White Paper frankly conceding the impossibility of reconciling existing policy with the ends either of peace or human rights. The White Paper would detail the steps the United States has resolved to take to help democratic forces within the country unite and assume control of their destiny. Specifically, the statement would recognize that real power remains in the hands of the officer corps and that it has thus far failed to purge itself of criminal elements, to root out right-wing death squads and to reconcile itself to democracy. The U.S. statement would endorse the Franco-Mexican proposition that the FDR/FMLN is a legitimate political force with a substantial social base and draw the necessary conclusion about the opposition's participation in the renewal of the country's political and social institutions. After conceding the legitimate fears of both the government and the opposition, the White Paper would offer military and economic assistance to all groups demonstrating their commitment to a negotiated settlement. Next, it would propose concrete steps for suspending hostilities and beginning negotiations.

In this initial redefinition of policy, the United States would not have to specify all the means it is prepared to use to protect the negotiating process. It would be useful, however, to state categorically that the United States would regard opponents of negotiations as persons pursuing ends inimical to important U.S. interests, to the democratic values embodied in the Charter of the OAS, and to the defense of human rights in El Salvador. Moreover, the United States should be prepared to recognize a transitional regime and, in conjunction with other democratic states, to assist in creating a climate conducive to continued evolution toward an institutionalized democracy. In addition to seeking support among OAS members and European allies, the United States should invite Cuba to assist in bringing about a negotiated settlement. If Havana accepted the invitation in good faith, it would help deliver the guerrillas to the negotiating table and to press them toward compromise.

Good faith acceptance would be consistent with Cuban interests. In the first place, a democratic, center–Left regime is the best it can hope for in El Salvador now that the United States seems committed against a guerrilla victory. This being apparent even to the Salvadoran Left, Cuba's cooperation with the American initiative would not be construed as a betrayal. Moreover, participation would immediately lower the temperature in U.S.–Cuban relations and effectively eliminate the threat of direct, military confrontation. Finally, it might reopen the door, closed at the time of Angola, leading ultimately to the normalization of relations. For one or more of these reasons, in recent months Cuba has signaled its readiness to assist in engineering a negotiated settlement.

Conclusion

If the administration announced it was prepared to seek the objectives and take the steps outlined above, the Cubans, the Nicaraguans, and the Salvadoran Left, including most or all of the guerrilla groups, would enter negotiations conducted under the auspices of the Contadora States. Most of the Salvadoran Left would settle for temporary power sharing followed by elections. And, even if most guerrilla leaders decided to opt for war, the democratic Left's participation in government and elections, the demonstration that democracy could be made to work in El Salvador, and the reforms implemented by a center–Left government would drain the reservoir of sympathizers and recruits on which the armed Left must rely.

Without that reservoir, they soon would become little more than a problem for the police.

The United States can negotiate the neutralization of Nicaragua. Accepting neutralization would not mean abandoning Nicaragua to unchecked authoritarian rule. While the United States would agree to end military harassment, it would continue to treat the country as a pariah, denying the economic assistance and access to American markets necessary to transform Nicaragua into a prosperous polity—until the leadership moved toward objectives announced in the neutralization agreements. And in case of a serious deterioration of human rights, the United States can renew aid to the rebels who then would inevitably reemerge.

America should not underestimate either our material or symbolic assets. A United States ready to lavish aid on a politically plural Nicaragua (even if the Sandinistas rule as a consequence of electoral success) and unencumbered by association with the remnants of the Somoza order, will exert profound influence on the Nicaraguan political system. And if the United States, in the meantime, has succeeded in superintending a settlement of the civil war in El Salvador, the prospects for democracy in Nicaragua will be enhanced.

As it blunders after military solutions without counting the cost to the people of Central America, this administration unintentionally demonstrates the difference between a ruthless and a wise diplomacy.

In the debate over this country's Central American policies, the word "symmetry" has done as much or more than any other concept to cloud minds. So it is with some unease that I note, in closing, the essential symmetry of my proposals for dealing with Nicaragua and El Salvador.

The symmetry of ends is unmistakable—relatively just, relatively stable, broadly participatory political orders. While there cannot be a perfect symmetry of means, the means I proposed are symmetrical in their most crucial albeit negative feature, namely, this administration's relinquishment of its search for military victory.

I do not, of course, recommend a symmetrical insistence on power sharing as the ne plus ultra of negotiations. Why? Quite simply because, in El Salvador's case, power sharing is the only way of halting the slaughter and of constructing just and democratic institutions. In the case of Nicaragua, by contrast, an insistence on (as distinguished from incentives to) power sharing is likely to prolong the killing with little prospect of advancing America's ultimate objective and with considerable risk of making it unobtainable. Moreover, in Nicaragua the objective, including power sharing, appears more likely to evolve in the aftermath of a negotiated settlement that deals only glancingly with domestic political arrangements.

The moral and pragmatic reasons for differential treatment with respect to the content of negotiations seem self-evident. But mindful of the confusion the very word *symmetry* appears to sow, perhaps I should more fully recapitulate the differences between these cases, since it is precisely those differences that make the claim for symmetry literally nonsensical. Treating different cases as if they were the same is just as asymmetrical as treating identical cases differently.

Two differences are fundamental. One is character—the history, as well as the institutional and class bases—of the regimes in Managua and San Salvador. A second is the relative autonomy and capacity of the rebels. Since the latter is really a function of the former, in the end the differences are one.

The problem Washington faces in El Salvador does not stem from the ideological vagaries or idiosyncratic awfulness of a few, identifiable people. Rather, the problem is inherent in the struggle to wrench power from a self-perpetuating and self-controlled military institution and an oligarchy with precapitalist roots. In supporting the latter coalition, the United States struggles against history. America wages war against the very forces whose triumph will mark another stage in the modernization process and will, ironically, make Salvadoran society more like our own. A vast aid program conceived as a substitute for rather than a concomitant to deep political and social change will only strengthen the forces bidding to crack the society's ancient mold. I refer not primarily to the guerrillas (who are only the cutting edge of change) but to all classes struggling to shape the nation's institutions to their needs.

An oligarchy, clinging not only to its money but to its status as a force above the law, and a parasitic officer corps are incompatible with a relatively modern political and social order. They cannot survive in an authentic participatory political system. They know that. And so to save the stinking hulk of the *ancien régime,* they will fight to the last priest, peasant and reformer. They will fight, that is, as long as the Reagan administration allows them to believe that it won't let them sink.

The Sandinistas, conversely, are an expression of the new forces pushing relentlessly against worn out structures of life and thought. In part because the Sandinistas share many (but not all) widely popular objectives—opportunity open to merit; general access to education and medical care; a more even distribution of income and wealth—the armed opposition seems unable to ignite a broadly based revolt.

But the Sandinistas' grip on power also owes something to the educative value of experience. Made stupid at first by their ideology, the Sandinistas have gradually and partially adapted to the character of Nicaraguan and international reality.

No doubt some among them still dream of pressing society into a Marxist mold. The Central American wars sustain their dreams. For in the peace the United States and the Latin and European democracies can help create, irreconcilables of the Left and Right alike will depart from the historical stage into a deserved obscurity.

Notes

This chapter was originally published in *Central America: Anatomy of Conflict*, Robert Leiken, Ed., Pergamon, 1984.
1. "Nicaragua: Threat to Peace in Central America," U.S. Department of State, Bureau of Public Affairs, Current Policy No. 476, April 12, 1983.
2. Dickey, C., "Latins Find U.S. Policy Confusing," *The Washington Post*, July 25, 1983. p. A1.
3. "Juridical Foundations to Guarantee International Peace and Security of the States of Central America: Official Proposal of Nicaragua Within the Framework of the Contadora Process," Nicaragua Minister of the Exterior, October 15, 1983.
4. Article 6 of "Draft Treaty to Guarantee Mutual Respect, Peace and Security Between the Republic of Nicaragua and the United States of America," ibid, p. 9.
5. Tyler, P., "Sandinistas Propose Security Accords to U.S.," *The Washington Post*, October 21, 1983, p. A1.
6. "Draft Accord to Contribute to the Peaceful Solution of the Armed Conflict in the Republic of El Salvador," esp. Articles 1–5, *supra*, note 3, pp. 27–30.
7. They believed it in 1984, when I wrote the above. The importance in December 1986 of continuing U.S. aid to the much larger, better trained and armed forces guarding the status quo is unclear.
8. See generally Fagen, R., "The End of the Affair," *Foreign Policy*, No. 36, Fall 1979, p. 178.
9. If the Sandinistas hold municipal elections in 1987, if they allow the internal opposition to contest mayoralty races, and particularly if the opposition manage to elect some mayors who are allowed to exercise power, this conclusion will be more subject to doubt.
10. See Ullmann, R., "At War with Nicaragua," *Foreign Affairs*, Fall 1983.
11. In response to a question at a semipublic forum about what he would do in the event of a U.S. invasion of Nicaragua, Eden Pastora responded: "I would fight alongside my people."
12. "A Secret War for Nicaragua," *Newsweek*, November 8, 1982, p. 42.
13. Since my personal sympathies run to the progressive democrats moved by the practices and policies of the Sandinista leadership to collaboration with the FDN, I arrived at this prescription with great reluctance.
14. See e.g., Crossett, B., "Castro Says U.S. Seeks to Deploy Troops Under Guise of Maneuvers," *The New York Times*, July 27, 1983, p. A1.
15. *The New York Times*, December 7, 1980, sec. 4, p. 3.
16. "Remarks Prepared for Delivery by the Honorable Fred C. Iklé, Under Secretary of Defense for Policy, to Baltimore Council on Foreign Affairs, September 12, 1983." News Release, Office of Assistant Secretary of Defense for Public Affairs, p. 4.

17. See, e.g., Dickey, C. and McCartney, R., "Little Hope Seen for Salvadoran Peace," *The Washington Post,* September 4, 1983, p. A1.
18. Ibid.
19. Loferedo, G., "The Central American Crisis: Mexico's Role in the Search for a Negotiated Settlement," paper prepared for the Latin American Task Force of the Congressional Black Caucus, U.S. House of Representatives, Washington D.C., March 14, 1982, p. 14. See also "Position of the FDR-FMLN's Political-Diplomatic Commission on Elections and Political Solution," July 22, 1981, and Zamora, R., "Saving Salvador," *The New York Times,* January 22, 1982, p. A31.
20. See Farer, T., "Manage the Revolution?" *Foreign Policy,* No. 52, Fall 1983, pp. 96-117.
21. Gelb, L., "U.S. Aides See Need for Big Effort to Avert Rebel Victory in Salvador," *The New York Times,* April 22, 1983, p. A1.
22. See Kissinger, H., *White House Years,* Little Brown, 1979, pp. 663-678; *Years of Upheaval,* Little Brown, 1982, pp. 409-13; Sigmund, P., *The Overthrow of Allende and the Politics of Chile, 1964-1976,* U. of Pittsburgh Press, 1977, pp. 113-123.

22

Contadora

A seeming contradiction lies at the heart of the approach of the Contadora group (Columbia, Mexico, Panama, and Venezuela) toward the conflicts in Central America. All four members oppose the proliferation of Soviet-style regimes in the Western Hemisphere; all four would prefer to see a more open political system in Nicaragua; and none would welcome a radical revolutionary triumph in El Salvador. Yet all not only steadfastly oppose U.S. military intervention to achieve these goals, but also worry about the Reagan administration's depiction of Central America as one front in the global confrontation between East and West. And they are frightened by the degree to which their backyards already have been militarized.

These disagreements with Washington concern far more than the relative efficiency of different policy tools or an interesting academic dispute over the origins of turmoil in the region. Instead, they reflect a judgment by the Contadora countries that current U.S. policies threaten their futures more than do radical forces in the small countries of Central America. Specifically, they fear that even a direct U.S. military intervention that liquidated the armed Left in El Salvador and drove the Sandinistas into the mountains would be far more likely to destroy their own fragile political orders than the triumph and survival of revolutionaries in two comparatively unimportant Central American countries. Understanding why the Contadora countries feel this way is one step toward designing a more realistic and appealing U.S. policy for the region.

The centrist elites that rule the Contadora countries view the comparatively open frameworks they have built as their best hope for preserving their own power bases, as well as sparing their countries the agony of civil strife. They feel secure enough to withstand the reverberations of nearby revolutions. But they are convinced that full-scale war in Central America would upset the balance of interests that is the sole guarantor of their democracies. By ignoring these calculations, the United States has put itself on a collision course with countries that share its security concerns and that could be useful partners.

The relatively mild and relatively open political orders of the Contadora states are nonetheless brittle. They are neither powerfully institutionalized—with the possible exception of Mexico—nor cushioned by a widely accepted democratic ethos and idiom. For important groups in all of these countries, the rule of law (*estado del derecho*), competitive politics, and other aspects of human rights are essentially means for promoting their own interests, not transcendent ends. And other groups, which currently acquiesce in rule by centrist elites, plainly chafe under these restraints, awaiting opportunities to break free. The Center holds, but precariously.

Evidence of fragility in these countries abounds. In Columbia, militarization of the judicial system and other deviations from democracy were reported in 1980 and 1981 by Amnesty International and the Inter-American Commission on Human Rights. The "creeping coup," as some Columbians called these developments, was not just the army's idea. Although part of the traditional governing elite urged the incorporation of new groups demanding access to political power, another segment demanded firmness in the face of threats. The bitter dispute within both traditional parties—Liberals and Conservatives—over a general amnesty and concurrent negotiations with guerrilla leaders exemplified the centrifugal forces threatening a moderate political order.

In Mexico, a striking sign of the uneasiness of the civilian political elite is the fiercely nationalistic government's remarkably low-key response to the Guatemalan army's repeated raids miles into Mexico to kidnap refugees suspected of having guerrilla connections. The government's moderation stems at least partly from fear that a major diplomatic confrontation will heighten pressure for military participation in policymaking. Another, even clearer, sign of tension is the continuing harassment of opposition political parties, despite the apparently sincere efforts by recent Mexico leaders to loosen slightly the country's political joints.

Ideological wars in neighboring countries threaten these fairly conciliatory, progressively more inclusive political orders and buttress the advocates of closure by force. They dramatize issues concerning the distribution of wealth and power that the Contadora states, to varying degrees, have managed to mute. The threat of war tends to give these issues a dangerous prominence. Moreover, a feeling of ideological fraternity and a practical interest in exploiting the emotions aroused and sharpened by the neighboring conflict invariably encourage both poles of the political spectrum to indict the Center's instinctive neutrality, thereby adding yet another issue to the agenda of latent internecine conflict.

As long as the conflict is localized, however, the centrist Contadora establishments seem able to manage these pressures. But they would prefer not to face them at all. Therefore, they will support the emergence of political orders that, like their own, can produce enough change, distribute enough income or opportunity, or co-opt enough members of the potential counterelite to evade entrapment in the procrustean alternatives of hideous repression and civil war. These fears are never openly admitted by the Contadora regimes, for governments rarely advertise their structural weaknesses. But in private conversations, the anxieties shared by leading figures in these states are clear.

Deep U.S. involvement in Central America's civil wars would accentuate the centrifugal forces always threatening to rip apart political order in the Contadora states and in their Central American sibling, Costa Rica, even if Washington scrupulously avoided efforts to align the Contadora governments with its policies. Significant segments of the educated elite throughout the Caribbean Basin are by now animated by any major American initiative. The long history of U.S. involvement in their countries' destinies; the deep infiltration of American culture into their lives; the dense economic networks on which individual, family, and national well-being depend; and the profusion of personal ties and personal experiences (for example, Disneyland, Bloomingdale's, and the Inter-American Defense College) generate on the Right an instinctive deference to U.S. preference and perspective and on the Left an instinctive hostility. Once galvanized by a local American initiative, both factions pressure their governments to pursue a foreign policy consistent with their incompatible inclinations, thereby underscoring and intensifying their endemic hostility and shaking the foundations of tolerance.

Since the United States, like any other state, will try to marshal diplomatic support and to neutralize potential opposition among regional actors, the decision to intervene anywhere in the region entails more subtle, but potentially destabilizing, forms of intervention everywhere in the region. America unavoidably becomes an active participant in the domestic politics of each state, driven by its objectives and its points of leverage—particularly the military or people in business who are either export-oriented or linked with U.S. corporations—to collaborate with the Right and to inflame the Left. In addition, Washington is continually tempted to apply pressure directly on the governing centrist coalition—as some advisors urged President Ronald Reagan to do at the height of the Mexican financial crisis.

The consequent domestic polarization is best illustrated by Honduras, whose fragile semidemocracy nearly collapsed under the weight of American determination to turn the country into a base for U.S. operations supporting El Salvador and opposing Nicaragua. Power within the military tilted toward General Gustavo Alvarez Martinez and his colleagues, who composed the faction that was most belligerent, most authoritarian, most closely tied to extremist business leaders (this faction also had connections with the Reverend Sun Myung Moon), and most eager to convert the country into an American subsidiary. Power within the society appeared to gravitate to the military. Rightist paramilitary units and leftist guerrillas suddenly leaped onto the hitherto quiet local stage. The phenomenon of disappeared persons made its now-predictable appearance. One could see more than the end of the country's flirtation with democracy; one could see Honduras slipping for the first time into the nightmare world of private and public terrorism.

The country's remission, initiated by the military's expulsion of Alvarez, resulted in part from the general's quirky character and, according to press reports too numerous to be discounted, the imperiousness of U.S. Ambassador John Negroponte, whom many in Honduras believed better suited for the British Colonial Service in the days when its representatives ruled over more than a few large rocks. The experience of Honduras also suggests that even in a desperately poor, vulnerable country, ideas of national dignity and interest limit American influence.

Honduras' longer-term future is still uncertain. But the country remains an illustration of the dangers to domestic equilibriums that the Contadora states have been trying to avoid by confining Central America's violence and discounting its alleged ideological and geopolitical significance.

A Settlement Without Victors

A related motive behind Contadora, at least for the more progressive elements in each country's governing coalition, undoubtedly is concern for the message that would be sent by the repression of the Salvadoran rebels, unaccompanied by significant reform, which would be the likeliest result of military victory over the insurgents. As their U.S. and West European counterparts have done since their own welfare states emerged, Contadora elites are debating how much reform is necessary to maintain calm among the popular classes. If El Salvador ultimately demonstrates that the traditional U.S. guarantee of survival in the event of elite miscalculation is still good and that Nicaragua is an anomaly, the position of those who discount the need for substantial concessions will be reinforced.

It is true, however, that a collapse of the Salvadoran military and the emergence of a ferociously vengeful and radically redistributive government inevitably would heighten the paranoia of the wealthier classes and thereby augment the ranks of the far Right in all the Contadora states. This was precisely the effect throughout the hemisphere of Fidel Castro's triumph in Cuba. The sudden prestige acquired by advocates of revolution now produced a spiral of violence that left most of Latin America in the hands of governments pursuing rigidly conservative ends with ruthlessly immoderate means.

Centrist elites in the Contadora states apparently are betting that, at least for the short term, the United States will supply enough aid to prevent an outright rebel victory. In the meantime, these elites seek U.S. and West European support for efforts to manage a settlement without victors—the only outcome they believe will not strain but rather will reinforce their respective political systems.

At root, it is fear of direct U.S. intervention that has shifted Columbia, Panama, and Venezuela away from their traditional posture of compliance with U.S. policy; moved Columbia to raise its low diplomatic profile; and propelled the traditional lone wolf, Mexico, into coalition diplomacy. Also cementing the Contadora states into a coherent diplomatic agent has been the shared conviction that, to the extent their ends coincide with America's, they can be achieved by means more compatible with Contadora interests than the ones Washington has stubbornly employed.

Obviously, the Contadora states are no more eager than the United States to have Soviet power camped on their doorsteps. But they agree with many American critics of U.S. policy that overthrowing the Sandinistas and exterminating the Salvadoran Left are not needed to prevent that outcome. Their judgment rests on confidence in the will and capability of the United States to deter any Central American government from offering itself as a Soviet base and to deter the Soviet Union from accepting such an improbable offer.

Although their views on how best to promote counterpart regimes in Central America are not entirely uniform, all the Contadora states reject the Reagan scenario, according to which pluralistic regimes will be the residue left by the military defeat of the Sandinistas and the Salvadoran opposition.

Mexico has most explicitly disparaged this scenario and, in fact, sees it as a recipe for promoting extremism. Like many U.S. critics of Reagan administration policy, Mexican foreign-policymakers believe that military pressure, coupled with political and economic isolation, will strengthen the Sandinista regime's most Leninist elements by helping to justify severe restrictions on a range of democratic freedoms. Even in democracies, civil rights do not prosper in wartime.

But the Contadora countries have more self-interested reasons for rejecting isolation and military pressure, exercised through the contras, as a policy for dealing with Nicaragua. They fear that the intensified Sandinista repression that could result from an escalation of the U.S.-organized and armed threat might loosen domestic political restraints on direct U.S. intervention—the worst possible outcome from the Contadora perspective.

These countries do not seem to envision a Sandinista defeat by any other means. Rather than relying, apparently futilely, and no doubt dangerously, on military force, the Contadora regimes would have the United States, acting in conjunction with them, use political and economic means to enlarge the existing obstacles to building a Leninist state: Nicaragua's open and dependent economy; its position squarely in the traditional zone of American influence (which would appear to discourage Soviet-bloc aid beyond levels required to assure the regime's bare survival); its strong Roman Catholic tradition and general cultural orientation toward the West, especially the United States; and the porosity of its frontiers (there cannot be a Nicaraguan Berlin Wall to prevent the flight of the skilled and energetic).

Castro exploited just such an exodus to consolidate Marxist rule in Cuba. The Sandinistas are unlikely to pursue a similar strategy. Indeed, Sandinista leaders regularly concede the failure of the Cuban economic model and insist on Nicaragua's need for a mixed economy to fight poverty and achieve development. But the Sandinistas clearly have not even faced, much less resolved, the problem of how to win private-sector support for their development objectives without giving that sector a significant political role. When faced with the threat of political emasculation, entrepreneurs in most countries turn their attentions to the covert export of capital.

Castro solved this problem by fully socializing the economy and by imposing draconian controls. These options do not seem open to Nicaragua's revolutionary elite. In the first place, Castro survived in part through huge infusions of Soviet aid. At present, Moscow shows no inclination to provide aid on a comparable scale, partly because of economic strains and partly because of an accurate appreciation of Nicaragua's marginal strategic value—especially given evident U.S. will and capacity to preempt militarily any Soviet effort to establish a strategic military presence in the country. Precisely because Nicaragua is not part of the Soviet bloc—not a Marxist state—it cannot invoke the principle of bloc solidarity. And any effort to satisfy the requisite criteria of institutional and ideological purity and deference to Soviet leadership would repel support from democratic socialists and powerfully encourage decisive U.S. intervention.

In addition, the Sandinistas cannot consolidate support among a large class of landless laborers by transferring to them a cornucopia of confiscated wealth, as Castro did for his island's sugar-cane cutters. Nicaragua possesses neither a comparably deprived class nor a relatively vast infrastructure of affluence. The blacks and Indians of the Atlantic Coast do represent relatively deprived groups. But because they have always distrusted the Spanish-speaking majority, and because they were generally left alone by the late dictator Anastasio Somoza Debayle, their attitude toward the revolutionaries has tended to spread across the spectrum between indifference and hostility.

Finally, Nicaragua does not possess a single charismatic leader able to rally and sustain mass support for forms of social organization sharply at odds with traditional culture and traditional institutions, above all the Catholic church.

Although the Contadora colleagues all oppose big-stick diplomacy and favor more pluralistic regimes in Central America, their visions of desirable political systems for the area are no less diverse than their own political orders. Mexico, for example, would feel more comfortable than Colombia and Venezuela with a single dominant party incorporating all important peasant and trade union leaders, controlling the armed forces, and limiting political competitors to the status of a permanent minority. Panama probably would not object to a political order in which the armed forces effectively guaranteed the bounds of political choice.

While the partners probably differ in their conception of the good society, their differences are undoubtedly narrower than a superficial comparison of their recent history and formal political institutions would indicate. All the Contadora countries are heirs to the Spanish tradition of centralized power and the Catholic vision of an organic, rather than a Lockeian, contractual society. All are governed by elites little influenced by the egalitarianism of the American and French revolutions. They vary in their assessment of the speed with which emerging social groups should be brought into the power structure. But these differences do not correspond neatly to the degree of formal political competition each regime allows. Thus, the Contadora states have not had to cross great ideological divides to arrive at a common diplomatic front.

The strongest evidence of the priorities of the Contadora states is the basic Central American peace plan they have developed. That the top priority of these countries is not assuring any specific outcome to the conflict but preventing U.S. military intervention by containing regional wars is clear from their continuing emphasis on limiting arms imports and foreign advisors. Their conviction that Honduran support for Nicaraguan contras fighting the Sandinistas is the most likely detonator of regionwide conflict has led the Contadora states continually to strive to end this assistance. In return, they want Nicaragua to refrain from organizing or aiding insurgents and from expanding its military in ways threatening to Honduras.

Isolating the conflict in El Salvador also serves the Contadora interest not only in keeping U.S. combat forces out of Central America but also in discouraging any sort of foreign involvement tending to convert internal conflicts into international conflicts. By insisting that the conflict be seen and treated as an essentially domestic struggle rather than as an aspect of U.S.-Soviet relations, the Contadora states hope to isolate the conflict symbolically. Contadora proposals of what amounts to collective repudiation of aid to all insurgents in the region are especially helpful in symbolically and operationally isolating El Salvador's civil war.

The Contadora commitments to democratization are not merely cosmetic. These countries believe that continuing civil wars will ultimately undermine whatever legal and diplomatic walls they manage to construct. Moreover, absent direct and sustained U.S. intervention, they do not see how Central Americans can achieve domestic and regional harmony—the prerequisites for renewed economic growth—unless each of the embattled Central American states opens its political process.

But the conditions for institutionalizing pluralism in El Salvador, Guatemala, and Nicaragua are hardly auspicious right now. So while the commitments proposed by the Contadora group are serious, they are not functionally integral to the envisioned process of containment. On the contrary, the group views an insistence on the immediate achievement of authentic pluralism as an obstacle to containing the fighting. Therefore, the recent unilateral imposition by Washington of a trade embargo on Nicaragua is inconsistent with the Contadora priorities because its purpose appears to be either to achieve instant democracy or to facilitate the destruction of the Sandinista regime.

A Historic Crossroads

The Contadora group symbolizes the emergence of politically potent indigenous forces in the Caribbean Basin—forces that, unlike Cuba, are not beholden to an extrahemispheric power. The group is a symbol precisely because it has managed to become a significant actor. Yet the ultimate significance of its effort remains to be seen.

In terms of the kind of raw economic and military power the United States is able to deploy, the Contadora group's assets are trivial. If unreasoning passion and a reckless disregard for costs inspired the Reagan administration to impose a Pax Americana on Central America, the Contadora states could do nothing but bob in the wake of the ensuing disaster. But at this point they retain some capacity to influence Washington, in part by influencing the actions of the Central American states and in part by reiterating to Washington the depth of their collective hostility to U.S. intervention.

Given its theories and passions, the Reagan administration has shown notable restraint in the Central American wars. Fear of a direct confrontation with the Soviet Union and the fall from power of former Secretary of State Alexander Haig, Jr., explain much of Washington's loss of interest in directly threatening Cuba, the supposed source of all regional turmoil. But concern about superpower confrontation cannot explain the administration's failure to send U.S. warplanes into combat over Nicaragua and El Salvador or to use identifiably American troops to help the contras establish a "liberated sector" in Nicaragua, complete with a provisional government.

The immediate cause of restraint has been congressional and public opinion. But the unusual resistance of Congress and the American public to the Great Communicator's entreaties arguably stems in part from opposition to more militarized diplomacy voiced by many NATO allies and the Contadora states. The latter may loom larger in U.S. calculations because they are among the dominoes the administration supposedly is protecting—and hence cannot be dismissed with charges of ignorance or gratuitous meddling. Moreover, unlike the West Europeans, the Contadora countries are not constantly indicted as demanding but unappreciative free riders on American power. And because they are, in general, very ably represented in Washington and because on several occasions they have had access to high officials, including the President, Contadora leaders also may have sowed some doubts within the administration about the prudence of its preference.

In addition, the formation of a united front has unquestionably affected U.S. policy in Central America by reinforcing each Contadora country's confidence in its preferred policies and by influencing the political environment in Central America itself. Without mutual reinforcement and the political safety found in numbers, the individual Contadora states would have had more difficulty resisting administration pressure to adopt its view of the crisis in Central America and its solution. Had two or three of the Contadora states succumbed and the holdout been silenced, leaving Washington free to define reality and extinguish any sense of alternatives, Central American enthusiasts for military solutions in the region would have found themselves in psychologically and politically more commanding positions.

For a moment in September 1984, when the Contadora group presented its draft treaty and Nicaragua immediately declared its willingness to sign, this precedent-shattering consortium seemed to have built the foundations of regional peace in the narrow space left by Washington's indecision. But by swiftly mobilizing opposition among the other Central American states, the administration underlined the gross disparity in power between the United States and the Contadora states. At this point the Contadora group may be approaching the limits of its role. The main capacity for initiative outside of Washington may now lie primarily with the Central American actors themselves.

The draft treaty, even as revised, remains the most promising focal point of local diplomacy. But the amendments proposed by Costa Rica, El Salvador, and Honduras in October 1984, in the so-called Tegucigalpa draft agreement, tend strongly to slow and weaken the process of military de-escalation and negotiation. Whereas the September draft, which Nicaragua had declared it was prepared to sign without reservation, called for an indefinite arms freeze, the Tegucigalpa proposals would limit the freeze to 60 days, leaving open the prospect of a renewed arms race. Firm timetables set forth in the September draft for the departure of foreign military advisors engaged in training and operations and for the elimination of foreign bases and schools are missing from the Tegucigalpa proposals. The proposed amendments also would permit foreign military exercises, which are proscribed in the September draft.

Some of the October amendments appear to have been designed to dilute the influence of the Contadora group. According to the September draft, disputes that could not be resolved by the foreign ministers of the five Central American countries would be referred, for good offices, to the Contadora foreign ministers. But under the Tegucigalpa amendments disputes would be appealed from the five Central American foreign ministers to a larger group made up of the original five, plus the four Contadora ministers. Finally, some roles assigned by the September draft to the Contadora-sponsored Commission on Verification and Control would be assumed by an "Ad Hoc Disarmament Group" composed of representatives of the five Central American states and four unspecified countries "that have not participated in the Contadora Group negotiating process."

These amendments are compatible with two interpretations. One is that they flow from genuine fears of Nicaraguan noncompliance and are therefore designed to assure the treaty's efficacy. The other is that they flow from a conviction, encouraged by Washington, that Sandinista survival is incompatible with the interests of Nicaragua's neighbors and therefore that the new proposals are designed to assure either that there will be no treaty or that any treaty that might emerge will not inhibit U.S. intervention.

The tremendous ideological, political, and economic influence of the United States in Central America makes the second interpretation a distinct possibility. Yet the first is plausible as well. For the capitalist and military elites of Central America are divided between those who have lost their hearts in Miami and those with a passion for an autonomous, national existence. And the latter know they are at a historic crossroads. U.S. intervention can guarantee the status quo for another generation. All that will be lost is national dignity. For some soldiers and politicians in Central America, that price now seems too high. Perhaps the real contribution of the Contadora states has been to underline the price and to reinforce the belief that it need not be paid.

Note

This chapter was originally published in *Foreign Policy,* No. 59, Summer 1985.

Index

Abrams, Elliot, 99
Afghanistan, xxvii, xxix-xxx, 57, 233
Aguilar, Andres, 94
Alliance for Progress, 70
Alvarado, General Juan Velasco, 146. *See also* Peru
American Convention on Human Rights, 73, 80-81, 110, 118, 147
Angola, xviii, xxix-xxx, 4, 12
Argentina: 11, 37, 41, 133; IACHR Investigation, 111

Ball, George, 234
Barre, General Siad, xvii. *See also* Somalia
Beckett, Sir Eric, 184
Bosch, Juan, 49
Bowett, Derek, 179-84
Brazil: 11-12, 29-30, 37-39, 41, 70, 193; economy, 41, 139; Indians, 39
Brownlie, Ian, 177, 179
Brzezinski, Zbigniew, 90
Bush, George, 235

Cambodia, 4, 117, 233
Cardenas, Lazaro, 37, 134. *See also* Mexico
Carter, Former President James, xxvi-xxx, 3-4, 6-7, 9-10, 14, 23, 32, 34, 41-42, 50-51, 53-55, 57, 91-92, 94, 96-97, 242, 261
Castro, Fidel, 90, 120, 139, 142, 236. *See also* Cuba
Catholicism: 46, 231, 267; influence in Latin America, 255
Central America: 219-90; External forces, role of, 230-31; Neutralization, 246-48
Central Intelligence Agency, 139, 210, 228
Chile: xx, 11, 29, 37, 41, 89-90, 114; "democratic" model, 119; demobilization of population, 37; Henry Kissinger, 88-89; IACHR Investigation, 87; U.S. Aid to, 88

China: xvi-xvii, 46, 132, 143; Revolution, xvi; U.S. relations, xvi; U.S.S.R. relations, xvi
Clark Amendment, 4
Cold War, xiv, xvi, xviii, xxvii, xxx, 3, 201, 212
Colombia, 11, 34, 71
Congo, 12
Contadora Group, 280-90
Conservatives: xx, xxv-xxvi; agreement with, xxii, xxv-xxvi; U.S. influence on, xx-xxi
Costa Rica, 9, 34, 54, 71, 95, 220-21
Contras, 210-11, 216, 265-66
Cuba: 4, 137-40, 144-45, 200, 223, 235; capacity for evolution, 144-45; economy, 40, 137-40; individual autonomy: 140-43; organs of popular power, 141; revolution, 241; welfare, 137-39
Czechoslavakia, xxiv, 46, 199

D'Amato, Anthony, 157, 159, 164-66, 168, 170-72
Democracy: form and substance; 235-38, 243, 250-51, 253-59
Dickey, Christopher, 261
Dobrinyin, Ambassador, xix
Dominican Republic: 34, 49, 71, 198, 234; U.S. occupation, 197-99
Duarte, Napoleon, 243, 249. *See also* El Salvador

Economics: 13, 21, 23, 26, 30-31, 51; conditions in Latin America, 26
Ecuador, 30, 71
Eisenhower Administration: 48; Dulles, John Foster, 48
Elections: xxi; as a human right, 80-81; as expression of popular will, 117-21, 124-31, 226-28; manipulation of, xxi, 235-38
El Salvador: 36, 55, 59, 71, 114-15, 221, 225,

234-37, 260; potential for democracy, 243; elections, 235-38, 250-51. *See also* elections; IACHR Investigation, 91-94, 225; Liberal infatuation with, 249-52; military, 36, 256-57; Napoleon Duarte, 249-59, opposition, 54; potential for liberal reform, 226, 253-59; power sharing, 239, 271-74; U.S. aid, 232-33, 240
Enders, Thomas, 232, 261, 268
Ethiopia: xvii-xviii, 10, 12; as an American defeat, 8, 11; relations with U.S.S.R., xxix, 10

Finland Option, 246-47
Foley, Thomas: 235; on El Salvador, 235
Force, xxviii. *See also* international law

General System of Preferences (GSP), 30
Grenada, 71
Guevara, Che, 4, 241
Guatemala: xxii, 4, 38, 58, 71, 90, 114-15, 143, 227-29, 236; Coup of 1954, xxiii, 4; elections, 236

Haig, Alexander, 59, 63
Haiti, 22, 71, 90, 114, 145
Hewlett, Sylvia, (study of Brazil) 39
Higgins, Dr. Rosalyn, 193
Honduras: 71, 115, 229-30; military, 229-30
Human rights: 52, 57-58, 70, 79-81, 113; American Declaration, 70; Argentina, 111; Brazil, 39; Colombia, 117-18; Costa Rica, 220-21; Cuba, *See* Cuba; El Salvador, 54; Guatemala, 54; Honduras, 229-30; Inter-American Commission, *See* Inter-American Commission; Nicaragua, *See* Nicaragua; Panama, 89-91; Peru, *See* Peru; relationship to Human Welfare, 124-55

Imperialism: direct verses indirect; 245-46
India, xxix, 13
Indonesia, xviii
Inter-American System, 23-25, 30, 71
Inter-American Commission on Human Rights (IACHR): 69, 72, 74, 79, 86; composition and authority, 72-73; country reports, 75-76; doctrine, 79-85, 112-21; impact of Commission, 85; no other international proceeding requirement, 74; observations in Loco, 76, 87; principal activities, 69; prior exhaustion requirement, 73-74; procedure, 74-75
International Court of Justice: 73; U.S. verses Nicaragua, 212-16
International Law: case of Nicaragua, xiii-xiv, 206-18; conflicting theories, 191-92; nature of, 157-72, 206-7; regulating intervention, 190-96; relation to national interest, 206-7; role of custom, 157-72; use of force, 174-89, 197-205
Iran, xxvii, 8-9, 13, 32
Iraq, 12
Israel, 12

Johnson Administration, 197

Kennan, Ambassador George, 18-23
Kirkpatrick, Ambassador Jeane, xix-xxiii, xxv, 32-36, 53, 56-58, 89, 96, 99, 142
Kissinger, Henry: xix, xxviii, 4, 18; policy towards Chile, 4, 88-89

Lauterpacht, Hersch, 176-78
Lasswell, Harold, 160-61
Law of Nations, 177
Law of Peace, 175
Liberalism: 44; self-determination, 44
Liberation theology, 122

Mao Tse Tung, xxvii, 47. *See also* China
Marcos, Ferdinand, 22. *See also* Philippines
Martin, John Barlow, 197
Mengistu, Haile Mariam, 10-11
Mexico: xxiii, 11-12, 37, 71, 134, 195; Catholic church, 34; economy, 139; Institutional Revolutionary Party (P.R.I.), xxiii, 34, 121
McDougal Myres, 160-61, 165-68
McNamara, Robert, 200
Military Establishment, 220-21, 226-28, 239-40
Morality: role in foreign policy, 18-22
Monroe Doctrine, 25
Motley, Langhorne, 240
Moynihan, Senator Patrick, xix
Mozambique, 12

Neorealism, 6, 13-17
New Republic, The, 232, 240

Index

Nicaragua: xxvii, 8-11, 14, 32, 71, 94, 221, 262; Carter policy toward, 9-10, 52-54, 264; Democratic National Front (FDN), 265; Democratic Revolutionary Alliance (ARDE), 265; IACHR investigation, 94-97; Miskito Indian resettlement, 115-16; National Guard, 222; neutralization, 268-69; power sharing, 143; Reagan Administration demands, 261-63; Somoza, Anastazio, 221-22; U.S. Contra Aid, 18, 261
Nigeria, xxix, 12
Nixon, Former President Richard, xix, xxviii

O'Donnel, Guillermo, 37
Organization of American States (O.A.S.), 24-25, 27, 30, 34, 70-72, 77, 84, 92, 95-96, 110, 199
Organization of Petroleum Exporting Countries (OPEC), 6, 16

Pahlavi, Shah Mohammad Reza, 4, 6-7, 33. *See also* Iran
Panama: 9, 54, 71, 89; Canal Treaty, 24; IACHR Investigation, 89-91
Peron, Juan, 37, 45, 111, 133
Peru, 30, 34, 36-37, 71, 146
Pinochet, General Augusto, xx, 37, 87-89, 119
Pluralism: in Mexico, xxiii-xxiv
Podhoretz, Norman, xix
Poland, 46, 57
Pope John Paul II, 84-85
Porter Convention, 178

Reagan, President Ronald, xviii, xxix, 6, 18, 22, 28, 42, 44, 56, 58-59, 63, 99, 139, 145, 232, 234-35, 255, 260, 263-64, 269
Refugees: causes of, 38
Revolution, xxvi
Rio Treaty of reciprocal assistance, 24, 25
Robelo, Alfonso, 40
Rogers, William, 24, 88-89
Romero, Carlos Humberto, 91-92. *See also* El Salvador
Roosevelt, Eleanor, 109-10, 122
Rule of Recognition, 157-58

Said, Edward, 166-67

Sandinistas, 96-97, 119, 223-24, 263, 266
Saudi Arabia, 15
Singapore, xviii
Social Darwinism, 45, 59, 109, 122
Somalia, xvii, 12; Soviet relations, xvii, 10; war with Ethiopia, xvii
Somoza, Anastasio, xxvii, 6, 9-10, 36, 53-54, 94-97, 221, 222
South Africa, xxix, 58
South Korea, xxvi
Stepan, Alfred, 37
Stone, Julius, 179, 184-85
Stone, Richard, 243, 270
Strategy: effect of regime change, xvi-xviii; effect of technological change, xv-xvi

Taiwan, xxvi
Terrorism: xx, 83, 85; definition of, 83; human rights and, 84
Thailand, xviii
Torrijos, Omar, 89-90. *See also* Panama
Torture: 98; rationalizations of, 100-8
Truman Administration, 46-48
Tucker, Robert, 9
Turner, Admiral Stansfield, xxvii. *See also* C.I.A.

United Nations: 99, 201; charter of, 25, 178-85, 199-200
United States: xviii, xxviii, xxx, 11, 14, 26, 29, 31, 33, 38, 45, 117, 246; contadora attitude toward, 284-90; and Cuba, xviii, 38; Dominican intervention, 197-200; El Salvador relations with, 242-43; influence on Central America, xxii, 53, 97; intervention, 4, 25, 44, 52, 200; missile crisis, 200-2; Nicaraguan relations with, 9, 212-16, 240; position in Third World, xx, 3-5, 16; strategic position of, xviii
U.S.S.R.: xxix, xxx-xxxi, 6, 14, 46, 57, 117, 195, 200-1; and China, xxx; and Ethiopia, xvii, 10-11; Hungary Invasion, 197; and missile crisis, 202; Third World relations, xiv, xxviii, xxx, 5, 13, 16; U.S. attitudes, xxx-xxxi
Uruguay, 41, 90

Vance, Cyrus, 4
Vattel, 175

Venezuela: 11, 30, 34, 70-71; contadora, 280-90
Vietnam, xvii-xviii, xxx, 4, 16, 47, 49, 57
Victoria, 175

White, Robert, 253

Yale School, 161-64
Young, Andrew, xxviii, 4
Yugoslavia, xxiv, 143-44, 200

Zaire, 16, 49
Zimbabwe, 4, 12